P9-BZC-576

The Rough Guide
History of

Spain

Rough Guides online

www.roughguides.com

credits

Rough Guides series editor: Mark Ellingham
Text editor: Joe Staines
Production: Julia Bovis and Dan May
Cartography: Katie Lloyd-Jones
Proofreading: Ken Bell

cover credits

Front – Equestrian statue of Philip III by Giambologna and Pietro
Tacca, Madrid
Back – Spanish Civil War poster

publishing information

This edition published November 2003 by
Rough Guides Ltd, 80 Strand, London WC2R ORL

distributed by the Penguin group

Penguin Books Ltd, 80 Strand, London WC2R ORL
Penguin Putnam, Inc. 375 Hudson Street, New York 10014, USA
Penguin Books Australia Ltd, 487 Maroondah Highway, PO Box 257,
Ringwood, Victoria 3134, Australia
Penguin Books Canada Ltd, 10 Alcorn Avenue,
Toronto, Ontario, Canada M4V 1E4
Penguin Books (NZ) Ltd, 182–190 Wairau Road,
Auckland 10, New Zealand

Typeset to an original design by Henry Iles
Picture research by Eleanor Hill of Lovely

Printed in Spain by Graphy Cems

No part of this book may be reproduced in any
form without permission from the publisher
except for the quotation of brief passages in reviews.

© Justin Wintle, 2003
512 pages includes index

A catalogue record for this book is available from the British Library.
ISBN 1-85828-

3 1984 00214 2659

The Rough Guide

History of

Spain

by Justin Wintle

New Lenox
Public Library District
120 Veterans Parkway
New Lenox, Illinois 60451

series editor
Justin Wintle

To Michael and Loutfia

acknowledgements

The author wishes to express his indebtedness to Jonathan Buckley, editorial director of the Rough Guide reference division; Joe Staines, a text editor sent from heaven whose greater knowledge of Spanish art proved a blessing; Eleanor Hill for her indefatigable picture research; Daniel May for typesetting; Katie Lloyd-Jones for preparing the maps; Ken Bell for proofreading; Matt Milton for indexing; and also Richard Trillo, Claire Southern and Demelza Dallow in marketing and publicity. The author also wishes to thank Professor John Hamilton Frazer for setting him straight about Antoni Gaudí.

contents

introduction

introduction

The **Iberian peninsula**, consisting of Spain and its smaller neighbour Portugal, forms a sub-continental 'annexe' at the south-western extremity of Europe, attached to it by a relatively thin neck of land, surmounted by the high **Pyrenees**. Across the north of the peninsula runs a line of mountain ranges – the Asturias and the Cantabrians, as well as the Pyrenees – which have provided a largely impregnable haven for those determined to resist political centralization. In the centre, a high and mainly arid plateau – the *meseta* – is broken up by further mountain chains, Spain's famous *sierras*. In the south is a more fertile, subtropical landscape, watered by the Guadalquivir and other rivers. There are significant **rivers** elsewhere in the peninsula – the western Tajo (Tagus), the more northerly Duero, and the Ebro, flowing eastwards into the Mediterranean. In addition, Spain is adjacent to Africa, separated from it by the narrow **Straits of Gibraltar**, the gateway between the formidable Atlantic ocean and the calmer, civilizing Mediterranean.

In pre-history the peninsula acted as an overflow for groups of settlers pushing into Europe from the east. These spread through the land, but enjoyed little contact with each other. Later, more certainly identifiable peoples – the Beaker People, the 'Urn Burial Folk', and the Celts – arrived. But even as the **Celts** took up residence in the north and west of the peninsula, the great civilizations that had evolved in the eastern and central Mediterranean began taking an interest in Iberia, drawn by its southerly deposits of copper, gold and silver. First the **Phoenicians**, **Greeks** and **Carthaginians**, then, most critically, the **Romans**.

In the second and first centuries BC, the peninsula came

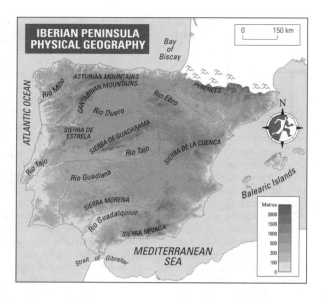

IBERIAN PENINSULA
PHYSICAL GEOGRAPHY

0   150 km

Bay of Biscay

ATLANTIC OCEAN

ASTURIAN MOUNTAINS

CANTABRIAN MOUNTAINS

PYRENEES

Rio Miño

Rio Ebro

Rio Duero

SIERRA DE ESTRELA

SIERRA DE GUADARAMA

SIERRA DE LA CUENCA

Rio Tajo

Rio Tajo

Balearic Islands

Rio Guadiana

SIERRA MORENA

Rio Guadalquivir

SIERRA NEVADA

MEDITERRANEAN SEA

Strait of Gibraltar

Metres
2000
1500
1000
500
200
100
0

N

to be regarded as a single, potentially cohesive territory, once the Celtiberi and other 'indigenes' had been pacified. As Rome's first great colony outside Italy, **Hispania** furnished a model for how other colonies elsewhere should be managed, and so played an integral part in the evolution of the empire itself. The Romans also brought with them a sense of civic pride, routine justice, the Latin tongue, a network of roads and other engineering projects, and, from the 3rd century AD onwards, **Christianity**.

All this survived the collapse of the empire in the 5th century, when Hispania was overrun by a succession of 'barbarians' from the north – the Vandals, Alani and Suevi. It was the

Visigoths, though, who made the land their own. Relatively few in number, they abandoned their 'barbarian' customs, preferring not only to adopt the Latin tongue, but also to leave existing administrative arrangements intact as a means of efficiently governing their Romano–Iberian subjects.

In the 7th century close bonds developed between the **Catholic Church** and an elective monarchy in the process of adopting hereditary succession. As a result, Visigoth Hispania emerged as the most stable territory in Europe, even a precursor of later medieval kingdoms. But then, at the beginning of the 8th century, another, longer–lasting invasion occurred. The peninsula was overrun by the **Arabs** and their **Berber helpers**, driven by a thirst for booty, and by their **Islamic faith**. Although, to begin with, al-Andalus, as Hispania now became, was answerable to the Caliph in far-off Damascus or Baghdad, it gradually distanced itself from the Middle East, and in 929 its Umayyad amir, Abd al-Rahman III, proclaimed a separate **caliphate**.

Under its Umayyad rulers **al-Andalus** developed into an enviably tolerant society. Jews as well as Christians could retain their faith, and **Córdoba** emerged as one of the most populous and cosmopolitan cities in Europe. But the Umayyads by no means had Spain to themselves. In the Asturias and Cantabrians autonomous Visigoth enclaves survived, coalescing into a succession of **Christian kingdoms** that slowly recaptured lands to the north of the Duero and Ebro rivers. At the same time the Franks wrested control of what became known as the **'Spanish March'** in the north-east – effectively modern **Catalunya**.

Slowly the Christian kingdoms reconquered the entire peninsula. Everything changed from around 980, when the Muslim dictator **al-Mansur** seized power in Córdoba and waged a ferocious *jihad* against the kings that profoundly altered not only the complex equilibrium of Iberian affairs, but also, it has been argued, the entire edifice of Muslim-Christian relations. For the Christian states responded in kind. Against *jihad* they practised their own brand of holy war – **the crusade** – which inspired the great crusades launched to recover the Holy Lands in Palestine.

By 1250, following the capture of **Seville** by Fernando III of León-Castile, all that remained of Muslim Spain was the amirate of **Granada** in the south. But Christian militancy was by no means the only cause of the collapse of al-Andalus. By asserting his own, personal authority al-Mansur had fatally undermined the caliphate, exposing it to the ravages of two groups of Islamic fundamentalists, the **Almoravids** and **Almohads**, both issuing out of north Africa. But while the Christian kings took full advantage, they also feuded amongst themselves, and it was not a single state that emerged. Rather it was three distinct larger states – **Castile**, **Aragon** and **Portugal** – together with several smaller principalities, among them Navarra.

The country now called Spain only began to emerge in 1469, with the marriage of **Fernando of Aragon** to **Isabel of Castile**. The same two monarchs completed the *Reconquista* by finally dismantling Granada in 1492, the same year in which they sponsored **Christopher Columbus's** epoch-making voyage to the New World.

The new nation was set to enter the most extraordinary period in its history. Under the rule of **Carlos I** and **Philip II**, Fernando and Isabel's **Habsburg** successors, Spain became, in the 16th century, not only the most revered power in Europe, but the founder of an **American empire**. Although Portuguese adventurers had established trading colonies as far away as India, it was Spain that led the way in colonizing vast stretches of territory overseas, so that its *conquistadores* – men like **Hernán Cortés** and **Francisco Pizarro** – may rightly be credited with initiating the era of European global dominance that lasted beyond the Great War of 1914–18.

Yet, spectacular as their exploits were, the price paid for them was heavy. In the Americas both the indigenous population and the ecology suffered cruelly. Nor did Spain itself reap anything like the full benefit of the vast amounts of **silver and gold** carried back across the Atlantic. Much of it went to royal bankers in Italy, the Netherlands and Germany. Significantly, Carlos I of Spain was also the Holy Roman Emperor Charles V – a man who ruled more of Europe than any other man since the Roman emperors, and who therefore had to bear the costs of endless continental wars.

Well before Philip II's death in 1598 the Spanish throne was bankrupt. Largely this was because Philip, in his self-appointed role as defender of the Catholic faith, had embarked on multiple wars of his own – against the **Ottoman Turks**, but also against those whom he saw as Christian infidels, Europe's new **Protestant rulers**. Most costly of all was the prolonged struggle to prevent the Spanish Netherlands falling into 'rebel' hands.

During the 17th century Spain entered a period of gradual decline that was only partially reversed by the advent of a new ruling dynasty – the **Bourbons** – in the 18th century. Now the dark inflexibility of many of Spain's institutions became plainly apparent. If the empire had been floated on an astonishing tide of confidence, the same confidence had been grounded in an intolerance that was both religious and racial. In 1492, Fernando and Isabel had expelled Spain's **Jews**. Subsequently Spain's **Muslims** and *moriscos* – Moors who had converted to Christianity – were also forced out. Most famously, the **Inquisition**, used as an instrument of political as well as intellectual and doctrinal oppression, sometimes resorted to torture.

The great empire was anything but outward-looking in its instincts. Nor did the acquisition of empire resolve the differences Spaniards felt between themselves. Catalans especially resented the overweening prestige of Castile. But rather than create a framework in which different voices might carry weight, the throne obstinately clung to its self-importance. The Bourbons, a junior branch of the ruling dynasty of France, sought to perpetuate a Spanish version of the *ancien régime*, and so accelerated decay. At the beginning of the 19th century Spain experienced the ignominy of invasion by the armies of **Napoleon**, and although the country was liberated by British forces in 1814, no true recovery followed. In the early 19th century a series of **colonial uprisings** stripped Spain of all its American possessions except Cuba, exacerbating political turmoil at home that lasted well into the 20th century.

Little by little Spain's military emerged as the arbiter of its politics, despite the humiliating loss of both Cuba and the Philippines in 1898 during a brief war with the **United States**. Yet even though Spain became one of Europe's more backward nations, change and modernization could not be entirely excluded. During the latter stages of the 19th century parts of the north industrialized, and Catalan **Barcelona** emerged not only as a thriving cultural centre, but also as a hotbed of revolution.

By the 1920s Spain's inner contradictions could no longer be contained. Unrest was everywhere. In 1923 an army general, **Primo de Rivera**, installed a military dictatorship to stem the tide of socialism. When this failed, a republic was declared, and progressives briefly held the stage. This, however was too much for the army, which, in 1936, plunged Spain into a searing civil war.

Crucially, the **Spanish Civil War** was internationalized from its outset, at a time when Europe was being pulled apart by right-wing and left-wing extremists. The **Soviet Union** and the **International Brigades** supported the Republic, but were no match for the fascist **General Franco**, strongly backed by **Adolf Hitler** and **Benito**

Mussolini. Following three years of carnage, El Caudillo, as Franco became known, emerged triumphant.

Under Franco, Spain became for a while a pariah state. The **Cold War**, however, led to a partial rehabilitation, as Washington, never shy to support right-wing regimes in any quarter of the globe, recognized in Franco a useful ally against the USSR, and long before the Generalismo's death in 1975 Spain had begun reintegrating with Europe. Increasingly Franco's regime was seen as irrelevant, especially after he made clear that he should be succeeded by **Juan Carlos,** a Bourbon claimant to the vacant throne. In 1978 a new constitution was promulgated, which not only made Spain a modern democracy, but also extended autonomy to Catalunya and other provinces.

Overnight Spain jumped from being behind to somewhere in the vanguard of European politics. Today, following the country's admission to the **European Union,** and two decades of steady economic growth, the nation is, for the first time in centuries, in profit, to the great advantage of its 50-odd million inhabitants. Poverty and social inequalities persist in some areas, but memories of Franco and the devastation he caused are enough to deter widespread upheaval, except among a dwindling band of militant Basque separatists.

Justin Wintle, 2003

author's note

The spelling of proper nouns in this book (i.e. Spanish places and historical figures) follows current Spanish usage, complete with accents, in nearly every instant. For example King Pedro is preferred to King Peter, Juana to Joanna, and Catalunya rather than Catalonia. Anglicization only occurs when a figure or place is particularly well known by the English form of the name. Thus all kings with the Spanish name Felipe are called Philip, Castile is preferred to Castilla, and Aragon to Aragón. When an English adjective derived from a Spanish noun occurs, the accent is dropped e.g. the adjective relating to the city of Córdoba is Cordoban, that relating to León is Leonese.

list of maps

1: From the beginnings

up to 206 BC

The early history of Spain is inseparable from the early history of the **Iberian peninsula** as a whole, which in turn is closely bound up with developments in western Europe and the Mediterranean. Indeed, the peninsula has been so heavily affected by external influences, that Spanish society retains a markedly 'composite' character even to this day. Its location at the western extremity of Europe, with only the vast **Atlantic Ocean** beyond, has meant that those peoples who first entered the peninsula had nowhere further to push on to. Yet the peninsula's terrain is large enough and its climate sufficiently diverse to encourage regionalism. Up to and beyond its conquest by the **Romans**, in the 3rd century BC, **Hispania** (as the Romans called it) consisted of many different communities with their own customs and traditions often living in isolation from one another.

Two **physical features** were of particular significance. Firstly, there was no single great life-sustaining river system in the peninsula, but rather a number of different rivers, notably the **Duero** and **Tajo** (Tagus) in the north-west and west, the **Guadalete** and **Guadalquivir** in the south, and the **Ebro** flowing into the Mediterranean in the east, which promoted the emergence of several discrete centres of human settlement. Secondly, the peninsula is naturally compartmentalized by the presence of high mountain ranges, or *sierras*, that served to keep peoples apart – the more so as much of the interior of the peninsula, being a raised plateau known as the **meseta**, is not especially fertile.

In the far north, too, were three mountain ranges – from west to east the **Asturias**, the **Cantabrians** and the **Pyrenees** – that at many points in Iberian and Spanish history have provided refuge for those determined to maintain their independence. On the other hand, as human technology developed, the presence of substantial mineral deposits – copper and silver in the south, tin and iron in the north – not only encouraged the emergence of intra-peninsula trade networks, but also attracted the attention of more advanced metal-working civilizations: the **Phoenicians** and **Greeks**, as well as the **Romans**.

Inexorably the lands that would, in the future, form the Spanish nation were drawn into the Mediterranean world of antiquity, which meant also being drawn into a world of far greater political sophistication and organization. Yet by the beginning of the first millennium BC the Iberian peninsula was already ethnically and genetically complex, the result of successive waves of incomers spread over thousands, even tens of thousands, of years.

Whether, or to what extent, the peninsula was inhabited by man's hominid ancestors is unknown, but almost certainly there were **Neanderthal** settlements – cavemen who survived by hunting and foraging. Then, between thirty and forty thousand years ago, *homo sapiens sapiens*, or modern man, began entering Spain from southern France, entirely displacing its previous inhabitants. These too were cave-dwelling hunter-gatherers, who over time brought with them new skills and abilities, and began constructing simple dwellings for themselves.

By the fifth millennium BC the two main characteristics of the **Neolithic Revolution** were present in Spain: agriculture, and the domestication of animals. By the third millennium Iberians had begun smelting copper and silver. Around 2500 BC the **Beaker People**, who had already established their culture in the Rhineland, France and Britain, made their way into Spain, to be followed several hundred years later by the equally distinctive **Urnfield folk**. More significantly still, during the first millennium BC the **Celts** arrived, establishing settlements and spreading their iron-working culture across large swathes of the north and west.

In the same period the south and east opened up to the **Phoenicians** and the **Greeks**, who created permanent trading colonies, notably at **Cádiz** (known to the ancients as Gades) and **Emporion** (present-day San Marti d'Empúries). As a result the more productive parts of the peninsula began merging with the more developed world of the middle and eastern Mediterranean. While the Phoenicians and Greeks brought with them urbanization, the written word, new religious faiths and rituals, and advanced technologies for the manufacture of bronze and ceramic artefact, neither sought territorial dominion. Rather they encouraged those whom they encountered to organize themselves. In the Guadalquivir river valley especially, the inhabitants responded by putting copper and silver mining on a mass industrial footing, by building their own townships, and by forging larger political units, including perhaps the first indigenous kingdom, **Tartessus**.

There was still no sense of a wider Iberian identity, however, even though, during the course of the first millennium BC, the peninsula developed into a vital link between the burgeoning Mediterranean economy and an **Atlantic seaboard trading system** that reached as far north as the British isles and Scandinavia. Least of all did the intrusion of outsiders inspire any kind of collective resistance. Rather Iberia was, and continued to be, a patchwork of tribes speaking different languages and following different customs.

This all began to change as a consequence of the rivalry between two of the big players of the developed ancient world: the **Carthaginians** and the **Romans**. In 237 BC **Hamilcar Barca** left Carthage in North Africa with a band of followers specifically to carve out an *imperium* for himself in southern Spain – an action that immediately aroused Rome's apprehensions. During the long war that ensued Hamilcar's son **Hannibal** attempted the destruction of Rome itself, over-running much of Italy; and Rome responded by launching a counterattack in the Iberian peninsula.

Rome emerged victorious, but had a tough decision to make. Should it wind down its military presence in Iberia, or consolidate its power there in order to prevent a Carthaginian resurgence? After agonizing debates in the senate it was decided to adopt the latter course, and **Hispania** was declared a *provincia*. But although Hispania (the Latin equivalent of the Greek Iberia) eventually became one of Rome's most prosperous, and least querulous, colonies, it would take a century at least to 'pacify' its interior.

c.750,000 BC At the beginning of the **Lower Palaeolithic** archeological period, Europe's climate is dominated by the recurrence of **'ice ages'**, at intervals of between 70,000 and 80,000 years. During each period of glaciation the north of the continent is covered with ice, spreading as far south as the **Pyrenees** and **Cantabrian** mountain ranges in the northern part of the Iberian peninsula. At each glacial maximum, the ice-cover reaches the **Ebro** river and further south. When an ice age occurs, sea levels drop by as much as 100 metres, enlarging the area of the European land-mass and altering Europe's coastlines. At times the Iberian peninsula is joined to Africa across what will become known as the **Strait of Gibraltar**, the narrow sea-passage between the Mediterranean and the Atlantic Ocean.

Man's early ancestor, **homo erectus**, has evolved in Africa, and some groups have migrated into Europe. Such hominids dwell in caves, are hunter gatherers, and are able to fashion crude flint and pebble tools. The periodic recurrence of the ice ages however means that the colonization of lands to the north of the Pyrenees by *homo erectus* and his successor *homo sapiens* is discontinuous.

c.300,000 BC *Homo sapiens*, having also evolved in Africa, makes his first appearance in Europe. He has a larger head and smaller teeth than *homo erectus*, but continues to live in caves.

c.200,000 BC **Neanderthal Man**, evolves in Europe, with a cranial capacity (brain size) the equivalent of a modern human's. Like his predecessors he lives in caves and survives by hunting and foraging, but is better adapted to cold climates. His tools, now made of bone and ivory as well as flint and other stones, are a marked improvement on those that have gone before. Neanderthal man uses a short wooden spear tipped with various kinds of head for killing game. In the Iberian peninsula, the mammoth, the woolly rhinoceros and the giant deer are among the meats that provide human sustenance. As well as packs of wolves, lions roam the terrain.

The arrival of Neanderthal Man marks the end of the Lower and the beginning of the **Middle Palaeolithic** archeological periods.

c.50,000 BC The end of the Middle Palaeolithic and beginning of the Upper Palaeolithic archeological periods is marked by the advent of homo sapiens sapiens. Within no more than 15,000 years, homo sapiens sapiens displaces the European Neanderthals, who become extinct. Homo sapiens sapiens himself has evolved in Africa, but reaches Europe primarily through the Near East, although it is possible a secondary migration occurs from North Africa directly into the Iberian peninsula. The earliest evidence of homo sapiens sapiens in Spain occurs in the Pyrenees and other parts of the north, indicating immigration from southern France.

Homo sapiens sapiens is more agile than Neanderthal Man, almost certainly has a greater capacity for speech as well as other forms of communication and, as significantly, is more strongly **sexually dimorphic**. He also dramatically extends the repertoire of tool making, introducing fresh elements of **design** that include **decoration** seemingly for its own sake. The surfaces of his flint and stone tools are sometimes polished, and soon he will begin producing simple **figurines**, possibly as playthings for children, but later to become a vehicle for mythic or 'religious' sentiment.

For at least 25,000 years *homo sapiens sapiens* continues living in caves in relatively small groups, based perhaps on an instinct for the extended family. The dispersal of artefacts made in one area and found at sites in another, at distances of up to 100 miles, suggests an early form of trade by exchange between clans and prototribes.

c.22,000 BC 'Venus' figurines – miniature female figures sculpted out of stone – are present in large numbers at archaeological sites in Iberia's northern mountains.

c.18–14,000 BC In the Pyrenees and Cantabrians, as well as in southern France, *homo sapiens sapiens* begins decorating the walls of the caves he lives in with vivid hunting scenes, giving rise to the celebrated Upper Palaeolithic **'cave art'**.

c.16,000 BC As the 'last' ice age attains its glacial maximum, the coastline of the Iberian peninsula extends forty or fifty miles further into the Atlantic than its present-day contours. Although the Pyrenees and Cantabrians are again covered with ice, and the central plains become a sort of tundra, the south remains well-forested. However, *homo sapiens sapiens* has learned to survive freezing weather conditions, taking advantage of seasonal migrations of animal herds to acquire sustenance.

c.10,000 BC The 'last' ice age recedes and Europe's climate takes on its present characteristics amidst widespread natural reforestation. Mammoth, woolly bison and the great deer shortly become extinct, but lesser mammals, in particular the horse, auroch, pig (or wild boar) and smaller species of deer, prosper, as does *homo sapiens sapiens*, who now colonizes nearly all parts of the continent. In the Iberian peninsula the pine and the oak become the main varieties of tree in the plains and river valleys.

The Upper Palaeolithic archeological period ends, and the **Mesolithic** begins. Perhaps for the first time in Europe man begins exploring ways of living outside caves, constructing simple dwellings from natural materials. He also begins building boats, adopts the bow–and–arrow for fighting and domesticates the dog as a hunting animal. He begins designing animal-traps and fashioning woven garments from plant fibres as a substitute for animal skins. It is also probable that from an early stage of the Mesolithic period he starts managing the natural environment to his own advantage, clearing spaces for the benefit of specific nutritional plants.

c.8000 BC Around this time 'rock art' flourishes in the Spanish Levant (the eastern seaboard of Iberia on the Mediterranean), with an extraordinarily animated series of paintings being found at **Cueva de los Caballos** (see p.9). Pebbles decorated with animals and other forms are also commonplace.

c.7000 BC Improved boat-building and navigational techniques enable the first human settlements on the **Balearics** in the western Mediterranean, islands that in modern times form part of Spanish territories.

Iberian Cave and Rock Art

Although the most celebrated cave-paintings by prehistoric or Stone Age man were discovered at Lascaux in the French Dordogne in 1940, others have been found at 30 or so sites in northern Spain, the most significant being at **Altamira**. As at Lascaux, Iberian cave-art depicts a variety of animals – bison, deer, mammoths, wild horses, ibex, and (more rarely) bears, wolves and lions. That these are usually depicted in full flight, with only the occasional token human figure in attendance, suggests that such paintings are primarily hunting scenes, though the reason they were painted remains a mystery. While some scholars have suggested they were merely decorative, others have attempted to extrapolate a religious cult, with the painted caves functioning as Upper Paleolithic temples.

   In most cases the paintings were executed in the deeper recesses of a cave complex, possibly as a means of passing away the severe winters that marked either the onset or passing of the last 'great' ice age. What is not in doubt is the artistic and technical excellence of the paintings themselves. Movement, energy and power are all effectively captured, while the pigments used – colours derived from iron ochre, and the black outlining and shading from manganese oxide – must have been particularly striking by whatever form of lighting the cave-dwellers used.

   Cave-painting seems to have died out in the northern mountains once the last ice age had passed, but curiously it revived in the form of **rock art** in the Spanish Levant sometime around 8000

c.6000 BC Excavation of large-scale 'cemeteries' in the Iberian peninsula suggests that some Iberians have begun living in larger social units than hitherto. The evidence also shows that a variety of dwellings have come into being, among them primitive huts supported by wooden poles as well as animal skin tents.

c.5000 BC During the course of the 5th century BC the Neolithic Revolution begins to impact on Iberia. Iberi-

BC. This time, however, the subject-matter was significantly more human, although an important exception is the portrait of an injured bull at Cueva Remigia. At Cueva de los Caballos a series of scenes depicts men and women engaged in dancing and warring as well as in hunting. Most poetically, at Cueva de la Arania a couple is caught in the act of taking honey from a wild beehive in a tree. Yet in none of these do the human figures come close, either in their detail or in their individual expressiveness, to their bestial forbears in northern Spain.

ROBERT HARDING

Bison are the most numerously depicted animals in the Altamira caves

ans start husbanding **herd animals** and planting imported grain seeds. Sheep and goats are introduced, and coarse **pottery** is produced at many sites around Spain's coast-line. A majority of the population however continues to subsist as hunter-gatherers, and as yet there is no evidence of any habitation larger than a small village. Large parts of the Iberian interior remain at best only very sparsely populated.

c.4000 BC The Atlantic seaboard of Iberia is particularly affected by the spread of a distinctive west and north–west European **megalithic culture** – so called because of its penchant for structures composed of large, heavy stones (megaliths) that clearly require a degree of communal enterprise for their assembly. Many large **stone burial chambers** are built, some in the form of **dolmens** above the ground, others as sunken or semi-sunken tombs lined with rough-hewn slabs of stone.

Over the succeeding millennium, megalithic burial monuments spread to many parts of Spain, to become part of a widely diffused 'common culture'.

Los Millares

In 1889, a Belgian mining engineer, **Louis Siret**, began excavating a series of pre-historic sites in south-eastern Spain that, over the next forty-five years, revealed an extensive and distinctive 'Copper Age' culture, known as **Los Millares** after its largest site, close by the Andarax River in Almería. Although Siret wrongly believed that Los Millares was the product of Phoenician colonization (see p.18), further excavations, combined with carbon-dating and other modern research techniques, have confirmed it to be an important and in some ways unique pattern of settlement. Whether 'Los Millares' was a truly 'indigenous' culture, as some Spanish pre-historians argue, or was the result of an intrusion by unidentified outsiders, remains unresolved. Metal-working skills undoubtedly helped create a wealthier, more diversified and more socially stratified human environment; but the evidence also suggests that the Los Millares sites – over 25 in number and spread over a wide geographic area – originated long before their inhabitants began using copper.

 Los Millares itself may or may not have been a political centre, with other close-by sites as satellites. Three semi-circular concentric walls, replete with bastions, central gateway and a watch-tower, enclose an area of approximately 400 metres in the centre of which is a raised, flattened mound that shows the

c.3500 BC In Iberia polished stone **axe-heads** are manufactured, and (in the south) plant-fibre **textile** production becomes steadily more sophisticated. Excavation of an important archeological site at Cueva de los Murciélagos (near Almería) will reveal fully clothed corpses, and **woven baskets** filled with poppy flowers.

c.2600 BC As megalithic tomb-building continues, a distinctive, relatively advanced culture that lasts the best part of a thousand years emerges in south-eastern Spain. Known as **Los Millares culture** from its primary archeological site, this is typified by unprecedentedly extensive fortifications and communal cemeteries furnished with

remains of a rectangular edifice that formed some kind of citadel. Around this are the circular stone bases of what must have been mud-and-wattle crafted huts. But while these arrangements may have guaranteed the peaceful and productive co-existence of at most just a few score individuals, of equal significance is an adjoining cemetery, sometimes called a 'necropolis' ('city of the dead'), three times the size of the living settlement, and clearly the object of intensive labour and material investment.

The cemetery contained tombs of various kinds, including megalithic family sepulchres, from which have been recovered an array of 'grave goods' including such copper artefacts as chisels, awls and daggers. But there is also an array of artefacts made from alabaster, silex, amber and jet, as well as flint and other materials of the neolithic or 'Stone Age'. Most telling are examples of finely worked ivory, apparently restricted to a wealthy elite, which can only have come from Africa, thus indicating inter-continental trading links. And if Los Millares was, in prehistoric terms, a 'multi-media' society, it also enjoyed a varied diet. Bone and grain analysis points to a community that kept pigs, sheep and cattle as livestock, drank milk, hunted red deer, and grew legumes as well as barley.

'advanced' grave goods, reflecting an exaggerated respect for departed **ancestors** that perhaps denotes the emergence of a primitive religion. Los Millares and related sites also provide evidence for the Iberian peninsula's first endeavours at metallurgy. **Copper** is extracted from surface deposits located in the Sierra Nevada and other local mountain ranges, smelted and fashioned into simple implements.

Soon afterwards, a similar and probably related Copper Age culture evolves in the southwest of the Iberian peninsula, extending northwards along the Atlantic seaboard into the Algarve and other parts of present-day Portugal, with a principal archeological site at **Villa Nova de São Pedro**. Although copper artefacts are far less plentiful, fortifications are more extensive and weapons more plentiful.

c.2400 BC During the course of the second half of third millennium BC much of northern and western Europe plays host to an enigmatic group named the **'Bell-Beaker people'** after the distinctive inverted-bell shaped pottery drinking vessels found at widely dispersed grave sites. The Bell-Beaker people reach the Iberian peninsula perhaps around 2400 BC, apparently across the Pyrenees as well as along the Atlantic seaboard, and bell-beakers become a common find in different types of grave and burial site in various parts of Spain until around 1600 BC.

c.2200 BC Stone is used in eastern and southeastern Spain, particularly in the Almería and Valencia regions, for the construction of **rectangular dwellings**, and also for building defensive walls around the perimeters of such settlements.

c.1700 BC The advent of the European Bronze Age coincides with the emergence of a distinctive culture in south-eastern Spain, known as **El Algar** from its primary site in Almería. El Algar culture, found also in Granada and

The Bell-Beaker People

The **Bell-Beaker People** are one of the abiding mysteries of European prehistory. In the archeological record, 'bell-beakers' are found in graves across northern Europe, in the British Isles, along the Atlantic seaboard, and in many parts of the Iberian peninsula, as well as in the present-day Czech Republic. Because of their spread pattern and carbon-dating, it is deduced that these distinctive ceramic drinking vessels originated somewhere in the **German Rhine Valley**. While early beakers are ornamented on the outside with a simple 'cord' pattern, made by impressing a length of cord on wet clay before being fired, later beakers are more ambitious, often incorporating 'local' pottery styles.

Many of the graves and tombs from which bell-beakers have been recovered are those of single males, and the presence of leather jerkins and a sometimes rich array of primitive weapons, including bows-and-arrows and, at a later date, copper daggers, suggests that the Beaker People may have been a **migrant warrior caste**. On the other hand scant evidence has been produced to show that the Beaker People were a 'race apart' from those they mingled with, and there is virtually no evidence of any social disruption (or realignment) caused by the Beaker People during the 800 or so years during which bell-beakers were interred with the dead. Rather it seems bell-beakers were merely absorbed into such societies and settlements as they penetrated. This in turn has led some prehistorians to characterize the Bell-Beakers as primarily a **trading phenomenon**, possibly associated with mead or some other alcoholic beverage, the production of which may have spread with the vessels specifically designed for drinking it. There may even have been no Bell-Beaker People as such at all.

Murcia, lasts for approximately 600 years and is characterized by the production of large **pottery storage jars**, as well as by such **bronze implements** as relatively crude knives, daggers, swords and halberds. El Algar people also work **silver**, found in the Sierra Nevada and elsewhere, fashioning diadems worn by women. Bracelets and earrings figure prominently among their grave goods, and for the first time a few **gold artefacts** are present. Flint- and copper-work however persist, suggesting a continuity of life style and people with the preceding period. Unlike their Los Millares predecessors, the El Algar people inter their dead, usually in stone lined pits or cists, in a crouching position. Their cemeteries are also notable for an apparent distinction between an elite, buried with substantial quantities of artefact, and a commonalty buried with few if any goods. Other pits are used for storing food – mainly cereals – during what seems to be a period of sustained **population growth**. El Algar itself is constructed on a fortified flattened hilltop, indicating that the Iberian peninsula's most 'advanced' inhabitants are still reluctant to create settlements on valley-floors or directly by a river.

c.1600 BC Metal-working spreads among long-established human settlements in the Spanish Levant, probably as a result of contacts with El Algar culture to the south. A limited supply of mineral resources however restricts growth, and the people of the Levant continue depositing their dead in caves and crevices, usually at a distance from their habitations, indicating either an insurmountable fear of death, or a low regard for ancestors, or both.

Around this time the first *motillas* are constructed in La Mancha. Known also as *morras*, and as the 'Towers of La Mancha', *motillas* consist of artificially raised mounds, on average 10 metres high and 80 metres in diameter, on top of which a look-out post and sometimes other facilities (even a temple of some kind) are erected. Around the base of each *motilla* are the remains of stone-based dwellings, protected by a perimeter wall. In parts of La Mancha *motillas* are spaced at regular intervals, 15 kilometres or so apart, suggesting a federation of like-minded settlements. A handful of imported metallic artefacts have been recovered, and the *motilla* settlements specialized in trading animal skins. The *motillas* are inhabited for somewhere in the region of 300 years, but are then inexplicably abandoned.

c.1500 BC Bronze production spreads from the southeast Iberian peninsula to the south-west, including areas around Huelva and Badajoz, where the most abundant copper deposits are located. Even at the principal site of this 'secondary' bronze age society, **Atalaia**, grave goods are significantly less copious than in El Algar settlements. Conversely, around Alentejo especially, a vogue develops for impressively carved stone **stelae** (memorial plinths), depicting axes, swords and other Bronze Age weapons.

c.1300 BC The **'Iron Age'** arrives in Europe with the emergence of 'Hallstatt' culture to the north of the Alps. In the succeeding centuries relatively advanced metallurgy techniques will be carried into Western Europe, and eventually Iberia, by the **Celts** (see p.26), who also possess a distinctive pantheon of gods and goddesses. Compared to either France or the British Isles, however, the Iberian peninsula lags well behind in the 'race for iron'.

In Iberia itself decorated stelae are carved out of stone to mark the graves of outstanding individuals – presumably clan and tribal leaders.

c.1200 BC Around this time a new phenomenon affects northern Europe, namely the **'Urn People'**, characterized by the custom of interring the cremated remains of their dead in well-decorated ceramic urns that are often buried in fields – hence the term 'Urnfield culture'. Within a century urn burial spreads from France into northeastern Spain and becomes established particularly in the lower Ebro valley (in present-day Catalunya) as well as in Aragon and Rioja. Like the Bell-Beaker

People (see p.13) the Urn People (or 'Folk' as they are often called) seem to have made their first appearance in the Rhine Valley. Continuing for approximately six hundred years, they are associated in their later phases with the use of **iron**. Tweezers, razors and iron spearheads belonging to the Urn People are the first iron artefacts to appear in the Iberian archeological record. Of equal significance, theirs are also the first settlements in Spain to consistently construct their dwellings on an oblong or rectangular pattern, sometimes called the **'Indo-European room'**.

In the northwest, to the south of the Asturian and Cantabrian mountains, and mainly in the Duero River valley, a highly decorated and advanced pottery-type emerges, known as **Las Cagotas style** after its principal archeological site. Examples of the same pottery type sometimes appear in sites on the Guadalquivir River and elsewhere in the south, indicating the further emergence of exchange-trading patterns in the Iberian peninsula.

c.850 BC As bronze production spreads along the European Atlantic seaboard and coastal trading routes develop in the Mediterranean, so bronze products made in the southern Iberian peninsula become more widely dispersed. Helmets, spears and daggers are diffused throughout Spain, including Galicia in the north-west. Iberian 'leaf-blade' swords will be found at sites as far east as Italy.

In the centuries ahead, much of the developing **Mediterranean trade** will be conducted by Phocaea, Samos, Rhodes and other **Greek city states**, which from around this time enter a period of revival and expansion. Pushing westwards, Greeks establish first trading posts, then permanent colonies in Italy, Sicily and Sardinia, and later in southern France and eastern Iberia – a sphere of interest that will become known as **Magna Graecia**. Already however another, and more advanced, outward-looking trading civilization has developed in the Syrian Levant (present-day Lebanon), known as **Phoenicia**. Better sailors than the Greeks, the Phoenicians advance westwards along the coast of North Africa, absorbing much of the historic culture of Egypt.

814 BC Phoenicians from the city of Tyre found a new trading settlement at **Carthage**, on the coast of present-day Tunisia. It is possibly from Carthage that the first large-scale Phoenician expeditions are sent to Iberia, drawn by reports of great deposits of copper and silver in the southern sierras. According to the 1st century BC Greek historian Strabo, the third such expedition, undertaken perhaps before the close of the 9th century BC, leads to the founding of **Cádiz**, known among the ancients as **Gades**, on an island (later joined to the shore) close to the mouth of the Guadalete river west of the Strait of Gibraltar (associated by the Greeks and Romans with the Pillars of Hercules).

Like Carthage, **Gades** soon develops into an important port settlement, to become Spain's first true city. The Phoenicians erect temples to their deities, notably Melqart and Astarte, as well as to the Greek hero Heracles (Hercules), and Gades becomes the centre of a Phoenician trade network that successfully taps into the mineral resources of southwestern Iberia. As importantly, Phoenicians gain access to the highly fertile lower Guadalquivir river basin. Other trading colonies are created along the southern coast east of Gibraltar, including Málaga, Baria (modern Villaricos), Abdera and Sexi. In return for copper and silver, they trade a variety of advanced artefacts, including Greek and Egyptian vases, as well as cloths dyed purple – conventionally associated with Phoenician material culture. The Phoenicians may also be responsible for introducing Iberians to the production and consumption of **wine**.

The Phoenicians

The Phoenicians were a **Semitic** people whose nearest cousins, based on the linguistic evidence, were the Canaanites and Israelites. They first emerged as a distinctive community during the third millennium BC, constructing settlements in the Syrian Levant (present-day Lebanon and parts of Israel), some of which – Tyre, Sidon, Byblos and Beirut – became great cities during the course of the second millennium. There was no Phoenician nation as such, only a federation of small monarchies increasingly dominated by **merchant fraternities**. For much of their early history the Phoenicians were subject to Egyptian rule, but around 1500 BC they asserted their independence and rapidly became the principal traders not only in the Near East but subsequently, thanks to their maritime expertise, throughout the Mediterranean. As well as exotic goods of their own manufacture, including perfumes and a purple linen that used a striking dye extracted from the **murex snail**, they established themselves as carriers of Greek products. They colonized Anatolia, Cyprus, Sardinia and parts of the North African coast, where **Carthage** became an important city in its own right during the period of classical antiquity before eventually being destroyed by Rome.

The rise of 'Phoenicia' coincided with the unfolding of the **European Bronze Age**, and it was this that propelled them even further westwards. Clearly, by the late 9th century BC, the Iberian

In time more and more Phoenicians settle in southern Iberia and intermarry with Iberians. Many Iberians adopt Phoenician religious beliefs and rites, perhaps their language, and also their square or rectangular architecture.

800 BC In south-western Iberia, away from the incipient Phoenician settlements, crudely carved and decorated stone *stelae* become more numerous. A warrior and his weaponry are commonly depicted, with special

peninsula had acquired a reputation as a land full not only of vital copper but also of silver, and even lead, and it was this that persuaded the **Tyrenians** – always the most adventurous of the Phoenicians – to embark on a fresh expansion that took them beyond the Strait of Gibraltar and into the Atlantic.

The risks involved paid handsome dividends. Within a century of the founding of **Gades** (Cádiz) mineral ores from southern Iberia became a mainstay of the burgeoning Mediterranean economy. As well as copper and silver, and later tin derived from trade that reached as far north as the British Isles, the **Guadalquivir river valley** especially proved a bountiful source of vegetable oils, wine and other agricultural produce. Such was the Phoenicians' success that in time first the Greeks, and then the Romans, followed in their footsteps. But although the Phoenicians were primarily interested in the economic exploitation of a backward country, their impact was decidedly beneficial. By building twenty or more **coastal trading stations** they introduced the Iberian people to an altogether higher standard of living that was soon copied, adapted and replicated in parts of the Iberian hinterland. The Phoenicians also brought with them a Semitic script, the first time **writing** of any sort appeared in the Peninsula. Indeed, it is no exaggeration to say that it was the Phoenicians who brought Iberia within the pale of Mediterranean civilization.

prominence given to round shields with a characteristic 'v' indentation on their facial inner rings. Whether such *stelae* are produced as memorial stones for outstanding chieftains or as territorial markers is unclear, but historically they are associated with the emergence of a shadowy tribal federation (or even kingdom) called **Tartessus**, centred on the lower Tajo, Guadiana and Guadalquivir rivers.

Tartessus

As it became apparent during the 8th and 7th centuries BC that the Phoenicians had gained access to an invaluable source of copper and silver in southern Iberia, so the legend of a fabulously rich kingdom at the western extremity of the Mediterranean became current. Most commonly the name given this ancient El Dorado was **Tartessus** (Tartessos). In early Greek writings the same name was given to a city somewhere in the lower Guadalquivir river basin, although there is no archeological evidence for the existence of even a large township in pre-Phoenician times. The historian Herodotus, writing in the 5th century BC, extrapolated the figure of **Arganthonios**, said to have ruled Tartessus for eighty years from the late 7th century BC; while the Roman historian Justinus, writing in the 4th century AD, claimed that an even earlier king, **Gargoris**, was the first man to collect wild honey from the forest. But whereas such myths have no verifiable foundation – Herodotus has been dubbed the 'father of lies' as well as the 'father of history' – ironically 'Tartessus' became a reality once the Phoenician presence was established.

The **Phoenicians** had no interest in creating an empire; rather they preferred to build secure coastal trading stations. From these they bartered their own imported goods – sometimes little more than trinkets – for the valuable minerals of the interior they had come for. To win over the 'locals' they doubtless distributed lavish gifts in the first instance, and may, with their superior weaponry, have offered limited military protection to their new 'allies'. But as this, or some trading mechanism like it, evolved, so the indigenous population of southern Iberia must have realised it was to their advantage to organize themselves more thoroughly. To satisfy Phoenician demand, a sizeable workforce of miners, smelters and carriers was called for, and it was in these circumstances that Iberian society became more highly stratified than hitherto, perhaps even giving rise to local **kingships**. Whereas when the Phoenicians first arrived, the Tartessians still lived in small communities in round huts of wattle and daub, during the 7th and 6th centuries these gave way to larger settlements and the use of stone and mud-bricks to construct rectangular dwellings. The Tartessians were equally impressed by the Phoenicians' superior pottery, much of which was Greek anyway, and soon began producing high-grade burnished ceramics of their own, including painted vessels known as Carambolo-style. At the same time, the Tartessians expanded agricultural production, not just to feed the foreign settlers, but also to provide choice foodstuffs for export to eastern markets, so that little by little Tartessus justified its reputation as an Iberian cornucopia.

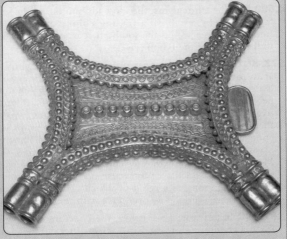

ARCHIVO ICONOGRAFICO, S.A./CORBIS

Golden pectoral, or chest piece; part of a haul of Tartessian treasure found at El Carambolo near Seville in 1958

c.655 BC The Carthaginians establish a colony on **Ibiza** (known to the ancients as Eivissa), one of the Balearic islands.

c.650 BC Archeological evidence strongly suggests the existence of a newly created indigenous Iberian township or city at Huelva (La Joya), sometimes taken to be the capital of Tartessus. Some individual graves, filled with local artefacts as well as luxury goods derived from the Eastern Mediterranean through the Phoenicians, reflect the emergence of a regional **Iberian nobility** or upper class.

620 BC According to Greek chronology based on the work of the historian Herodotus, **Arganthonios** becomes king of Tartessus, and reigns for eighty years until his death in 540 BC.

c.600 BC The **Phocaeans**, the most adventurous of the seafaring Greeks, establish a trading colony at **Massalia** (modern Marseilles) on the southern coast of France close to the mouth of the Rhône river.

573 BC The Syrian Levant is overrun by the Babylonian army of **King Nabocodonozor** (Nebuchadnezzar). Those Phoenicians who can, flee to **Carthage** which now becomes the 'new Tyre', as well as the centre of a distinctive later Phoenician culture. The Carthaginians expand their business interests in southern Iberia, and their trading contacts with the Greek city-states. Greeks and Phoenicians frequently carry each other's wares across the Mediterranean, although later conflict between Carthage and the Greek 'tyrants' of **Syracuse** (in Sicily) will lead to maritime tensions, as a result of which Carthage endeavours to assert a monopoly over trade with southern Iberia.

c.570 BC In this year, if not before, the Phoceans of Massalia form a trading colony at **Emporion** (literally meaning 'emporium') in the Golfo de Rosas (Bay of Roses) on the far northeastern coast of present-day Spain. As Emporion grows into an important western Mediterranean port city, (made rich by exporting wine, oils and textiles), other smaller Greek colonies are founded on the eastern Iberian coastline, in present-day Catalunya, Valencia and Alicante. Although the Phoenicians have introduced southern Iberia to Greek products and some Greek ideas (including religious rituals), the development of Emporion links eastern Iberia to classical antiquity at a time when the northern and western parts of Iberia are, in one way and another, being colonized by the **Celts**. As a result the Peninsula becomes broadly divided between two different civilizations and cultures, the one deriving from the 'advanced' Mediterranean world, the other from the now dominant peoples of northwestern Europe.

Initially founded on an island, Emporion is soon transferred to a nearby site on mainland Iberia, where the

> **"** The Phocaeans were the pioneer navigators of the Greeks, and it was they who showed their countrymen the way to the Adriatic, Tyrrhenia, and the Spanish peninsula as far as Tartessus. They used to sail not in deep, broad-beamed merchant vessels but in fifty-oared galleys. When they went to Tartessus they made themselves agreeable to Arganthonios, the King, who had ruled the place for eighty years, and lived to be a hundred and twenty. Indeed, this person took such a fancy to them that he asked them to quit Ionia permanently and settle wherever they liked on his own land; the Phocaeans, however, refused the offer, whereupon the king, hearing that the Median [i.e. Persian] power was on the increase in their part of the world, gave them money to build a wall round their town. And he must have given them a great deal, for the wall of Phocaea is of pretty considerable extent, and constructed of large stone blocks fitted together. **"**
>
> Herodotus, *The Histories*, trans. Aubrey de Sélincourt

Greeks enter into a close protective relationship with a people known as **Indicetans**.

c.560 BC The Phocaeans, now deploying fearsome 50-oared war vessels, create a trading settlement at **Alalia** in Corsica, intended as a forward staging post for the trade with Iberia.

544 BC The **Persians**, seeking to invade Greece, occupy Asia Minor and lay waste several Greek cities, including Phocaea. The Phoceans take flight, joining their kinsmen in Massalia, Alalia and Emporion. The Greeks' increased trading activities in the western Mediterranean, aimed at supplying Athens and other mainland Greek city-states, draw them into open competition with the Carthaginians, as well as with the **Etruscans** of north Italy, who have significant commercial interests in the south of France.

c.535 BC The Carthaginians and Etruscans form an alliance against the 'western' Greeks. Following a sea battle off Alalia, the Greeks claim a victory but such is the damage to their fleet they subsequently abandon Corsica and concentrate on expanding their activities in southern Italy and France. Massalia becomes a main entrepôt on a new overland trading route connecting the Mediterranean to the Bay of Biscay, giving the Greeks access to tin deposits of **Galicia** in northwestern Spain.

The Carthaginians meanwhile, now enjoying naval supremacy in the western Mediterranean, extend the number of their trading colonies in southern Spain. Among the new settlements is **Cartagena**, known variously as Mastia Tarseion and 'New Carthage', encroaching on the Greek-controlled Spanish Levant.

509 BC The western Greeks and Carthaginians conclude a treaty that defines their respective spheres of interest in Iberia. The Greeks are excluded from direct trade with the southern peninsula, but are confirmed in their eastern peninsular possessions.

PETER OSZWALD, BONN

Limestone figure of a warrior found at Cerrillo Blanco and probably made in the first half of the 5th century BC

c.500 BC Archeological and other evidence suggest that the traditional tranquillity of Tartessus breaks down, and that for several decades violence becomes endemic in southwestern Iberia. Probably as a result of such conflict a warrior elite emerges, accelerating the emergence of a southern Iberian aristocracy.

c.480 BC The **Celticization** of western and northwestern Europe enters a new phase with the arrival of **La Tène culture**, which, with its metallurgical refinements and

The Peninsula Celts

Scholarly opinion about the **Celts** is divided between those who see them as a phenomenally successful group of warrior peoples who overran large swathes of western and north-western Europe during the first millennium BC, and those who regard 'Celticization' as having been primarily a process of cultural transformation. In some areas Celts clearly established themselves as a dominant, even exclusive population, while in others there is scant record of a wholesale displacement of pre-existent peoples even where Celtic culture, epitomized by the production and use of high-metal work, survives. But whatever else it was, the Celtic diaspora was not a deliberate programme of pillage and conquest accomplished within a relatively brief time-frame. Rather the Celts spread westwards slowly and unevenly, in fits and starts, from a homeland in central Europe, their formidable fighting abilities moulded around intense loyalty toward individual war-leaders.

Eventually the Celts reached Iberia, entering the peninsula from France across the Pyrenees, and also down the Atlantic seaboard. By the 4th century BC their culture extended over much of the north and west, including as far south as the Algarve in present-day Portugal. Along the **Ebro** and **Tajo** (Tagus) rivers Celtic remains have been found in great profusion; these include iron swords, shields and helmets as well as stoneware incised with characteristically Celtic curvilinear decorative motifs. In other

striking ornamentation of weapons and other artefacts, displaces the 'Hallstatt culture' of the earlier 'proto' Celts. As well as the British Isles and France, the La Tène Celts make their presence felt in the north of the Iberian peninsula.

c.450 BC From around this time **larger stone carvings** ('monumental statuary') are present in the archeological record of present-day Andalucía and Valencia as well as Tartessus. Notable examples include the life-size 'Dame of El Cerro de los Santos' and the figure of a bull from Sagunto.

---

areas very little has been unearthed. Since there is also an overlap at some sites between Celtic and Urn Folk materials, it has been argued that the number of Celts who came to Iberia were relatively few. Conversely surviving place names, particularly in Lusitania, attest a fairly widespread use of the **Indo-European** Celtic language.

While descriptions of the Iberian Celts by Greek and Roman authors do exist, notably by Diodorus of Sicily, these often seem to mix fantasy and fact. From them we learn that the Celts cleaned their teeth with urine, left the bodies of their warriors unburied so their souls could be released by vultures, suspended the heads of their enemies from doorposts, and chopped off the hands of their captives to offer to **Lupus** (god of the underworld), **Matres** (Mother Earth), **Epona** the horse-goddess and other deities. Such stories were often prompted by the Celts' fearsome reputation, but we do know that the Celts were sometimes employed as mercenaries by the western Greeks, and perhaps by the Phoenicians. Equally, while the **Celtiberri**, **Pelendones**, **Carpentani** and **Lusitani** undoubtedly were Celtic, others living in 'Celtic Iberia' – for example the Olcades, the Astures and the Vascones (Basques) – were not. On the eve of the Roman conquest, Iberia was still very much a patchwork of different peoples speaking different tongues; sometimes absorbing, sometimes spurning their immediate neighbours' customs.

> ❝ ... a peculiar practice is followed by them [the Celts] in the fashioning of their defensive weapons; for they bury plates of iron in the ground and leave them there until in the course of time the rust has eaten out what is weak in the iron and what is left is only the most unyielding, and of this they fashion excellent swords and such other objects as pertain to war. The weapon that has been fashioned in the manner described cuts through anything which gets in its way, for no shield or helmet or bone can withstand a blow from it because of the exceptional quality of the iron. ❞
>
> Diodorus of Sicily, *Library of History*, trans. C.H. Oldfather and Charles L. Herman

c.400 BC A proliferation of hill forts in Galicia and other parts of northern Spain confirms that Celtic settlements have taken root in the Iberian peninsula. Around this time **Rome**, one among many central Italian city-states modelled, begins building a wider polity that threatens the security of the Etruscan civilization to its north.

During the century ahead, Gades (Cádiz), effectively an autonomous Phoenician city-state, achieves pre-eminence as a supplier of finely worked jewellery and other luxury products (including a liqueur known as *garum*) to Mediterranean markets, in addition to the metalware it already exports.

348 BC The Carthaginians and western Greeks conclude a fresh treaty whereby the Greeks agree not to trade directly with anyone south of Cartagena. The Greeks however retain their monopoly over the Spanish Levant, which has become an important source of grain and salt for export to Italy and Greece itself.

La Dama de Elche, discovered in Valencia in 1897, is all that remains of what was probably a full-length figure. Carved from sandstone during the 4th century BC, a cavity in its back suggests possible funerary usage

c.325 BC The Greek traveller **Pytheas** explores Europe's Atlantic coast from the Strait of Gibraltar to the British mainland, which he circumnavigates.

264 BC When Greek cities in Sicily come under attack from Carthage, the **Roman republic**, now in control of the whole Italian peninsula, intervenes to defend them, sparking the first **'Punic' war** that lasts 25 years, the word 'Punic' being a Latin corruption of the Greek term for 'Phoenician'.

The Iberians

If the Celts were almost unassuageable in their violence and treachery towards the Romans, the so-called 'Iberians' of southern and eastern Spain swung decidedly the other way. Long exposed to Phoenician and Greek influences, in the 5th and 4th centuries BC such peoples as the Oretani, Bastetani and Libyphoenices, not to mention the 'original' Tartessians, exhibited a willingness to adapt elements of classical civilization to their own ends and traditions. It was however the **Turdetani**, inhabiting the middle and upper reaches of the Guadalquivir, well away from the previously developed seaboard, who made the greatest strides forward. Archeological excavations reveal up to two hundred townships, including the origins of **Seville** and **Córdoba**, which in some cases afforded paved streets and double-storeyed buildings of varying size and function, ranging from ordinary dwellings to larger residences and storehouses for grain, salted meats, olive oil and wine.

These **townships** were sited at regular intervals in the river basin, and an additional feature was the erection of watch-towers outside their walled perimeters that may have been used as communication points between settlements as well as for defensive purposes. While agriculture and mining continued to be the primary economic activities, these produced sufficient wealth to promote the emergence of both an indigenous aristocracy and specialized, often highly skilled craftsmen. Amongst the latter were those who catered for the needs of several **religious cults** that took root throughout the region. In some cases the gods worshipped were Greek or Phoenician, in others either local

241 BC The first Punic War ends with the defeat of Carthage. Rome gains control of Sardinia and Corsica, and begins trading directly with the Greek city-ports of Iberia. Tensions between Rome and Carthage continue however as each side vies for control of the western Mediterranean.

deities or cultural hybrids, including a widely disseminated **'mother goddess'** who perhaps harked back to a very distant past indeed, but who was also sometimes merged with the Carthaginian Tanit as well as the Phoenician Astarte.

To appease the gods, worshippers offered not only purifying libations at altars, but also **votive figurines** representing warriors, ordinary folk and animals. These were either cast in bronze and copper or carved from stone. Shrines and temples were constructed in a variety of places: sometimes in the open, sometimes in the mountains and sometimes in caves and grottoes. In the Sierra Morena two mountain cave shrines at **El Collado de los Jardines** (Santa Elena) and **Los Altos del Sotillo** (Castellar de Santiesteban) were almost certainly the end-points of laborious pilgrimages that must themselves have been a form of self-cleansing. At **Cerro de los Santos** at Montealagre in the south-east another shrine seems to have catered especially for the sick. Among a remarkable series of stone statues are several finely dressed women bearing beakers, as well as individual limbs presumably requiring urgent curative attention. Most arresting of all though are the near-monumental remains of what has been called a Tartessian 'sanctuary-palace' at **Cancho Roano** (Zalamea de la Serena near Badajoz), with a central structure measuring over 500 square metres. Here the main object of worship appears to have been an unadorned pillar, though its precise meaning is, like the non-Indo-European language or languages spoken by the southern Iberians, something that is lost in time.

238 BC In North Africa, Carthage experiences temporary weakness as a result of a revolt amongst its Libyan mercenaries. Rome takes advantage by annexing the western Mediterranean island of Sardinia.

237 BC A Carthaginian military aristocrat, **Hamilcar Barca**, leaves Carthage with his son **Hannibal** and other followers, takes control of Gades and Tartessus/Turdetania, and extends Carthaginian influence on the Mediterranean shoreline as far as Alicante. Unlike his Phoenician and Carthaginian predecessors, Hamilcar is intent on carving out a territorial empire in the Iberian peninsula. His actions are seen as a direct challenge to Roman strategic interests.

228 BC Hamilcar dies and is succeeded in his Iberian territories by his son-in-law **Hasdrubal Barca**, who continues the Carthaginians' expansionist policies. Determined to control the western Mediterranean, Hasdrubal creates a powerful naval base at **Cartagena** (New Carthage).

225 BC The **Gauls** (Celts settled in present-day France) stage an invasion of northern Italy and threaten Rome. Following negotiations between Carthage and Rome, Hasdrubal agrees not to advance his armies northwards beyond the Ebro river.

221 BC Hasdrubal is assassinated by a Celtiberian slave. His brother-in law (and son of Hamilcar) **Hannibal** becomes

> The Romans, seeing that Hasdrubal was in a fair way to create a larger and more formidable empire than Carthage formerly possessed, resolved to begin to occupy themselves with Spanish affairs. Finding that they had hitherto been asleep and had allowed Carthage to build up a powerful dominion, they tried, as far as possible, to make up for lost time.

Polybius, *The Histories* (Book II)

the ruler of the Carthaginians in Iberia, assisted by his brothers, Mago and another Hasdrubal.

220 BC The people of **Saguntum**, a Greek colony on the eastern coast north of present-day Valencia, appeal to Rome for protection against Carthaginian aggression. The Roman senate offers Saguntum its friendship and warns Hannibal not to cross the Ebro.

219 BC Hannibal attacks Saguntum, and then marches north, crossing the Ebro on his way into Gaul through the Pyrenees. A Roman army under **Publius Scipio** attempts to halt Hannibal on the Rhône, but fails.

218 BC As the **Second Punic War** between Rome and Carthage gets under way, the Roman Senate, fearing that Hannibal will make an alliance with the Gauls (who still exert a powerful influence in northern Italy), decides to dispatch an army to Iberia commanded by Publius Scipio's brother Gnaeus. At the same time Rome declares Iberia a Roman *provincia* called **Hispania.** Gnaeus Scipio lands with 20,000 troops at the old Greek port of Emporion, from where he begins a slow but successful campaign against Hannibal's brothers Mago and Hasdrubal.

Hannibal himself continues his advance through Gaul, crosses the Alps and begins campaigning in northern Italy. In November he defeats Roman forces at **Ticinus** and **Trebia**. Many of his troops however are mercenaries, and Hannibal is dependent on silver from Iberia to pay for them.

217 BC Gnaeus Scipio is joined by his brother Publius in Iberia. By establishing military control over the north-east they are able to disrupt Hannibal's supply lines. An important Roman base is founded at **Tarraco** (modern Tarragona).

215 BC A Carthagininian army commanded by Hannibal's brother Hasdrubal is defeated on the Ebro by the Scipios. Hostilities between Rome and the Carthaginians spread to

Sicily and Sardinia. Roman seapower limits Carthaginian manoeuvres.

212 BC Gnaeus Scipio captures **Saguntum**.

211 BC The Roman campaign in Iberia suffers a severe setback when both Publius Scipio and Gnaeus Scipio are killed in separate battles. The Romans are pushed back to the Ebro, but, squabbling between themselves, Hannibal's brothers fail to press home their advantage.

At the end of the year Publius Scipio's 25-year old son, also called Publius but later known as **Scipio Africanus**, takes over command of Roman forces on the Ebro, with Junius Silanus as his able lieutenant.

209 BC The younger Scipio conducts a brilliant campaign against Cartagena (New Carthage), attacking the port city by both land and sea. Cartagena falls, and supplies to Hannibal in Italy are cut. Many Iberian chieftains, impressed by Scipio's generalship, begin siding with the Romans against the Carthaginians.

208 BC Campaigning in the southwest, Scipio inflicts a crushing defeat on Hannibal's brother Hasdrubal at **Baecula** at the head of the Guadalquivir valley.

206 BC In the culminating engagement of the Iberian campaign Scipio defeats Hannibal's brother Mago at **Ilipo** (near present-day Seville). The Romans occupy Gades (Cádiz) as well as the whole of the Guadalquivir valley and drive Carthaginian forces out of southern Hispania. In the same year a Roman township is founded at **Italica** (modern Santiponce, also near Seville) as a colony for veteran centurions who have fought in Iberia. In Rome itself, Hispania is confirmed as a 'province' (*provincia*). Before returning to Rome, the younger Scipio strengthens alliances with Iberian leaders as a means of preventing a Carthaginian return. There is a revolt among the Ilegestes, but this is quickly suppressed.

2: Roman Spain

206 BC–415 AD

Within four years of **Scipio Africanus**'s culminating victory over the **Carthaginians** in the Iberian peninsula **Hannibal** – already forced to withdraw to north Africa – was defeated. The Carthaginian threat defused, Rome could breathe again. Yet there remained the problem of what to do in the west. Should **Hispania** be left to itself or brought more permanently within the Roman sphere? To maintain a colony in Hispania would tie up men and other resources, and Rome's experience at maintaining possessions outside Italy was slight. On the other hand, given that roughly half Iberia's population was Celtic, and that the **Celts** in Gaul had shown themselves as much a menace to the republic as the Carthaginians, it made sense to try and reduce the risk of a pan-Celtic coalition forming. Moreover, Hispania was rich in minerals and other goods that were needed if Rome was to progress from being a successful city-state into something larger. At the least, Hispania could be made to pay for itself. At best, it could be made to yield a profit without imposing intolerable exactions on its inhabitants.

Although the details are sketchy, the party in favour of turning Hispania into a Roman *provincia*, spearheaded by Scipio himself, won an important debate in the **Senate** in 201 BC. At any rate, after that date there was little further talk of withdrawing troops from the peninsula, and it became accepted that Hispania would henceforward form part of the Roman world. Even so, the conquest, or pacification, of Hispania was a slow, drawn-out process that lasted well over a century. To begin with the Romans divided the province into two: **Hispania Citerior** ('Nearer Spain'), consisting of the Mediterranean seaboard and its hinterlands; and **Hispania Ulterior** ('Further Spain'), consisting of the south and southwest. In both, the majority of the population were Iberian, long used to the civilizing influences of the Mediterranean world, and who were therefore more inclined than not to welcome the Romans, both as new trading partners and as guarantors of their peace. But the 'two Spains' only accounted for half the peninsula. The north and the west of the country were mainly inhabited by Celts, among them the **Celtiberi** and **Lusitanians**, and throughout the 2nd century BC bringing these people to heel proved a major undertaking.

Nonetheless, the Romans persevered, and serving in Hispania became an attractive option for career soldiers and politicians alike. But just as, by the opening decades of the 1st century BC, the job of extending Roman rule over the whole peninsula was largely completed, so Hispania became involved in a series of **civil wars** that convulsed Rome itself, leading eventually to the acclamation of **Augustus** as emperor in 27 BC, and bringing the republic to an end. First, a bitter war was fought between the followers of **Marius** and the dictatorial **Sulla** in the 80s and 70s; then there was an equally protracted contest between **Julius Caesar** and **Pompey** in the 40s; and finally there was a power-struggle between Caesar's adopted heir **Octavius** (the future Augustus) and **Mark Antony** in the 30s.

In all these internecine wars Hispania was seen as an invaluable asset, either because of its wealth and manpower or as a refuge. But if Hispania sometimes paid dearly for its involvement – 49 BC in particular was a year of widespread devastation – once the emperor-system had been established it reaped the reward of almost four centuries of peace. This stability was marred only by the occasional intrusion of various peoples from **north Africa**, and, more threatening in the long-term, such 'barbarians' from the north as the Suevi and the Alani who, crossing the Rhine, managed to penetrate deep into neighbouring **Gaul** (France). But because Hispania had only the one narrow land frontier with Gaul, it was generally spared the border fighting inflicted on Roman provinces elsewhere; and it was not until the greater barbarian invasions of the **Goths** and the **Vandals** of the late 4th and 5th centuries AD that Spain's security was thrown into brutal jeopardy.

During the imperial period, Hispania, now an important provider of wine and olive oil, became fully integrated with the empire at large, to the extent that many leading figures of the Roman world could claim Roman-Iberian descent, among them the emperor **Trajan** (the first 'provincial' to accede to the throne), his Antonine successors, the emperor **Theodosius**, and such writers as **Seneca**, **Martial** and **Lucan**. Significantly, in 74 AD the Flavian emperor Vespasian extended the *Ius Latii*, or 'Latin Right', to the native inhabitants of Spain, putting them on an equal footing with the peoples of Italy. Yet even by then, distinctions between Romans settled in Spain and indigenous Iberians had become blurred, partly through marriage, and partly through previous grants of special rights to individual towns and cities. Rather, under imperial Roman rule, Iberian society evolved into a complex hierarchy. Nominally, at the top were the senior governors and administrators, sent from Rome for fixed periods, and also a number of senatorial families who had acquired estates in Hispania. Next came those who, though born in Spain, could claim special privileges by virtue of their Roman or Latin descent. Then there was a local Iberian aristocracy, then the *hoi polloi* of ordinary Iberian commoners or 'freemen', and finally a large number of bondsmen and slaves. But, by the 3rd and 4th centuries, thanks largely to the inclusive **meritocracy** that held the empire together and prolonged its life, such distinctions often went by the board. Much of Hispania had become urbanized, and within such cities as **Emerita Augusta** (Mérida), **Caesar Augusta** (Zaragoza), **Toletum** (Toledo) and **Corduba** (Córdoba) status and opportunities were alike fluid.

All told, Hispania was transformed under Roman rule, mainly because the Romans supplied a common culture to which, in time, all Iberians could subscribe. At its heart was a system of **encoded laws**, applied uniformly, and applied impartially. As well as dozens of **new towns and cities** the Romans built a network of **roads** that for the first time connected the disparate parts of the peninsula, and which helped erode the strongly tribal complexion that had existed hitherto. As importantly, the Romans furnished a **common tongue** for all to speak, to the extent that, with the exception of Basque, all the languages spoken in the peninsula today – Spanish, Catalan, Galician, Portuguese – are derivatives of Latin. More importantly still, toward the latter stages of their imperium the Romans introduced the Iberians to **Christianity**, which became their enduring religious faith, and which also, in times ahead, served as a bond with the rest of Europe.

206 BC The victorious **Publius Cornelius Scipio** (Scipio Africanus) returns to Rome, but leaves much of his army behind in Hispania under the command of **Cornelius Lentulus**. As well as strategic considerations, Hispania's rich mineral and other resources encourage some Roman leaders, including Scipio, to consider establishing a permanent **colony** or *provincia* in the Iberian peninsula.

205 BC Scipio is elected consul by the Roman senate – an appointment that strengthens the faction of those who want to incorporate Hispania into Rome's incipient empire.

204 BC As **Hannibal** continues to wage war against the Romans in Italy, Scipio crosses to North Africa to attack Carthage itself.

202 BC Scipio inflicts a decisive defeat on Hannibal at **Zama** in North Africa but chooses not to destroy Carthage. This brings the **Second Punic War** to an end, and the number of Roman troops in Hispania is subsequently reduced.

201 BC After much debate the Roman Senate decides to maintain a presence in Hispania, even though the Carthaginian threat has passed. This is partly because of Hispania's wealth, but also for long-term strategic reasons to do with the potential risk of the **Gauls** in France forming alliances with their Celtic counterparts in Iberia.

197 BC As Roman control over the Iberian peninsula spreads outwards from the eastern coast and the Guadalquivir river valley, Hispania is divided into two provinces: **Hispania Citerior**, covering the northeast and east; and **Hispania Ulterior**, in the south and southwest. Each province has its own military governor, usually a *praetor*, initially appointed for one year, then later for two.

195 BC Roman forces in the two provinces of Hispania, seeking to consolidate their control, encounter resistance from various peoples and tribes of the interior. The consul **Porcius Cato** assumes personal command of military operations in the peninsula, campaigning against both the **Celtiberi** and the **Turdetani**.

194 BC As their revolt spreads, the Turdetani are joined by the **Lusitani** (Lusitanians) in southwest Spain.

185 BC Following successful campaigns against the Celtiberi, the Romans establish a garrison at **Toletum** (Toledo).

179 BC The Romans create a settlement at **Corduba** (Córdoba). Roman troops campaign against the Lusitani in the southwest.

175 BC Roman troops begin campaigning in the **Duero valley**, pushing Rome's authority into the *meseta* and towards the northeast.

Around this time Celtiberian townships begin minting their own coinages in bronze and silver, either to pay for hostilities against the Romans or to render tribute.

170 BC After thirty years of campaigning Rome has brought most of the Iberian peninsula under its control. Pockets of resistance continue in the north and west, while the northeast (**Galicia**) remains to be 'pacified'.

155 BC A fresh revolt against Roman rule among the **Lusitani** in Hispania Ulterior begins.

154 BC A second major revolt against Roman rule begins in the interior of Hispania Citerior among a confederation of Celtiberian tribes. The revolt lasts 18 years, and is known among Roman historians as the Numantinum Bellum (**Numantine War**), named after the principle Celtiberian township Numantia (on the Ebro).

150 BC The Lusitanian revolt ends when **Sulpicius Galba**, the praetor of Hispania Ulterior, massacres its leaders, having invited them to a meeting to discuss peace terms.

146 BC The Lusitani again revolt, under the leadership of **Viriathus**, whose guerrilla tactics become legendary not just in Hispania but throughout the expanding Roman empire.

In North Africa, Carthage is destroyed by Scipio Aemilianus, bringing to an end the **Third Punic War** begun in 150. Henceforward the Carthaginians play no further significant role in history. In the same year **Greece** falls under Roman administration.

145 BC The consul **Quintus Fabius Maximus** arrives in Hispania to restore order. Although he enjoys some success against the Lusitani, he fails to capture Viriathus.

143 BC Viriathus forms an anti-Roman league that includes some rebellious Celtic tribes.

139 BC The Roman consul **Sevilius Caepio** induces three of Viriathus's closest allies to murder him. Following Viriathus's death, the Lusitanian revolt collapses, but the rebellion of the Celts continues.

138 BC **Junius Brutus** campaigns in the northwest and begins bringing Galicia under Roman control.

134 BC Rome dispatches its finest general, **Scipio Aemilianus**, to Hispania to subdue the Celtiberians and their allies. Scipio Aemilianus surrounds Numantia with a ring of seven fortresses, forcing the city to surrender, although many Numantians kill themselves rather than submit to Roman authority. Following Scipio's victory, the Celtiberian revolt collapses, and the two provinces of Hispania enter a period of **relative peace** that lasts half a century, although Roman forces continue campaigning in the Spanish hinterlands to bring so far unpacified peoples under Roman control..

125 BC Around this time an estimated 40,000 workers are involved in the extraction and smelting of **silver** in the region around Carthago Nova (Cartagena). Ten thousand pounds of silver are remitted to Rome annually, based on a tax-rate of five percent of produce.

123 BC The Roman consul **Caecilius Metellus** conducts operations against **pirates** who have infested the western Mediterranean from Iberian ports, and also from bases in the **Balearic Islands**. New townships are created at Palma and Pollentia on Mallorca, peopled with settlers drawn from Hispania Citerior.

120 BC Construction begins on the **Via Domitia**, a road connecting Italy with Hispania Citerior through southern Gaul (France).

110 BC Unrest, in the form of brigandage and cattle rustling, develops among the Lusitani in Hispania Ulterior, but is not deemed sufficiently threatening for reinforcements to be sent from Rome.

102 BC Continuing unrest among the Lusitani is compounded by a rebellion among some Celtiberians, but again the problem is contained by Roman forces already present in Iberia.

98 BC The consul **Titus Didius** campaigns against the **Arevaci**, a Celtic people living between the upper Duero and Ebro river valleys who until now have maintained their independence.

91 BC Rome's authority is challenged on home ground by the **Socii**, a confederation of Italian cities determined to reassert their historic autonomy.

87 BC The four-year War of the Socii (or **'Social War'**) is brought to a conclusion by the Roman commander **Lucius Cornelius Sulla**. Sulla uses his victory to impose a personal dictatorship over the Roman Republic which quickly sparks first political, then armed, opposition, led by **Gaius Marius**. The rivalry between Sulla and Marius plunges the Roman world into a civil war which spreads to Hispania. The same conflict is also the first in a series of domestic conflicts leading to the dissolution of the republic in favour of an emperor-system later in the century.

84 BC Marius dies, but his followers continue to oppose Sulla and his faction.

83 BC **Quintus Sertorius**, a supporter of the Marian faction, is appointed *praetor* in Hispania Citerior. Sertorius rapidly wins over his Iberian subjects through a series of lenient **tax reforms** and through his charismatic personality. In the same year however Sulla resumes power in Rome, having defeated Mithridates VI of Pontus to the east of Greece.

Sertorius (c.123–72 BC)

Arguably no other individual Roman had as great an impact on Spain as **Quintus Sertorius**. Born in Nurcia in northern Italy, he trained in law and gained a reputation for oratory in Rome before going off to Gaul to fight against unruly Teutons and Cimbri. During these campaigns he lost an eye in battle – a wound which, according to **Plutarch**, he was proud to display as a badge of courage. Returning to Rome, Sertorius made steady progress as a **military administrator** in the expanding Republic, and so inevitably became caught up in the civil war that erupted in 87 BC. Siding with **Marius**, Sertorius used his position as governor of **Hispania Citerior** to oppose **Sulla**, whose dictatorial aspirations he regarded as profoundly unrepublican. When Sulla's party gained the ascendancy in Rome Sertorius began building a personal fiefdom in the Iberian peninsula that for a few years functioned as a virtually independent state, with its own senate of some 300 mixed Iberians and Romano-Iberians. At Osca (Huesca) he set up a school for the sons of prominent Iberian chieftains, so that they too could become lawyers and jurists; and as well as forging a new political compact in Spain, Sertorius strove to create an army in which native Iberians were trained to perform to the same standard as Romans.

By these and other means Sertorius 'romanized' the Spanish as no previous governor or commander had done, and it seems that he was genuinely popular among those he ruled over. More questionable was his alleged willingness to enter into an alliance with Rome's great enemy in the east, **Mithridates VI of Pontus**, and some commentators have suggested it was his ambition to create a permanently independent Hispania once Sulla's faction had been seen off. But it was **Pompey**, Sulla's most gifted protégé, who in the end put paid to Sertorius's ambitions. Outmanoeuvred in 74 BC, Sertorius fled to the hills, where he waged guerrilla warfare before finally being murdered by his own lieutenant M. Perperna. About this last period of his life very little is known, enabling the legend of an intractable mountain warrior with a small band of followers to grow – an unlikely scenario given Sertorius's attested commitment to discipline Roman-style and abstemious personal habits.

> **❝** He [Sertorius] was also highly honoured for his introducing discipline and good order amongst them, for he altered their furious savage manner of fighting, and brought them to make use of the Roman armour, taught them to keep their ranks, and observe signals and watchwords; and out of a confused number of thieves and robbers, he constituted a regular, well-disciplined army. He bestowed silver and gold upon them liberally to gild and adorn their helmets, he had their shields worked with various figures and designs, he brought them into the mode of wearing flowered and embroidered cloaks and coats, and by supplying money for these purposes, and joining with them in all improvements, he won the hearts of all. **❞**
>
> Plutarch, *Lives*, trans. A.H. Clough

81 BC Apprehensive about Sertorius's growing strength in Hispania, Sulla orders **Caius Annius** to expel him. Sertorius flees to Africa, but returns to Hispania Ulterior at the invitation of the Lusitani, who acclaim him their supreme commander. For eight years the Roman authorities attempt, but fail, to dislodge Sertorius, who now becomes master of the Iberian peninsula.

79 BC **Quintus Caecilius Metellus Pius** arrives from Rome with a large army, but is unable to either capture or defeat Sertorius.

78 BC Sulla dies, but the Roman civil war continues as his protégé Gnaeus Pompeius – better known as **Pompey the Great** – crushes a rebellion led by Aemilianus Lepidus. Lepidus flees to Hispania with his supporters, many of whom join Sertorius following Lepidus's death.

77 BC Pompey arrives in Hispania to take personal command of the campaign against Sertorius, but is defeated by him at **Lauro**, south of Saguntum. As a result of his victory, Sertorius exerts control over the Ebro valley.

74 BC The war in Hispania turns against Sertorius when, with fresh reinforcements, Pompey defeats his army, probably near **Sigüenza**. Although Sertorius survives the battle, he is forced to concede most of his territory to Pompey, and is limited to conducting guerrilla-type operations against his enemy.

72 BC The Sertorian War ends when Sertorius is murdered by his second-in-command **Perperna** during a banquet at his base-town **Osca** (Huesca). Pompey reasserts direct Roman authority over both Hispanias, and founds **Pompaelo** (Pamplona) as a township for non-Roman subjects. Fresh campaigns against the Celtiberi are undertaken by Pompey's subordinate, **Pupius Piso**.

68 BC The young **Julius Caesar** serves as a district officer in Hispania Ulterior under the proconsul Antistius Vetus.

67 BC Pompey is given sweeping powers to clear the Mediterranean of a fresh infestation of **pirates**. Large Roman fleets are based in **Gades** (Cádiz) and the Balearic islands as well as elsewhere.

66 BC Following his success in suppressing piracy Pompey is sent east by the Roman senate to combat a resurgent Mithridates.

62 BC Having created a new province in Syria, Pompey returns to Rome where his prestige secures him near dictatorial powers. Julius Caesar is appointed praetor of Hispania Ulterior, where he achieves the final pacification of the Lusitani and consolidates Roman authority in the western Iberian peninsula.

> **❝** The province of Western Spain was now allotted to Caesar. He relieved himself of the creditors who tried to keep him in Rome until he had paid his debts by providing sureties for their eventual settlement. Then he took the illegal and unprecedented step of hurrying off before the Senate had either formally confirmed his appointment or voted him the necessary funds. He may have been afraid of being impeached while still a private citizen, or he may have been anxious to respond as quickly as possible to the appeals of our Spanish allies for help against aggression. At any rate, on his arrival in Spain he rapidly subdued the Lusitanian mountaineers, captured Brigantium, the capital of Galicia, and returned to Rome the following summer in equal haste – not waiting until he had been relieved – to demand a triumph and stand for the consulship. **❞**
>
> from Suetonius, *The Twelve Caesars*, trans. Robert Graves (1957)

60 BC To offset their rivalries, which threaten to return the Roman world to civil war, Pompey, Caesar and Licinus Crassus form the **First Triumvirate**, agreeing to share power.

59 BC Caesar leaves Hispania to become consul for the first time. In the following year he begins campaigning in **Gaul**.

55 BC Pompey and Caesar are given command over Hispania and Gaul respectively for a five year term as Crassus is dispatched to the east to campaign against the Parthians. Since peace prevails in the Iberian peninsula, Pompey remains in Rome, governing his territory through subordinates.

50 BC Crassus and his army are annihilated at **Carrhae** fighting the Parthians. Crassus's death removes the last restraint between Pompey and Caesar, who begin contesting supreme power in the Roman world.

49 BC Having pacified all of Gaul, in February Caesar marches his army into Italy, crossing the small river **Rubicon** on the way, and occupies Rome. When Pompey, now in Greece with a large army of his own, refuses to acknowledge Caesar's authority, Caesar marches back through Gaul to Hispania to ensure support in the west. In Hispania Citerior, he easily overcomes a group of Pompey's supporters at **Ilerda** (Lleida), and isolates two of Pompey's generals, Afranius and Petreius, in the Ebro valley. M. Varro, another Pompeian, surrenders Hispania Ulterior to Caesar, who marks his 'victory' by granting **Gades** (Cádiz) the status of a Roman *municipium* (municipality). Appointing **Cassius Longinus** as his proconsul, Caesar leaves Hispania to prepare for a campaign against Pompey. Cassius's repressive policies however stir almost immediate revolt amongst some Iberians, and a mutiny among his soldiers.

48 BC On 29 June Caesar crushes Pompey's forces at **Pharsalus** in Thessaly, and becomes undisputed master of the Roman world after Pompey is murdered in Egypt.

47 BC On Caesar's behalf, **Aemelius Lepidus** restores order in Hispania Ulterior. Attempting to flee by sea, Cassius is drowned.

46 BC Two of Pompey's surviving sons, **Cnaeus** and **Sextus Pompeius**, begin a revolt against Caesar in Hispania. First they besiege **Carthago Nova** (Cartagena), then they create a base for themselves in the Guadalquivir valley (Baetica). At the end of the year however Caesar himself lands in Hispania with an army to crush the rebellion.

45 BC In March, Caesar defeats Cnaeus Pompeius at **Munda**; but although Cnaeus is soon captured and killed, and Caesar re-establishes his authority over Hispania, Sextus Pompeius escapes.

Before leaving Hispania, Caesar creates further Roman *coloniae* (colonies) at **Tarraco** (Tarragona), **Carthago Nova** (Cartagena), **Hispalis** (Seville) and elsewhere.

44 BC Fearing that Caesar intends to abolish the republic, a group of conspirators led by Decimus Brutus and Gaius Cassius assassinate him on the steps of the Senate on 15 March – known as the **Ides of March**. On hearing this news, Sextus Pompeius sets up a base in Sicily.

43 BC To maintain order in the Roman world, **Marcus Antoninus** (Mark Antony), **Marcus Lepidus** and **Gaius Octavius** (Caesar's grandnephew and adopted son) form the **Second Triumvirate**. Responsibility for governing Hispania is given to Lepidus.

42 BC Brutus and his followers are defeated by Antony and Octavius at **Philippi**.

41 BC A Berber leader called **Bogud** crosses from north Africa to Hispania Ulterior and begins raiding Roman and Iberian settlements, possibly with the encouragement of Mark Antony.

39 BC The triumvirate comes to terms with Sextus Pompeius, who is allowed to continue as the effective ruler of Sicily, Sardinia and Corsica. Pompeius however uses the ports under his control to harry shipping in the western Mediterranean.

38 BC As the Second Triumvirate disintegrates, Octavius strips Lepidus of his authority in Hispania. Realising that, like Julius Caesar before him, Octavius is intent on establishing a dictatorship, Mark Antony withdraws to **Egypt**.

36 BC Octavius's loyal commander **Marcus Vispanius Agrippa** defeats Sextus Pompeius at sea. Lepidus attempts to gain control of Sicily, but his followers are persuaded to defect to Octavius. Lepidus is imprisoned at Circeii until his death in 13 BC.

32 BC Octavius musters support in Rome by demonstrating that Mark Antony intends to establish a separate empire in the east with his lover **Cleopatra**, queen of Egypt. Once again the republic is plunged into civil war.

31 BC Octavius triumphs over Antony at **Actium** in September and becomes sole master of the Roman world.

27 BC In January Octavius is proclaimed *imperator* (emperor) by the Roman senate, and adopts the personal title **Augustus**. Soon afterwards he makes his way to the Iberian peninsula to oversee a campaign designed to pacify the **Cantabri** and **Astures** in the mountainous north.

25 BC Satisfied that he has succeeded in bringing the Cantabri and Astures under control, Augustus returns to Rome. In a symbolic ceremony the gates of the Temple of

ROBERT HARDING

Built around 15 BC, the Teatro Romano at Mérida was a gift to the city from Agrippa

Janus are closed, meaning that **peace** pertains throughout the empire. In Hispania Ulterior a major Roman township, **Emerita Augusta** (Mérida**)**, is founded for veteran legionaries on the upper reaches of the Guadalquivir. Perhaps in the same year another colonia called **Caesar Augusta** (Zaragoza) is founded on the Ebro.

22 BC The newly pacified Cantabri and Astures stage a second revolt. Augustus dispatches Agrippa to restore order.

19 BC Agrippa quells the Cantabri and Astures. In the northern mountains only the **Vascones** (**Basques**). inhabiting parts of the Pyrenees, remain independent, but they are not considered so serious a threat to warrant further campaigns.

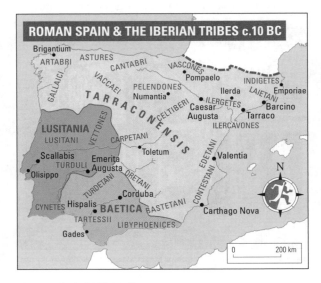

ROMAN SPAIN & THE IBERIAN TRIBES c.10 BC

It is around this time that Hispania is reorganized into three provinces: **Tarraconensis**, including the old Hispania Citerior, but now extending across the entire north; **Baetica** in the central southern region; and **Lusitania** in the west and southwest. Tarraconensis and Lusitania are designated 'imperial provinces', belonging directly to Augustus, while Baetica belongs to the 'people and senate' of Rome. The administrative capitals of the three provinces are **Tarraco** (Tarragona) in Tarraconensis, **Emerita Augusta** (Mérida) in Lusitania, and **Corduba** (Córdoba) in Baetica.

14 AD Augustus dies (19 August), and is succeeded as emperor by his adopted son **Tiberius**. On 17 September Augustus is declared to have become a god by the Senate, an initiative that quickly inspires the spread of his worship throughout the empire, including the three provinces of Hispania.

c.15 At about this time the Greek geographer **Strabo** writes an account of the Iberian peninsula that reflects rapid urbanization in those areas closely controlled by Rome, and the continuation of hilltop settlements in remoter areas.

37 The emperor Tiberius dies and is succeeded by his depraved nephew **Gaius Caligula**. Hispania however is sufficiently far removed from the Roman court not to suffer any of Caligula's cruelties at first hand.

41 Caligula is assassinated by his guards. He is succeeded as emperor by another nephew of Tiberius, the stuttering **Claudius**.

44 St James the Apostle is executed by the Judean puppet ruler Herod Agrippa I for preaching the divinity of Jesus Christ. St James will be later adopted as the patron saint of the Spanish.

54 Claudius dies, supposedly poisoned by his empress Agrippina. Agrippina's 16-year-old son **Nero** becomes emperor. Actual power however is wielded by the pre-

Seneca the Younger (c.4 BC–65 AD)

Rome in the mid 1st century AD was dominated, politically and intellectually, by a native of Corduba (Córdoba), **Lucius Annaeus Seneca**. Known as Seneca the Younger, since his father, a noted rhetorician, shared the same name, he spent his childhood in Hispania, but was brought to Rome in his teens, and then taken to Egypt, by an ambitious and well-connected aunt. As a young man he pursued a conventional path to high office by studying law, but in 41 AD was exiled to **Corsica** by the emperor Claudius for allegedly seducing the imperial niece Julia Livilla. Only in 49 was he recalled to Rome at the insistence of the empress Agrippina, whereupon Seneca became tutor to Agrippina's son **Nero**. When Nero became emperor in 54, Seneca remained at his side, and effectively ran the empire with his close friend **Sextus Afranius Burrus**, prefect of the Praetorian or household guard. Under their administration important fiscal and judicial reforms were introduced, and the empire prospered. However, he was unable to oppose Nero's increasingly tyrannical temperament, and one of Seneca's less welcome duties was to arrange Agrippina's murder in 59. He may also have had a hand in the death of Burrus in 62. In the same year he 'retired' from public life, and in 65 was commanded by Nero to commit suicide after being implicated by his enemies in a plot – an order he obeyed promptly and, by all accounts, with exemplary dignity.

Seneca died rich – by today's reckoning a multi-millionaire, his wealth accumulated through property speculation and by lending out the proceeds. According to the 3rd century historian Dio Cassio, he even prompted Boudicca's (Boadicea's) revolt in Britain when he called in various loans he had made. He is however chiefly remembered as a writer whose professed **Stoic** philosophy, opposed to the fun-loving, pleasure-seeking philosophy of the Epicureans, paints a grim and often violent picture of the world. Some forty of Seneca's works have survived, divided between essays and treatises of a distinctly moralizing character, and ten dramas, composed for recitation rather than performance. From the 16th to the 19th centuries Seneca was widely admired throughout Europe, not least because his tragedies were often the only specimens of **classical drama** available to playwrights. Shakespeare's *Titus Andronicus* and Webster's *Duchess of Malfi* are both recognizably Senecan, and among others strongly influenced by him were Calvin, Montesquieu and Rousseau, as well as St Augustine and St Jerome from an earlier age. Hispania could boast other famous authors from the 1st century AD, including the scurrilously epigrammatic **Martial**, and the 'silver' poet **Lucan**, whose unfinished *Pharsalia* attempted an epic account of the civil war between Julius Caesar and Pompey. Both belonged to Seneca's circle. It is Seneca himself however who Spaniards think of as the first true Spanish writer.

ARALDO DE LUCA/CORBIS

Marble bust of Seneca the Younger

> **"** If a true picture of our life should be flashed before your mind, you would think that you were seeing the representation of a city that had just been stormed, in which all regard for decency and right had been abandoned and only force holds sway, as if word had gone out to cause universal confusion. Fire is not idle, the sword is not idle; all crime is free from the law; not even religion, which has protected its suppliants in the midst of hostile invasion, affords any check upon those rushing to seize plunder. This one strips a private house, this one a public building, this one a sacred place, this one a place profane; this one breaks down, this one leaps over; this one, not content with a narrow path, overthrows the very walls that block his way, and reaches his booty over ruins; one ravages without murdering, another bears his spoils in a hand stained with blood; everyone carries off something that belongs to another. **"**
>
> Seneca, *De Beneficiis* ('On Benefits'), trans. John W. Basore

fect of the Praetorian Guard, **Sextus Afranius Burrus**, and by Nero's Iberian-born tutor, **Lucius Annaeus Seneca**.

68 Emperor Nero commits suicide in June after being sentenced to death by the Senate, which now recognizes **Servius Sulpicius Galba**, the governor of Tarraconensis in Hispania since 60 AD, as emperor. Galba departs for Rome, where he promotes Romano-Iberians to high office, but the severity of his policies rapidly alienates those senators who have supported his elevation.

69 The Praetorian Guard proclaims Galba's former ally **Marcus Salvius Otho**, who has served as governor of Lusitania, emperor. But although Galba is quickly murdered, Otho survives only until April, when he dies fighting another claimant to the throne, **Aulus Vitellius**. Vitellius's reign is also short-lived. In July Titus Flavius Sabinus Vespasianus is proclaimed emperor in Egypt. Known as **Vespasian**, and the founder of the **Flavian dynasty**, by December Vespasianus is the master of Rome. Despite the factional upheavals that have beset the Roman empire during the 'year of the four emperors', little or no disorder is experienced in Hispania.

75 The emperor Vespasian extends the *ius Latii*, or **Latin right**, to the 'free- born' people of Hispania. Originally granted to Rome's Italian allies in 338 BC, the *ius Latii* enables non-Romans to participate in local affairs, to advance their careers in the military, and to take advantage of other opportunities, including rights of legal redress, in the Roman world. As such it underpins the

> ❝ [Galba] ruled Tarragonian Spain for eight years, beginning with great enthusiasm and energy, and even going a little too far in his punishment of crime. He sentenced a money-changer of questionable honesty to have both hands cut off and nailed to the counter; and crucified a man who had poisoned his ward to inherit his property. When this murderer begged for mercy, protesting that he was a Roman citizen, Galba recognized his status and ironically consoled him with: 'Let this citizen hang higher than the rest, and have his cross whitewashed.' As time went on, however, he grew lazy and inactive; but this was done purposely to deny Nero any pretext for disciplining him. In his own words: 'Nobody can be forced to give an account of how he spends his leisure hours.' ❞

Suetonius, *The Twelve Caesars*: Galba, trans. Robert Graves (1957)

meritocracy of the empire during the period of its greatness. The *ius Latii* however is not extended to slaves and bond-servants.

79 The emperor Vespasian is succeeded by his son **Titus**.

81 Titus is succeeded by his brother **Domitian**.

96 The emperor Domitian is stabbed to death by a servant in Rome on 18 September. The following day the elderly senator **Cocceius Nerva** is proclaimed emperor.

98 In October Nerva adopts Ulpius Trajanus, a native of Hispania known as **Trajan**, as his son and co-emperor. Around this date work begins on the construction of the great **aqueduct** at Segovia.

99 Nerva dies in January, and Trajan becomes sole emperor. The first non-Roman to rule the Roman empire, he founds the **Antonine dynasty**. During Trajan's reign an

KIT KITTLE/CORBIS

The aqueduct at Segovia was built to carry water from the Río Frío some 18 kms out of town. It is made from large granite blocks held together without mortar

The Emperor Trajan (53–117 AD)

In 99 AD a 'provincial' became sole emperor of the Roman empire. That man was **Ulpius Trajanus**, a native of the relatively small city of Italica in Baetica. Yet Trajan's elevation to supreme power was neither accomplished by force, nor to the Roman world was it an unpalatable surprise. By the end of the first century Hispania was sufficiently integrated into the Roman orb to be regarded indeed as a *provincia*, not a mere colony, and Trajan's father, also named Ulpius Trajanus, was a well-respected and honoured member of the **Roman establishment** who had served as a consul, and as a governor of Syria and Asia, as well as of Baetica itself.

Although born in Hispania, of possibly mixed Romano-Iberian ancestry, Ulpius Trajanus Jnr spent little of his childhood in the peninsula. Rather he accompanied his father on his various postings, and under the emperors Vespasian and Domitian came to prominence in his own right. By 89 he was in command of a legion back in Hispania. In 91 he himself became a consul, and in the same year accepted the job of governor of **'upper' Germany**. By 98, when he was made co-emperor by Nerva, he had gained the trust of both Rome's military and political lobbies.

As emperor, Trajan left his mark in several ways. He restored good relations between the throne and the senate; he pleased the people by lowering taxation, at the same time instituting the first state-funded programme for the provision of poor and needy children in Italy; he expanded the empire by pacifying **Dacia** (present-day Romania), and by driving the Parthians back into eastern Iraq; and he encouraged public works empire-wide. In Rome itself he commissioned a new forum that included amongst its many monuments the eponymous **Trajan's Column**, a pillar adorned with a spiral frieze depicting the triumph of Roman arms during the Dacian campaigns of 101–106. He also founded the **Antonine dynasty** which lasted 96 years and is conventionally regarded as the high point of the empire. In retrospect the fact that a 'colonial' like Trajan could become emperor explains in part the longevity of the empire itself. Within the empire's boundaries doors tended to open rather than close.

imposing stone bridge across the Tajo is constructed at Alcántara near Cáceres.

117 The emperor Trajan dies on 8 August and is succeeded by his cousin and adopted son Publius Aelius Hadrianus, known as **Hadrian**. During Hadrian's reign his home town **Italica** in Baetica is comprehensively rebuilt as a showcase Roman city, with a new forum, amphitheatre, public baths, sports centre and other facilities, and also a monument to Hadrian's now deified predecessor. Italica becomes admired as the greatest city in the west; but because it is sited on an unstable clay bed, its heavy structures will soon collapse, and within a century it is abandoned.

138 Hadrian dies, and is succeeded by his adopted son Titus Aurelius Fulvius Boionus Arrius Antoninus, known as **Antoninus Pius**.

161 Antoninus Pius dies, and is succeeded by his adopted son **Marcus Aurelius**.

170 **Mauri** tribal warriors cross over to the Iberian peninsula from North Africa and ravage Baetica, causing widespread havoc. The raids continue for three years until the Mauri are expelled.

175 A second wave of Berber incursions from North Africa strikes at the south.

176 The emperor Marcus Aurelius dies and is succeeded by his son **Commodus**. A cruel and rapacious man, Commodus will be seen by future historians as the emperor under whose rule the Roman empire first begins to weaken.

185 For the first time there is evidence that **Christian** communities may be established in Spain. The legend begins to grow that St James the Apostle (**Santiago**) journeyed to and preached in the Iberian peninsula during the lifetime of Christ.

186 Maternus, an army deserter, forms a brigand band in southern Gaul and ravages towns and cities, sometimes venturing into Tarraconensis.

188 The Mauri return to Baetica and resume their raids against cities and settlements.

192 On 31 December Commodus is strangled by Narcissus, a court wrestler, at the instigation of his empress Marcia. Commodus's death brings to an end the rule of the Antonines, and ushers in a period during which the imperial throne is regularly contested by rival commanders, to the detriment of the state. Commodus's death also marks the waning of the influence of Romano–Iberians in Rome itself.

197 The reigning emperor, **Septimus Severus**, orders the elimination of his personal enemies throughout the empire. Several senators are stripped of their estates in Baetica.

212 The emperor **Caracalla** issues the *Constitutio Antoniniana*, an edict that confers Roman citizenship on all his 'free' subjects throughout the empire. Since in Hispania especially the distinctions between Romans and non-Romans are already blurred the edict causes relatively little practical change.

217 Caracalla is murdered by mutinous army officers. In the east, the empire is threatened by the gathering might of the **Persians**.

250 The reigning emperor **Decius** institutes a persecution of Christians throughout the empire. In the same year perhaps a people known as the **Goths** begin impinging on the empire's Danube border. From around this time too the Roman economy is seriously undermined by persistently debased coinage. Declining wealth leads to lower living standards in the cities of Hispania which also suffer from improvements in the export economy of Rome's north African provinces.

Despite Decius's persecution, **Christianity** begins to take root in the Iberian peninsula. Already there are significant Christian congregations in Tarraco (Tarragona), Emerita Augusta (Mérida) and other towns and cities, inspired and sustained by Christian communities in north Africa.

260 The empire temporarily fragments after the emperor **Valerian** is captured by Persians. Among various rivals for power **Latinius Postumus** creates a Gallic empire that includes much of Hispania.

270 Lucius Domitius Aurelianus, known as **Aurelian**, becomes emperor and begins reimposing Rome's authority over the western provinces. The empire's northern borders however become prone to attacks by the Franci (**Franks**) and Germani, who sometimes penetrate as far south as Tarraconensis.

278 Around this time two Germanic tribes, the Franks and the Suevi, cross over the Rhine and plunder parts of Gaul. Some Franks and Suevi reach as far as Tarraconensis in the peninsula, but are swiftly driven out.

284 Aurelius Valerius Diocletianus Jovius becomes emperor after the latest imperial assassination. Known as **Diocletian**, he will rule for 21 years, doing much to restore the integrity of the empire, even though he prefers to base his court at Nicomedia in Bithynia.

293 As a result of administrative reforms promulgated by Diocletian Hispania is divided into five imperial provinces: **Tarraconensis** in the northeast; **Carthaginensis** in the centre and southeast; **Baetica** in the south; **Lusitania** in the southwest and west; and **Gallaecia** (Galicia) in the northwest.

298 As tribal unrest erupts among the Berbers of north Africa reinforcements are sent to Hispania to protect the Strait of Gibraltar.

300 37 delegates, representing 37 different Christian communities in Hispania, attend a church council at Iliberis (modern Granada), more generally known as the **Council of Elvira**. The Council issues a series of edicts designed to promote **Christian practice**. Christian women are forbidden to marry non-Christians, gambling and money-lending are prohibited, and Christians are advised to avoid intimacy with **Jews**. While actors are told they must abandon their profession if they wish to remain in the church, reformed prostitutes are welcomed into urban congregations.

303 Diocletian enters Rome for the first time. Wishing to further strengthen the empire by reviving worship of the 'pagan' gods, he issues an edict banning Christianity. A great **persecution of Christians** follows, although the western provinces are only lightly affected,

305 Diocletian abdicates on 1 May. **Galerius Valerius Maximanus** and Flavius **Valerius Constantius** become co-emperors in his stead.

306 The co-emperor Constantius dies in Britain, where his son Constantinus, known as **Constantine**, is immediately acclaimed his successor. When Maxianus refuses to acknowledge Constantine the Roman world is plunged into acrimony and civil war, although as so often in the past Hispania is spared the immediate consequences of conflict.

312 Constantine marches on Rome and on 28 October defeats his enemies at **Milvan Bridge** – a victory that makes him undisputed emperor in the west, and which he attributes to the intervention of the Christian deity. Claiming to have seen a cross in the sky above the battle, he adopts the slogan 'By this sign shall you conquer' ('In hoc signo vinces').

313 Constantine, closely advised by an Iberian Bishop **Hosius** and his co-emperor in the east **Licinius**, formally adopts the Christian religion. By the **Edict of Milan** previously confiscated property is restored to Christians throughout the empire.

324 Following a decade of rivalry and civil war, Constantine triumphs over Licinius, whom he executes.

325 Constantine, now the sole ruler of a reunified empire, convenes the **Council of Nicaea** to determine Christian orthodoxy. The council, presided over by Hosius, bishop of Coduba (Córdoba), upholds the 'doctrine of consubstantiality' between Father and Son. The **Arian doctrine**, of the Alexandrine priest Arius, maintaining the inferiority of Christ to God, is repudiated, even though it is thought the emperor is a secret follower. Arianism however survives, and will later be embraced by the **Goths**.

330 Constantine formally adopts **Constantinople**, a city he himself has built on the shores of the Bosporus, as the capital of the empire. Dedicated to the Holy Trinity and to the Virgin Mary, Constantinople rivals Rome as a centre of power, and presages the permanent division of the empire. In`the east, a stronger economy, supported by Antioch (Syria) and Alexandria (Egypt), and greater wealth mean that increasing numbers of Romans are persuaded to abandon Rome.

337 The emperor Constantine dies, and the empire is divided among his three sons.

In Hispania, restoration work begins on the municipal circus at Emerita Augusta (Mérida), capable of holding 25,000 spectators.

360 The **Huns**, a Central Asian nomadic warrior people, overrun the territory of the **Alani** between the Caucasus and the Urals. As the Alani, an Iranian people, are pushed westwards into eastern Europe, so population pressures on the Roman Empire's frontiers are exacerbated. Very quickly the Hunnish expansion begins affecting the Goths, inhabiting northeast Germany (**Visigoths**) and southern Russia (**Ostrogoths**), the **Vandals**, living to the north of the Goths, and the **Suevi**, in central Germany and Slovakia.

361 Flavius Claudius Julianus, known as **Julian the Apostate**, becomes emperor and attempts to restore pagan worship by outlawing Christianity.

363 The emperor Julian is killed fighting the Persians. **Jovian**, his successor, immediately sets about reversing Julian's pro-pagan policies, so that Christianity resumes its status as the empire's official religion.

372 St Damasus, the Iberian-born bishop of Rome, convenes an ecclesiastical council which formally condemns Arianism as a heresy.

375 A scholarly ascetic known as **Priscillian** begins preaching an idiosyncratic form of Christianity in Baetica, Lusitania and Galicia. His doctrines particularly attract wealthy and female followers, and are soon perceived as heretical by the ecclesiastical establishment in Hispania.

376 As the Huns continue pressing westwards, the **Visigoths**, already driven out of their homelands and now massed along the northern banks of the **Danube** in the abandoned Roman province of Dacia, are permitted by the Romans to cross the river and settle as refugees. In return they are required to supply the Romans with tribute and military service. Resettled, however, the Visigoths, led by **Athanaric**, are badly treated by local Roman commanders who demand extortionate prices for foodstuffs, and then insist on being paid in kind with 'slaves'.

378 The Visigoths revolt against their Roman masters and on 9 August win a resounding victory at **Adrianopolis** (modern Edirne in Turkey), killing the eastern 'co-emperor' **Valens**.

To suppress the Visigoths, **Theodosius**, an Iberian-born commander, is summoned from Hispania by the emperor Gratian to replace Valens as emperor in the east.

379 With the aid of German mercenaries Theodosius suppresses the Visigoth revolt. The Visigoths are now recognized as 'confederates' of the Romans in the Balkans. Resettled in Moesia, they begin converting to Christianity, although it is the Arian, not the Nicene, creed they adopt.

Despite Theodosius's success in restoring peace in the east, the empire is undermined by major rebellions in Gaul, and by sedition among its western commanders.

380 A church council convenes at Caesar Augusta (Zaragoza) and censures **Priscillian**. Notwithstanding, Priscillian is elected bishop of Ávila, and the church in Hispania is divided between his followers and adversaries. **Hyginus**, the bishop of Mérida and Priscillian's principal opponent, appeals to the 'western' co-emperor Gratian, who imposes a ban on Priscillianism. Driven out of Hispania, Priscillian begins preaching in southern France. Brought to Rome, he persuades Gratian that his views are not heretical.

The eastern emperor Theodosius formally adopts the Nicene creed after recovering from an illness. From this date the suppression of paganism and the fostering of a uniform **'Catholic'** Christian faith, based on the Nicene principle of the 'consubstantiality' of God the father, Christ and the Holy Ghost, become central to Theodosius's policies.

383 **Magnus Maximus**, a Roman commander of Iberian descent, challenges the power of the emperor Gratian in the west and establishes an imperium of his own in Gaul and Hispania that lasts five years. Maximus, wishing to support Christian orthodoxy, agrees to reopen the case against Priscillian.

Priscillian (c.340–385)

The 3rd and 4th centuries were the great age of early Christian martyrs, victimized by intermittent attempts to restore pagan worship in the Roman empire. **Priscillian**, however, was the first Christian to be condemned to death for heresy by fellow Christians, who, however much they quarrelled on points of doctrine, had hesitated to use the final sanction against each other.

The precise nature of Priscillian's allegedly diabolical teachings is far from clear, since much of what we know about him is derived from the writings of his detractors. It seems he denied any separation – except in name – between God the Father and God the Son, contrary to the doctrine of the Holy Trinity; and from this he may have moved towards an even more 'unorthodox' position by proposing an essential dualism between matter (equated with evil) and spirit (equated with good). But the problem is that dualism simply became the litmus test of heresy, so it may be Priscillian is assumed to have been a dualist just because he was castigated as a heretic.

What is more certain is that in late 4th century Spain Priscillian created an ascetic and somewhat secretive movement that the church authorities found threatening. His followers abjured luxury, wine, sexual pleasures and even marriage, and possibly it was this holier-than-thou attitude, combined with the fact that many of his admirers were drawn from the upper echelons of Romano-Iberian society, that irritated those who had their own interests to protect. A serious campaign was waged against him by several Spanish bishops, and despite the intervention of St Martin of Tours, who regarded it as an ecclesiastical matter and not a civil one, Priscillian was tried and executed by order of the emperor **Maximus**. Killing Priscillian did not provide a solution to the problem, however, since many now regarded him as a martyr and Priscillianism survived well into the 6th century, especially in **Galicia**. More broadly too, the fate of Priscillian provided Christianity with an unfortunate precedent, since it replaced argued refutation of a man's ideas with licensed murder.

> **❝** If any credit could be allowed to confessions extorted by fear or pain, and to vague reports ... the heresy of the Priscillianists would be found to include the various abominations of magic, of impiety, and of lewdness. Priscillian, who wandered about the world in the company of his spiritual sisters, was accused of praying stark naked in the midst of the congregation; and it was confidently asserted that the effects of his criminal intercourse with the daughter of Euchrocia had been suppressed by means still more odious and criminal. But an accurate, rather a candid inquiry, will discover that, if the Priscillianists violated the laws of nature, it was not by the licentiousness, but by the austerity of their lives. They absolutely condemned the use of the marriage bed; and the peace of families was often disturbed by indiscreet separations. They enjoined ... a total abstinence from all animal foods; and their continual prayers, fasts and vigils inculcated a rule of strict and perfect devotion. **❞**
>
> Edward Gibbon, *The History of the Decline and Fall of the Roman Empire*

384 Priscillian is condemned as a heretic in his absence by a church synod convened at **Bordeaux** in Gaul.

385 Priscillian appeals in person to Maximus who confirms the ruling of Bordeaux and orders the execution of Priscillian and six of his followers for the sins of immorality and sorcery. Although opposed to Priscillian's beliefs, St Ambrose of Milan criticizes his principal accusers who are subsequently excommunicated by Pope Siricius.

388 Maximus is defeated and killed by the combined forces of the emperors **Valentinian I** (Gratian's successor in the west) and **Theodosius**, who is now married to Valentinian's daughter.

391 Valentinian I dies, and **Eugenius**, a pagan, becomes emperor in the west.

392 Aurelius Clemens Prudentius, a lawyer and official promoted by Theodosius, retires from public life to devote himself to study. Among his surviving works, the *Psychomachia*, personifying a contest between Faith and Idolatry, is the first Christian allegory. Prudentius will also be remembered for his Christian hymns and lyric poetry, some of which were set to music, after his death in the early 5th century.

> **"** Father of spirits, whose divine control
> Doth bind the soul and body into one;
> Thou wilt restore this body now undone;
> For once it was the mansion of a soul,
> Where dwelt the glowing wisdom of thy son. **"**
>
> Prudentius, from *Liber Cathemerinon*, trans. Percy Dearmer

394 Theodosius leads an army largely made up of Visigoths into Italy and overthrows Eugenius. Rather than promote a new co-emperor Theodosius assumes the title of sole emperor of the whole of the Roman empire – the last time it will be 'unified'.

395 Theodosius dies in January, and the Roman empire is again divided east and west, this time permanently, between his two young sons, **Arcadius** and **Honorius**. Guided by his regent **Stilicho**, a Romanised Vandal, Honorius establishes his court at **Ravenna** instead of Rome.

Theodosius 'the Great' (347–395)

The defeat and death of the eastern emperor Valens in 378 at the hands of the barbarian Visigoths at **Adrianopolis**, within an easy march of Constantinople, sounded alarm bells throughout the empire. Yet even as it seemed the empire must collapse, a fresh infusion of Spanish blood appeared to save the day, at least for a generation. **Theodosius**, a Romano-Iberian who claimed descent from Trajan (see p.57), was born and spent his childhood in **Galicia**. Like Trajan, he benefited from the exploits of his father, Flavius Theodosius, a commander who fought successful campaigns, first against the Picts and Scots in Britain, then in Gaul and the Balkans. By his mid-thirties the younger Theodosius was himself a commander, and gained fame by suppressing a Sarmathian revolt in 374. But in the same year he retired from public life, after his father was executed as a result of political infighting.

Following Adrianopolis, Theodosius was persuaded by the western emperor **Gratian** to abandon the quiet of his Spanish estates and take Valens's place. Within a year he had brought the Visigoths to heel, and had become emperor of the east. Ten years later he joined forces with Gratian's successor, Valentinian, to crush his fellow-Spaniard Magnus Maximus; and in 394 he became **sole emperor**. Yet Theodosius's military and political achievements were to prove short-lived. His sons, who inherited the imperial mantle, were weak-minded, and those whom Theodosius had appointed to administer their affairs quarrelled amongst themselves. In retrospect, too, Theodosius's policy of relying on Teutons, Goths and other 'barbarian' soldiers to fight his wars was a liability. In fact, he had little choice since by the late 4th century most 'Romans' were exempt from military service. Perhaps by 400 the empire was simply too far gone for any one individual, however talented, to mend. Yet Theodosius did have a lasting influence. With the help of **Bishop Ambrose of Milan**, he sought to impose uniformity of Christian faith throughout his imperium, preferring the Nicene creed, promulgated by the Council of Nicaea in 325, to all other versions of Christianity, including Arianism. As a result, although the empire crumbled in the west, there was a stronger sense of Christian orthodoxy than perhaps had prevailed hitherto, and it is from the reign of Theodosius that the term **'Catholic'** gained currency. At any rate it was because of this presumed achievement, as well as his rebuilding of **Constantinople**, which survived as an imperial capital for another thousand years, that the soubriquet 'the Great' became attached to his name.

WERNER FORMAN/CORBIS

Detail from a silver dish, the 'Missorium of Theodosius', made to celebrate the 10th anniversary of the Emperor's coming to power

397 The Visigoths, led by **Alaric**, attempt to settle in northern Greece, but are turned back by Stilicho.

401 The Visigoths begin ravaging the northern plains of Italy, but are again repulsed by Stilicho.

406 In the north of the western empire, the Vandals, in alliance with the Suevi and the Alani, cross the Rhine and begin ravaging Gaul.

407 In Britain, **Constantine III** is proclaimed emperor in opposition to Honorius. As the western empire becomes factionalized between followers of the rival emperors, civil war breaks out in the provinces of Hispania before Constantine is able to add the Iberian provinces to his territories.

408 Led by Alaric, the Visigoths advance southwards toward **Rome**. Honorius, fearful that he is about to be overthrown, orders the death of Stilicho, his most capable commander. Only when Honorius agrees to pay Alaric tribute do the Visigoths withdraw from outside Rome's walls.

As the western Roman empire enters into its final period of decline, fewer than 8000 legionnaires are stationed in the five provinces of Hispania.

409 Honorius is forced to acknowledge Constantine III as his co-emperor in the west. Constantine however is unable to prevent the Vandals, the Suevi and the Alani from entering **Tarraconensis** in September. Meeting scant resistance, the 'barbarians' begin plundering Hispania. The Vandals and Suevi overrun **Galicia**, the Vandals alone overrun **Baetica**, the Alani overrun **Lusitania** and parts of **Carthageninsis**. Only in Tarraconensis, where a Briton named **Gerontius** is proclaimed emperor, are Romans able to maintain partial control.

410 In August, at the head a Visigoth army, Alaric enters and **sacks Rome**, which is plundered of much of its wealth. Alaric dies soon afterwards, however, and leadership of the Visigoths passes to his brother **Athaulf**.

411 Throughout the year the Visigoths plunder central and southern Italy. In Hispania, the 'local' emperor Gerontius kills himself in Tarraco (Tarragona) when his house is besieged by a murderous mob. In Rome, the emperor Honorius naively urges the Visigoths to recover the western provinces on his behalf. Constantine III marches on Rome, but is murdered by agents of Honorius shortly after entering Italy.

412 Having despoiled Italy, but hard-pressed to feed his soldiers, Athaulf leads the Visigoths into southern **Gaul** where they establish a kingdom that is 'federated' with Rome. As Honorius's ally, Athaulf succeeds in restoring order in his new territory.

413 The Visigoths take control of Narbonne.

414 Athaulf marries the emperor Honorius's half-sister **Galla Placidia**, whom he has previously abducted during his Italian campaigns.

415 The Visigoths cross the **Pyrenees** into Hispania, where they war against the Vandals and Alani. Unlike their foes, the Visigoths are converts to Christianity, and their eventual conquest of the Iberian peninsula will ensure at least religious continuity in the collapsed Roman province.

3: Spain during the period of the Visigoths

415–711

The **Roman empire**, which lasted well over 600 years, collapsed within the space of fifty years – between the sack of Rome in 410 and the assassination of Emperor Valentinian III in 455. The most significant cause was the impact of the so-called **'barbarians'**, a catch-all term used to describe very disparate peoples, among them the Goths (subdivided into Ostrogoths and Visigoths), the Vandals, the Franks and, most fearsomely of all, the Huns. Each impinged across different parts of the empire's northern and eastern frontiers, and each pursued its own trajectory in relation to the Roman empire. Paradoxically the Germanic **Visigoths**, whom Alaric had led through the gates of Rome in 410, soon became Rome's allies, even its policemen. Moving westwards into southern France, they provided a buffer against the Franks in the north, and it was a Visigoth king, Theodoric I, who finally put paid to Attila the Hun, at Chalons in 451. Similarly, the Visigoths were used by Rome to restore control over **Hispania**. As early as 411 the emperor Honorius had encouraged the Vandals, the Alani and the Suevi, who had broken into Gaul across the Rhine, to settle in Hispania; but the continuing rapacity of the Vandals and Alani was a cause of continuing concern.

The Visigoths first entered Hispania in 415, but up until 429, when the Vandals and Alani departed *en masse* for north Africa, they were unable to do much more than re-establish control over the northeastern province of **Tarraconensis**.

There then followed a strange lull, when Rome persuaded the Visigoths not to intervene further in Hispania, and when the **Suevi** enlarged their influence in the western peninsula. But although formally the Visigoths had entered into a *foedus* (federation) with Rome, by 454 relations had soured to the extent that the Visigoths regarded themselves as a separate nation; and it is from this date that the Visigoth conquest of Hispania began in earnest.

If their previous campaigns in Tarraconensis had given the Visigoths a taste for Spain, then it offered the additional attraction of a safe refuge from the bellicosity of the **Franks**, who persistently attacked the Visigoth kingdom of Tolosa (Toulouse) in Aquitania (Aquitaine) in southwestern France. Yet the Visigoth conquest was long drawn-out and fraught with setbacks. Although the Romano-Iberians in the east, south and southwest generally accepted Visigoth dominance, the independence of the Suevi in Galicia continued at least until 576, while the **Vascones** (Basques), clinging on to their mountain strongholds in the Pyrenees, never were subjugated. In addition, the **Byzantines** – the inheritors of the eastern Roman empire – also attempted a conquest of Hispania, creating a province of their own in **Carthaginensis** in the southwest that lasted from 534 to 615.

The Visigoths, then, by no means had it all their own way. Even so, once the Byzantines, now hard pressed by the Persians in the east, had been forced to withdraw, Visigoth hegemony over most of the peninsula was assured. What is striking however is the extent to which the Visigoths abandoned the custom and culture that had originally accompanied them two centuries earlier, when they crossed over the Danube from Dacia – perhaps because numerically they were always at a disadvantage. At no point did the Visigoths make up more than five percent of the Iberian population, estimated at around seven million in 700. Rather than attempt to impose their own style of government, they largely opted to leave existing systems intact, so that for a majority of Romano-Iberians Visigoth rule represented continuity with the past rather than radical change. In time too the Visigoths ceased speaking their own language, adopting a late Latin tongue instead, and in 589 they forsook **Arianism** – a version of Christianity that downplayed the divinity of Christ and which the Visigoths had embraced early in the 5th century – in favour of **Roman Catholicism**.

As significantly, the Visigoths groped their way towards **hereditary monarchy**. Traditionally the Gothic peoples 'elected' their leader each time his predecessor died, sometimes amid scenes of rivalrous blood-letting – a custom caricatured as the *morbus Gothicus*, or 'Gothic disease', by such Christian commentators as Gregory of Tours. Attempts by successive Visigoth rulers in Spain to establish a royal dynasty as often as not met with opposition from the Visigoth elite; yet by 700 the principle of hereditary succession, strongly supported by Catholic churchmen, was more or less in place. As a result of this, and of the other accommodations the Visigoths had made with their Catholic Romano-Iberian subjects, by the beginning of the 8th century Hispania exhibited many of the characteristics conventionally associated with later Christian medieval nation-states, and might well have further evolved into a new centre of European civilization at a time of continuing instability elsewhere in the continent.

In the event, any such outcome was derailed by the **Arab-Berber Muslim conquest** of 711 – carried out with such startling rapidity that, in the past, historians were tempted to dismiss 'Visigoth Spain' as an irrelevant interlude. Today however, although it remains the case that documentary and other evidence for the period is fairly thin – for example, virtually nothing is known about the lives of ordinary, rank-

and-file Visigoths — a consensus has emerged that the Visigoth nobility were the preservers, not the destroyers, of what they found in the land they came to control, for all that they rewarded themselves with two-thirds of the Roman senatorial estates they coveted.

415 **Athaulf**, king of the Visigoths in southern Gaul and Tarraconensis (north-eastern Spain), is murdered by a fellow Goth while inspecting his royal stables at Barcino (Barcelona). Leadership of the Visigoths passes to one of his assassins, Sergeric, but he is quickly displaced by **Walia**, who resumes relations with Rome. Giving an undertaking that the Visigoths will serve Roman interests, Walia arranges for the return of Athaulf's widow Placidia to Ravenna, to rejoin her half-brother the emperor **Honorius**.

417 Promised a supply of corn by Honorius, Walia adopts a policy of slaughtering non-Gothic 'barbarians' (the Vandals, Alani and Suevi) in Hispania.

418 Walia recovers **Baetica** from the Vandals, but is then ordered by the co-emperor Constantius to withdraw to Gaul, where the Visigoths create a 'kingdom' centred on **Tolosa** (Toulouse). As the Visigoths depart, the **Suevi** move down from north-western Spain and occupy parts of Baetica.

423 The emperor Honorius dies in Ravenna without a direct heir. For two years the western empire is plunged into a succession crisis.

425 Honorius's nephew Valentinian III establishes himself as the western emperor. In Hispania the **Vandals** embark on three years of raids and plundering that terrorize the Romano-Iberian community. They also overrun the Balearic Islands.

428 The Vandals, having abandoned Galicia to the Suevi, and determined to assert control over the south, sack **Seville**.

429 In May, the Vandals, under the leadership of **Gaiseric**, leave Hispania *en masse* to settle in north Africa, where they successfully overrun Roman forces. North Africa provides copious grain supplies, and by sequestering these the Vandal conquest further undermines the western empire. In Hispania itself the Suevi move into those areas vacated by the Vandals.

436 A Roman army commanded by **Litorius** advances into southern Gaul to destroy the kingdom of the Visigoths, but is defeated outside the Visigoth capital Toulouse.

Advancing eastwards across north Africa, the Vandals occupy Tunisia and begin threatening Roman Sicily.

439 The **Suevi**, led by their king Rechilla, capture **Mérida** from its Romano-Iberian defenders.

The Visigoths agree to renew their federation with Rome, despite festering ill will between them.

441 The Suevi capture Seville. In the province of **Tarraconensis** a mainly 'peasant' revolt, raised in opposition to the continuing rule of Rome, is put down by Asturius, a Romano-Iberian commander.

442 The Suevi overrun the province of **Carthaginensis**. Except for Tarraconensis they now control nearly all the Iberian peninsula.

443 A second uprising among the *bagundae* (armed peasants) of Tarraconensis is crushed by Marobaudes, a 'barbarian' from Baetica who has been raised in Rome.

446 A Roman army led by Vitus is sent to Hispania but fails to reclaim territory from the Suevi.

448 Rechilla, king of the Suevi, dies a pagan. He is succeeded by his son, **Rechiarius**, a convert to Roman Catholicism.

449 Rechiarius agrees to marry a daughter of the Visigoth king **Theodoric I**. As he journeys to Toulouse to attend his wedding Rechiarius conducts a quick campaign against the **Vascones** (Basques) in the Pyrenees.

451 Led by Theodoric I and the Roman general Aetius, a combined Visigoth-Roman army inflicts a crushing defeat on the Huns at **Campa Catalaunici** (Chalons) in Gaul, decisively halting the advance of the Huns into western Europe. Theodoric is killed during the battle. The Hunnish leader **Attila** survives the fight, but his death two years later further undermines the Huns' confidence.

Theodoric is succeeded as king of the Visigoths by his eldest son **Thurismund**, who keeps Toulouse as the seat of royal power.

453 Thurismund is murdered by his brothers Theodoric and Frederic. Theodoric becomes king as **Theodoric II**.

454 Theodoric II's brother **Frederic** leads an army into Tarraconensis, the beginning of a long campaign to win control of all Hispania for the Visigoths.

455 In March, the emperor Valentinian III is assassinated. His death, which is followed by a period of sustained confusion in Italy, during which the **Ostrogoths** gain an upper hand, is conventionally held to mark the final collapse of the western Roman empire.

456 Theodoric II takes personal command of the Visigoth campaign in Hispania. He defeats King Rechiarius of the Suevi at **Parambo** (near Astorga) and enters **Braga**, the capital of the Suevi, on 22 October. In December Rechiarius himself is captured at Portucale and put to death.

> He is well set up, in height above the average man, but below the giant. The nose is finely aquiline; the lips are thin and not enlarged by undue distension of the mouth. Every day the hair springing from his nostrils is cut back; that on the face springs thick from the hollow of the temples, but the razor has not yet come upon his cheek, and his barber is assiduous in eradicating the rich growth on the lower part of his face. Chin, throat and neck are full, but not fat, and all of fair complexion; seen close, their colour is fresh as that of youth; they often flush, but from modesty, and not from anger. His shoulders are smooth, the upper- and fore-arms strong and hard; hands broad, breast prominent; waist receding. The spine dividing the broad expanse of back does not project, and you can see the springing of the ribs; the sides swell with salient muscle, the well-girt flanks are full of vigour. His thighs are like hard horn; the knee-joints firm and masculine; the knees themselves the comeliest and least wrinkled in the world.

Sidonius Apollonaris, describing Theodoric II in a letter to his brother-in-law, from The Letters of Sidonius, trans. O.M. Dalton (1915)

457 Theodoric II captures Mérida and occupies **Lusitania** in the south-west of the peninsula. He returns to Toulouse in May, and the Suevi continue to resist the Visigoths in Galicia.

458 The Visigoths establish control over the whole of **Baetica** in the south.

459 Theodoric II returns to Hispania to oversee further campaigns against the Suevi. As the Visigoths extend their power in Spain, and begin acquiring landed estates, they rely upon the existing Romano-Iberian administration as a means of government.

465 Theodoric II promotes **Remismund** as the 'puppet' ruler of the Suevi, loyal to the Visigoths. The Suevi court is coerced into accepting **Arian Christianity** (see p.62).

466 Theodoric II is murdered in Toulouse by his brother **Euric**, who becomes king of the Visigoths. Almost immediately he is faced with an uprising among the Suevi as Remismund renounces his allegiance to the Visigoth throne.

469 Euric assembles a large army in Gaul and marches into Hispania to campaign against the Suevi.

Death of **Hydatius**, a Galician-born cleric whose writings provide an important source for the history of the Iberian peninsula in the first half of the 5th century.

470 Led by Euric, the Visigoths establish firm control over most of the Iberian peninsula, placing garrisons in the more important towns and cities. The Suevi however, always prone to rebel, remain strong in the west – in Galicia and Lusitania – while Euric himself is soon obliged to return to Gaul, where his kingdom is threatened by the

> ❝ I must confess that formidable as the Goth may be, I dread him less as the assailant of our walls than as the subverter of our Christian laws. They say that the mere mention of the name of Catholic so embitters his countenance and heart that one might take him for the chief priest of his Arian sect rather than for monarch of his nation. Omnipotent in arms, keen-witted, and in the full vigour of life, he yet makes this single mistake – he attributes his success in his designs and enterprises to the orthodoxy of his belief, whereas the real cause lies in mere earthly fortune. ❞
>
> Sidonius Apollonaris, describing Euric in a letter to the Bishop of Aix, c.473, from *The Letters of Sidonius*, trans. O.M. Dalton (1915)

growing power of the **Franks**. In an effort to hold his Gallic territories together, Euric rotates his court between Toulouse, Arles and Bordeaux.

475 Euric authorizes a new **law code**, based mainly on existing Roman law but with some Visigoth additions. While the Visigoths remain subject to their own customs, the main purpose of the Codex Euricanus is to ensure continuity among his 'Roman' subjects, both in Gaul and in Hispania. Euric's determination to uphold **Arianism** however creates long-term resentment among many of his Catholic subjects.

476 The last of the western Roman emperors, **Romulus Augustus**, is forced to abdicate his throne at Ravenna.

484 Euric dies, and is succeeded as king of the Visigoths by his less forceful son **Alaric II.**

493 **Clovis**, king of the Franks since 485, begins warring against the Visigoths in Gaul, driving them out of **Toulouse**. An ardent Roman Catholic, Clovis projects himself as the protector of the Romano-Gauls against the 'heretical' Arian Visigoths.

498 The Franks enter **Bordeaux** and put its Visigoth governor to death. Continuing Frankish victories encourage many Visigoths to settle in Hispania, particularly in **Segovia** and **Toledo** and their environs.

506 Alaric II issues a revised law-code, based partly on the *Codex Theodosianus* of the emperor Theodosius (see p.68), intended to reassure his non-Gothic subjects of their rights, including the right to follow the Roman Catholic form of Christian worship.

507 Clovis inflicts a heavy defeat on the Visigoths at **Vonglé** (near Poitiers). During the battle Alaric II is killed. Alaric's young son **Amalaric** is proclaimed king, but his older half-brother **Gesalaic** seizes power. Gesalaic is quickly driven out of Narbonne by the Franks, and flees to Barcelona, where he is killed.

509 With the help of the Ostrogoths, who now rule Italy, the Visigoths regain control of Narbonne, giving rise to a new Visigoth province in southern Gaul known as Narbonensis, later **Septimania**. Alamaric is restored to his throne, but during his minority the Ostrogoths assume overall command in Hispania, where **Thiudis** is given the powers of a regent. Amalaric himself remains in Narbonne.

511 The Frankish king Clovis dies. The partitioning of his territories among his four sons relieves some of the pressure on the Visigoths.

516 A Catholic church council convened at **Tarragona** authorizes abbots and bishops to regulate the relations between monks and the 'secular' world at a time when monasticism is spreading in Hispania. **St Donatus**, fleeing Vandal rule in north Africa, sets up a monastery for seventy of his followers in Carthaginensis.

526 As the Ostrogoths' hold over Italy and the remains of western empire deteriorates, following incursions by the Lombards, Amalaric assumes the full powers of kingship over the Visigoths.

527 Hoping to forge peaceful relations with the Franks, Amalaric marries **Clothilde**, the sister of Childebert of Armorica.

531 A Frankish army drives Amalaric out of Narbonne. Like Gesalaic before him, Amalaric flees to Barcelona where he is murdered. **Thiudis**, formerly Amalaric's Ostrogoth regent in Hispania, assumes the kingship.

534 Having broken the back of Vandal power in North Africa the previous year, the **Byzantines** (from the 'eastern' empire based at Constantinople) take possession of the

Balearic Islands, preparatory to mounting a campaign to restore 'Roman' rule in the west.

541 A Frankish army crosses the Pyrenees and lays siege to **Zaragoza**. When the siege fails, the Franks return to Gaul.

546 The Byzantines threaten to invade Hispania, but are prevented by uprisings in Italy and north Africa.

548 In June Thiudis is murdered in Seville, and **Thiusdiscus** – an unrelated Ostrogoth – is proclaimed king.

549 Thiudiscus too is murdered in Seville, and the Visigoth nobility elect **Agila**, one of their kinsmen, as king. However, Agila, a fervent Arian, is challenged by another Visigoth, the Catholic **Athanagild**.

550 A Pannonian Greek, later known as **St Martin of Duma**, begins a 30-year mission among the Suevi. Persuading their leaders to become Roman Catholics, he founds several churches and monasteries in Galicia, and expunges the last vestiges of **Priscillianism** (see p.65).

552 During the reign of the strong reforming eastern emperor **Justinian**, Byzantine forces 'recover' much of **Carthaginensis** from the Visigoths. Assisted by the Byzantines, Athanagild displaces Agila as king of the Visigoths, but renounces his Catholic faith in favour of Arianism in order to win the support of his fellow barons.

554 In March the fugitive Agila is murdered by his own followers. The Byzantines occupy **Córdoba**, which becomes the capital of the **Byzantine province of Hispania**. Forced out of Córdoba, Athanagild re-establishes himself at **Toledo**, which now becomes the capital of Visigoth Spain. Warfare between Visigoths and Byzantines continues.

567 Athanagild dies without heir. **Liuva** is proclaimed king of the Visigoths in Narbonne, but declines to visit Hispania.

568 The Visigoth strongman **Leovigild** takes Athanagild's widow Godawintha as his wife and is proclaimed king in Toledo. Leovigild has two sons by a previous marriage, **Hermenegild** and **Reccared**, both of whom will become Catholics. Rather than attempt to re-unite the Visigoth kingdom, Leovigild energetically pursues the war against the Byzantines.

572 The Visigoths, led by Leovigild, recapture Córdoba from the Byzantines, who are pushed back toward the Mediterranean, making **Cartagena** their new provincial capital. In the same year the Narbonnese king Liuva dies and Leovigild becomes king of all the Visigoths.

Leovigild (d.586)

During the course of the late 6th and 7th centuries the Visigoth kingdom in Hispania emerged as the most cohesive in Europe. Although this was accomplished by a series of capable kings, including Athanagild, Reccared and Sisebut, most of the credit is usually given to **Leovigild**. When he came to the throne in 586 large parts of Hispania still eluded Visigoth control, but by greatly reducing the territory and influence of the **Byzantines** in Carthagenensis; overpowering the kingdom of the **Suevi** in Galicia; and imposing Visigoth authority over such northern montagnards as the **Sabi**, Leovigild managed to win renown for both himself and his crown. The first Visigoth ruler to adopt the insignia of kingship, he rebuilt Toledo as a royal capital, and raised an entirely new city, called Reccopolis after his second son, thirty or so miles east of modern Madrid. The central episode of his reign, however, was the 'Catholic' revolt of his oldest son **Hermenegild**, which brought into sharp focus one of the principal differences between the ruling Visigoths and their Romano-Iberian subjects.

Doubt surrounds Hermenegild's motives, some regard his 'conversion' to Catholicism as merely opportunistic, others think that he acted out of real conviction. For his part, Leovigild, though prepared to face down the rebellion militarily, initially sought a

573 Having contained the Byzantines, Leovigild begins campaigning in **Cantabria** to assert Visigoth rule in northern Hispania.

574 Leovigild overcomes resistance in Cantabria and begins campaigning against the Suevi in **Galicia**.

576 The Suevi agree that Leovigild should become their overlord, although Suevi kings continue to rule locally.

577 Leovigild campaigns in the south, crushing a rebellion in the **Sierra Morena**. Following his victories he proclaims his two sons as 'associate' kings as a means of establishing a dynasty. His eldest son Hermenegild is sent

religious compromise. At a council of Arian bishops convened in Toledo in 580, Leogivild modified Visigoth Arian doctrines, conceding Christ an equal status to God the Father, though still refusing to acknowledge the third element of the Catholic Trinity – the Holy Spirit. Simultaneously, by decreeing that henceforward Visigoths and Romano-Iberians could inter-marry, he removed one of the longest surviving barriers between the ruling elite and their subjects. With these concessions Leovigild aimed to promote unity in Hispania, and at least one Catholic bishop, **Vincent of Zaragoza**, came over to his side. Other Catholic bishops, however, notably **Masona of Mérida**, remained obdurate: their belief was non-negotiable, the more so as it represented the common culture of the great mass of Romano-Iberians. In the event Masona was exiled, and Hermenegild's revolt crushed. Yet within three years of Leovigild's death the rebel cause triumphed when **Reccared** converted to Catholicism, and persuaded many of his Visigoth peers to do the same. In retrospect Leovigild's reign was one of transition, during which it became increasingly apparent that the best and perhaps only way for the Visigoth monarchy to establish itself on a truly Spanish footing was to abandon Arianism altogether.

to Seville as governor of the former Roman province of Baetica.

580 **Hermenegild** raises a 'Catholic' rebellion against his father in Seville, requesting support from the Byzantines in Cartagena. Leovigild summons a council of Arian bishops at Toledo, and makes concessions to Catholicism (see p.64).

St Martin of Duma dies.

581 When Hermenegild fails to win Byzantine support, his father Leovigild decides to let him alone and concentrate on quelling the fractious Vascones (Basques) in the Pyrenees. As a result of Leovigild's campaign, many Vascones flee northwards into France, where they become known as **Gascons**.

583 As Hermenegild's revolt spreads among Catholics in Córdoba and other southern cities, Leovigild turns his attention towards his son.

584 Hermenegild's forces are defeated by Leovigild outside Seville. Hermenegild flees the battlefield, but is soon captured in Córdoba.

585 When Hermenegild refuses to renounce his Catholicism, his father orders him to be put to death at Valencia where he is being held. Leovigild then resumes campaigning in the north, where a fresh revolt among the Suevi has erupted. Leovigild defeats the Suevi and abolishes their monarchy, so that, nominally at least, the Visigoths once again rule all Spain. Meanwhile his younger son **Reccared** campaigns against the Franks in Gaul. To defend Narbonne, he attacks and sacks the former Visigoth capital Toulouse.

586 Leovigild dies in Toledo in May. According to legend he converts to Catholicism on his deathbed. He is succeeded by Reccared who is proclaimed 'king of all the Goths and Suevi' by his followers.

587 To heal the rift between Arians and Catholics, Reccared summons the church leaders of both persuasions to his court. During the **Council of Toledo** that follows, Reccared proclaims his own conversion to **Catholicism**, which henceforward becomes the official religion of Visigoth Hispania.

588 Reccared puts down a rebellion led by those Visigoth nobles who have refused to renounce Arianism. Observing his success, the Byzantines reinforce Cartagena.

599 **Pope Gregory I**, known as 'the Great', sends gifts to Reccared from Rome, by way of acknowledging the Visigoth king's full inclusion in the Catholic Church.

600 The scholar **Isidore** becomes Bishop of Seville, and is appointed papal *vicarius* in Hispania by Gregory the Great.

601 In December Reccared dies in Toledo and is succeeded by his eighteen-year-old son **Liuva II.**

603 Liuva II is overthrown by a group of Visigoth grandees dismayed by the young king's unwillingness to fight the Byzantines. **Witteric**, secretly tolerant of Arianism, assumes the throne. Despite his efforts the Byzantines hold on to Cartagena.

610 In April Witteric is assassinated during a feast at Toledo. Another Visigoth grandee, **Gundemar**, becomes king. Gundemar fights against the Vascones as well as the Byzantines.

612 Gundemar dies, apparently of natural causes, and **Sisebut** is proclaimed king of the Visigoths. An admirer of Isidore, Sisebut will be remembered as a pious and cultured monarch whose achievements include the authorship of a life of the Gallic saint Desiderius.

It is during Sisebut's eleven-year reign that Isidore completes the first version of his history of the Visigoths, *Historia Gothorum* as well as his *De virii illustribus*.

615 Sisebut forces the **Byzantines** to surrender Cartagena, and orders the city's walls to be levelled. The Byzantine province of Hispania, which has lasted sixty-three years, is brought to an end by his victory, although some 'Greek Romans' remain in Spain as subjects of the Visigoths.

Sisebut turns his attention to the northern mountains, where unrest still affects the Pyrenees, Cantabrians and Asturias.

621 Sisebut dies suddenly in February, possibly killed by medicines he has been prescribed. During his reign restrictions against **Jews** (mainly concentrated in southern towns and cities) have been imposed, barring them from owning Christian slaves, marrying Christian women and holding most public offices. Conversely, Jews who convert to Roman Catholicism are guaranteed property and other rights equal to those enjoyed by Christians.

Following Sisebut's death his son **Reccared II** is proclaimed king, but is murdered within a few weeks by Visigoth conspirators who resent hereditary succession. He is replaced by **Swinthila**, the son of Reccared I and the most able of Sisebut's commanders. Swinthila immediately begins expelling those Byzantines that have remained in Spain.

625 Swinthila concludes a lasting peace with the Byzantine Empire, which is too distracted by its war with the Sassanian Persian Empire to contemplate recovering Hispania. As well as the Balearics, the port city of Ceuta, on the north African coast close to the Strait of Gibraltar, remains in Byzantine hands.

626 Isidore presents Swinthila with a revised version of his chronicle *Historia Gothorum*, and also his tract **De laude**

> Of all the lands that extend from west to India, thou are the fairest, Oh sacred Hispania, ever-fecund mother of princes and peoples, rightful queen of all the provinces, from whom west and east draw their light. Thou art the honour and ornament of the world, and the most illustrious part of the earth, in thee the glorious fecundity of the Visigothic people takes much delight and flourishes abundantly... With good reason in another time golden Rome, chief of the peoples, desired to possess thee; but even though Roman valour, victorious, might first take thee as a bride, the driving race of the Goths came later and carried thee off to love thee, after many victorious wars fought over the vastness of the earth. That race delights in thee even today, secure in the happiness of its domain, with regal dignity and greatness of wealth.

St Isidore, *De laude Hispaniae*, from *Historia Gothorum*, trans. Theodore Mommsen

Hispaniae ('In Praise of Spain'), which predicts a glorious future for Hispania under its Catholic Visigoth kings.

In the same year Swinthila campaigns to drive the **Vascones** (Basques) out of Tarraconensis, where some of them have strayed from their strongholds in the Pyrenees.

631 The severity of Swinthila's rule provokes a cabal of Visigoth grandees, led by **Sisenand**, to invite King Dagobert of the Burgundian Franks to help them overthrow the king. Once Swinthila has been deposed, Sisenand is proclaimed king, and Dagobert and his men are paid off and return to Gaul.

632 In June, the founder of **Islam**, Muhammad, dies at Medina in Arabia. In his wake the Arab peoples, brought together and inspired by their new faith, embark on a series of conquests that will carry Islam into the Mediterranean world as well as into the Middle East and Central Asia.

633 During the **Fourth Council of Toledo**, presided over by Isidore, Sisenand prostrates himself before Hispania's assembled bishops and pleads forgiveness for his usurpation of the throne. The same council takes steps to exclude those suspected of Arianism from ecclesiastical positions, and, in an attempt to create uniformity of faith in Spain, places further restrictions on Spanish Jews.

637 In the scramble for power that follows Sisenand's death, **Khintila** uses force to overcome his rivals.

St Isidore (560–636)

Canonized in 1598, and declared a Doctor of the Church by Pope Innocent XIII in 1722, **St Isidore** was the outstanding figure of 7th century western Christendom. As a scholar, he produced a formidable output of books and treatises that were put in order and preserved by his disciple, St Braulio of Zaragoza. Chief among these was the twenty-part *Etymologiae* ('Etymologies'), an attempt to summarize all existing knowledge, ranging from theology to natural history, agriculture, architecture, cosmology and anthropology, and which, foreshadowing the 'seven liberal arts', inspired university syllabuses in much of medieval Europe. Other works include his *Historia Gothorum* ('History of the Goths') and *Synonima* ('Synonyms'), a handbook for contemplative meditation.

Prolific though he was as an author, Isidore was also active in the public arena and had a lasting impact on Spanish politics. Succeeding his brother, St Leander, as **bishop of Seville** in or around 600 AD, he sought to refurbish the Visigothic monarchy along quasi-theocratic lines by making the crown a divinely sanctioned institution that – like the Church itself – could reinforce

In the same year King Dagobert of the Burgundians campaigns against the Vascones settled in Gaul, driving many of them back into the Pyrenees.

639 Following two years' internecine warfare among the Visigoth leaders, Khintila is deposed and Tulga, strongly supported by the Romano-Iberians, usurps power. His reign is short-lived, however, as he in turn is ousted by another Visigoth strongman, **Khindaswinth**. Khindaswinth is illiterate, speaks only Gothic, is unsparing toward his rivals, and is mistrusted by both Catholic bishops and the Romano-Iberian community at large.

645 Eugenius is appointed Bishop of Toledo at Khinaswinth's insistence, despite having lampooned the king in

the bonds between man and God. His greatest triumph came in 633, when he presided over the fourth great **ecclesiastical council at Toledo**. Personally accepting King Sisenand's supplication for forgiveness following his usurpation of the throne two years earlier, Isidore used the occasion to cement a new partnership between church and monarchy.

At the same council Isidore took fresh steps to suppress 'heresy', particularly **Arianism**, and enforce **liturgical uniformity** in the Spanish church: henceforward the same version of the Catholic Mass would be celebrated throughout the peninsula. As a result, nowhere else in Europe was Catholic orthodoxy as well entrenched as it was in Spain. Although within a century of his death in 636, Isidore's achievements seemingly lay in ruins because of the Muslim conquest of Spain, when Christian Spain did revive, it did so in terms Isidore would have recognized and approved. The *Reconquista* ('reconquest') was led by kings who were very much Catholic kings – rulers who strove to overcome the 'infidel' for the glory of a closely defined faith they shared with those they ruled over as much as for any personal gain.

a book of ballads written three years earlier. Catholic priests, still fearing for their safety, leave Hispania.

649 Khindaswinth pursues a more conciliatory policy toward the Church as he seeks to have his son **Recceswinth** recognized as 'associate' king. Recceswinth has been educated by Catholic priests at Zaragoza, and helps soften the impact of his father's harsh rule.

653 Khindaswinth dies in November and **Recceswinth** becomes king.

In the same month Recceswinth convenes the eighth great council of bishops and Visigoth commanders at Toledo in order to affirm his accession to the throne. By kneeling before the assembled clergy he revives a ritual that binds the fortunes of crown and church. Pardoning his father's enemies, Recceswinth declares that the lands he has inherited from his father are to be regarded as a royal, not a personal, patrimony. He also concedes that it is ultimately the council's prerogative to elect or appoint a new king. The same council however stipulates that a ruler's son may be appointed an associate king provided the agreement of a great council is secured.

654 Supported by the Vascones, the Visigoth nobleman **Froila** raises a rebellion in the north. As he besieges Zaragoza the Vascones ravage the Ebro Valley. The rebellion collapses when Recceswinth relieves Zaragoza and orders Froila's execution.

Recceswinth promulgates the *Forum iudiciorum*, a law code that will survive into the Middle Ages as the basis of Christian government in Spain.

657 Recceswinth's queen **Recceberga** dies at the age of twenty-two without providing him with an heir. Recceswinth does not remarry, and the remaining fifteen years

PRIVATE COLLECTION

Polychromatic votive crown of the Visigoth king Recceswinth, with his bejewelled name hanging from the lower rim

of his reign are clothed in obscurity, although priests working out of Zaragoza are effective in re-enforcing the Catholic faith in Galicia and Lusitania.

The *Forum Iudiciorum*

Both in Gaul and in Hispania Visigoth rulers sought stability.
However, those whom they ruled over already had a system of
government based on **Roman law**, and to have arbitrarily
imposed **Gothic law**, which was based on custom rather than the
written word, would have been to risk unrest and even turmoil.
The short-term solution was to allow the two systems to run
parallel, Gothic laws for the Visigoths, and (in Hispania) Roman
laws for Romano-Iberians. In the longer term, particularly after
King Reccared had abandoned Arianism in 589, a synthesis was
forged that resulted in the *Forum Iudiciorum* issued by **King
Recceswinth** in 654. Recceswinth, though, was not the first
Visigoth ruler to issue a comprehensive legal code. Other codes
have survived, either in part or in full, from the reigns of Euric (476)
and Alaric II (506), and scholars now think that the *Forum
Iudiciorum* itself was based on 'lost' codes promulgated by
Leovigild and Khindaswinth, just as, in turn, it formed the basis of
a revised code issued by Erwig in 681.

Jurisprudence, then, was a central preoccupation of Visigoth
monarchs for over two hundred years, and Recceswinth's
achievement should be seen as the culmination of a lengthy
process rather than as the inspiration of one court. That said,
the **Forum Iudiciorum** (also called *Liber Iudiciorum*, or 'Book of

662 Muslim Arabs launch their first attacks against Sicily in
the central Mediterranean.

666 A great council is held at Mérida in order to mark the
'reconstitution' of the Catholic Church in **Lusitania**.

672 In September Recceswinth dies in Toledo. Ignoring the
bishops, a group of Visigoth dukes and counts (*duces* and
comes) proclaim **Wamba** as king, despite his protests that he
is too young. Wamba travels to Toledo to be anointed by
its bishop. According to the *Historia Wambae* ('Chronicle of

Judgements') does hold a special place in history, not only because its detail and range make it unique in western Europe for the time, but also because it survived the Muslim conquests to become the legal bedrock (called the *fuero juggo*) of the **later Christian kingdoms** of the Asturias, of Leon and Castile, and medieval Portugal. Blending Roman law with elements of Visigoth custom and accumulated ecclesiastical or **canon law**, Recceswinth's compilation aimed to provide laws that applied throughout the territories under his dominion without regard to ethnicity. Among its many provisions was the outlawing of all other law books, possession of which could incur a fine of 30lbs of gold. But if this now seems draconian, in other respects it was distinctly liberal. Even for serious crimes the death penalty is rarely recommended, fines and compensation being preferred. Of equal significance are the provisions made for administering justice. Judges are to be appointed for hearing and determining cases, but their authority is derived from the king himself, so that there can be no doubting that the ultimate source of justice is the throne. Conversely, kings too are required to abide by the laws they have sanctioned. By such adjustments, the traditional dictatorship of Visigoth leaders was tempered by Roman legalism.

Wamba'), at the first splash of oil a sweet scent and a swarm of bees are released from his head.

673 In Visigoth Gaul, the Count of Nîmes, **Hilderic**, mounts a revolt against the new king. Wamba sends a Geek Byzantine called **Paul** to negotiate with Hilderic, only to discover that Paul has had himself proclaimed king in Nîmes. Wamba interrupts a campaign against the Vascones and marches into Septimania. Paul is captured at Nîmes' Roman amphitheatre and taken back to Toledo.

In November Wamba makes all his male subjects, including priests, liable to military service. At the same time he takes measures to repair and extend the defences of Toledo.

680 During an illness, Wamba abdicates and is tonsured as a priest, designating **Erwig**, the half-Greek husband of a niece of Khindaswinth, his successor. When Wamba recovers later in the year he tries to reclaim the throne, but is forced by Erwig to retire permanently to a monastery at Pampliega, outside present-day Burgos.

681 The **twelfth great council** to be held at Toledo confirms Erwig as king of the Visigoths, although a minority of Visigoth commanders express their support for Wamba as rumours spread that he only abdicated because he was drugged while ill. The same council affirms previous church rulings (canon law) discriminating against Jews, and adopts measures that place the primacy of the Bishop of Toledo beyond doubt. Henceforward all other bishops in Hispania must be consecrated by the 'metropolitan' bishop.

An Arab Muslim commander, **Uqba ibn Nafi**, leads a warband through present-day Algeria and Morocco and reaches the Atlantic Ocean. As a result, the Mahgreb (present-day Morocco and Algeria) begins to come under Islamic rule.

687 Erwig dies in September. His son-in-law **Egica**, a nephew of Wamba, is proclaimed king.

688 According to some later chroniclers, retrospectively seeking an explanation for the calamity that will befall Visigoth Hispania in 711, the peninsula is ravaged by **famine and plague**.

691 A Visigoth aristocrat called **Suniefred** attempts to seize the throne from Egica, but his 'rebellion' proves short-lived.

694 The eighteenth council of Toledo, fearful that Jews may offer clandestine support for the advancing Muslims, orders their removal from ports on Hispania's eastern and southern shores.

697 Egica appoints **Witiza**, his son by another marriage, as his 'associate' king.

698 The forceful commander **Hassan ibn al-Nusayr** assumes control of the Muslim-Arab campaign to establish Islam across north Africa. As a means of pacifying the native Berbers, he promises them booty if they convert to Islam and enlist in his army.

700 Witiza is anointed associate king by the Bishop of Toledo.

702 Egica abdicates in favour of Witiza, who becomes sole king. Soon afterwards the Visigoths occupy **Ceuta**, the north African port city, most probably at the request of its Byzantine governor, who realizes he cannot hold the city against the Muslim Arabs without support.

705 In Damascus (Syria) **Caliph al-Walid**, ruler of Islam, declares that Ifriqiya (modern Libya and Tunisia) is a Muslim province in its own right, separate from Egypt. He also authorizes **Musa ibn Nusayr**, governor of Ifriqiya in succession to Hassan ibn al-Nusayr, to complete the Arab conquest of the **Maghreb**. As ibn Nusayr advances westwards, his army is strengthened by **Berber tribesmen** who have converted to Islam.

710 Following Witiza's death in February, attempts are made to enthrone his young son **Olmond**, but the boy is quickly pushed aside by the Visigoth aristocracy in Toledo, who prefer **Duke Roderic** (possibly a grandson of Khindaswinth). Roderic is accepted as king by Witiza's brothers, but the Visigoths in Septimania (Narbonne) reject him, and proclaim one of their own, Akhila, as king. The port city of Gerona also declares against Roderic. According to Arabic

A page from the 10th century *Codex Vigilanus*. The two upper rows depict the last Visigoth monarchs, the bottom row shows the monks who produced the codex

sources, one of Roderic's rivals, **Count Julian**, approaches ibn Nusayr's deputy commander **Tariq** for military assistance against the king. Muslim and Visigoth forces clash for the first time as Tariq advances on **Ceuta**, which surrenders to him in June, possibly at the instigation of Count Julian.

In July another of ibn Nusayr's commanders, **Tarif ibn Mulluk**, leads four ships carrying about four hundred Berbers across the Strait of Gibraltar on the first Muslim raid against the Hispanic mainland. They plunder a small area of the south before returning to Ceuta. Despite the possibility of a more serious Arab-Berber incursion, King Roderic allows himself to be distracted by a revolt among the **Vascones** in the north.

711 A much larger Arab-Berber force of around 7000 men is assembled by Tariq and lands in Hispania, possibly at or near **Algeciras.** By the time Roderic hears this news in May, further reinforcements of 5000 men have been sent by ibn Nusayr. Abandoning his campaign against the Vascones, Roderic prepares to march south.

4: The Islamic Conquest

711–1099

At the turn of the 8th century Hispania, or the **Kingdom of Toledo** as it is sometimes called, was the most stable state in western Europe. Under Visigoth rule the Iberian peninsula was relatively well-ordered, and relatively homogenized, although in the Pyrenees the Vascones (Basques) remained a law unto themselves. Across the land at large, **Roman Catholicism** prevailed, at least in towns and cities, sustained by a hierarchical church with the 'metropolitan' Bishop of Toledo at its apex. The same church supported – and was supported by – the Visigoth monarchy, which seemed to be on its way to becoming the preserve of a single royal dynasty. Yet within barely a decade of the beginning of the new century everything was turned upside down.

The vehicle of Visigoth Hispania's demise was its invasion in 711 by an Arab-led **Muslim army** composed mainly of north African Berber tribesmen who had earlier converted to Islam – part of a much larger series of 'Arab' conquests that, as well as spreading westwards across north Africa, had already swallowed up Syria, Iraq and Persia, and was knocking on the doors of Byzantine Constantinople.

With astonishing speed an empire had been and was being forged. But unlike its predecessors, the Arab-Muslim empire was based on a dynamic religious creed, and not just on the anticipated profits of territorial acquisition. Historically there can be no doubting the linkage between conquest and faith. Islam's founder, **Muhammad**, was himself a warrior. By the time of his death in 632 he had unified the disparate tribes of the Arabian peninsula into a cohesive entity, partly by force of arms, partly by diplomacy, and partly by the ideology he disseminated. Following his death the process of unification and expansion begun by Muhammad continued.

In many instances expansion was accompanied by naked rapacity. Existing kingdoms and cities were plundered and looted. But while the Huns, the Vandals, and the Goths themselves had all practised pillage, none of these tribal conglomerates brought with them the promise of spiritual certainty and redemption, or sought to convert the conquered to the conqueror's way of thinking. Everywhere that Islam triumphed a programme of **mosque building** was swiftly installed, and the civilization that emerged was sometimes more humane than at least some of its predecessors, with special emphasis placed on the succour of women and orphans.

The army that crossed over from Africa was led by mainly Yemeni Arabs, and had at its core a mixed Arab-Syrian cohort; but its rank-and-file were recently converted 'Berber' tribesmen (named after the Latin for barbarian) drawn from the peoples of the Maghreb (present-day Morocco and Algeria). But after a series of initial, stunning victories, the Muslim regime established at **Córdoba** soon ran into difficulties. Berber loyalty could not be taken for granted, and the Arab leadership itself reverted to clan and tribal rivalries.

More seriously still, from a Muslim viewpoint, in the mountainous north of the Iberian peninsula conquest proved illusory. In the Asturias, the Cantabrians and the Pyrenees enclaves of Christian resistance persisted – oppositional remnants that eventually furnished a springboard for the **Christian *Reconquista***, or reconquest, of the whole of Hispania.

Al-Andalus, as Muslim Hispania became known (the word literally means 'land of the Vandals'), also proved the limit of Islamic expansion, in western Europe. Having taken the peninsula by storm Islamic forces almost immediately campaigned beyond the Pyrenees. Although at first they again made startling headway, easily over-running the Visigoth Gallic province of Septimania, their defeat by the Franks in 732 effectively prevented further expansion.

It was a salutary lesson. It also laid the foundations for what became a remarkable passage in Spanish history. Defeated in France, the Muslims of Spain – known also as the **Moors**, because many of them had emanated from the former Roman province of Mauretania in Africa – set about consolidating what they had already gained. For a while al-Andalus, under **Umayyad** rule, became what it had been before: the strongest state in Europe.

The reason for this had much to do with numbers. Since the invaders could never outnumber the native inhabitants, after the initial ravages of war an extraordinary compromise set in. **Christians**, as well as **Jews**, were permitted to retain their faith. Restrictions were placed upon them, but from early on the Umayyad rulers of Iberia recognized that tolerance towards those described in the Koran as the 'People of the Book' was the most likely means of enduring success.

Out of this disposition arose an even more extraordinary social development. As Arabs and Berbers and other Muslims settled into their new surroundings, so ethnic and religious divisions blurred. Some of the Christian population converted to Islam, to become *muwallads*; others retained their faith, but adopted Arab custom and the Arab tongue, and these became known as **Mozarabs**. An added complexity was the presence of slaves, called **saqaliba**, who might come from almost anywhere, and who might rise to high position.

In time, cultural collision gave way to cultural exchange. Just as Christians and Jews contributed to the wellbeing of al-Andalus, whether as hired officials or as craftsmen helping assemble such incontrovertible symbols of Muslim rule as the **Great Mosque of Córdoba**, so al-Andalus became a conduit for the revival of European learning, based on the import of Greek and Arab texts from the Middle East.

How different was Islam from Christianity? During the eleventh century battle lines between the two monotheistic faiths hardened on both sides. Beforehand, the emergent Christian states of northern Spain jockeyed for advantage, both *vis-à-vis* al-Andalus, and amongst themselves. Yet the same period is also pitted with at least temporary alliances between Christian and Muslim strongmen. If mutual pillaging became endemic, it was practised by all, as the opportunity arose. But then, once the fact of Muslim occupation had been established, opportunism, particularly at the clan and dynastic level, was the order of the day, much as it was in the rest of early medieval Europe, and early medieval Islam.

The Muslim Settlement 711–866

In the wake of the Arab conquest perhaps between 150,000 and 200,000 Muslims took up residence in the Iberian peninsula, alongside an existing population numbering between five and seven million. Later further immigrants would arrive, but it is unlikely the ratio between Hispanics and non-Hispanics was ever much below 5:1. The majority of immigrants were **Berbers**, drawn from the nomadic and semi-nomadic peoples of the Maghreb. Many took Christian wives, to compensate a dearth of available Muslim brides. Further, it is possible that as many as seventy percent of those Hispanics still living under Muslim rule in the year 1000 had undergone at least nominal conversion to Islam. But since conversion usually meant adopting an Islamic name, it

becomes exceedingly difficult to extrapolate precise demographic trends from surviving records.

Historians are faced by similar difficulties when trying to
piece together a narrative of the conquest itself, later mythol-
ogized by Muslim historians and Christian chroniclers alike.
Whilst Islamic writers tended to view the conquest as a ful-
filment of a uniquely Islamic mission, Christian moralists
often saw it as God's rebuke on a people and a church fallen
into disrepute, epitomised by an injunction issued by King
Witiza in 702 that Christian clergy should marry – even
though Witiza's decree merely followed a lead that had
already been taken in Constantinople.

The only half-way creditable near-contemporaneous
source for the events of 711 and their immediate aftermath is
an unfinished Latin document compiled in Córdoba a generation later, known as *The Chronicle of 754*. While this pur-
ports to be a 'universal' history in the manner of St Isidore's
Historia Gothorum (itself a continuation of a history begun by
St Jerome), it attests the ferocity of Musa ibn Nusayr and
other Arab leaders. Christians were either put to the sword
or crucified; cities were sacked; and the countryside laid
waste.

Are such descriptions unduly apocalyptic? Probably not, if
only because it is hard to conceive how the Arab and Berber
Muslims (known also in western Europe as **Saracens**) should
have achieved so much so fast except by terror. Yet the
Chronicle also mentions one Theodemir, a Visigoth nobleman who, having valiantly resisted the invaders, then came to
terms with them, and was permitted to keep his estates
intact. And this, historians contest, was also a common pattern, and for much the same reason. For unless they co-
opted some at least of Hispania's existing stake-holders into
their regime, how else could the Arabs hope to maintain
control over such a large and potentially unruly territory?

The Arabs obtained their ends by combining crude military might with real-politik. To ensure their supremacy they hurriedly constructed fortified citadels, known as **alcazars**, in all the main towns and cities. But they also, wherever possible, allowed their conquered subjects to go about their customary lives without further molestation.

In the mountainous north however enclaves of undefeated Christians persisted, defending themselves, as the need arose, by guerrilla warfare. Gradually these coalesced into two important autonomous principalities: the Kingdom of the **Asturias**, and the Kingdom of **Pamplona-Navarra**. In addition, in Catalunya, east and south of the Pyrenees, the Frankish empire established a dependency known as the **Spanish March**.

In the long term the narrow northern territory, stretching from the Mediterranean to the Atlantic, survived and prospered just because it backed onto the emergent and equally Christian Frankish empire. In the interim however the Spanish Christian states eked out a precarious existence by exploiting weaknesses in the Islamic state of al-Andalus.

711 As King **Roderic** of the Visigoths campaigns against the Vascones (Basques) in the north, the governor of the Islamic province of Ifriqiya (Africa), **Musa ibn Nusayr**, orders an army to cross the narrow strait separating present-day Morocco from Spain. Commanded by **Tariq ibn Ziyad**, a Berber, this force is composed of Berber as well as Arab and Syrian soldiers. Roderic hurries south to meet Tariq's army, but is routed on 19 July in the **Guadalquivir river valley**, possibly at a site near Medina Sidonia. While the fate of Roderic is unknown – Muslim historians claim that only his white horse with a golden saddle inlaid with rubies and emeralds is found on the battlefield – many Visigoth nobles are slain, leaving the way open for Tariq to begin the conquest of Hispania. As a result of his success, the outcrop of rock at the mouth of the Mediterranean will become known as *Jebel Tariq* (the mountain of Tariq), later corrupted into the name **Gibraltar**.

712 As word reaches him that Tariq has taken Córdoba, Musa ibn Nusayr, apprehensive about his subordinate's ambitions, crosses over to the peninsula with reinforcements to assume command. To maintain protocol he has Tariq flogged, but allows him to retain his rank of deputy commander. Musa captures Seville and Medina, and then advances on Toledo, laying waste the upper Guadalquivir. As Sindered, the **Archbishop of Toledo**, flees – 'more like a hireling than a shepherd' according to the *Chronicle of 754* – votive crowns offered to successive Visigothic kings by a religious community are hastily buried at nearby Guarrazar. These will be unearthed in 1857.

> 66 Who can relate such perils? Who can enumerate such grievous disasters? Even if every limb were transformed into a tongue, it would be beyond human nature to express the ruin of Spain and its many great evils…Leaving aside all of the innumerable disasters from the time of Adam up to the present, which this cruel, unclean world has brought to countless regions and cities – that which, historically, the city of Troy sustained when it fell; that which Jerusalem suffered, as foretold by the eloquence of the prophets; that which Babylon bore, according to the eloquence of the scriptures; that which finally Rome went through, martyrially graced with the nobility of the apostles – all this and more Spain, once so delightful and now so miserable, endured as much to its honour as to its disgrace. 99

from *The Chronicle of 754*, trans. Kenneth Baxter Wolf (1990)

Islam

Islam, the faith of Muslims, began with the teachings of **Muhammad** (c.570–632), an Arabian warrior-politician known as 'The Prophet' who asserted that the 114 *suras* (chapters) of the **Koran** came to him as a divine revelation through the medium of the archangel Gabriel, from 610 until shortly before his death. Islam literally means 'obedience', which should be rendered to Allah, an Arab word originally meaning 'high god'. Of crucial significance – as the presence of Gabriel suggests – is that long stretches of the Koran rework the ideas and histories of both **Judaism** and **Christianity**, so that from its inception Islam was intimately identified with the established monotheistic tradition. Indeed, Jews and Christians were to be tolerated by Muslims as *ahl al-kitab* – 'People of the Book'. Muhammad also asserted, however, that the revelation he had received specifically superseded all other revelations; and much of the Koran is concerned with defining the social regulations of the ideal Muslim community, or *umma*, giving Islam a political edge notably lacking in the Christian New Testament.

Largely because of this, early Muslim clerical scholars were prompted to extrapolate the second mainstay of Islam from the Koran – the **Shariah**, or Islamic Law, covering nearly every aspect of everyday life in exhaustive detail, including rights of inheritance, rules of taxation, even dress codes. Yet despite the painstaking legalism of the *Shariah*, and because theological speculation has often been discouraged inside Islam, the Muslim faith has often won adherents by the clarity and directness of its principal requirements, summarized from early on as its **Five**

c.713 Having taken Toledo, Musa ibn Nusayr and Tariq march north into the **Ebro valley**, where Zaragoza falls to the Muslims. Musa and Tariq begin separate campaigns to flush Visigoth remnants out of the northern mountains, but before they can consolidate their gains the Umayyad caliph **Walid I**, jealous of their success, recalls them to Damascus. Taking

Pillars. These are: a profession of faith (or spoken acknowledgement that there is one god only, Allah, and that Muhammad is his messenger); regular prayer; fasting during the 'holy month' of Ramadan; the giving of alms for the benefit of the poor and needy; and a willingness to make a pilgrimage to Mecca, Muhammad's birthplace, at least once during the believer's lifetime.

Not included among the Five Pillars is *jihad*, variously translated as 'personal struggle' and 'holy war'. Yet the essentially Old Testament concept of *jihad* is most often aired in several of the Koran's *suras*, and has often been invoked by those termed fundamentalists, extremists, radicals and fanatics to justify and promote wars of aggression. Of these, the most spectacular and far-reaching occurred during the century after Muhammad's death, when Islamic and Arab expansionism coincided, creating a unified empire that stretched from Central Asia to the shores of the Atlantic, governed from Damascus by a caliph who combined supreme political and religious authority. These conquests included the Iberian peninsula; but once the first exactions of invasion were past, the ethos of Muslim rule was markedly tolerant, at least in **al-Andalus**, of which Hispania now became a part. Jews and Christians were permitted to retain their faith and customs. It has, though, been argued that there were good practical reasons for this. On the one hand by not converting to Islam non-Muslims were liable to pay a special and lucrative Koranic tax called the *jizya*; on the other, the ratio between conquerors and conquered was always in the latter's favour.

captives and a huge booty of bullion and jewels with him, Musa leaves his son **Abd al-Aziz** in charge of the campaign.

c.714 Although Musa ibn Nusayr is formally disgraced by the caliph in **Damascus** for having overreached his authority, Abd al-Aziz is confirmed as governor of Ifriqiya and commander of the Iberian conquest.

c.715 Having already overrun Málaga and Elvira (later Grana-da) in the south-east, Abd al-Aziz continues campaigning against remaining Visigoth strongholds. Like his father how-ever he too is recalled to Damascus, where his marriage to King Roderic's daughter has aroused suspicions of un-Islam-ic behaviour. But before he leaves Spain he is assassinated by his own followers in Seville. He is replaced as *amir* (gover-nor) by **Ayub ibn Habib**. Over the next thirty years eighteen new amirs will be appointed. Few retain the office for more than two years, and some for only a few months.

718–21 During the governorship of **As-Samh ibn Malik al-Khaulani**, territories in the conquered peninsula are distributed among Arab and Berber soldiers by lot. Notwithstanding this arrangement the Arabs gain the best estates in the south, while the Berbers are given poorer estates, especially in central Spain and the north. As-Samh captures Barcelona and Narbonne, and personally supervis-es the first attacks on the kingdom of the **Franks** (modern France).

c.720 As the last Visigoth outposts are overrun the whole of the Iberian peninsula, and also the erstwhile province of **Septimania** in southwestern France, falls into Muslim hands. Henceforward those parts of Spain and Portugal under Islamic rule – along with parts of the Mahgreb – are known as **al-Andalus**.

721 **As-Samh** is killed besieging Toulouse in southern France. His Arab commanders elect Abd al-Rahman ibn Abd-Allah al-Ghafiki as replacement governor before the caliph in Damascus can appoint his own nominee.

722 Just as the Muslim Arab conquest of the peninsula seems complete, either in this year or possibly in 718, a surviving Visigoth noble, **Pelayo** (or Pelagius), stages a rebellion in the mountainous north (near the Picos de Europa). Pelayo defeats a Muslim army at **Covadonga**, a victory that

Covadonga

Despite the nationalist hype that often surrounds the **Battle of Covadonga** and its victor **Pelayo** in Spanish literature, even the date of this apparently momentous event remains uncertain. Covadonga was fought either in 718 or 722, or some time in between, and was probably more of a skirmish than a large-scale military engagement. While it is accorded generous treatment in the 10th century Asturian *Chronicle of Alfonso II*, it is unmentioned in the *Chronicle of 754*.

As both Romans and Visigoths had learned to their cost, the mountainous north and its hardy inhabitants – Basques, Cantabrians and Galicians among them – were intractable at the best of times, and the most effective way to maintain peace was by persuasion and concession. The Arabs, more used to fighting in the desert, would have been reluctant to conduct a prolonged campaign in unfamiliar and hostile terrain, made all the worse by cold and rain; and in any case there was much still to be done in the lands already occupied.

Covadonga's true significance lies in its symbolic association with the creation of the **Kingdom of the Asturias** and the subsequent Christian reconquest of the peninsula. Just as the wooden cross reputedly worn by Pelayo during the battle would later be encased in gold by Alfonso III and revered as an icon of the *Reconquista*, so would Asturias one day transmute first into León, and then Castile. The battle also inspired a medieval verse epic, now lost, and the legend that the Virgin Mary appeared during the fight to inspire the Christian soldiers. In reality, however, in the first centuries of its existence the kingdom of the Asturias showed no special inclination to sustain a holy war against al-Andalus, and only expanded its territory during intervals of Muslim disarray. There is also the suggestion that Pelayo, who had been expelled from the court of the Visigoth King Witiza, might well have resisted Spain's hegemonic power whatever its character or identity.

enables him to found the small but independent Christian **Kingdom of the Asturias**. While it is probable that the

> Then Alqamah ordered his men to engage in battle. They took up arms. The catapults were set up. The slings were prepared. Swords flashed. Spears were brandished. Arrows were shot incessantly. But on this occasion the power of the Lord was not absent. For when stones were launched from the catapults and they neared the shrine of the holy virgin Mary, which is inside the cave, they turned back on those who shot them and violently cut down the Chaldeans [i.e. Muslims]. And because the Lord does not count spears, but offers the palm of victory to whomsoever he will, when the Asturians came out of the cave to fight, the Chaldeans turned in flight and were divided into two groups. There Bishop Oppa was immediately captured and Alqamah killed. In that same place 124,000 of the Chaldeans were killed. But the 63,000 who were left alive ascended to the summit of Mount Auseva and came down to Liébana through Amuesa. But they could not escape the vengeance of the Lord. For when they reached the summit of the mountain, which is over the bank of a river called the Deva, next to a village called Cosgaya, it happened, by a judgement of God, that the mountain, quaking from its very base, hurled the 63,000 men into the river and crushed them all.

from the *Chronicle of Alfonso II* (c.920), trans. Kenneth Baxter Wolf (1990)

Asturias and neighbouring Galicia in the far north-west of the peninsula have eluded Muslim rule since 711, the Battle of Covadonga will be celebrated as the first step in the *Reconquista*, or Christian reconquest of Spain.

725 Driving further and further into the kingdom of the Franks, Muslims sack Autun in Burgundy.

728 As the Arab or 'Saracen' threat to western Europe grows, Berber tribesmen stage an anti-Arab revolt in the Maghreb.

730 A Muslim army ravages Avignon.

731 **Abd al-Rahman al-Ghafiki** is confirmed as amir of al-Andalus by the Umayyad caliph Hisham in Damascus.

732 Having invaded Aquitaine, Abd al-Rahman al-Ghafiki and his Muslim army are convincingly defeated by the Frankish king **Charles Martel** near Poitiers. During the battle of Tours, as it is later called, Abd al-Rahman al-Ghafiki is killed. Although Arab incursions into France will continue for several years, the event marks both the beginning of the Carolingian dynasty in France and the containment of Islam in western Europe to the Iberian peninsula.

737 In the Asturias, King Pelayo is succeeded by his son **Fafila**.

739 The amir of al-Andalus, Ukbah ibn al-Hejaji, is deposed by his army commander **Abd al-Malik ibn Kattan**, himself a former amir (732-4) until disgraced for excessive cruelty. The outbreak of a further and major revolt by Berbers in the Maghreb adds to the confusion in al-Andalus.

King Fafila of the Asturias is killed by a bear, and is succeeded by his nephew Alfonso (known as 'the Catholic'), the son of Duke Peter of Cantabria and Ermosinda, daughter of King Pelayo. **Alfonso I**, claiming descent from King Leovigild of the Visigoths (see p.84), establishes his court at Cangas and conducts campaigns against towns garrisoned by Berbers in Galicia. To the south he orders the evacuation by Christians of the Duero River valley, thus creating a wasteland buffer zone between his own realm and al-Andalus. In response the amir creates a cordon of fortified 'marches' across what is quickly perceived as the viable northern frontier of al-Andalus.

> **❝** I saw Adam in my dream, and I said to him: 'O Father
> of mankind! Men generally agree that the Berbers are
> descended from thee.' 'Yes, it is true, but none dispute that
> Eve was at that time divorced from me.' **❞**
>
> Khalf ibn Faraj as-Samir of Almería, c.1080

740 Berber unrest spreads from north Africa into the Iberian peninsula, fuelled by their 'unequal' treatment
following the conquest. There is also conflict within the
Muslim leadership, between those already settled in al-
Andalus and Syrian reinforcements sent from Damascus
under the command of **Balj ibn Bishr**, a Yemeni Arab,
to quell the Berber rebellion. Feuding becomes endemic, as does slave-taking and cattle-rustling. Although
Christians are not directly implicated, some migrate to
the Christian north, and even to France. In the north
itself, the mainly Basque Christian citizens of
Pamplona expel its Arab governor.

741 Balj ibn Bishr captures Abd al-Malik, and has him crucified in Córdoba between a pig and a dog. Blood feuds
between tribally differentiated Arabs in al-Andalus
continue.

742 Balj ibn Bishr defeats Abd al-Malik's sons, but is himself
killed in battle. Arabs in al-Andalus now divide into two
factions, the 'indigenous' **Beladiun** and the 'arrival'
Shamiun.

747 **Yusuf al-Fihri** of the Beladiun asserts control over al-
Andalus, ending inter-Arab conflict. Despite an agreement
that the amirate should alternate between the two factions
annually, Yusuf massacres his Shamiun rivals and rules for
another nine years.

750 In Damascus, the enfeebled Umayyad caliphate is over-thrown by Abu al-Abbas, who founds the **Abbasid** caliphal dynasty. But although al-Abbas endeavours to exterminate every member of the Umayyad clan, one of them, **Abd al-Rahman**, escapes to the Maghreb.

756 Abd al-Rahman crosses from the Maghreb into Spain with his followers and joins forces with those opposed to Yusuf al-Fihri. He marches on Córdoba, defeats the amir, and re-establishes Umayyad rule over Spain. Although the Spanish Umayyads avoid issuing any challenge to the Abbasid caliphate, in effect al-Andalus becomes an autonomous Islamic state, with Córdoba as its capital. Taking the title amir, Abd al-Rahman will rule for 32 years. But although he eventually succeeds in reimposing a unified authority in al-Andalus, his almost constant struggles against Arab rivals present the emergent Christian states in the north with opportunities for expansion. To combat this, Abd al-Rahman appoints military governors along his land frontiers. But as these governorships become hereditary, so they will pose a threat to the amir's authority in Córdoba.

757 Alfonso I of the Asturias is succeeded by his son **Fruela I** 'the Cruel'. Fruela expels the remaining Berbers from Galicia, but also wars against Basques in Cantabria – a conflict partially defused by his marriage to a Basque aristocrat, Muena.

759 In southwestern France a major revolt against Muslim rule is sparked by the massacre of Arabs and Berbers in Narbonne. As Narbonne is handed over to the Frankish king **Pepin**, Charles Martel's son, anti-Muslim sentiment spreads into north-eastern Spain.

762 The Abbasids abandon Damascus, preferring **Baghdad** as the caliphal capital.

763 Abd al-Rahman quashes an Abbasid attempt to foment revolt in al-Andalus.

The Great Mosque of Córdoba

The **Great Mosque** of Córdoba, begun in the late 8th century and called *La Mezquita*, is regarded as not just the principal architectural monument of early Muslim Spain, but also one of the finest creations of Islamic architecture anywhere. At the heart of its conception is a mysteriously lit prayer-hall whose roof is supported by a forest of two-tiered, horse-shoe arches, each one decorated with alternate voussoirs of brick and stone. Despite the incongruous presence of a Christian building, inserted into the centre of the mosque in the early 16th century, there is no clear focal point for the eye to dwell upon. The chamber is at once centrifugal, and self-imploding. Its message is in its diffused evenness. Yet the tranquillity that greets the modern visitor belies a complex history.

When **Abd al-Rahman I** made Córdoba his capital the site was already occupied by a Christian church dedicated to St Vincent, and for a while this was shared by Muslims and Christians. Then, despite Muslim injunctions against the building of new churches, the Christians agreed to vacate the premises provided they could rebuild outside the city. St Vincent's was demolished, and work on the mosque began in 785. The original building consisted of a rectangular prayer-hall with a courtyard of slightly smaller dimensions in front. Roman and Visigothic columns and capitals were reused within the interior, and there was a greater emphasis on the *mihrab* (the prayer-niche indicating the direction of Mecca) than is now the case, with the central aisle which led to it being wider than the other ten aisles.

As the population of Córdoba increased, so enlargements to the building became a necessity, and a number of significant additions occurred under successive rulers. Those carried out under the caliphate of **Al-Hakem II** (between 962 and 966) are the most spectacular, and represent Córdoba's artistic apogee. The building was extended southwards, culminating in a new, horse-shoe arched *mihrab* richly decorated with stucco reliefs and mosaics. The domed chambers in front of the mihrab – encrusted with exquisite Byzantine mosaics of gold, rust-red, turquoise and green – constitute the *maqsura*, where the caliph and his retinue would pray.

Following the fall of Córdoba, in 1236, the mosque was converted to Christian use; and in 1526 the 'cathedral' was further 'modified' by the addition of a *coro* (choir) and chapter wall, in effect creating a building within a building. The work was sanctioned by Carlos I (Charles V), but when he saw the results he felt compelled to exclaim: 'You have built here what you or anybody else could have built anywhere, and in so doing have destroyed what is unique in the world.'

PRIVATE COLLECTION

A 19th century engraving of the Great Mosque of Córdoba

> **Light is admitted by the doors, and several small cupolas; but nevertheless the church [i.e. the Great Mosque] is dark and awful; people walking through this chaos of pillars seem to answer the romantic ideas of magic, inchanted knights, or discontented wandering spirits.**
>
> Henry Swinburne, *Travels through Spain in the Years 1775 and 1776* (1779)

768 Fruela I of the Asturias is succeeded by his cousin **Aurelius**, while among the Franks King Pepin is succeeded by **Charlemagne**.

In al-Andalus, Umayyad authority is weakened by renewed Berber revolt in the Maghreb, led by the Miknassa tribal strongman **Chakya**.

774 Aurelius of the Asturias is succeeded by a nobleman called Silo, who establishes his court at Pravia.

776 Chakya's Berber revolt ends when his followers murder him and send his head to the amir in Córdoba.

777 Abd al-Rahman crushes a second Abbasid attempt to foment rebellion.

778 At the request of the Muslim governor of Zaragoza, rebelling against Abd al-Rahman, **Charlemagne** marches into Spain at the head of a Frankish army. When the governor of Zaragoza reneges on his alliance, Charlemagne withdraws to France through the Pyrenees. The rear of his army, however, under the command of Count Roland, is mauled at the (First) **Battle of Roncesvalles** by combined Muslim-Basque forces. Out of this engagement is born the medieval chivalric French verse epic *Le Chanson de Roland* ('Song of Roland').

Beatus of Liébana composes the first of three versions of his Latin *Commentary on the Apocalypse*, in the belief that the world must soon end.

BRITISH LIBRARY

The four horsemen of the Apocalypse. An illumination from a manuscript copy of Beatus's *Commentary* copied by the monks of Silos in the early 12th century

780 Abd al-Rahman reduces Zaragoza and reasserts Muslim control over the Ebro valley.

781 An Abbasid army sent from Baghdad to destroy the Umayyad amirate is routed by Abd al-Rahman's forces. The severed heads of the Abbasid commanders are sent to the caliph al-Mahdi, who reputedly exclaims: 'Allah be praised for placing a sea between us.' Taking advantage of Muslim infighting Emperor Charlemagne's son **King Louis of Aquitaine** raids the Catalan region of north-eastern Spain.

783 Mauregatus, an illegitimate son of Alfonso I, seizes the Asturian throne following the death of King Silo.

785 The **Adoptionist Controversy** erupts when Elipandus, archbishop of Toledo, is upbraided by fellow Iberian eccle-siastics for the unorthodoxy of his views.

788 At his own behest Abd al-Rahman is succeeded as amir by his younger son **Hisham I** at the expense of his eldest son Suleyman. Turmoil ensues as dynastic infighting erupts.

In the Asturias Mauregatus is succeeded by Aurelius's broth-er **Vermudo I**, known as 'the Deacon' because of his piety.

791 Vermudo I abdicates in favour of **Alfonso II**, son of Fruela I and his Basque consort Muena. Known as 'the Chaste', Alfonso will rule for 52 years, relocating his court to **Oviedo**. Alfonso will also foster contacts with the Frankish empire.

In the same year Hisham I, having overcome his brothers, recommences campaigns against the Christian north.

793 Frankish forces are expelled from Gerona and Narbonne by the amir's army.

794 A communal war between Christians and Berbers in Tarragona is brought to an end when Arab forces intervene

The Adoptionist Controversy

In 780 the Archbishop of Sens sent a cleric called **Egila** to al-Andalus as a peripatetic bishop charged with reviewing the state of the church in Spain. Egila had no difficulty in identifying a local heretic, **Migetus**, who taught that not only Christ but also King David and St Paul were divine incarnations. **Elipandus**, as bishop of Toledo, and therefore head of the church in Spain, agreed to condemn Migetus, but in doing so committed an apparent heresy of his own when he wrote that Christ in his human form was only the *adopted* son of God. Having thus strayed into unorthodoxy Elipandus was duly condemned not only by an ecclesiastic council in Frankfurt, but also by Pope Hadrian I. Since however the church in Spain, now under Muslim supervision, enjoyed a life and routine of its own, Elipandus was personally unaffected by the storm he had created. He continued in office until his death, whereupon 'Adoptionism' more or less disappeared. In hindsight, though, the controversy was much more than a mere theological spat. Through its ramifications can be seen the determination of the emergent Roman Catholic Church to maintain and extend doctrinal orthodoxy in western Europe, the more so if, as some historians believe, Egila journeyed to Spain with, at the least, the papacy's approval. For the moment the Spanish Church remained relatively immune to outside intervention; but the will of the papacy to intervene, which would one day return Spain squarely into mainstream Catholicism, was already gathering strength.

after Christians are massacred. Tarragona itself however is abandoned as a Muslim garrison. An Arab army raids and destroys much of Alfonso II's Oviedo.

As the Adoptionist Controversy spreads, Bishop Elipandus is condemned by an ecclesiastical council summoned at Frankfurt by Charlemagne.

795 Arab Muslim forces continue to prevail against Alfonso II.

796 Hisham I is succeeded by **al-Hakem I** as amir of Al-Andalus. Al-Hakem bolsters his power by expanding his palace guard, by creating a regular (and largely Christian)

The Umayyads

As the Arab empire expanded in the 7th century, so the matter of who should rule over Islam became an acute issue. Some wanted a leader to be elected according to traditional tribal practice, others a succession of the Prophet Muhammad's blood relatives. Out of this conflict eventually emerged an enduring schism in Islam, between majority **Sunnis** and minority **Shiites**. The exigencies of territorial administration meanwhile necessitated an institution more or less akin to conventional kingship. The structure that took shape was called the **caliphate**, presided over by a caliph invested with absolute temporal power, but in theory at least subject to the censure of Islamic clerical scholars, or *ulama*.

In 661, after a period of civil war, the caliphate fell into the hands of **Muawiyya**, the governor of Syria, and a member of the **Umayya clan**. Muawiyya established his court at Damascus, and to give his rule a semblance of Islamic legitimacy launched a first, albeit unsuccessful, campaign against Christian Constantinople (Byzantium). He also established the principle of hereditary succession, so that for ninety years the caliphate passed to Muawiyya's descendants, until in 750 they were displaced by a rival dynasty, the **Abbasids**. The Islamic conquest of the Iberian peninsula therefore was essentially an Umayyad undertaking, and until 756 al-Andalus was administered by governors either sent from or approved by Damascus. When the Abbasids endeavoured to liquidate their Umayyad rivals, one of them, **Abd al-Rahman**, escaped westwards, made his way to Africa, and finally seized control of both the Maghreb and the Iberian peninsula. The hereditary amirate he founded lasted until 1031, having finally severed all links with Damascus in 929 when **Abd al-Rahman III** proclaimed himself Caliph of Córdoba.

slave-army of 1000 cavalry and 5000 infantry, and by instituting a network of spies in Córdoba, where he adopts a luxurious lifestyle unprecedented among his predecessors.

799 Pamplona, having reverted to Muslim rule at an unknown date, is again 'liberated' when its governor, a member of the **Banu Qasi clan**, is murdered along with other Arab officials. Pamplona re-emerges as an independent Christian kingdom ruled by **King Inigo Arista**.

801 Louis of Aquitaine captures the Catalan city of **Barcelona** and its surrounding territory. As a result the foundations of a Franco-Spanish 'march' are laid.

802 Amrus ibn Yusuf is sent by the amir to quell revolt in the north. The city of Pamplona is sacked, but the Christian kingdom of Pamplona survives.

803 A revolt by the Banu Qasi clan in Tudela is suppressed by the amir.

805 Al-Hakem I crushes a conspiracy against him in Córdoba. 72 ringleaders are publicly crucified.

806 Pamplona voluntarily submits to the suzerainty of King Louis of Aquitaine. Around Pamplona however the Basques will create the independent kingdom of Navarra.

In Toledo, on 16 November, known as the 'Day of the Ditch', al-Hakem I orders the massacre of 1500 potentially rebellious, mainly Arab citizens.

812 Following the death of Amrus ibn Yusuf, the Banu Qasi clan plan to take over the al-Andalusi 'northern march' which Amrus has strengthened.

813 The year traditionally ascribed to the discovery of the supposed tomb of St James the Apostle at Padrón on the Ría de Arousa. A church erected by Alfonso II to house the saint's remains marks the beginnings of **Santiago de Compostela** as a site of Christian pilgrimage.

Santiago de Compostela

Santiago is the Galician name for St James – the brother of St John, and one of the earliest disciples of Christ. Sometimes known as St James 'the Greater' (to distinguish him from a disciple with the same name), he is reputed to have preached the gospel in **Roman Hispania** by, among others, Beatus of Liébana (see p.119), although there is nothing in the Bible to support this. What the Bible does recount (in *Acts of the Apostles*) is the fact that James was executed 'with the sword' by King Herod Agrippa I in Jerusalem, probably around 44 AD. According to legend, his remains were then transported to Jaffa, and from thence by boat to Iria Flavia (modern Padrón) in Galicia.

With the Muslim conquest of the peninsula, the tradition of St James as a 'Spanish' saint gained a new lease of life. Although there is no reliable evidence for the story, around 813 a hermit named **Pelayo** apparently rediscovered the saint's tomb, guided by a vision of stars over a field. 'Campus Stellae', which is Latin for 'field of stars', may be the origin of the name Compostela, or it may derive from 'compositum', the Latin for burial place. Following confirmation of the discovery by Bishop Theodemir of Iria Flavia, Alfonso II of the Asturias commissioned a modest earthen shrine-church. This was later replaced with a much larger stone edifice by **Alfonso III**, and it is during his reign that **Santiago de Compostela** emerged as one of the most important of all Christian pilgrimage sites. The cult of St James also functioned as a form of anti-Muslim propaganda: one myth was that at the **battle of Clavijo**, Ramiro I was assisted to victory by the appearance on a white charger of Santiago, who by destroying thousands of the enemy earned himself the soubriquet 'Matamoros' ('Moor-killer').

814 In France, the emperor Charlemagne is succeeded by his son **Louis I**, formerly King of Aquitaine.

816 A revolt against Frankish rule in Pamplona is suppressed.

Although **al-Mansur** destroyed Santiago de Compostela in 997, he left the tomb itself undisturbed, enabling a third structure, the great Romanesque cathedral that still stands, to rise from the dust of its predecessors. By the time of its consecration in 1211 Santiago had already become a holy place in western Christendom. Subsequent visitors included St Francis of Assisi in 1214, and the mystique of St James was further bolstered by the creation of the crusading **Order of Santiago** (see p.170). As the modern nation of Spain slowly coalesced so the Apostle became its patron saint, despite the improbability of his actual remains being anywhere near the western Mediterranean.

ORONOZ

Romanesque tympanum from the cathedral of Santiago de Compostela showing St James as the 'Moor-killer'

818 Al-Hakem I crushes urban unrest in Córdoba by levelling an entire suburb.

822 Abd al-Rahman II succeeds Al-Hakem I as amir. He expands the Córdoban bureaucracy, and models his court on that of Baghdad, instituting Abbasid etiquette. A highly cultured man and a keen bibliophile, Abd al-Rahman II becomes patron to the noted singer and musician, Ali ibn Zaryab (known as **Ziryab**), an exile from Baghdad. Zaryab establishes a conservatoire, and is largely responsible for the introduction of many refinements into the Iberian amirate.

824 At the second **battle of Roncesvalles** the Franks are defeated by mainly Basque rebels. Pamplona again becomes an independent kingdom, soon adding Navarra and the county of **Aragon** to its territory.

827 Bernard, the Frankish count of Barcelona, crushes a Catalan-Visigoth revolt with the help of Abd al-Rahman II.

The Franco-Spanish March

Although much of the border between Spain and France is dominated by the high, and in places impassable, **Pyrenees** mountain chain, both west and east of the Pyrenees are relatively low-lying plains that, until the Umayyad conquest of Spain, afforded successive waves of human migration to the Iberian peninsula. From 711 however that process was briefly reversed. The heartlands of western Europe were threatened with Arab invasion and Arab settlement, precisely through the Iberian gateway. While the **Battle of Tours** in 732 effectively ended such a prospect, it was natural that, as the Empire of the Franks (i.e. France) expanded and consolidated its power, it should look to secure its southwestern borders. The options available were to bolster the emergent but vulnerable Christian states in northern Spain, or to directly annex frontier territory. Both options were tried. It was, however, the creation of a Franco-Spanish 'march' from the time of King Louis of Aquitaine's capture of **Barcelona** that had the greatest consequences. In time, as well as Barcelona, other French-administered counties were added, including Ausona, Gerona, Cerdanya, Pallars and Ribagarca. Barcelona however remained the linch-pin, and its count, known as the **Marchi**o, was the effective regional overlord. From 878 this

840 As the Cordoban court grows in stature it exchanges envoys with Christian Byzantium.

842 In the Asturias, Alfonso II dies without issue. In an intense struggle for the succession, **Ramiro I**, a son of Vermudo I, defeats his rivals. His eight-year reign will be marked by continuous factional infighting, but also by a revival of monasticism that draws a number of Christians from al-Andalus.

In al-Andalus, **Musa ibn Musa** of the Banu Qasi stages a rebellion against the amir, temporarily forming an alliance with the king of Pamplona.

position became hereditary, enjoyed by Count Wilfrid and his descendants, all of them uncharacteristically loyal to the French crown in an age of feudal self-aggrandisement.

Although the Franco-Spanish counties frequently suffered Muslim attack, and became entangled in the rivalries of the Christian states, over a period of three centuries their relative stability played a critical role in nurturing and sustaining contacts between Spanish Christians and Christendom proper. It was largely through this 'French gate' that Benedictine, Cluniac and Cistercian **monastic orders** spread into the Iberian peninsula, and with them the authority of the Papacy. As a result, the *Reconquista*, when finally it got fully under way, was perceived as an international as well as national undertaking. Similarly the umbrella of French rule helped preserve Catalan identity. Nor was the traffic all one way. The great monastic houses in France attracted members not only from the March, but through the March from deep within al-Andalus. These brought with them the books and learning that had seeped into Spain from the Middle East, among them **ancient Greek texts**, that helped make possible the '12th Century Renaissance' and its attendant revival of European culture.

The west end of San Miguel de Lillo near Oviedo, probably built as the palace chapel of Ramiro I

ROBERT HARDING

843 Abd al-Rahman II leads an army against Musa ibn Musa, whom he defeats before marching north to sack Pamplona.

844 The amir reinstates Musa ibn Musa as governor of the northern Muslim marches. In return Musa campaigns against the **Vikings**, who, having been repelled by Ramiro I of the Asturias, sail a fleet of 54 vessels up the Guadalquivir and assault Seville.

847 Musa ibn Musa resumes his revolt against Córdoba and effectively establishes an autonomous kingdom centred on Zaragoza. Married to King Garcia of Pamplona's daughter, Musa maintains his independence by making alliances with Christians as well as other rebellious Arabs.

850 Ramiro I of the Asturias is succeeded by his son **Ordoño I** who, taking advantage of Muslim disunity, begins extending his Christian kingdom onto the *meseta* south of the Cantabrian mountains. As well as occupying León and Astorga, Ordoño strikes eastwards along the upper Ebro valley, but is hindered by the alliance between Musa ibn Musa and Pamplona.

The Cordoban Martyr Movement

In the mythology of the *Reconquista* the fifty or so Christians executed in Córdoba in the 850s are collectively regarded as saints. The first was the monk **Perfectus**, who was beheaded in 850, the most famous **Eulogius**, who met the same fate in 859. Yet on the evidence available it appears they deliberately courted martyrdom. Eulogius, for example, the chronicler of the movement, was repeatedly told by his 'Muslim inquisitors' that, provided he stopped promulgating his fervently anti-Islamic opinions in public, he would be set free and left alone. Nor was any pressure put on him or any other of the martyrs to abjure their Christian faith. Rather it would seem the **Cordoban Martyrs** actively sought their own deaths by persistent provocation, without any encouragement from Church authorities. Indeed, the bishop of Seville, far from condoning Eulogius and his associates, condemned them from the pulpit. Even so the episode sheds light on communal tensions within al-Andalus. As the Muslim conquest consolidated, so the pressure mounted on indigenous Christians to adopt Muslim customs, if not necessarily to convert to Islam. Thus were born the **'Mozarabs'**, Arabized Christians who retained their faith. On top of this, the Church in Spain was subject to many restrictions under Muslim rule. Bells could not be rung, nor could any new place of Christian worship be built, while attempting to convert a Muslim was a capital offence. In such circumstances the wonder of it is perhaps there were, relatively, so few martyrs. As for St Eulogius, his remains were removed to Oviedo in 883, to become part of a growing treasury of Christian relics.

In Córdoba the Christian monk **Perfectus** becomes the first of the **Cordoban Martyrs** when he is executed for persistently denouncing the Prophet Muhammad in a marketplace.

851 Isaac, formerly a high-ranking official of the amir, denounces Islam at the monastery of Tabanos outside Córdoba and so becomes the second Cordoban Martyr.

852 Muhammad I, succeeding Abd al-Rahman II as amir, purges his court of Christian and *muwallad* officials.

856 Musa ibn Musa sacks Barcelona and takes two Frankish counts prisoner.

858 Muhammad I pays the Vikings a heavy ransom for royal women snatched from the north African amirate of Nakkur.

859 The Vikings again raid Seville, and plunder Algeciras. Muhammad I responds by ordering the construction of a new fleet.

Eulogius, author of *Apologeticum Martyrum* ('Defence of the Martyrs'), and leader of a literary Latin revivalist movement in al-Andalus, becomes the most eminent of the Cordoban Martyrs when he is executed for his diatribes against Islam.

861 Repelled by Muhammad I's fleet, the Vikings resume their raids on the Christian north. **King Garcia of Pamplona** is captured and ransomed for 60,000 gold pieces.

862 Ordoño I defeats the combined forces of Musa ibn Musa and King Garcia at **Albeda** and imposes Asturian rule on the Alva valley.

Following Musa's death in the same year Muhammad I re-establishes an al-Andalusi march in the Ebro valley.

866 Ordoño I is succeeded by **Alfonso III**, known as 'The Great'.

The Rise of the Christian Kingdoms 866–1099

By the middle of the 9th century Ummayad rule in the Iberian peninsula was seemingly secure, underpinned by an unbroken succession of capable and militarily accomplished amirs who, from the accession of Abd al-Rahman I in 756, had successfully developed al-Andalus independently of first the Umayyad caliphate in Damascus and then the Abbasid caliphate in Baghdad. Yet although culturally the best was still to come, with the flowering of **Córdoba** in the 10th century, by around 866, the year of **Alfonso III**'s accession to the Asturian throne, the storm-clouds were already gathering.

Alfonso III, called 'the Great', is regarded as one of Spanish history's heroes. A strong and devout monarch, he oversaw the **Christian repopulation** of the Duero valley. He also effectively opened up **Castile** (literally 'land of the castles', from the Arabic al-Qila) as a Christian territory; and it was Castile that, in the remote future, would furnish the backbone of the Spanish nation. But in itself Christian aggrandizement in the north was not a critical problem for the Cordoban amirate. Annually almost, Muslims and Christians fought each other, if only because warfare was virtually a way of life, affording chances of material and human booty, and keeping young bloods out of greater mischief.

The Umayyads however faced other problems. Because the amir also ruled territories in the Maghreb, he had to concentrate some of his energies and resources in that quarter. But while tribal uprisings were containable, now new kinds of turbulence festered in north Africa: firstly the emergence of the **Fatimids**, a Shiite Islamic dynasty who themselves had pretensions of ruling an extensive empire; and secondly ideological ferment – **Islamic reformers** who sought to restore the original purity of their faith by incubating their fanaticism in *ribats*, or military-religious camps located in distant or inaccessible places.

The al-Andalusi Umayyads stood up to the Fatimids, who, after a while, turned their attentions eastwards, founded Cairo and opened a fresh, important chapter in mainstream Islam. They also resisted the Norsemen, **Vikings** who regularly raided the peninsula's western and southern coasts of Iberia. But concurrently there were domestic troubles. Muslim rule over al-Andalus depended on local governors ensconced in strongly fortified towns often many days' or weeks' journey from Córdoba. Some of these governors were Arabs, some were Berber generals, others *muwallads* or even freed slaves. Such men, unless carefully controlled from the centre, were liable to rebel, for purely selfish reasons. By exercising autonomy they could keep taxes and other dues belonging to the amir for themselves. In the borderlands with the Christian states especially, where loyalties were notoriously ambiguous, there was always scope for an appointed strongman, or his successor son, to abrogate power.

The accession of Alfonso III coincided with a series of such rebellions: by the Banu Qasi; by Abd al-Rahman ibn Marwan; and most threateningly of all, by Umar ibn Hafsun.

All these circumstances undermined the status quo, and Alfonso III wasted no time taking advantage, first by filling the no man's land between his own and the amir's state with Christian settlements, and then by warring purposefully against the amir's strongholds. As a result he at least doubled the size of his domains, so that what had been the Kingdom of the Asturias became the **Kingdom of León**, with more than a foothold on the central northern *meseta*. But his very success inspired an equal reaction. If **Abd al-**

Rahman III failed to retake every lost territory, by overcoming his own Muslim rebels, and by determinedly waging war against the Christian kingdoms, he restored the prestige of al-Andalus.

So assured was Abd al Rahman III that in 912 he proclaimed himself caliph, severing the last formal link with Baghdad. By the time of his death in 962 even the Christian kings acknowledged his Iberian overlordship. Yet the accession of a minor, his grandson Hisham II, fourteen years later, and the assumption of power by Hisham's regent **al-Mansur**, set in motion the forces that eventually destroyed the Umayyads, and offered the Christian north fresh opportunities for aggrandizement.

Al-Mansur campaigned against the Christians with a ruthlessness not seen since the conquest of 711. He also allowed the Cordoban caliphate to degenerate, in order that his own family might rule in the caliph's name. But when his son, the equally warlike Abd al-Malik, died in 1008, al-Andalus began breaking up into thirty-odd 'statelets' ruled over by upstart governors and others called *taifas*, or 'party kings'.

The Christian states, including the now enlarged kingdom of Pamplona-Navarra, again asserted themselves, and in 1085 the great prize of Toledo fell to Alfonso VI of León-Castile. With its capture the river Tajo became the new frontier between Christian and Muslim rule.

Everywhere the tension was rising, and both al-Mansur's and Alfonso VI's campaigns had strong elements of holy war about them. This new colouring was confirmed by the eruption into the peninsula of the **Almoravids**, a revivalist Islamic force that had been moulded in a Moroccan *ribat*; and by the militant pope Gregory VII's 1095 declaration of a **Christian Crusade** to recover the 'Holy Land' of Palestine from Muslim control.

866 Under Alfonso III's rule, the kingdom of the Asturias will be significantly enlarged. The Duero valley is repopulated with Christian subjects, and Castile brought under royal control. His armies will penetrate deep into the western peninsula, conducting campaigns around Braga, Oporto and Viseu in modern Portugal. During his reign, Alfonso becomes the first Christian king to specifically articulate the concept of the *Reconquista*. In his capital Oviedo he consciously revives elements of Visigoth kingship, whilst endowing several new monastic foundations, including San Salvador de Valdedios.

868 Abd al-Rahman ibn Marwan, a *muwallad* nicknamed al-Djilliki ('the Galician'), and governor of Mérida, rebels against the amir. Mérida's fortifications are dismantled after the rebellion is put down.

872 Musa ibn Musa's son Mutarrif, having openly rebelled against the amir, is captured and crucified in Córdoba. Mutarrif's brother Ismail however remains at large, and re-establishes Banu Qasi control of the Ebro valley for three generations.

877 Ibn Marwan, restored to the amir's favour, again revolts after fortifying Badajoz, in Extremadura.

878 With assistance from Alfonso III, ibn Marwan defeats an army sent against him by the amir. As a larger force is prepared against him he seeks refuge in the Asturias.

In Frankish Barcelona, **Wilfrid 'the Hairy'** becomes count, establishing a hereditary succession that nonetheless remains loyal to the French crown.

880 The son of a powerful *muwallad* landlord of the Ronda region, **Umar ibn Hafsun**, returns to al-Andalus having fled to the Maghreb the previous year. With his ruthless followers he establishes an independent court at **Bobastro** that will last fifty years.

883 Ibn Hafsun temporarily surrenders to the amir and agrees to serve in his army. Derided by Arab commanders on account of his Visigoth ancestry, he returns to Bobastro and creates an even stronger breakaway court by mobilizing Berber and Christian peasants against Cordoban rule.

884 The seasoned rebel ibn Marwan re-establishes himself at Badajoz.

In the north, **Burgos** is founded as the administrative capital of the emergent Asturian **county of Castile**.

c.885 In Baghdad, the Islamic geographer **Ibn Khurradadhbih** writes of al-Andalus as a land rich in slaves and furs.

886 Muhammad I is succeeded by his son al-Mundhir as amir. Throughout al-Andalus there is growing restlessness, especially among the *muwallads* of the south.

888 Al-Mundhir is succeeded by **Abd Allah**, another son of Muhammad, possibly by a Christian slave consort. Abd Allah marries Onneca, a Navarrese Christian princess.

Abd Allah dispatches a force against ibn Hafsun, capturing and then crucifying a *muwallad* commander between a dog and pig in the traditional way. Undeterred, ibn Hafsun continues to expand his territory, so that soon it will stretch from Cartagena to Gibraltar.

890 Despite the death of ibn Marwan, Badajoz and its surrounding lands remain independent of Córdoba for another four years.

897 Mohammed ibn Lope, a member of the Banu Qasi clan, exacts control over Toledo in opposition to the amir.

c.900 Around this time the Ismailis, a Shiite (or Shia) sect, begin proselytizing in north Africa, to the eventual consternation of its 'orthodox' Sunni rulers.

c.901 Construction begins on the monastic church of **San Miguel de Escalada** near León, an important example of Mozarabic architecture.

905 Following many years' factional infighting, **Sancho Garces** establishes the Jiminez royal dynasty in Pamplona.

906 Toledo is returned to Cordoban rule after Mohammed ibn Lope's son, having styled himself 'king', is murdered by its citizens.

907 The last male of the Banu Qasi family dies fighting Christian Catalans.

910 Alfonso III, now an old man, is deposed by his sons, one of whom, **Garcia**, becomes King of the Asturias.

In the north African Islamic province of Ifriqiya an independent Shiite sultanate emerges under the rule of **al-Mahdi** ('the guided one') who founds the Fatimid dynasty, named after the prophet Muhammad's daughter Fatima.

912 Abd Allah is succeeded as amir by his grandson **Abd al-Rahman III**. Notwithstanding his largely Hispanic-Basque ancestry, Abd al-Rahman III gives himself the honorific title *al-Nasir li-dini 'llah* – 'he who fights victorious in the faith of Allah'.

In Ifriqiya, the Fatimids found a capital city in present-day Tunisia called al-Mahdiya, and threaten disruption to trading routes in the western Mediterranean sea and northern Saharan desert.

914 **Ordoño II** accedes to the Asturian throne. He founds the *meseta* city of **León**, and takes his court there, thus inaugurating the Kingdom of León. In Rioja he competes with King Sancho Garces of Pamplona to acquire fresh territory.

Abd al-Rahman III (891–961)

Abd al-Rahman III, by common consent the greatest of the Muslim rulers of Spain, became amir aged 21, having been singled out by his grandfather Abd Allah as the member of the Umayyad royal family most likely to restore the dynasty's fortunes. Although it took him twenty years' continuous campaigning, the young ruler did indeed succeed in reimposing the rule of Córdoba over all of al-Andalus, moving first against **ibn Hafsun** and reducing his territories fortress by fortress, then mopping up other recalcitrants. Simultaneously he waged war against the Christian kingdoms of the north, and against Fatimid power in Africa in order to defend his possessions in the Maghreb.

It was largely because of the Fatimid threat that, in 929, Abd al-Rahman III was persuaded by his advisers to adopt the supreme title Caliph. Under the amir's care, **Córdoba** blossomed into one of the foremost cities of the world, rivalling Byzantium in its glory and renown. He extended the Great Mosque, and built a large new palace complex, the Madinat az-Zahra. He also replenished the fabric of Umayyad government, wisely rotating those whom he appointed to govern the provinces of his realm. He was less successful in reversing the Christian gains that had occurred during the reigns of his predecessors, and his signal victory at **Valdejunquera** in 920 was followed nine years later by ignominious defeat at **Simancas**, when he barely escaped with his life.

Despite the ongoing hostilities, in 958 the Christian kings travelled to Córdoba to pay Abd al-Rahman III personal homage, a reflection – it has been claimed – of the fair-mindedness with which he treated both his Christian and his Jewish subjects. But of this too much can be made. The world on which Abd al-Rahman III had such an impact had yet to be riven by overtly religious and racial hatred, and interestingly the amir – red-haired, blue-eyed and fair-skinned – was himself of mixed Arab-Iberian descent. Nor did he lack the ruthless streak. In 949 he did not hesitate to order the execution of his own son for plotting rebellion. In paying their respects, therefore, the Christian kings may simply have been acting in their own best interests.

917 Ibn Hafsun dies and is clandestinely given a Christian burial. Within ten years his autonomous principality will be dissipated by his feuding sons.

920 On 26 July Abd al-Rahman III leads an army north and defeats the combined forces of the kingdoms of Asturias-León and Pamplona-Navarra at **Valdejunquera**, south of Pamplona. In Córdoba the heads of slain Christians, placed on spikes, are displayed in public. Booty is shared out among the amir's soldiers, according to Islamic law. Christians taken prisoner are either ransomed or sold into slavery, according to their rank.

924 Ordoño II is succeeded as King of León by Fruela II, a younger son of Alfonso III.

925 Fruela II, dying of leprosy, is succeeded by his brother Alfonso IV.

927 To bolster his position in north Africa, Abd al-Rahman III captures the port city of **Melilla**. In the peninsula, his forces finally recapture Bobastro. Ibn Hafsun's body is disinterred and crucified in Córdoba.

929 Abd al-Rahman III declares himself *kalipha* (caliph), and formally breaks with the Abbasid caliphate of Baghdad. In the same year he strengthens his fleet operating in the Mediterranean. His motivation is most probably to 'send a message' to the Fatimids in north Africa.

Hasdai ibn Shaprut is appointed director of customs, and court physician to Abd al-Rahman III. As the founder of a centre for spiritual studies, he attracts many Jewish scholars and poets to Córdoba, inaugurating a 'Golden Age' for Spanish Judaism.

931 After Abd al-Rahman III recaptures the port city **Ceuta** in the Maghreb, the Fatimids begin turning their attention eastwards, towards Egypt.

In León, Alfonso IV vacates his throne in favour of his younger brother Ramiro, and then reclaims it. In the ensuing struggle Alfonso and the three sons of Fruella II are blinded, and **Ramiro II** becomes king.

In the same year **Fernan Gonzales** becomes Count of Castile. Although he is Ramiro's vassal, over the coming decades he skilfully exploits tensions between León and Pamplona. His gathering strength is further consolidated by the marriage of his son Ordoño to Ramiro's daughter Urraca.

936 Abd al-Rahman III orders the construction of a new palace-city, **Madinat az-Zahra**. Located thirteen kms northwest of Córdoba, it functions both as his residence and as his administrative headquarters.

939 Seeking to avenge Valdejunquera, Ramiro II roundly defeats Abd al-Rahman III at **Simancas** (near Valladolid). During the battle the amir loses his copy of the Koran and vows never to fight again. Subsequently Ramiro II takes possession of the Rioja region and Salamanca.

944 Abd al-Rahman III builds a naval shipyard at Tortosa in the Ebro estuary.

947 Among gifts brought to Córdoba by an envoy from Byzantium is a copy of **Dioscorides**' treatise on medical botany, *De materia medica*, written in the 1st century AD. Just one of an increasing number of Greek texts finding their way to al-Andalus, Dioscorides's work is translated into Arabic with the help of Hasdai ibn Shaprut.

950 In León, Ramiro II is succeeded by his son Ordoño III, but only after King Sancho of Navarra-Pamplona intervenes to end a civil war between his sons. As the Christian states feud among themselves, León becomes a virtual vassal of the amir.

955 Ordoño III is succeeded by his brother **Sancho 'the Fat'**.

Córdoba

A settlement had existed at **Córdoba** since Carthaginian times, and during the Roman empire it was one of four judicial centres, as well as an entrepôt where boats sailing up the Guadalquivir could unload their cargoes ready for transportation up the Via Augusta to Hispania's northern cities. Small wonder then that in 756 **Abd al-Rahman I**, the first of the Ummayad amirs, had preferred Córdoba to Seville as his capital, or that his successors retained it as the focal point of al-Andalus.

By 950 AD Córdoba was one of the world's great conurbations. With a population of 700,000 or more, some 100,000 shops and houses, as many as 3000 mosques, it covered an area that may well have measured as much as 144 square miles. This was watched over by the *munyas*, country mansions of the rich dotting the slopes of the Sierra Córdoba to the north. In the centre was a walled city, dominated by the **Great Mosque** (see p.116). Outside its walls were endless suburbs and great palace complexes, the most prestigious of which was Abd al-Rahman III's *Madinat al-Zahra*, a city and palace combined. Noted for its opulence, its interiors glittered with gold and silver, and its throne room was illuminated by a giant bowl of mercury that refracted sunlight streaming down from angled windows.

Through Córdoba's streets thronged Muslims, Jews and Christians, drawn from either across the peninsula, or from much further afield. This was a highly cosmopolitan place, renowned as a centre of **international trade**, famous for its silks, brocades, leatherwork and jewellery, and also for the production of **manuscript books**, diligently copied by mainly female scribes

956 With the resumption of Viking raids on the Iberian peninsula, Abd al-Rahman III develops a naval base at Almería.

957 In León, King Sancho is deposed by Ordoño IV, known as 'the Bad'.

whose skill rivalled that of their male Christian contemporaries. Public baths abounded, and everywhere there was a feeling of cleanliness, reinforced by the ubiquitous presence of Islamic clerics. But there were also Christian churches and synagogues, and despite occasional eruptions of intercommunal tension, the inhabitants seem to have been adept at getting along with each other on a day-to-day basis – an inheritance perhaps of the city's ancient foundation.

ORONOZ

An exquisite example of embroidered silk, probably produced at Madinat al-Zahra in the 10th century

960 Having fled to Córdoba, and, with Hasdai ibn Shaprut's help, Sancho the Fat is restored to his throne, ousting Ordoño IV.

Around this time **Recemund**, a Christian monk and high official, compiles the *Calendar of Córdoba*, an account of contemporary agricultural practices in al-Andalus.

961 Abd al-Rahman III is succeeded as Caliph of Córdoba by his son **al-Hakem II**, who will be remembered for his patronage of literature and learning. During his reign the palace library becomes one of the greatest in the world, its catalogue listing over 400,000 titles, from as far afield as Persia.

966 A fresh spate of Viking raids on the peninsula's Atlantic coast, lasting five years, is generally contained by the caliph's fleets.

970 Death of Count Fernan Gonzalez, Count of Castile.

972 **Gerbert of Aurillac**, a French scholar, returns home after ten years' study in Barcelona. He takes with him knowledge of the abacus, transmitted to Spain from China via the Middle East, and traditionally considered the beginning of a revived interest in **mathematics** in western Europe.

976 Al-Hakem II is succeeded by **Hisham II**, his eleven-year old son by a Christian consort. To ensure stability a three-man regency is established, consisting of first minister al-Mushafi; a senior military commander called **Ghalib**; and Ghalib's son-in-law Abu Amir Muhammad ibn Abi Amir al-Mafari, better known as **al-Mansur** ('the victorious'), or Almanzor among the Spanish. Al-Mushafi, tainted with Berber blood, is quickly side-lined as al-Mansur and Ghalib conspire together.

977 Al-Mansur gains prestige by leading a campaign against Christian León.

978 Al-Mushafi is imprisoned and subsequently murdered. Ghalib and al-Mansur begin quarrelling.

979 As science in al-Andalus flourishes, **Maslama al-Madjriti**, a native of Madrid, adapts the great Islamic

ORONOZ

This ivory box, produced at the palace city of Madinat al-Zahra, was a gift from al-Hakem II to his consort Subh. The profusion of ornately carved foliage and animals suggests an association with fertility

mathematician **al-Khwarizmi**'s astronomical tables to the Córdoba meridian. Maslama will also be remembered for a treatise on the **astrolabe**, and his translation into Arabic of the work of the Greek astronomer **Ptolemy**.

981 Ghalib is killed in battle after relations with his son-in-law deteriorate into open factional warfare. Assuming the powers of a dictator, and encouraging the young caliph Hisham II to waste his energies in a life of debauchery, Al-mansur transfers the government of al-Andalus to the **Madinat al-Zahira** ('Shining City'), a new palace complex to the east of Córdoba he has been building since 978. Al-Mansur's ambition however remains fixed on subduing the Christian states.

al-Mansur Muhammad ibn Abu Amir (938–1002)

Claiming descent from an Arab family that had participated in the conquest of 711, **al-Mansur** has been charged by historians not only with bringing the Cordoban caliphate into disrepute, but also with undermining the very viability of Muslim al-Andalus. Starting out as a professional letter writer, he became the favourite, and perhaps the lover, of the mother of the boy-caliph Hisham II. It was however his connection with the veteran commander **Ghalib**, whose daughter he married, that catapulted **Muhammad ibn Abu Amir** into power, as a member of a three-man council of regency. By 981 that triumvirate had reduced to one, al-Mansur himself, who henceforward ruled al-Andalus as a warlord dictator. Like Abd al-Rahman III (see p. 137), he undertook almost continuous military campaigns – reputedly 57 in number – in order to bolster his authority. But unlike his Umayyad predecessor he targeted the northern states with such ferocity that he earned the soubriquet 'scourge of the Christians'. In sharp contrast, his approach to Córdoba's African possessions was relatively easy-going: authority

985 Al-Mansur sacks Barcelona and massacres its Christian citizens.

987 Al-Mansur plunders the Leonese garrison of Coimbra in present-day Portugal.

988 Al-Mansur plunders Zamora, León and Sahagun.

995 Al-Mansur captures the Castilian count Garcia Fernandez, who dies shortly afterwards. Astorga and Carrión are razed.

997 Al-Mansur penetrates Galicia and sacks Santiago de Compostela.

998 Al-Mansur appoints his son **Abd al-Malik** to govern his African possessions from the city of Féz.

was delegated among local tribal rulers in order to free up manpower and other resources for his Iberian wars. Dispensing with the palace guard, which at this time was composed mainly of Slavic slaves and mercenaries, he relied instead on a standing army 60,000-strong, made up of imported Berbers and Christian converts. An outwardly devout, even zealous, Muslim, he regularly and pointedly consulted with Córdoba's *faqihs* (religious judges). This however may have been a political device, to offset his contempt for the caliphate itself, just as he reduced commodity taxes to court popularity. Islamic commentators have deplored the excessive cruelties of his style of warfare, which seem to have been governed as much by an appetite for plunder as by any sense of 'holy' war. In retrospect he may be seen as a transitional figure, presaging the end of Umayyad rule both in Spain and in Africa, and upsetting the complex accommodations between Muslims and Christians that had evolved during the first three centuries of the Islamic occupation.

999 Alfonso V, a minor, accedes to the throne of León. Al-Mansur campaigns against Pamplona-Navarra.

1000 Sancho III, known as Sancho 'the Great', accedes to the throne of Pamplona-Navarra. Under Sancho's rule, Navarra becomes the strongest of the Christian states and engulfs its immediate neighbours. Encouraging contacts with Europe north of the Pyrenees, Sancho develops the pilgrimage route to Santiago de Compostela, and sponsors Cluniac reform of the monasteries within his territories.

The population of the Iberian peninsula at this time is around seven million, with non-Hispanics forming probably no more than a fifth of this figure.

1002 Al-Mansur dies at Medinaceli on his way back to Córdoba after ravaging Rioja. His son **Abd al-Malik** assumes his father's offices and continues campaigning against the Christian states.

1003 Abd al-Malik plunders Catalunya.

1004 Abd al-Malik plunders Castile.

1005 Abd al-Malik plunders León.

1006 Abd al-Malik plunders Aragon.

1008 The onslaught against the Christian states abruptly ceases with the death of Abd al-Malik, possibly poisoned by his half-brother Sanchuelo. The resulting confusion will prevail in al-Andalus for twenty years.

1009 In an attempt to rekindle the prestige of the Cordoban caliphate, **Muhammad II**, a grandson of Abd al-Rahman III, usurps the sybaritic Hisham II and destroys al-Mansur's Medina al-Zahira palace complex. Berber commanders however propose **Sulayman**, another grandson of Abd al-Rahman III, as a rival caliph. With the help of Sancho Garcia, the count of Castile, Sulayman marches on Córdoba in November. Mohammed II flees to Toledo, where he enlists the support of the Christian counts of Barcelona and Urgel.

1010 Muhammad II's coalition defeats Sulayman's. As the 'Year of the Catalans' unfolds, Muhammad retakes Córdoba, only to be murdered there in July. Hisham II is restored to the caliphate, but almost immediately Sulayman lays siege to the capital. Meanwhile in southern al-Andalus Berber generals begin carving out personal kingdoms.

1011 As the **siege of Córdoba** enters its second year, the plight of its inhabitants is worsened by plague and flooding. To purchase food Hisham II sells off much of the royal library.

1013 After two-and-a-half years' siege Córdoba surrenders. Many of its surviving citizens are massacred as Sulayman's mainly Berber troops rampage through the city. Hisham II disappears, presumed killed. Sulayman is confirmed as caliph, but is forced to award provincial governorships to his Berber commanders.

1014 Berber generals create autonomous fiefdoms at Algeciras, Málaga, Ronda and other cities. Zawa ibn Ziri, the Berber general granted the governorship of Elvira, founds **Granada**, a new citadel in the foothills of the Sierra Nevada. Civil administrators also usurp power, notably Sabur al-Saqlabui, a former Persian slave who now rules over Badajoz, Santarem, Lisbon and the Algarve.

1015 Mujahid al-Amiri, al-Mansur's former admiral operating out of Denia in southern Valencia, conquers Sardinia.

1016 Sulayman is beheaded by a coterie of Berber generals. Although a succession of 'puppet' caliphs follows, the Cordoban caliphate is essentially ended as al-Andalus disintegrates into a congress of warring factions.

Mujahid al-Amiri is expelled from Sardinia by a coalition of Italian forces. He retains control however over the **Balearic Islands** (which include Majorca, Minorca and Ibiza).

1020 Alfonso V sets his seal to the *Fueros* **of León**, the earliest surviving document of its kind (see p.186).

1027 Alfonso V of León is succeeded by **Vermudo III**.

1031 Hashim III, the last Umayyad caliph of Al-Andalus, is expelled from Córdoba. Henceforward the many local rulers of the fragmented Muslim realm in the peninsula are known as *taifas*, or 'party kings', from the Arabic *maluk al-tawa'if*, 'ruler of a faction'. While Arab families generally maintain control of the central cities, Berber warlords dominate southern al-Andalus, and 'slave' generals assume local power in eastern al-Andalus.

1034 **Sancho III** of Navarra, having already seized the county of Castile, and having the counties of Aragon, Sobrarbe and Riborgorza under his patrimony, wars against Vermudo III. He occupies León and declares himself 'emperor'.

1035 Sancho III's ambitions over Christian Spain are cut short by his death. Instead of bequeathing a unified kingdom to a single heir, he divides his realm among sons. Navarra is given to Garcia III, Castile to Fernando I, Aragon to Ramiro I, and Sobrarbe and Ribagorza to Gonzalo.

1037 Vermudo III, having been permitted to return to the throne of León, is defeated and killed by Fernando I of Castile at the **Battle of Tamara**, following which Fernando is proclaimed King of León and Castile. Now ruler of the strongest of the Christian states, Fernando begins exploiting the weaknesses of a divided al-Andalus by demanding substantial payments of gold – protection money – from individual *taifas*.

1039 In the Maghreb, the Islamic revivalist preacher **Ibn Yasin** begins proselytizing among the Sanhaja tribes living in the west on the fringes of the Sahara desert. Driven out by them, he founds a *ribat* (religious community) on the Atlantic seaboard. His sect, called *al-Murabitun* ('people of the ribat'), but better known as the **Almoravids**, combines strict religious observance, simplicity of lifestyle and military discipline.

c.1040 The number of al-Andalus's statelets ruled over by *taifas* begins to dwindle as the stronger consume the weaker. Those that survive include Granada and Seville in the south; Badajoz, Toledo and Valencia in the centre; and Zaragoza in the Ebro valley. Of these, Seville, where the Abbadid family rule, is the most powerful. As a semblance

Seville

In al-Andalus **Seville** nearly always played second fiddle to **Córdoba** once it had been abandoned as a capital city in 756, but in the 11th century it experienced a revival as the stronghold of the leading *taifa* regime. Seville's natural advantage was twofold. Firstly it was the market centre of Spain's most fertile region, rich in a variety of produce, particularly olive oil, prized throughout the Mediterranean trading system, but also *qermazi*, a crimson dye made from crushing the kermes beetle abundant in nearby ilex forests. Secondly, sited on the lower Guadalquivir, Seville could control at least some of Córdoba's food and commodity supplies. Out of these circumstances was born the short-lived but flamboyantly wealthy **Abbadid dynasty**, founded by Muhammad ibn Ismail in the 1020s, and continued by Ibn Abbad, al-Mutadid and al-Mutamid. Under these autonomous rulers Seville flourished, as the different *taifa* states vied with one another not only for political and military power, but also for cultural and artistic pre-eminence. But its assets were also its liabilities. Having shown its potential, Seville became the object of predators from the Maghreb. First the Almoravids, then the Almohads came in conquest, and it was not until the late 15th century that, as the launch pad for Christian Spain's conquest of the Americas, Seville came truly into its own.

of peace returns so economic activity picks up. The emergence of a handful of relatively strong courts also encourages artistic production.

1042 Al-Mutadid succeeds his father Ibn Abbad as the ruler of Seville, whose territories he will expand to incorporate Mertola, Huelva, Niebla, Algeciras, the Algarve, Moron, Arcos, Ronda and Carmona.

In present-day Morocco, Ibn Yasin launches his Almoravid movement to conquer the Sanhaja tribes who had previously spurned him.

1045 Ramiro I of Aragon annexes Sobrarbe and Ribagorza after the murder of his brother Gonzalo.

1055 Fernando I of León-Castile occupies Lamego and Viseu (in present-day Portugal), and sells their Muslim inhabitants into slavery.

1059 With the Sanhajas 'converted', leadership of the Almoravids passes to **Abu Bakr** following the death of Ibn Yasin. Abu appoints his cousin **Yusuf ibn Tashufin** commander of the northwestern sector of his territory. Yusuf establishes a new base at Marrakesh.

1064 Fernando I of León-Castile, whose 'crusade' now gains papal support, captures Coimbra, expelling its Muslim inhabitants.

> ❝ What makes me feel humble in Spain
> Is the use of the names Mutasim and Mutadid there.
> Royal surnames not in their proper place:
> Like a cat that by blowing itself up imitates the lion. ❞
>
> Ibn Sharaf (d. 1068), quoted by Ibn Khaldun in *Muqaddimah*,
> trans. Franz Rosenthal (1958)

In the same year **Ibn Hazm** of Córdoba, the best known Muslim intellectual of his age, dies.

1065 Fernando I dies as he prepares to conquer Valencia. His succession is disputed among his sons. **Alfonso VI** is captured and imprisoned by his brother **Sancho II** of Castile.

1066 In Granada, several hundred **Jews** are massacred by Muslim authorities on the grounds that it is un-Islamic for a Muslim to serve members of another faith.

1069 Al-Mutadid of Seville annexes Córdoba to his territories, but dies soon afterwards. He is succeeded by his similarly expansionist son **al-Mutamid**.

c.1070 Death of the poet and philosopher Solomon ben Yehuda ibn Gabirol (known as **Avicebron**). His best-known philosophical work, *The Well of Life,* attempts to explain the universality of matter through a synthesis of Judaic scripture and neo-Platonic thought.

1072 After a protracted power-struggle, Alfonso VI overcomes his brothers to take the throne of León-Castile. Supported by **St Hugh of Cluny**, Alfonso will support the foundation of several Cluniac monasteries in his territories.

1074 Pope Gregory VII persuades Alfonso VI to adopt the exact rituals of the Roman Catholic Church throughout his kingdom.

1078 The *taifa* state of Seville attains its maximum extent when al-Mutamid captures Murcia.

1079 In north Africa, Yusuf ibn Tashufin captures Tangier for the Almoravids.

Alfonso VI marries Constance, daughter of Duke of Burgundy. His daughters Urraca and Teresa will marry Constance's cousins Raymond and Henry.

Ali ibn Ahmad ibn Hazm (994–1064)

As Córdoba emerged as a centre of artistic and cultural excellence, so the Muslim occupation and settlement of Spain provided Islam with many distinguished writers and intellectuals. Outstanding among these was the polymath **Ibn Hazm**. Of the 400-odd books credited to his name, some forty survive, exhibiting an astonishing assuredness across a multiplicity of disciplines. Ibn Hazm was at once a jurist, a theologian, a philosopher, a historian and a poet of genuine sensitivity. At the same time he was a keen polemicist whose championing of Umayyad rule at precisely the time the Umayyads were being written out of the al-Andalusi script sometimes made him an isolated and contentious figure. Born in Córdoba, he claimed descent from a high Persian-Arab family that had accompanied the invasion of 711, although modern research indicates that Ibn Hazm was in fact a fourth generation *muwallad*. His father was a trusted and high-ranking official at the court during the rule of al-Mansur, and consequently the son enjoyed unusual privileges in his upbringing. It was in these circumstances that Ibn Hazm's identity as an Umayyad loyalist was forged. After the collapse of Umayyad power in 1008 he was forced to leave the capital, and spent most of his adulthood at Manta Lisham near Seville. From

1081 Expelled from León-Castile, **Rodrigo Diaz**, otherwise known as **El Cid**, embarks on a mercenary warlord career by offering his services to the Muslim ruler of Zaragoza.

1083 Yusuf ibn Tashufin extends his hold over present-day Morocco by capturing Ceuta.

1084 On behalf of Zaragoza, Rodrigo Diaz campaigns successfully against the Christian state of Navarra-Aragon.

1085 Alfonso VI captures Toledo after its *taifa* ruler al-Qadir falls into arrears with his *parias* (tribute). Although this sig-

1031 he began vigorously criticizing the *taifa* kingdoms, and was often imprisoned for his outspokenness. Echoing the Christian theme that the Islamic conquest had been in some sense a visitation of God's anger upon a corrupt and venal society, he equated the expansion of the Christian states in the north with Allah's displeasure at the dismemberment of the Cordoban caliphate. In his theological writings he attempted comparisons between Islam and Christianity, although his scholarly knowledge of Christian history and principles served only to reinforce his commitment to Islamic doctrine. As a jurist he followed and enriched the Zahiri school of thought, which insisted on grounding Islamic jurisprudence in a strict reading of the Koran, emphasizing the literal meaning of the text rather than any hidden meaning. Such affinities explain why perhaps Ibn Hazm has been more often ignored than noticed in the West. Tellingly the one work of his that did achieve an international, cross-religious readership was *Tawq al-hamamah* ('The Ring of the Dove') – an atypically humorous prose-and-verse discourse which shrewdly depicts how love can thrust its victims into states of self-deceptive denial, and which may have been inspired by a youthful obsession with Hisham II's harem on the part of its author.

nal victory for the Christians advances their territory to the Tajo river, it also encourages the remaining *taifas* in al-Andalus to turn to the Almoravids for support.

1086 In October Yusuf ibn Tashufin enters the peninsula with an Almoravid army and convincingly defeats Alfonso VI at **Sagrajas** (near Badajoz). Toledo however remains part of León-Castile, and Rodrigo Diaz is rehabilitated at Alfonso's court.

Bernard de Sedirac (d.1124), a French Cluniac monk and ardent anti-Muslim, is appointed Bishop of Toledo.

El Cid (c.1043–1099)

The man known as **El Cid**, from the Arabic *al-sid* meaning 'lord' or 'master', was born **Rodrigo Diaz** into the lesser Castilian nobility at Vivar near Burgos. Through his mother's royal connections he was raised at the court of Fernando I, and first achieved prominence when he was appointed standard-bearer to the newly crowned **King Sancho II** of Castile. Given command of the king's troops, he quickly enhanced his reputation as a soldier, and had little difficulty transferring his allegiance to **Alfonso VI** of León who ousted Sancho in 1072. In spite of his advantageous marriage to Alfonso's niece Jimena, Diaz's position at Alfonso's court was undermined both by his arch-rival Count Garcia Ordoñez as well as by his own haughtiness. His downfall came in 1081, when he rashly attacked the *taifa* statelet of Toledo, which was then under Alfonso's protection. Exiled from León-Castile, his response was to turn himself into a mercenary, offering his services, in the first instance, to the *taifa* ruler **al-Mutamin of Zaragoza**.

For the next eleven years Diaz amassed a fortune, fighting Muslims and Christians alike, until, in 1092, taking advantage of internal disarray in **Valencia**, he seized the city and its surrounding lands for himself. Apart from briefly aiding Alfonso against the Almoravids in 1086, Diaz remained essentially a freebooter until his death. In this respect he was no different from a dozen other self-made warlords of the period. What set him apart was the brilliance of his generalship, and a political acumen that enabled him to anticipate the shifting alliances of those around him. Such qualities, devoid of the Christian partisanship later associated with his name, were sufficient to turn him into Spain's premier medieval hero. When Valencia returned to Muslim rule in 1102 his remains were carried to Castile, to become the object of veneration at the monastery of San Pedro de Cardena. His exploits, massively distorted, were further celebrated in the chronicle *Historia Roderici* ('The Story of Rodrigo'), and in the epic poem *El Cantar de mio Cid* ('The Song of the Cid') – both from the 12th century. In these and other ways a ruthless predator was turned into a legend of the Spanish *Reconquista*.

1089 Tarragona is annexed by the French count of Barcelona.

Rodrigo Diaz is again exiled from León-Castile. Drawing on his accumulated war booty, he forms an army and sets about creating his own kingdom in the Levant region of eastern Spain, fighting both Muslims and Christians.

1090 Having halted the Christian advance, Yusuf ibn Tashufin begins campaigning against the 'corrupt' remaining *taifas*, overthrowing Abd Allah, the ruler of Granada, and his brother Tamim, the ruler of Málaga.

1091 The Almoravids capture Seville. Al-Mutamid, like other *taifa* rulers, is exiled to Morocco.

1094 The Almoravids capture Badajoz.

Rodrigo Diaz captures Valencia.

1095 At Clermont, pope Urban II preaches the **First Crusade**, a mission to recapture the Holy Land from Islamic rule.

> From his eyes the tears flowed
> When he turned his head and gazed at them.
> He saw the open doors and the gates pulled from their hinges,
> Empty pegs without furs or cloaks; no falcons or moulting hawks.
> The Cid sighed deeply, overwhelmed with cares.
> Then spoke in a clear and measured tone:
> 'I give thanks to you, Lord God, Father on high!
> A plot has been hatched against me by my evil enemies.'

The opening stanza of *The Song of the Cid*, trans. Roger Bardon (1953)

1099 In July, 40,000 Muslims and Jews are massacred in **Jerusalem** after the city falls to the Christian Crusaders.

Rodrigo Diaz dies of natural causes in Valencia, having been defeated by the Almoravids at Cuenca.

BETTMANN/CORBIS

Charlton Heston as the eponymous hero of the 1961 Hollywood epic *El Cid*

5: The Reconquista

1100–1479

I n the momentous medieval face-off between **Islam** and **Christianity**, each side seemed at times to mirror the other. On the one hand was the concept of *jihad*, or holy war against infidel transgressors; on the other the powerful notion of the Crusade, urged by no less a figure than the Pope. Both sides too evolved formidable fighting forces whose loyalty was as much to Allah or God as to any temporal ruler: in Islam the *ribat*; in Christendom the Knights Templars and other 'military-religious' Orders.

The **Reconquista**, the name given to the Christian recovery of the Iberian peninsula, was a vital part of the larger conflict, as well as being a struggle between two more or less ethnically discrete peoples, and two systems of government, for control of a specific territory each believed belonged to itself. The dates of the *Reconquista* however are indeterminate. Spanish patriots have sometimes located its inception at the **battle of Covadonga** (see p.111), just a few years after the initial Muslim conquest of 712; others have chosen subsequent, intermediate events as its true beginning.

Equally, there is disagreement as to when the *Reconquista* ended. Conventionally the chosen date is 1492, when Fernando and Isabel, the '**Catholic Monarchs**' of Castile and Aragon, triumphantly entered Granada, the last of the Moorish amirates. Yet by then **Granada**, representing only a small portion of the Iberian landmass, and having in any case only been established on Christian sufferance, was a shadow of what had gone before. Of far more significance was the capture of **Seville** in 1248, a victory that signalled the lasting dismemberment of al-Andalus.

Yet the *Reconquista* was not simply about the defeat of Islam in Spain. Just as much it heralded the full return of Hispania to the European fold, with something distinctive to contribute. The Iberian peninsula, from having become Europe's dispensable annex, came back at the end of the 15th century as an imperial power, unlocking the riches of the New World, and also as the unwavering champion of the beliefs and values of the **Roman Catholic Church**.

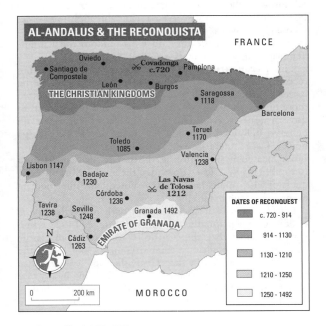

AL-ANDALUS & THE RECONQUISTA

FRANCE

Oviedo
Santiago de Compostela
Covadonga c.720
Pamplona
León
Burgos
THE CHRISTIAN KINGDOMS
Saragossa 1118
Barcelona
Teruel 1170
Toledo 1085
Valencia 1238
Lisbon 1147
Badajoz 1230
Las Navas de Tolosa 1212
Tavira 1238
Córdoba 1236
Seville 1248
Granada 1492
Cádiz 1263
EMIRATE OF GRANADA

N

0   200 km

MOROCCO

DATES OF RECONQUEST

c. 720 - 914
914 - 1130
1130 - 1210
1210 - 1250
1250 - 1492

In this larger, geopolitical context Pope Urban II's declaration of the **First Crusade** at Clermont in 1095, and the subsequent capture of Jerusalem and other cities in the Palestinian Holy Land, take on a special resonance for Spain. Papal backing for what amounted to a war against Islam, and the emergence of the Church Militant, attracted support for the Christian Kings in their struggle against Muslim al-Andalus, to the extent that the *Reconquista* became internationalized, and more urgent. Yet in its beginnings certainly the *Reconquista* predated the Crusades, and historians have argued, plausibly enough, that the very concept of the crusade was hatched in the peninsula.

In the century and a half that followed the fall of Jerusalem in 1099, the Iberian Christian kingdoms won back territories that had eluded them for the preceding four centuries. Moreover, this success counterbalanced failure in the 'Holy Land', since the Crusades – having begun so audaciously – ultimately came to nothing. Worse, the eventual fall of Constantinople in 1453 to a Muslim army, presaging the final collapse of the Christian Byzantine Empire and the coming of age of the **Ottoman Empire**, suggested that, for all the economic and cultural advances made by Christendom, its overall security was still in doubt.

For the future, Spain was to play an important part in containing Ottoman expansionism. In the interim it had domestic troubles to overcome. There was not one but several Christian kingdoms contending against al-Andalus, each with its own character and traditions. The period of the *Reconquista* was not just about the expulsion of Muslim rule from the Iberian peninsula therefore: it was also about the shape and nature of governments and societies to come.

During the course of the Middle Ages three principal Christian powers slowly emerged in Iberia: **Castile**, **Portugal**, and the **Crown of Aragon**. Of these, Castile grew out of the kingdom of León, which in turn had emerged from the kingdom of the Asturias; Portugal established itself as an independent monarchy having been a county of León-Castile; and the Crown of Aragon emerged as a portmanteau bloc, composed of the kingdom of Aragon, the French counties of Catalunya, the conquered territory of Valencia, and, for a while, Navarra.

By 1479 Castile was the largest, strongest and most prosperous of the three. But just to complicate matters, the Crown of Aragon had acquired interests in Sicily and the Kingdom of Naples; and Portugal had compensated for its relative inferiority by being the first post-Roman European state to acquire significant non-European colonies.

The reduction of al-Andalus 1100–1248

Although by 1100 the Christian kingdoms had made headway against al-Andalus, progress had been slow, and despite the **capture of Toledo**, they still controlled only the poorer northern parts of the peninsula. Nor did the disintegration of the **Umayyad regime** necessarily result in more substantial victories. Apart from the tendency amongst the Christian kingdoms to dissipate their energies and resources by squabbling with each other, there was a new threat on the southern horizon: militant Islamic revivalism, spawned in *ribats* in the Maghreb's inhospitable interior, and materializing in two successive waves of Muslim resurgence – the **Almoravids** and then the yet more potent **Almohads**.

But the Christian cause was given fresh backbone by the Papacy, as well as by a succession of warrior kings inheriting the Iberian thrones. In the 12th century **Alfonso VII** and **Alfonso VIII** of León-Castile together with **Alfonso I of Aragon** led the charge; and then, in the early 13th century, came the culminating campaigns of **Fernando III of Castile**, and **Jaume I of Aragon**. First the Castilians took Córdoba, then, after a famous siege, Seville fell in 1248, Valencia having succumbed to Jaume I ten years earlier.

Such victories, offsetting defeats in the Holy Land, were not entirely the result of Christian strength. The **Almoravids**, issuing out of Morocco on their own religious mission, proved little better than barbarian spoilers; while the **Almohads**, better organized and potentially more lethal, fell foul not just of a general unwelcome among the established Muslim community in al-Andalus, but also of family feuding amongst its leadership.

Even so, for a while it was a close run thing. The *Reconquista* might very well have reversed direction, and become an Islamic reconquest; indeed the great victory of **Las Navas de Tolosa** in 1212 was gained more by luck than by military superiority.

As it was, the Christians prospered. In hindsight all kinds of explanation can be invoked to explain that fact, not least a concerted stiffening of the Christian sinew, expressed most visibly in the creation of the three indigenous military-religious **Orders of Santiago**, **Calatrava** and **Alcántara**.

Yet even as the *Reconquista* unfurled, there were countercurrents. Victory did not necessarily unite the victors – sometimes it drove them apart as they pursued individual agendas. For a while León was divorced from its Castilian progeny, and in 1139, Portugal asserted its independence. Equally, there were those for whom the outcome of battles and the succession of kings, or the triumph of a particular faith, were not the be-all and end-all of existence. **Gerard of Cremona**, from the mid-1160s onwards, set about translating Arabic texts into Latin (the transnational language of Christendom), among them important works of pagan Greeks that had survived only because of the scientific curiosity of Gerard's counterparts in Islam. Later in the same century, the Cordoban Ibn Rushd, called **Averroës** in the West, not only resurrected **Aristotle**, but also, unwittingly, became the first scholar to define the long, unending debate between faith and reason.

1100 The **Almoravids**, having established themselves in the south of the Iberian peninsula, occupy Valencia, ruled since Rodrigo Diaz's death by his widow Jimena.

1104 **Pedro I of Aragon** is succeeded by his son **Alfonso I**, known as *El Battaldor* ('the Battler'). Alfonso will spearhead the war of reconquest against Almoravid al-Andalus; but his ultimate ambition, to lead a crusade to the Holy Land, will remain unfulfilled.

1106 **Yusuf ibn Tashufin**, leader of the Almoravids, dies.

Moses Sephardi, an eminent Jewish scholar, adopts the name Pedro Alfonso after converting to Christianity. He will be remembered for *Disciplina Clericalis*, a Latin compilation of Arabian and Indian folk-tales, the first of its kind in the West and an important influence on such later writers as Boccaccio and Chaucer.

1108 As the Almoravid campaign against the Christian north intensifies Alfonso VI's army is defeated at **Ucles**; but although the Almoravids continue to raid the Tajo valley they fail to capture Toledo.

1109 Alfonso VI of León and Castile dies and is succeeded by his daughter **Urraca**. Despite her marriage to Alfonso I of Aragon there is no question of the two kingdoms uniting. Meanwhile Urraca's sister **Teresa**, married to Henri of Burgundy, rules the dependent county of Portugal in the west of the Iberian peninsula.

1110 The Almoravids complete their conquest of al-Andalus with the capture of **Zaragoza** and the overthrow of the last *taifa* ruler. The Almoravid amir returns to Marrakesh, appointing governors to rule Islamic Spain in his stead.

The Almoravids

A persistent feature of Islamic history is the periodic eruption of geographically peripheral warrior sects determined to reassert what they consider to be the Muslim faith in its purest form. Such were the **Almoravids**, at least at their inception. The very word Almoravid derives from the Arabic *al-Murabitun*, meaning 'inhabitants of the ribat', where *ribat* denotes a combination of monastery and military camp. Assembled from tribal groups of the **Sanhaja** peoples living in the inhospitable interior of the Maghreb, the Almoravids were forged into a formidable fighting force first by **Ibn Yasin**, then by **Yusuf ibn Tashufin**. But their fundamentalist zeal was undermined by a thirst for conquest, and eventually the corrosive spoils of conquest. For the beleaguered *taifa* rulers of post-Umayyad Spain they represented an acute dilemma. The near-barbarian Almoravids were not wanted in al-Andalus, but the alternative was to be overrun by Christian infidels. In the event religious solidarity won the day. As al-Mutamid, the *taifa* amir of Seville, put it, 'I would rather drive camels in Morocco than tend pigs in Castile.' And so the reformist Almoravids arrived in Spain. They behaved however like brigands, and within barely a generation fell foul of their own greed. Nor, upon closer examination, were they quite as orthodox as they pretended. Although ibn Tashufin perpetually swore allegiance to the now ineffectual Abassid caliphate in Baghdad, it was soon noticed that the Almoravids' insistence on a strictly literal reading of the Koran had led them to attribute human qualities to Allah – the **'anthropomorphic' fallacy**. Because of that heresy, and because of the Christian crusaders' activities in Palestine, Islam did not rise up behind the Almoravids. Rather, from the moment they crossed over from the Maghreb into the more diverse world of al-Andalus they were a spent force.

1118 Alfonso I of Aragon, determined to take the fight to the Almoravids, gains papal approval through the ecclesiastical **Council of Toulouse** to launch a crusade to recover

Zaragoza. After a prolonged siege by a Christian army that includes French and other international elements, Zaragoza falls to Alfonso in December.

In the Maghreb **Muhammad ibn Tumart**, the son of a Berber chieftain, returns from a ten-year journey to the Middle East and begins planning the overthrow of Almoravid rule in north Africa. Failing to raise an immediate revolt, ibn Tumart takes to the Atlas mountains where he creates a new Islamic revivalist sect known at the **Almohads**.

1119 Alfonso I of Aragon captures the Valencian towns of Tudela and Tarazona. In Córdoba a Muslim revolt against Almoravid rule is swiftly and brutally suppressed.

1120 The diocese of **Santiago de Compostela**, already a major venue for Christian pilgrimage, is elevated to an archiepiscopacy by the papacy.

1121 Ibn Tumart is hailed as a *mahdi* ('guided one') by his followers and establishes an independent kingdom in southern Morocco.

1125 Continuing his campaigns in Valencia, Alfonso I of Aragon encourages disaffected Christians to leave al-Andalus and settle in the reconquered Ebro valley. Daringly he raids Granada in the south to 'liberate' Mozarabs, who return with him to his enlarged kingdom.

1126 The Almoravid amir, **Ali ibn Yusuf**, responds to Alfonso I's initiative by forcibly deporting al-Andalusi Christians to Morocco. Christians remaining in al-Andalus come under increasing harassment from Muslim authorities.

In León-Castile, Queen Urraca is succeeded by **Alfonso VII**. Like Alfonso I of Aragon, Alfonso VII pursues a militarily aggressive policy toward Almoravid al-Andalus.

1128 Afonso Henriques, the son of Teresa and Henri of Burgundy, becomes Count of Portugal on his mother's death.

1130 Ibn Tumart is succeeded by **Abd al-Mumin**, under whose leadership the Almohads will overthrow Almoravid rule in the Maghreb.

1134 Alfonso I of Aragon dies, having bequeathed his realms to the **Knights Templars**, the Holy Sepulchre (in Jerusalem) and other bodies of Christendom associated with the Crusades. Ignoring Alfonso's will, the Aragonese invite his brother **Ramiro II** to become king. Similarly the nobility of Navarra, joined to Aragon since 1076, elect a king of their own, **Garcia IV**, so that Navarra once again becomes independent.

1137 Ramiro II of Aragon dies without male issue. His young daughter Petronella is proclaimed queen, and betrothed to **Count Ramón Berenguer** of Barcelona, the ruler of the Franco-Spanish March. Berenguer becomes the administrator of Aragon during Petronella's minority, so that the two territories are effectively united from this date, to form the **Crown of Aragon**.

1139 Afonso Henriques repudiates the overlordship of León-Castile and proclaims himself **King of Portugal**, henceforth an independent state separate from the rest of 'Spain'. Shortly before this he inflicts a heavy defeat on the

> And so, on the last day of the month, early in the morning the castle was surrendered and the towers were filled with Christian knights, and the royal standards were raised above a high tower. Those who held the standards shouted out loud and proclaimed 'long live Alfonso, emperor of León and Toledo!'

The entry into Oreja, from *Chronica Adefonsis Imperatoris* ('Chronicle of Alfonso the Emperor'), trans. Simon Barton and Richard Fletcher

Almoravids, extending his own territories southwards along the Atlantic seaboard.

Alfonso VII of León-Castile begins his campaign into Muslim territory when he successfully besieges the Almoravid stronghold of Oreja near Toledo.

1140 By granting lands to some 'white monks' at Fitero, Alfonso VII sponsors the first **Cistercian** monastery in Spain. The Cistercians, a French religious order adept at creating agricultural communities away from towns and cities, will make a significant contribution to the *Reconquista* and the emergence of Spanish military-religious Orders through their disciplined 'settler' mentality and doctrinal opposition to Islam.

1142 The Abbot of Cluny, visiting the peninsula, persuades a resident English scholar, **Robert of Ketton**, to translate the **Koran** into Latin. Eventually printed in Zurich in 1543, Robert's is the first translation of the 'Book of Muhammad' into a western language.

1143 The death of Ali ibn Yusuf, the second Almoravid amir, precipitates a revival of local *taifa* rulers in al-Andalus as centralized authority collapses.

The Pope acknowledges Portugal as a discrete vassal state.

1144 As disillusionment with Almoravid rule spreads, Córdoba again revolts. There is also revolt in the Algarve, where **Ibn Qasi**, the founder of a revivalist sect known as *al-Muridan*, appeals to the Almohads in Morocco for military help.

1145 **Sayf al-Dawla**, son of the last *taifa* ruler of Zaragoza, and allied to Ibn Qasi, seizes control of Córdoba.

1146 Although the Almoravids reassert control over the Algarve, Ibn Qasi, supported by Almohad forces, captures Seville, and Alfonso VII of León-Castile occupies Córdoba. Meanwhile Muhammad **Ibn Mardanish**, a warlord known as *Rey Lobo* ('Wolf King'), seizes Murcia and Valencia. Aided by the Christian crowns, Ibn Mardanish will retain these provinces until his death in 1172.

1147 Assisted by the Genoese navy, Alfonso VII captures the port of **Almería**, giving León-Castile direct access to the Mediterranean for the first time.

Aided by English and Flemish Crusaders, the Portuguese king, Afonso Henriques, captures his country's eventual capital, the port-city **Lisbon**.

1148 The Almoravids recapture Córdoba; but Ramón Berenguer IV, at the head of a Catalan army, and with English help, takes Tortosa for Aragon at the mouth of the Ebro, and goes on to capture Lérida.

1151 When Ibn Qasi is murdered in Silves the Almohads take over control of his revolt.

1154 The Almohads seize Granada.

1157 The Almohads recapture Almería. In the same year Alfonso VII of León and Castile dies. His decision to divide his realms between his two sons **Fernando** and **Sancho** heralds sustained tension between the Christian states just as the Almohads are establishing themselves in the peninsula.

1158 Alfonso VII's son **Sancho III** of Castile dies and is succeeded by **Alfonso VIII**.

A group of Knights Templars withdraw from the defence of Calatrava, under assault by Muslims. The town however is heroically saved by a combined force of Castilians and Cistercian monks led by **Raimundo of Fitero**. As a result the first of Spain's indigenous military-religious orders, the **Order of Calatrava**, is founded.

1159 The town of **Gibraltar** is founded by the Almohads, and becomes their main bridgehead for the completion of their conquest of al-Andalus.

ORONOZ

An Almohad banner captured at the battle of Les Navas de Tolosa (see p.176)

The Almohads

Superficially the **Almohads** and the Almoravids were similar. Both originated in the mountainous deserts of the Maghreb, both began as a *ribat*, both relied upon a Berber following to swell their rank-and-file, and both claimed to be cleansers of Islam. But of the two it was the Almohads who offered the greatest threat to the Christian states. Their founding leader, **Ibn Tumart**, although of Berber origin, had spent long years in the Middle East, where he imbibed the revivalist thought of the Islamic theologian **al-Ghazali**. Like Ghazali, Tumart stressed the necessity of unity – the 'unity' of Allah as much as of those who believed in Allah – and it was from this that the Almohad sect derived its name, the Arabic word *al-Muwahhidun* meaning precisely 'upholders of Divine Unity'. But, influenced perhaps by contact with Sufism, the mystic wing of Islam, Ibn Tumart also preached **inner spirituality**. At the same time he was an outstanding commander, instilling a degree of discipline into his troops that dissolved tribal allegiances. For all these reasons – and because of Ibn Tumart's naturally charismatic personality – in the Maghreb at least he was hailed as the *mahdi*, the prophet-leader promised in the Koran who would restore righteousness shortly before the Day of Judgement.

Ibn Tumart duly proclaimed a *jihad*, not only against the troublesome Christians, but also against the corrupt and heretical Almoravids. It befell Tumart's successors however to institute Almohad rule in the Iberian portion of al-Andalus. Once that had been achieved, despite some stunning initial successes against the Christian states, the Almohad conquest unravelled almost as quickly as had the Almoravid. This time round, though, it was not despotic indulgence that led to downfall, but dynastic division. Even so, it is tempting to conclude that neither the Almoravids nor the Almohads were capable of tailoring their agenda to the needs and realities of a complex Muslim community that was detached from mainstream Islam and partly Hispanicized.

The Jewish philosopher **Moses Maimonides** (1135–1204) leaves Córdoba with his family as a result of Almohad persecution. He eventually settles in Egypt where he writes *Guide to the Perplexed*, and his codification of Jewish Law, the *Mishna Torah*.

1162 On the death of her husband, Count Ramón Berenguer IV, Queen Petronella abdicates in favour of their young son **Alfonso II** in order to cement the union of Aragon and the former Franco-Spanish March.

1163 The Almohad conquest is suspended following the death of Abd al-Mumin.

The Order of Santiago

If the Almoravids and Almohads were the product of Islamic militancy, on the Christian side there was a reciprocal development in the form of military religious orders. The first and largest of these were the 'Poor Knights of Christ and of the Temple of Solomon', better known as the **Knights Templars**, and founded in the wake of the capture of Jerusalem during the First Crusade. Originally convened around 1120 to protect pilgrims to the Holy Land, they were championed by the Cistercian monk **St Bernard of Clairvaux**, who also wrote the rules governing their strict 'monastic' existence. Soon the Templars switched their attentions to combat and, on the back of their famed courage, acquired massive estates and wealth, not only in Palestine and Syria, but also in Europe itself, particularly France. So powerful indeed did the Templars become, and so secretive were their deliberations, that by the early 14th century the only way to disband their organization was to level charges of heresy against them.

While some believe that Templar practices and traditions endure to this day through Freemasonry, more visibly they were outlived by three similar bodies their example inspired in Spain: the Orders of **Calatrava**, **Alcántara** and **Santiago**. Of these the

1165 Gerard of Cremona (d. 1187) forms a group of scholars in Toledo dedicated to the translation of Arabic, Syrian and Hebrew texts into Latin. Among the 70-odd scientific, mathematical, astrological and philosophical words translated by Gerard will be the *Almagest*, by the ancient Greek author **Ptolemy**, usually regarded as laying the foundations of European astronomy.

1164 The **Order of Calatrava** gains papal recognition.

1170 Fernando II of León founds a *hermandad* ('brotherhood') dedicated to further campaigns against Muslims among those who help him capture the town of Cáceres.

Order of Santiago, originating as a *hermandad* or brotherhood formed among those attacking Cáceres in 1170, and associated by name with Saint James the Apostle, became the richest and most prestigious. In 1174 **Alfonso VII** of León-Castile gave to the knights the town of **Uccles**, where their central monastery was established. Playing an important role in the military conquest of al-Andalus, the Order was able to exploit the Christian resettlement of central Spain, acquiring huge tracts of land it turned into pasturage for sheep. Like the Templars, the Santiago knights followed a Cistercian discipline and became a powerful political entity in their own right. By 1493 the Order's membership had swollen to tens of thousands, enjoying revenues that made them second only to the Crown of Castile in wealth. Calatrava and Alcántara too had prospered, so that between them the three Orders formed a state within the state. Rather than attempt to break them, however, **Queen Isabel** (see p.218) assumed control by the simple expedient of persuading each to adopt her husband **Fernando of Aragon** (see p.234) as its Grand Master. Thereafter the Orders were firmly part of the uniquely strong bonding between the Spanish throne and the Catholic faith.

1171 The Almohad conquest of al-Andalus is resumed under the leadership of **Yusuf I**. In order to attract wider support from Christendom, Fernando II of León renames the 'Knights of Cáceres' the **Order of Santiago**.

1173 With the exception of the Balearic islands, where Almoravid rule survives until 1203, the whole of al-Andalus submits to the Almohads who now campaign earnestly against the Christian kingdoms, in particular Portugal.

1185 Death of **Ibn Tufayl**, author of *Hayy ibn Yaqzan*, a philosophical romance set on a desert island that will influence Daniel Defoe's *Robinson Crusoe* (1719).

1187 In Palestine, the recapture of **Jerusalem** by the Muslim ruler of Egypt, **Saladin**, marks the beginning of the decline of the Christian crusaders.

1188 Fernando II of León is succeeded by his son **Alfonso IX**. In the same kingdom towns and cities are for the first times invited to send representatives to an enlarged meeting of the *curia regis* (king's council) or Cortes (see p.172).

1191 The Almohads capture the Portuguese township **Alcácer do Sal**, to the south of Lisbon.

Pope Celestine III, aware of the renewed Islamic threat in the Iberian peninsula, and anxious to heal divisions between the Christian states there, declares the whole region a crusading zone.

1192 Celestine III urges the Archbishop of Toledo to send Christian missionaries to Muslim cities, including Seville and Marrakesh.

1195 Muslim military supremacy seems confirmed when the Almohads inflict a crippling defeat on Alfonso VIII of Castile's forces at **Alarcos**.

1196 The Almohads launch raids deep into the Christian north, ravaging the land around the emergent Castilian city of Madrid. The Almohad ruler Abu Yusuf also persecutes 'unorthodox' Muslim scholars in his territories, including Ibn Rushd, better known in Europe as **Averroës**, who is banished from court.

1197 Almohad forces besiege but fail to take Madrid.

1199 Death of Averroës.

1202 As the Castilian crown debases its coinage to help finance its defensive wars against the Almohads, a Cortes convened at Benavente agrees to raise a new tax, *moneda foreda*, against further debasement. Like other emergency taxes of the period, *moneda foreda* will become a regular levy.

1203 The Almohad conquest of the Balearic islands removes the last bastion of Almoravid rule.

1207 **Pope Innocent III** brokers peace between the Christian states of the peninsula.

1212 In late May Alfonso VIII of Castile gathers a large and partly international Christian army at Toledo, and on 16 July, aided by Pedro II of Aragon and Sancho VII of Navarra, defeats the Almohads' main force at **Las Navas de Tolosa**. As a result of this victory the tide turns against the Muslim occupiers of Spain and the *Reconquista* enters its most successful period.

1213 The Almohad regime is undermined by revolt among **Banu Merlin** tribal warriors in the Maghreb, and by the accession of the resourceful **Jaume I of Aragon**, following the death of Pedro II. During his reign Jaume I will double the size of his territories, annexing the whole of Valencia to the Crown of Aragon. Famous for cutting out the tongue of the Bishop of Gerona, he will recount his flamboyant exploits in the self-congratulatory *Libre dels feyts* ('Book of Deeds'); but because of his military prowess against Islam he will place himself beyond reproach. According to legend Jaume's glory becomes such that Genghis Khan, the Mon-

Averroës (Ibn Rushd c.1126–1198)

That the acknowledged inspiration of the **'scholastic'** school of European medieval philosophy was a Muslim closely connected to the Almohad court at Córdoba suggests that, however much political antagonisms between Christianity and Islam hardened in the 12th century, intellectual exchange continued. Ibn Rushd, always known in the West as **Averroës**, was born into a family of Islamic jurists, and himself served as *qadi* (chief religious judge) both in Córdoba and in Seville. He also trained in medicine, and it was as a physician that he became intimate with the amir Ibn Yaqub. Recognizing in Averroës a man of exemplary learning, the amir asked him one day to explain Greek philosophy. When Averroës demurred, for fear of transgressing Islamic orthodoxy, Ibn Yaqub gave him permission to proceed anyway. Thus was born the great series of summaries of, and commentaries upon, works of **Aristotle**, written in Arabic but soon translated into Hebrew as well as Latin, that transformed Western learning by promoting firstly the credentials of analytical logic, and secondly, in the longer term, empirical scientific method based on Aristotelian observation of nature.

As well as several original treatises, among them *Tahafut at-tahafut* ('The Incoherence of Incoherence'), and a general medicine, Averroës also wrote a commentary on Plato's *Republic*. Yet as Averroës was acutely aware, to pursue philosophy at the level of abstraction practised by Plato and Aristotle was theologically dangerous, since 'truth' was supposedly revealed for all time in the Koran. His response to this conundrum was to seek to demonstrate that Aristotle's philosophy in particular was at one with the *Shariah* (Islamic Law), for all that the Greek pursued truth by other means. In similar, but not identical, fashion Averroës's greatest Christian admirer, **Thomas Aquinas**, elaborated the theory that philosophical enquiry necessarily deals with 'secondary' causes, and that any understanding of 'first' causes is indeed the preserve of theology. While both thinkers therefore finally – if circuitously – defended revelation, just by raising such issues they trod contentious ground. As the war between al-

Andalus and the Christian states intensified, Averroës was vilified by hard-line *ulama* (religious scholars); and in 1195 the amir Abu Yusuf banished him from Córdoba. Although Averroës was rehabilitated shortly before his death, and invited to Marrakesh, his star was never to shine as brightly in Islam as it has elsewhere.

Statue of Averroës in Córdoba

CORBIS

gol leader attacking Islam two thousand miles to the east, contemplates forming an alliance with him.

1214 Alfonso VIII of Castile is succeeded by **Enrique I**.

1215 The University of Salamanca is founded.

1216 The **Dominican Order** of friars is founded in Toulouse by **Domingo de Guzmán** (St Dominic) to combat heresy among the Cathars in southern France. In time the Dominican mendicants, along with their fellow Franciscans, will become a mainstay of the Catholic Church's evangelical movement.

1217 Enrique I of Castile is succeeded by **Fernando III**, a warrior king who matches Jaume I of Aragon in his deter-

Las Navas de Tolosa

For a generation the Almohads' crushing victory over Alfonso VIII at **Alarcos** in 1195 cast a shadow over the Christian cause in Spain; but, bent on avenging defeat, Alfonso eventually pulled off a victory of his own that reverberated throughout Christendom. From the beginning the campaign of 1212 was conceived as a crusade. For over a year **Rodrigo Jiminez de Rada**, the Archbishop of Toledo, bolstered the Castilian king by rallying international support, even persuading Pope Innocent III to threaten any Iberian Christian monarch who did not participate with excommunication. Beginning in May Toledo began filling up not only with Castilian, Leonese and Aragonese soldiery, but also with Knights Templars and others drawn from France, Germany, England and elsewhere. Not everything went to plan, however. The Almohad amir **Mohammed**, aware of the force being prepared against him, encamped on the plains of Las Navas de Tolosa, immediately south of the high Sierra Morena, directly on the road from Toledo to Córdoba, and fortified the main pass through the sierra so that the Christian army was effectively halted in its tracks. In these circumstances the French contingent, numbering perhaps 70,000, and oppressed by summer

mination to expunge Muslim power from the peninsula.

1219 Catalan merchants, sailing out of Barcelona, are recorded to be trading with Alexandria in Egypt.

1223 **Sancho II** accedes to the throne of Portugal. Joining in the *Reconquista*, he will establish the enduring boundaries of his kingdom.

1224 The passing of the Almohad amir **Yusuf II**, trampled to death by a cow in Marrakesh, provokes a succession crisis and the separation of Spanish and African al-Andalus.

1225 Work begins on the contruction of **León Cathedral** in the French Gothic style. Completed in 1302, it contains the finest stained glass windows in Spain.

heat, deserted almost to a man. It has also been suggested that the French and Templars, who wanted any captured Muslims put to the sword, had in any case fallen out with their Spanish hosts, who insisted prisoners be dealt with according to the more humane conventions of exchange and ransom prevalent in the peninsula. Only by finally enlisting the support of the King of Navarra was Alfonso able to make up lost numbers. Then, by a stroke of good fortune, a shepherd offered to lead his forces through a 'secret' pass, enabling them to descend on Mohammed on 16 July. Taken by surprise, the Almohad army was routed. At the end of the day Iberian bishops stood singing a *Te Deum* in a field carpeted with Muslim corpses. Yet the amir escaped, and, although Alfonso's troops went on to take a town or two, the **Battle of Las Navas de Tolosa** did not herald the immediate conquest of al-Andalus. Not until 1233, when another generation had gone by, and after the Almohad regime had imploded in a furore of dynastic squabbling, could the *Reconquista* be brought to a successful conclusion. Even so, the battle was psychologically decisive. Henceforward it was Christian, not Islamic, arms that enjoyed a reputation for invincibility.

1229 Jaume I of Aragon dispatches a fleet to recover the **Balearics** from Almohad rule. The fall of Palma on 31 December marks the beginning of an Aragonese-Catalan maritime empire in the Mediterranean. The government of the island of Mallorca (Majorca) is entrusted to **Dom Pedro**, an exiled member of the Portuguese royal family. Meanwhile, **Alfonso IX of León** successfully campaigns against the Almohads in Extremadura.

1230 Alfonso IX captures the strategically important Extremaduran cities of Mérida and Badajoz, but shortly after dies without a direct heir. His throne passes to his cousin Fernando III, who thereby presides over the **permanent reunification** of León and Castile.

As the Christian coalition against al-Andalus strengthens, the Almohad amir Muhammad fortifies Seville against anticipated attack.

1231 Dom Pedro captures Minorca, the second largest of the Balearic islands, and in so doing begins distancing himself from his master, King Jaume I of Aragon.

1234 Sancho VII of Navarra dying heirless, the Navarrese proclaim **Count Theobald of Champagne** their king, and so take the territory into the French sphere of influence.

1235 Dom Pedro completes the conquest of the Balearic islands by taking Ibiza and Formentera, and effectively establishes an independent kingdom.

1236 On 29 June Fernando III of León-Castile unexpectedly takes Córdoba after a group of Christian adventurers infiltrate its suburbs and appeal to him for help. The same evening the **Great Mosque of Córdoba** (see p.116) is consecrated as a Christian cathedral. Fernando also orders that the bells of Santiago de Compostela – looted by al-Mansur (see p.125) – be returned to their original home.

Towards the end of the year Jaume I of Aragon blockades and lays siege to the city of Valencia.

1237 As Almohad rule crumbles amidst dynastic feuding **Muhammad ibn Yusuf ibn Nasr** establishes an independent Muslim dynasty in the hill city of **Granada**. Over the course of the following fifteen years Granada expands to form an enclave amirate within Christian Spain that will survive under Nasrid rule until 1492.

1238 **Valencia** and its surrounding territories surrender to Jaume I of Aragon. Unlike his Castilian counterparts, Jaume allows the defeated Muslims to retain their faith, customs and rights, with the result that large parts of Valencia remain distinctly 'Moorish'.

1242 Resuming his campaigns, Jaume I captures Alcira in southern Valencia.

1243 Jaume I's forces take Jativa, and Castilian forces take Murcia.

1246 Campaigning successfully in the south, Fernando III of León-Castile lays siege to Seville in the autumn. To prevent the city being supplied by river, he commissions an entrepreneur from Burgos, **Ramón Bonifaz**, to build a fleet and blockade the Guadalquivir. In the same year Fernando's forces also besiege Jaén, in the hands of **Muhammad ibn Yusuf** of Granada. In return for relinquishing Jaén and becoming León-Castile's vassal, Muhammad is guaranteed the survival of his fledgling amirate.

1247 With the arrival of Bonifaz's fleet and the cutting of a pontoon bridge across the Guadalquivir Fernando III secures the encirclement of Seville.

A compilation of the *fueros* (see p.186) of Aragon is made under the supervision of Jaume I, detailing customary law, but interlaced with elements of Roman and Visigoth law supportive of monarchical authority.

Granada

From the Christian viewpoint **Granada** was a mistake. The last redoubt of Muslim rule in Spain, it stretched westwards from Almería to the Strait of Gibraltar, and was made possible by its first ruler **Muhammad ibn Yusuf ibn Nasir**'s consenting to become Fernando III's tribute-paying vassal in 1246. In the immediate term it provided shelter for tens of thousands of Muslims either fleeing – or unwilling to accept – Castilian rule, and in that sense probably averted greater resistance against the *Reconquista*. In the long run however it became a military threat to Christian Spain as its Nasrid amirs increasingly devoted their often scant resources to building complex and imposing fortifications. According to the Arab historian Ibn al-Khatib, by the mid-14th century Granada possessed 14,000 watchtowers, scattered throughout its territory. These however were not simply to warn of Christian attack. They were also designed to keep Granada's mainly Berber population under control. Instead of relying on a local soldiery for their security, the Nasrids recruited well-trained cavalry from Morocco. But such continuing connections with the Maghreb, and especially with the powerful **Merinids** there, only fuelled Christian apprehensions about the possibility of further full-scale invasions. Except for the latter half of the 14th century (when Castile was distracted by its involvement in Anglo-French wars), there was almost constant skirmishing along the Castile-Granada border, and in the 15th century a final reduction of the amirate became a priority of the Christian kingdoms. But although the **Fall of Granada** in 1492, wrought by Fernando and Isabella, was universally acclaimed in Christendom, the fact is that by then Granada was verging on collapse. Economically it was never self-sufficient, and depended on the export of such luxuries as sugar, almonds, raisins and, famously, silk. Gradually, though, the **Genoese** exerted a monopolistic control over Granada's external trade, forcing the amirs to raise taxation to levels that were socially corrosive and destabilizing. As the court became increasingly decadent, control at the local level passed into the hands of bosses known as *caciques*. In such circumstances it is surprising that Granada survived for as long as it did.

> We who are as good as you and together are more powerful than you, make you our king and lord, provided that you observe our *fueros* and our liberty, and if not, not.
>
> The traditional Oath of Allegiance to the King of Aragon made by his subjects during his coronation

1248 After a siege spanning three years **Seville** capitulates to Fernando III on 23 November, bringing to an end Almohad rule in the peninsula. Although Granada survives as a Muslim amirate and isolated pockets of Muslim resistance continue for at least a decade, the fall of Seville effectively cements the Christian *Reconquista*.

The Christian Settlement 1248–1479

The *Reconquista* was much more than simply the reduction and defeat of Muslim al-Andalus. It was a great military-religious movement upon which the character of Spain and the Spanish was founded. Yet by any fair assessment the character that emerged was contradictory as well as complex, and vulnerable to internal as well as external pressures.

Spain – or rather the conglomeration of disparate states that would eventually compose Spain – became at once intensely autocratic, but also legalistically conscious of the liberties and privileges belonging to its component communities and classes. In the two centuries that followed the Castilian capture of Seville in 1248 royal authority was both boldly asserted, and roundly challenged. As well as wars between the Christian kingdoms, there were civil wars within those states. At the same time the Iberian peninsula became more firmly welded to the fortunes of Christendom as a whole. It shared in the good times of a 13th century economic boom, but in the 14th century it suffered the profoundly destabilizing effects of the **Black Death**. In the same century too, all of the Iberian Christian states were dragged into the **Hundred Years War** between France and England.

Whatever else it brought, therefore, the *Reconquista* did not bring tranquillity. Despite the fall of Seville, the Muslim threat remained, both in the Maghreb, where the Merinids had established a potent Islamic dynasty, and also in **Granada**, where a supposedly emasculated amirate became, for a while at least, a renewed source of irritation.

Tragically, caught in the middle between Christians and Moors were the **Spanish Jews**, both those who abided by Judaism, and those who had converted to Roman Catholicism, known as *conversos*. With the enduring depression that set in following the Black Death, Jews of both kinds became the targets of racial prejudice and religious intolerance.

The violence and bloodshed that resulted were symptomatic of the divisions within Hispanic society. It was not a one nation-kingdom that had conquered al-Andalus, but three: León-Castile, Aragon and Portugal, each with it own traditions, and each with its own problems.

In the event, **Portugal**, once a county belonging to León, but now supported by England, clung on tenaciously to its independence, and so became historically detached from 'Spain'. Conversely, and against the rational odds, it was Castile, as León-Castile became known, and Aragon that eventually united, to become one of Europe's great powers.

In the context of medieval Christendom, Castile and Aragon were sharply differentiated. Apart from the Church, even the institutions they appeared to have in common developed in opposite directions. **Castile**, larger than Aragon in both population and territory, evolved as a pastoral frontier state. As it swallowed up the greater part of al–Andalus, it experienced a chronic shortage of manpower. To overcome this obstacle, the crown displayed a liberal hand in granting extraordinary rights, summed up in charters known as *fueros*, to those prepared to settle in forward territories. At the same time it encouraged the **Orders of Santiago**, **Calatrava** and **Alcántara** to partake of settlement, and by creating the **Mesta**, a union of sheep ranchers, ensured the growth of a wool industry that slowly but surely provided the foundation of Castile's wealth. Yet at the same time Castile's kings retained and augmented their royal power, most notably in their manipulation of the Castilian Cortes, or parliament; in the promulgation of a royal law code, the *Siete Partidas* of 1252; and in the steady accretion of royal taxes, among them the infamous *alcabala*, or sales tax, that made the Castilian monarchy the envy of its European rivals.

By contrast the **Crown of Aragon** was constitutionally weak, largely as a result of its conglomerate nature. Following its dynastic absorption of the Franco-Spanish March, and its capture of Valencia from al-Andalus, the Aragonese crown presided over three discrete territories. In each a Cortes, far from rubber-stamping royal policies, as happened in Castile, asserted its own will and its own prerogatives. Similarly Aragonese *fueros*, far from being appreciated as hand-downs from the throne, were regarded as embodying inalienable rights.

Aragon was also peculiarly vulnerable to economic vicissitudes. In the 13th and early 14th centuries **Barcelona**, and with it Catalunya, emerged as a principal maritime trading power in the western Mediterranean. But such pre-eminence was destroyed by the Black Death and the continuing rise of maritime Genoa in Italy, generating discontents that, in the 1460s, erupted in full-scale civil war between Barcelona's Biga and Busca factions.

Small wonder that the Kings of Aragon, enfeebled on their own doorstep, looked instead to acquire such overseas possessions as **Sicily** and **Naples**, adding to their domestic unpopularity by becoming absentee rulers. Yet periodically Castile too slid into civil war, partly because of resentment toward accentuated royal authority, but also because, in the later 15th century, of a dynastic dispute regarding the succession.

c.1250 The 'Usages of Barcelona', known in Catalan as the *Ustages*, are compiled from existing *fueros* (see p.186) and other documents, some dating back over a hundred years. Designed to be a comprehensive law-code for the Catalan people, the 'Usages' enshrine Catalan rights and privileges *vis-à-vis* their now Aragonese royal rulers; but because they are assembled by experts trained in Roman law, royal authority is also safeguarded in key passages, so that as a whole the 'Usages' are ambiguous as to the ultimate location of sovereignty in the Catalan state.

1252 Fernando III of León-Castile is succeeded by **Alfonso X**, known as 'the Wise' on account of his patronage of learning. Among other projects he promotes the translation of Arabic texts into the vernacular 'romance' language spoken by his subjects (rather than Latin). It is during his reign that **Castilian**, the basis of modern Spanish, emerges as a discrete language. Among the works commissioned by Alfonso X are the *Estoria de España* ('History of Spain') and *General Estoria* ('General History'). Also compiled in Castilian during his reign is the *Siete Partidas*, a comprehensive legal code that will progressively supply the Castilian Crown with precedents for its eventual assumption of absolute power. When it is first promulgated however it is resisted by elements of both the nobility and León-Castile's small urban population, to the extent that existing *fueros*, although contrary to the letter and the spirit of the *Siete Partidas*, go unchallenged.

> An emperor or king can make laws for the people of his dominions, but no one else has the power to make laws with regard to temporal matters except where they do so with their permission. Any laws that are made in any other way cannot be called laws or have the validity of laws, and are not to be regarded as valid at any time.

from *Las Siete Partidas del rey don Alfonso el Sabio*, trans. Angus MacKay

1258 The **Treaty of Corbeil**, concluded between Jaume I of Aragon and Louis IX of France, assigns the Franco-Spanish March, including the **county of Barcelona**, to the Crown of Aragon in perpetuity. The Crown's powers in Catalunya however are limited by existing laws and customary conventions, already enshrined in the *Ustages* (Usages) of Barcelona. Thus Jaume I's *de facto* status as Count of Barcelona is confirmed; but he is disqualified from using the term 'king' in Catalunya, and such powers as he has are granted on sufferance of the Catalan Cortes and other institutionalized bodies.

1264 As Leonese and Castilians begin settling in the south, Muslims continuing to live under Christian rule, known as **mudéjars**, launch a two-year revolt in the new provinces of Andalucía (from al-Andalus) and Murcia. But although Granada fuels the unrest by encouraging the Islamic Merinids to intervene from their bases in the Maghreb, the result of the revolt is a strengthening of Christian authority. Muslims are driven from their homes in the north, and some persuaded to return to Africa. In the south many Moorish towns are depopulated, although Seville, under Christian occupation, continues to flourish.

Fueros

Derived from the Latin *forum*, meaning 'open space', the term **fuero** was used in medieval Spain to describe a variety of charters issued by a ruler to particular groups of his subjects, and more rarely to his subjects as a whole. The earliest known such charter was the *Fuero de León*, issued in 1020, and between then and the end of the 14th century in excess of eight hundred such documents have survived. Most probably *fueros* had been drawn up before 1020, and it is routinely accepted that they were partly inspired by Visigoth law, particularly the *Forum Iudicorum*, known also as the *Fuero Juzgo* (see p.94).

In essence, a *fuero* specified subjects' rights, either communally or collectively, as well as their legal responsibilities and duties. *Fueros* were granted by both the crowns of León-Castile and Aragon (and later Navarra), and most commonly applied to **townships**, in which case they might also determine the institutions of municipal government. In Castile especially, the progress of the *Reconquista*, liberating vast tracks of under- or de-populated land meant that its rulers had to make significant concessions in order to attract settlers into 'frontier' territories, and so reduce the risk of Muslim resettlement. Exemptions from taxation were standard fare, and proffered benefits might include blanket pardons for crimes previously committed elsewhere – bigamy and even murder among them.

1265 During the Christian counter-offensive to the *mudéjar* rebellion, the southern Atlantic seaport of Cádiz is taken.

In Aragon, during a Cortes held at Ejea, Jaume I encounters opposition from his nobles, who have begun forming a 'league' to defend their interests against encroachments by the Crown. The king concedes that the **justicia** – the official responsible for administering justice in Aragon – should in future be chosen by the league and not appointed by himself.

Out of such arrangements, helped by the fact that Castile-León was relatively unaffected by patterns of feudal tenure, allowing free men to choose their lords, evolved a 'frontier culture', later exported to Spain's colonies in the Americas, where *fueros* helped establish Castilian settlements. But increasingly *fueros* were also used to codify existing customary law, particularly in Catalunya, where, although feudalism had developed as a result of the French settlement, towns and cities clung on obstinately to their traditional privileges. In the wider European setting, the interest in *fueros* as legal instruments is precisely in their constitutional implications. Like England's *Magna Carta* they restricted royal power, but also like *Magna Carta* nearly always to the advantage of well-defined interest groups, including the Church and the military religious Orders. Urban *fueros*, granted in Castile because of the military contribution made by municipalities to the *Reconquista* in terms of both soldiers and funds, generally legitimized bullying oligarchies, and so it would be wrong to emphasize their 'democratic' content. Nonetheless, the *fuero* became embedded in Spanish political culture as a symbol of liberty. Even the dictator Franco felt compelled to promulgate, in 1945, a *Fuero de los Espagnoles*, for the alleged protection of his subjects' personal rights.

1273 **Muhammad II** becomes the amir of Granada and at once sets about building new castles and other fortifications as relations between his principality and the kingdom of León-Castile deteriorate.

La Mesta, a 'union' of sheep-farmers under royal patronage, is founded in Castile (see p.211).

1275 Alfonso X of León-Castile leaves Spain in a futile endeavour to become **Holy Roman Emperor**. During his absence **Abu Yusuf Yaqub**, sultan of the Merinids in the Maghreb, mounts an invasion of southern Spain, assisted by Muhammad II of Granada. Two Castilian armies are defeated and bridgeheads are established at Tarifa and Algericas before the Merinids return to Africa.

1276 Jaume I of Aragon is succeeded by **Pedro III**, who immediately seeks support from Catalan merchants in the continuing struggle between crown and nobility. During Pedro III's reign Barcelona will rival Venice as the Mediterranean's busiest and wealthiest trading port.

c.1280 Alfonso X composes the *Cantigas de Santa Maria*, poems in praise of the Virgin Mary. The vividly illuminated manuscript reveals many aspects of the day-to-day lives of Christians, Jews and Muslims.

1282 During an unusually turbulent year, Alfonso X of León-Castile faces rebellion by his son, the *Infante* (crown prince) **Sancho**. While Sancho enlists the support of Muhammad II of Granada, Alfonso enlists the support of the Moroccan Merinids.

Pedro III of Aragon intervenes in **Sicilian affairs** and adds the island to his crown. Infuriated, the Pope first excommunicates him and then proclaims a crusade against him, proposing that **Charles of Valois** (heir to the French throne) should become King of Aragon instead. Pedro III manages to save his throne, but only by summoning a Cortes in both Aragon and Catalunya and making further constitutional concessions to his domestic political opponents.

1283 The anti-monarchical movement in Aragon, now known as the **Union of Aragon**, is reinforced when those representing the nobility and towns at a Cortes held in Zaragoza swear an oath to protect each others' privileges. Three months later Pedro III is confronted by a similarly organized opposition at a Catalan Cortes convened at

A Muslim and a Christian musician playing side by side. A page from the *Cantigas de Santa Maria*

Barcelona. In each case he is obliged to swear to uphold existing customs and *fueros*, and to agree that a Cortes should be summoned yearly. At the heart of Pedro III's difficulties is the disparate nature of the constituent territories of the Crown of Aragon, exacerbated by his expansionist policies in the Mediterranean.

1284 Alfonso X of Castile is succeeded by his formerly rebellious son **Sancho IV**.

1285 Pedro III of Aragon is succeeded by Alfonso III.

The Cortes

The existence of a nobility, the steady accretion of wealth and civil interests by the Church, the burgeoning costs of seemingly endless wars, and the growth of towns and cities – often on the back of enlarging domestic and international trade – all meant that the art of royal government became more complex, and often more difficult, as the Middle Ages wore on. Throughout Europe, monarchs depended on **royal councils** to administer their realms, but increasingly the advice proffered by such councils, generally made up of nobles, failed to reflect broader opinion. The solution, in England and France, was to assemble wider consultative assemblies called parliaments, and in Spain similar bodies called **Cortes**. As the word implies, a Cortes was just that: the king's court, only 'at large'. But although the Castilian Cortes predated its French and English medieval counterparts, its claims to enshrine the principle of representation are less well-founded. Critically the Castilian crown never conceded the principle that royal revenues were or should be dependent on any admission of grievances, presented by the Cortes as petitions. Rather the Castilian Cortes, summoned at the king's will (and so for long periods not summoned at all), first had to agree to whatever taxes the king needed; only then would he condescend to hear whatever 'legislation' the Cortes might propose. The Castilian throne also exercised autonomy by manipulating the agenda, and

1287 The Union of Aragon stages an 'invasion' of Valencia, and so wrings further concessions from Alfonso III and the Crown of Aragon in the form of the *Privilegio de la union*, which declares that henceforward the Union and not the King is the true guardian of Aragonese law.

1291 **Jaume II** succeeds Alfonso III of Aragon. During his 26 year reign the Catalan 'maritime empire' continues to expand in the Mediterranean, with trading colonies being established in Corsica and Sardinia as well as in Sicily.

by often choosing to summon only one or two of the Cortes's 'estates', i.e. the nobility, ecclesiastics or municipalities; and although the municipalities were represented in León from as early as 1188, those who represented them were far from being ordinary 'townsfolk'. With some skill therefore, the Castilian throne not only managed to keep its Cortes in check, but even used it to enhance its power.

The same was not true in the Crown of Aragon, where separate Cortes evolved for Catalunya and Valencia as well as Aragon itself. Although the histories of these three differ, each gained important concessions that in time became established prerogatives. The Aragonese Cortes generally declined to grant the king taxes until at least some of their grievances were redressed; and often the king was obliged to issue affirmations of existing privileges and *fueros* (see p.186). Nor did the Aragonese crown exercise the same degree of control over who could and who could not attend a Cortes. Indeed, the Catalan Cortes won the right to assemble regardless of whether it had been summoned. While some wanted an annual assembly, the impracticalities of this led to the creation of a standing committee, called the ***Disputacio*** ('Deputation') or *Generalitat*, that was capable of exercising near-sovereign power during periods of royal crisis or royal absence.

1292 Sancho IV of Castile captures the Merinid bridgehead port of **Tarifa**.

1294 The Merinids attempt to recapture Tarifa, but Tarifa is courageously defended by **Alfonso Perez de Guzmán** (known as 'Guzmán the Good'), who refuses to barter the port for the life of his son, a Muslim captive.

1295 Fernando IV succeeds Sancho IV as king of León–Castile, henceforth generally referred to simply as Castile.

Ramón Llull (1232–1315)

Born in Mallorca to Catalan parents, **Ramón Llull** (or Raymond Lully) became one of his era's greatest, if also most eccentric, polymaths. As a young man he was a glittering addition to the Aragonese court, writing poems in the French troubadour tradition, and a manual of chivalry widely translated in the Europe of his day. Aged 30, however, he experienced a personal vision of Christ that transformed his life. As a result he became deeply involved in the mystical traditions not just of Christianity, but also of Islam. He also became active as a missionary, participating in a movement (sponsored by the Papacy) to bring the Christian faith to Muslims. To this end he acquired a mastery of Arabic, to which he had already been exposed as a child by Mallorca's still largely Muslim population. With Jaume II of Aragon he established a small college on Mallorca dedicated to 'oriental studies', and his relentless campaigning on behalf of the scholarly study of Islam led to the founding of similar institutions at the universities of Salamanca, Paris, Oxford and Bologna.

Consistently revered among Catalans as the father of their robustly expressive language, Llull's *Libre de Amich e Amat* ('The Book of the Lover and the Beloved'), extracted from his

1296 In response to the growing trading power of the north European Hanseatic League, four towns on Spain's Atlantic north coast – San Sebastián, Laredo, Santander and La Coruña – form the *Hermandad de la marina de Castilla con Vittoria* as a rival trade cartel.

1300 As trade with northern Europe expands, the port city of **Bilbao** is founded on Spain's north coast.

1302 Catalan 'duchies' are established at Athens and Neopatras by Catalan mercenaries voyaging to Constantinople to fight Islamic incursions against the Byzantine empire.

1309 Fernando IV captures Algeciras from the Merinids. With the help of a Catalan fleet he then takes Gibraltar.

spiritual romance **Blanquerna** (1285), has long been regarded as a classic of medieval mysticism. His most important work, however, is the **Ars Magna** ('Great Art'), which employs elements of Islamic Sufi thought in an attempt to divulge the unity of creation. For Llull theology, philosophy and natural science are aspects of a single knowledge, just as the intellect, the will and memory are aspects of one mind, both triads corresponding schematically and literally to the Holy Trinity, the three manifestations of an undivided God. In attempting such syntheses, Llull was indebted to and enriched by an emergent **neo-Platonic** school of thought that pitted itself against the **Scholastics**' separation of primary and secondary causes, or orders of existence, derived from **Averröes** (see p.174), and which survived as a main thread in European culture until the 18th century (although Llull himself was condemned by Pope Gregory XI for 'confusing' reason and faith). According to legend, he was killed as an old man whilst preaching to murderously unreceptive Berbers in Tunisia, an irony – if true – since no one had done more than him to promote intercultural understanding.

1312 Alfonso XI succeeds Fernando IV as King of Castile.

1315 Death of **Ramón Llull**, Catalan courtier, writer and mystic.

> 'O bird that singest of love, ask thou of my Beloved, who has taken me to be his servant, wherefore He tortures me with love.' The bird replied: 'If love made thee not to bear trials, wherewith could'st thou show thy love for Him?'
>
> Ramón Llull, from *The Book of the Lover and the Beloved*,
> trans. E. Allison Peters

1323 Jaume II of Aragon begins the Aragonese conquest of **Sardinia**.

1327 Jaume II is succeeded by **Alfonso IV** of Aragon.

1333 In alliance with Granada, the Merinid sultan **Abul Hassan** recaptures Gibraltar and begins preparing a full-scale invasion of the Iberian peninsula.

1336 Alfonso IV is succeeded by **Pedro IV**, whose reign is spent trying to curb the influence and newfound powers of the Union of Aragon.

1337 France and England embark upon the **Hundred Years War**, a conflict that will spread into Spain.

1340 The long-threatened Merinid invasion of Spain is unleashed, and decisively repulsed by Alfonso XI at the **battle of the River Salado**. Following Salado, no further 'serious' attempt at the Islamic reconquest of Spain will be made.

1342 Alfonso XI begins fortifying Spain's southern coast, besieging Algeciras in the process. To finance his operations he persuades the Castilian Cortes to grant him an extraordinary tax, the *alcabala*. Like other war-taxes, the *alcabala* will become institutionalized as a regular levy raised without reference to the Cortes. Consisting of an urban sales tax, fixed at 5 per cent, but later rising to 10 per cent, it has been considered a forerunner of VAT.

1344 After a two-year siege, and despite the use of cannon by its Merinid defenders, **Algeciras** falls to Alfonso XI, to the general jubilation of Christendom.

Pedro IV of Aragon draws up the **Ordenaciòns de corte** ('Ordinations of the Court'), a pale attempt to provide the Crown of Aragon with an equivalent of the Castilian *Siete Partidas* (see 1252).

1348 The Great Plague, known also as the **Black Death**, enters Spain, most probably through Barcelona. While Castile will remain relatively unaffected, Valencia and particularly Catalunya are severely stricken. Following recurrences of the epidemic, Barcelona's population declines by half, and with it Barcelona's pre-eminence as a Mediterranean port. Across the whole land entire villages are emptied, and many monasteries abandoned. Castile's cartel of sheep farmers, the *Mesta*, benefits from the liberation of yet more grazing lands, and *mudéjars* (Muslims living under Christian rule) find new favour among their masters where they have hard skills to sell. Overall however Spain shares in the economic recession that grips Europe for the century that follows.

In Aragon in the same year, Pedro IV rescinds the *Privilegio de la union*, and makes a bonfire of related documents. When the Union of Aragon threatens general rebellion he stands his ground. Civil war is ended when both sides agree to concessions. Pedro reclaims some royal privileges, but concedes the continuing independence of the *justicia*.

In Castile, the Crown for the first time appoints **corregidores**, royal officials sent to towns to resolve local disputes. Whereas initially *corregidores* are dispatched 'by invitation', in time they will be imposed on every Castilian town and city.

1350 Alfonso XI of Castile dies of plague while laying siege to Gibraltar. He is succeeded by his unpopular son **Pedro I**, known as 'the Cruel'. Almost immediately Pedro is opposed by his illegitimate half-brother, **Enrique of Trastámara**. As the struggle between king and pretender balloons, Spain is dragged into the Hundred Years War. While Pedro, deprived of a promised French dowry after a brief and calamitous marriage to Blanche de Bourbon, enlists the support of England, equally swiftly Enrique attracts the backing of France, Aragon and the Papacy. In these circumstances the siege of Gibraltar is lifted.

A view into the Patio del Mexuar, a small section of the Alhambra – the great palace complex of the Nasrid dynasty

1354 Muhammad V accedes as amir of Granada. Under his direction the great palace-complex of Granada, known as the **Alhambra**, takes its final form.

1355 The forces of Enrique of Trastámara attack the *alcana*, the smaller Jewish quarter of Toledo, massacring over 1000 of its occupants.

1366 Enrique of Trastámara, continuing to enjoy the support of France and Aragon, and, having assembled an army at Montpellier that includes some English as well as other mercenaries, invades Castile, ousts Pedro I and proclaims himself King.

1367 With England's help Pedro I, having fled to Bayonne, returns to Spain and reclaims the Castilian throne.

1368 Enrique of Trastámara and Charles V of France formalize their alliance in the **Treaty of Toledo**. In return for military aid Enrique agrees to place a Castilian fleet at the service of the French in their war against the English.

1369 Enrique reinvades Castile, murders Pedro I at Montiel, and takes the throne as Enrique II. While Castile temporarily becomes virtually a French client state, Enrique courts popularity among Castilian nobles by removing several Jews appointed by his predecessor from their court offices.

1370 The **Order of St Jerome** (Jeronymites) is founded in Castile to promote reform in an increasingly corrupt Church. Unlike other monastics the Jeronymites expressly extol wealth as a means to accomplish good works. By the end of the century some twenty Jeronymite houses will have come into being.

1371 John of Gaunt, Duke of Lancaster and the son of King Edward III of England, marries Constance of Castile, the daughter of the former King Pedro I. As a claimant to the Castilian throne, the duke establishes a rival court at

> **"** Thou shalt make castels than in Spayne,
> And dreme of joye, al but in vayne. **"**
>
> Geoffrey Chaucer, *Romaunt of the Rose*, c.1371

Bayonne, and builds an anti-Trastamaran coalition with Aragon, Navarra and Portugal.

In Castile itself a Cortes agrees to a new judicial court, the **audencia**. As the highest lawcourt in the land the *audencia* is in reality a division of the king's *curia*, and accompanies him on his travels. Later however it will be given a permanent home, first at Segovia, then at Valladolid.

1372 A French-Castilian fleet inflicts defeat on the English at **La Rochelle**.

1374 Castilian warships raid the Isle of Wight off the south coast of England.

1377 Franco-Castilian warships inflict substantial damage on England's southern ports.

1378 The '**Great Schism**', lasting until 1429, begins as a rival papacy is set up in Avignon in opposition to Rome. Although the unity of the Catholic Church is damaged, the schism encourages such 'reformist' movements as the Jeronymites.

1379 Enrique II of Castile is succeeded by his son **Juan I**.

1380 A Franco-Castilian navy again attacks England.

1381 An English army lands in Portugal, but campaigns unsuccessfully against Castile.

1383 Juan I of Castile marries Beatriz, heir to the Portuguese throne. When **Fernando I** of Portugal dies five months afterwards, Juan claims his crown.

1384 The Portuguese nobility, unwilling to enter into union with Castile, proclaim **João of Avis** their king.

1385 Juan I is defeated by a combined Portuguese and English army at **Aljubarrota**, a battle conventionally regarded as the key to Portugal's continuing independence.

1386 Following the **Treaty of Westminster** between Portugal and England a Lancastrian army lands at La Coruña in Galicia, but fails to make headway against Castile after its ranks are devastated by disease.

1387 Pedro IV of Aragon is succeeded by **Juan I**.

John of Gaunt's daughter **Philippa of Lancaster** marries João I of Portugal.

1389 Spanish involvement in the Hundred Years War is ended by the Treaties of Leulingham and Monção. English claims to the throne of Castile, and Castilian claims to the throne of Portugal, are renounced. John of Gaunt is paid reparations amounting to £100,000, and an annual pension of £6000. Soon after Gaunt's daughter **Catherine of Lancaster** is married to Juan I of Castile's son and heir **Enrique**.

The monastery of **Santa Maria de Guadalupe** is taken over and reformed by the Jeronymites. The Jeronymites promote a local cult of the Virgin Mary, based on her supposed and frequent apparitions in the vicinity, and the monastery becomes a new centre for Christian pilgrimage.

1390 **Enrique III** succeeds Juan I of Castile.

1391 Beginning on 6 June in Seville, a wave of **anti-Jewish rioting** sweeps across the Iberian peninsula. Many hundreds of Jews are massacred, particularly in Valencia. While the immediate cause of the disturbances is attributable to the fiercely anti-Semitic preaching of Seville's archdeacon,

Feran Martinez, the pogrom exposes a multiplicity of social tensions, not least between Jews and *conversos* – Jews who have converted to Christianity. As well as a widespread resentment of individual Jews' success, there is a suspicion that many *conversos* have not completely abandoned their 'alien' faith. General economic decline, and an

BRITISH LIBRARY

A page from a mid-14th century Catalonian Haggadah showing the interior of a synagogue

ingrained Christian belief that Jews were responsible for Christ's crucifixion, contribute to the conflagration. In Barcelona anti-Jewish protests combine with radical discontent among the proletariat, and the city's administration is briefly overthrown. But the net result of '1391' is to encourage more Jews to become *conversos*, enabling them to pursue callings and professions previously barred to them.

1395 Juan I of Aragon is succeeded by his brother **Martin I**.

1398 Enrique III of Castile rules that only Castilian merchant vessels should porter Castilian goods and produce. Genoese merchants however continue to prosper in Seville and other southern ports, at the expense of the rapidly declining Catalan merchant empire.

1405 After a half-century interval, hostilities resume between Castile and Muslim Granada. The fighting however is half-hearted and inconclusive.

1406 Enrique III of Castile is succeeded by his one-year-old son **Juan II**. During John's minority his kingdom is effectively ruled by his uncle, **Don Fernando**.

1407 **Pedro López de Ayala**, the royal chancellor of Castile, and an accomplished writer, dies at Calahorra. He will be best remembered for his *Crónicas* ('Chronicles'), an unsentimental record of the events of his own time, and for his long satirical poem *Rimado de palacio*.

1409 **Sicily** is formally incorporated as a kingdom of the Crown of Aragon.

1410 Hostilities between Castile and Granada are brought to a conclusion with Don Fernando's capture of **Antequera**.

In Aragon, the death of the heirless Martin I induces a succession crisis that will last for two years.

Convivencia

Just as many Christians, known as **Mozarabs**, continued to live under Muslim rule following the conquest of 712, so many 'Moors', known as *mudéjars* ('one who remains'), lived under Christian rule as the *Reconquista* progressed. In day-to-day existence, however, it was the Muslims who came off worse. In many cases Castilian military success led to the expulsion of Muslims from captured territories (although the Aragonese conquest of Valencia was generally less punitive). Where Muslim communities were permitted to remain alongside their Christian neighbours, the social balance that resulted has been called *convivencia* – literally 'living together'. This entailed a degree of local self-government (sometimes even acknowledged in *fueros*), and the basic freedoms of worship, movement, property and trading were 'guaranteed', although such rights were often hard to sustain in Christian courts. Less positively there was an equal amount of restrictions and prohibitions: *Mudéjars* were required to practise such Christian rites as observation of the Sabbath; Christian families were banned from employing Muslim nannies; and any Muslim man who had sexual intercourse with a Christian woman was liable to be stoned to death. It was also a capital offence to convert, or attempt to convert, a Christian to Islam, and many mosques were consecrated as churches, depriving Muslims of their traditional community centres. In some cases Moorish communities were forcibly relocated, to lessen the risk of Muslim resurgence, and overall there was a tendency toward ghettoization and victimization. Even conversion by Muslims to Christianity was discouraged, since in an age when slavery was widely practised, this meant automatic manumission. Yet whatever their creed, Muslims did have an economic value, and those who kept their heads down, and allowed themselves to become 'acculturated', made at least as tangible a contribution to Christian society as previously Christians had made to Muslim society. Although never able to attain high or even middling positions in government, the 'Spanish Moors' made their presence felt as artisans and even architects, as witnessed by the minaret-like belfries of many medieval Christian churches.

1412 The Aragonese succession crisis is resolved when, by the '**Compromise of Caspe**', the crown is offered to the Castilian Don Fernando – **Fernando I of Aragon**. Although the two kingdoms remain separate, the greater part of the Iberian peninsula is now ruled by the Trastámara family. In Castile, Juan II's mother Catherine of Lancaster assumes the regency.

1415 The Portuguese capture of the Moroccan Merinid naval stronghold **Ceuta** puts the Strait of Gibraltar fully under Christian protection. As a result Genoese-Castilian mercantile activity expands to the further cost of declining Catalan maritime enterprise.

1416 Fernando I of Aragon is succeeded by his son **Alfonso V**, known as 'the 'Magnanimous'. During his 42-year reign Alfonso will become the most widely admired prince in the Christian Mediterranean, both as a patron of the arts and as a military leader willing to resist expansion by the Islamic Ottoman empire. Amongst Spaniards he will be less well regarded. While Valencia flourishes, Catalunya and Aragon itself experience economic stagnation.

1419 At the end of his minority Juan II assumes full power in Castile. When an English army occupies Normandy in northern France, he swiftly answers the threat to Castilian shipping by destroying a flotilla of Hanseatic League merchant boats at La Rochelle.

1420 Juan II of Castile falls under the sway of his anti-Aragonese courtier **Alvaro de Luna**, who encourages the king's preference for royal absolutism. For as long as policy is dominated by Alvaro, the Castilian Cortes will play little or no part in Castilian life. The Castilian nobility, however, resentful of Alvaro's hold over their monarch, and pursuing private feuds, soon reduce Castile to a patchwork of local wars.

Enrique of Portugal, known as Enrique O Navegador ('the Navigator'), begins dispatching fleets to explore the west coast of Africa with a view to establishing trading colonies – an initiative traditionally held to mark the beginning of European maritime expansion that by the close of the century will see Spanish fleets crossing the Atlantic.

1425 Inspired by the teachings of **Alonso de Mella**, a Franciscan monk, a heresy known as 'Free Spirit' spreads among Basque communities of northeastern Spain. Eventually eradicated in 1440, the heretics oppose marriage, advocate unrestrained sexual licence, and share their wealth and property.

1431 During a lull in Castile's domestic unrest, Alvaro de Luna leads a successful policing campaign against Granada, defeating the amir's army at **Higueruela**.

1435 As mercantile rivalry between Genoa and Barcelona degenerates into open warfare, the Catalans are crushed in the sea-battle of **Ponza**, confirming Genoese maritime supremacy in the western Mediterranean.

1440 Castile's grandees, increasingly impatient with Alvaro de Luna, begin combining in open rebellion.

1442 Alfonso V of Aragon gains control of **Naples**, where he becomes Alfonso I. A year later, to the detriment of his Spanish possessions, he establishes his court there.

1445 Alvaro de Luna inflicts a decisive defeat on the Castilian rebels, sometimes known as the 'Aragon Party', at **Olmedo**. Henceforward he rules despotically in King Juan II's name.

1447 Alvaro persuades the widowed Juan II to marry **Isabel of Portugal**.

1449 As communal tensions continue to simmer in Spanish cities, Toledo is gripped by a fresh outburst of anti-Semitism. The *conversos* bear the brunt of the violence, which is stirred up by the demagogue **Marcos Garcia de Mora** (known as 'Marquillos') who organizes an uprising aimed at seizing power in Toledo. The *conversos* are targeted on the pretext that their profession of Christianity is insincere, but it is now racial as much as religious intolerance that drives the crowd. Only when Marquillos is seized and executed is the uprising crushed.

1453 As opposition to Álvaro de Luna rekindles in the Castilian court, Isabel of Portugal persuades her husband to discard his favourite. Reluctantly Juan II agrees to his arrest and execution.

After a prolonged siege, the **fall of Constantinople** marks the final disbandment of the Byzantine empire, and the triumph of the Islamic Ottoman Turks. In Spain, *Reconquista* values are revived, to the detriment of Muslim Granada.

1454 Juan II of Castile dies, allegedly grief-stricken by the demise of Alvaro de Luna. He is succeeded by his son **Enrique IV**, sometimes called 'the Impotent'. Unable to control Castile's grandees, and unable to relinquish his father's absolutist pretensions, he will nonetheless endeavour to avenge Constantinople by renewing the war against Granada, for all that he surrounds himself with a guard of mainly Moorish soldiers.

In Catalunya disorder breaks out in Barcelona as a result of conflict between two factions competing for control of the city, the **Biga** and the **Busca**. The *Biga* represent the controlling oligarchy, made up of established merchant families and grandees; the *Busca* (sometimes called the 'royal' party) represent artisans, shopkeepers and workers, all generally excluded from municipal offices, but formed now into a powerful syndicate. The situation in Catalunya is further complicated by unrest amongst the *remensas* – peasants tied

The Jews of Spain

Although the *Reconquista* was directed against the Muslim occupation of Spain, the Jews were no less its victims. Famously, no sooner had Granada, the last bastion of Islamic rule in the peninsula, fallen to Christian arms in 1492 than Isabel, Queen of Castile, ordered the expulsion of every Jew from her territory (see p.244). Yet Jews had been present in Spain since the 1st century AD, and over the millennium-and-a-half that followed made a substantial contribution to Iberian life, while maintaining a distinctive community of their own. As a 'People of the Book' they were tolerated by the Umayyads, and individually many Jews prospered, either as craftsmen and artisans, or as merchants, financiers, doctors, lawyers, scholars, and sometimes as high-ranking officials. Nor, under Muslim rule, were they threatened by the steady expansion of the Christian north. Rather, with their extensive trading networks in Egypt, the Syrian Levant and beyond – in the 11th century there is reference to Tibetan musk in a Jewish inventory – Jews were an invaluable asset to the Islamic realm. In Toledo alone there were a dozen synagogues, and Jews were permitted to build new ones at a time when the erection of Christian churches was prohibited.

Similarly, the Jews flourished during the first centuries of Christian rule. In the south-eastern towns and cities where most Jews lived communal tensions were not unknown, but in the main ordinary Jews and Christians lived peaceably side-by-side. But by the end of the 14th century Spanish Jews were under attack. The

to the land and their overlords by feudal obligations – and by royal absenteeism.

1455 With papal approval Enrique IV of Castile embarks on a crusade to conquer **Granada**. Instead of direct assault he adopts a strategy of demoralizing Granada's Muslims by devastating the agricultural lands around Granada and other urban centres.

pogrom of 1391 marked the beginning of a sustained and ultimately systematic persecution. Why this happened is not fully understood. Many factors seem to have been involved: the growth of Christian militancy; the distrust and fear of an established but minority religion; the fact that as Semites Jews came from the same racial stock as Muslim Arabs; envy of the financial and political prominence achieved by some Jews; the economic hardships generated by the Black Death, setting citizen against citizen, and feeding racist instincts; and, amidst this catalogue, tensions between Jews and *conversos* – Jews who had converted to Christianity.

As regards the *conversos*, there was a particular difficulty, in that as long as unconverted Jews remained in Spain to 'tempt' them back into the Judaic fold, the sincerity of those who had converted was doubted; and indeed it was just such doubts that prompted the setting up of the Inquisition in 1478 (see p.220). It also appears that some *conversos* supported the expulsion of 1492. But the reality was that, post-1391, anti-Semitism became a populist cause in Spain. *Conversos* were derisively referred to as *marranos* ('swine'), and the notion of *limpieza di sangre* ('purity of blood') gained ground, to the extent that in Castile it became an unofficial but necessary qualification for official preferment, the more so as increasing numbers of Jews converted. One outstanding irony of the Jewish tragedy in Spain is that Isabel's own husband, Fernando of Aragon, had Jewish antecedents.

In Barcelona the conflict between *Biga* and *Busca* is temporarily resolved when the Crown intervenes in favour of the latter. Alfonso V of Aragon also decrees the freedom of the *remensa* peasants.

1458 Enrique IV of Castile abandons his campaign against Granada in order to concentrate on the growing factiousness of the Castilian nobility.

Alfonso V of Aragon dies, and is succeeded by his son **Juan II**. The Catalan and Aragonese nobility, in league with Barcelona's *Biga* faction, openly resist royal policy in their respective Cortes. Simultaneously the king is confronted by the expansionist policies of Louis XI of France. Mainly as a result of these pressures Juan II will spend less time than his father looking after his Mediterranean interests. He will also strive for a union between the crowns of Aragon and Castile as a solution to Aragon's problems.

1461 The **Prince of Viana**, Juan II's overly ambitious son, is arrested by his father on account of his support for the king's political opponents.

1462 Having become the figurehead of aristocratic opposition to Juan II, the Prince of Viana dies in prison. Immediately Juan II's enemies in Catalunya declare open revolt, sparking a ten-year civil war. The anti-monarchical *Biga* regain control of Barcelona.

Enrique IV of Castile, during a temporary respite from his domestic difficulties, captures the town of **Gibraltar** from Muslim control.

1463 Taking advantage of the civil war in Catalunya Louis XI of France occupies the Catalan counties of Cerdanya and Rossello (Cerdagne and Roussillon).

1464 Able to draw on the political and military support of Aragon, Valencia and also Mallorca, Juan II fares well against his Catalan opponents. Barcelona however remains in rebel hands, and fighting continues around the city.

1465 In January, following **civil war** in Castile between Enrique IV and a faction of grandees, the king accepts 'constitutional' terms imposed upon him by the rebels but revokes all concessions the next month. In June Enrique IV's opponents publicly 'depose' his effigy and proclaim his teenage half-brother Alfonso king.

1467 Unrest in Castile is exacerbated by local rebellion in the north-western province of **Galicia**, where an alliance of bandits, peasants and minor nobility begin destroying the fortified properties of the greater nobility. The revolt lasts three years, but is put down by the seigneurial lords themselves.

Anti-Jewish violence flares up in Toledo.

1468 Following the death of his half-brother the pretender Alfonso, Enrique IV concedes that his well-respected and unmarried sister **Isabel** should be named heir to the Castilian throne in preference to his own daughter Juana, widely believed not to be his child. At once speculation mounts as to a suitable husband for Isabel, the leading candidates being the French prince Charles of Valois; Juan II of Aragon's son and heir Fernando; and Alfonso V of Portugal (favoured by Enrique IV).

1469 On 19 October Isabel of Castile takes matters into her own hands by hastily marrying **Fernando of Aragon**, her cousin and at 18 one year younger than herself. The marriage takes place in Valladolid, and is made possible by the intervention of the archbishop of Toledo, Don Alfonso Carillo, who forges a document providing papal approval of the marriage despite the consanguinity of the betrothed. According to a marriage contract previously agreed at Cerva, Fernando undertakes to live in Castile and fight on behalf of Isabel, but not to claim the Castilian crown for himself. Almost immediately Castile is plunged deeper into civil war. Infuriated by news of the marriage, and now backed by important segments of the Castilian nobility, Enrique IV proclaims his daughter **Juana** (nicknamed *la Beltraneja* after her putative father Beltran de la Cueva) his heir, at the same time betrothing her to Alfonso V of Portugal. Enough nobles rally around Isabel however for her faction to survive.

1472 The civil war in the Crown of Aragon is brought to a close by the submission of Barcelona to Juan II following the defection of some *Biga* members to the royal cause. To ensure peace Juan II affirms the rights and privileges of his Catalan subjects, but he also reaffirms the freedom of the *remensa* peasants.

1473 The southern Castilian province Andalucí is gripped by anti-Semitism when, during a procession by a Marian fraternity through the *conversos* quarter in Córdoba, a blacksmith called **Alonso Rodriguez** tells the marchers that urine has been sprayed onto the image of the Virgin Mary from a *conversos* dwelling. The procession turns into a mob which sets about burning Jewish houses and murdering their inhabitants.

Printed books are manufactured in Spain for the first time.

1474 On 11 September Enrique IV of Castile dies, and his sister Isabel at once proclaims herself Queen.

1475 At the beginning of the year, backed by Alfonso V of Portugal and by the French crown, Juana *la Beltraneja* also lays claim to the throne, provoking a four-year **War of the Castilian Succession**. The 'Isabelline Party' however slowly prevails, not least because of the military and political talents of Isabel's husband Fernando.

1476 The war in Castile turns decisively in Isabella's favour when Alfonso V's Portuguese army is roundly defeated at **Toro**. To cement an alliance with the towns and cities of Castile, and to bring them under royal control, Isabella and Fernando create a unified **Hermandad**, or policing and judicial authority, presided over by the bishop of Cartagena. While in essence the *Hermandad* incorporates existing urban *hermandads* (brotherhoods) and other interest groups into a single crown-chartered body, its existence erodes the power and influence of the nobility over Castile's steadily expanding urban population. Over the coming decade the

The Mesta

One result of the *Reconquista* was that Castile became Europe's principal supplier of wool, the essential raw material of European clothiers. As territory was recovered from al-Andalus, the want of manpower to farm such land – much of which was sited on the relatively infertile *meseta* – meant that sheep grazing and transhumance (moving flocks between summer and winter pasturages) was favoured over more labour-intensive agriculture. This was boosted by unexpectedly rich returns following the introduction of the hardy, and extremely woolly, **Merino sheep** from North Africa around 1250. The accumulation of vast estates, in the hands of nobles, the Church or the military-religious orders, likewise facilitated the long treks of drovers between seasons. Simultaneously, as the medieval European economy grew, there were ready markets for Castilian wool and woollen cloths in Italy, England and the Netherlands, and from thence into central Europe and Scandinavia.

The development of a major industry in the Iberian peninsula brought prosperity to the emergent state of Castile, whose ruling house responded by reducing and overriding local tolls, and by prioritizing transhumance in return for a cut of the profits. Accordingly, in 1273, the **Mesta** was created, a super-*hermandad* that incorporated all those involved in sheep herding – both great and small – by royal warrant. In return, the Mesta paid annual dues to the Crown. The result was an even faster expansion of sheep grazing, and an even greater expansion of the Castilian economy, giving it a measure of protection against the Great Plague of the mid-14th century. But there was also a downside, fixed by legislation of 1502 that decreed that any land once used for sheep grazing should always be used for sheep grazing. Castilian agriculture lagged well behind what had been achieved on the same lands in Roman and even Visigoth times, and well behind the needs of Spain's growing population. In the short-term the problem was met by the acquisition of colonies in the New World; but in the long-term it meant a blighted interior.

Hermandad, with its wide-ranging powers of arrest and punishment, will become a principal instrument for restoring order in the kingdom.

The death of the **Grand Master of the Order of Santiago** (see p.170) at Uccles affords the throne further opportunity to enhance its power as well as revenues. Riding furiously from Valladolid, Isabel arrives at Uccles in time to secure Fernando's future assumption to the Grand Mastership.

1478 Courting popular anti-Semitism, Isabella inaugurates the **Spanish Inquisition** (see p.220) by sanctioning the establishment of a tribunal of the Holy Office in Castile. Although the papal Holy Office's declared purpose is to root out heresy within the Catholic Church, in Spain its energies are initially directed against '**New Christians**', ie converts from Judaism and Islam.

Isabelline forces begin occupying the Portuguese-owned **Canary Islands** in the Atlantic.

1479 On the death of Juan II his son Fernando accedes to the Crown of Aragon. Through Fernando's marriage to Isabel the thrones of Aragon and Castile are united, to form a composite kingdom subsequently known as **España** – Spain. With the connivance of the Archbishop of Toledo, Isabel seeks to increment royal power by summoning an ecclesiastical council with a view to wresting control over senior church appointments in both her own and her husband's territories.

6: Los Reyes Catolicos: The Spain of Fernando and Isabel

1479–1516

n **1479** the faction supporting the claim of **Isabel** (Isabella) to the throne of Castile conclusively triumphed over the faction supporting her niece **Juana** (*La Beltraneja*); and, on the death of his father Juan II, Isabel's husband **Fernando** (Ferdinand) succeeded to the Crown of Aragon. For the history of the peninsula this was a profoundly significant moment. It was not just that Castile and Aragon were joined, nor even that the two territories now found themselves ruled by two monarchs of unusual, even extraordinary, talents. Rather it was the way in which Fernando and Isabel shared an almost visionary sense of purpose which – if not in their own lifetimes – would forge a nation-state that, in the century after their deaths, often seemed to dominate western Europe, and much beyond.

Their marriage, contracted ten years before in 1469, was a political match characteristic of the **dynasticism** prevalent in Christendom throughout the Middle Ages. Nor should too much be read into Isabel's intervention in the matter of her own betrothal. If she chose Fernando in preference to a Portuguese or French prince, that followed from the advice of those around her. Fernando was her junior by a year, and the kingdom he would inherit was a lesser entity in almost every way than Castile. Isabel's strong character may simply have recoiled from the prospect of being allied to a crown equal to or greater than her own.

Unlike Castile, where royal absolutism was the coming mode, the **Crown of Aragon** was far less centralized. The 15th century had seen prolonged struggles between its rulers and its subjects, against a background of economic deterioration, especially in Catalunya; and it was the subjects who generally succeeded in defending a fabric of rights and privileges of almost breathtaking complexity. Indeed, it was principally because of Aragon's stagnation, and the political difficulties of the throne, that **Juan II** strove to secure his son's marriage to the heiress of Castile.

Yet the House of Aragon was not entirely without advantages. Quite separately from its Spanish interests, it had accumulated possessions in the Mediterranean, among them **Sardinia** and the **Balearic Islands**, and also the kingdoms of **Naples** and **Sicily**; and although currently the latter were ruled by the family's 'junior' branch, it was to be one of the triumphs of Fernando's reign to bring both Italian territories firmly under his personal aegis, in the process defeating the armies of one of Europe's stronger states, **France**.

Fernando also oversaw, in 1512, the repossession of **Navarra**, and its incorporation not into his own crown, but that of **Castile**. No other episode reflects perhaps the extent to which the political aspirations of his and Isabel's thrones had become merged. Yet in nearly all their institutions the kingdoms remained distinct; and tellingly Fernando was of far greater assistance to his wife in managing her realm than she was to him in his.

But there was one institution that straddled both: the **Church**. It was in this respect that Isabel and Fernando could most profitably make common cause. The attachment of the three religious-military orders of Santiago, Calatrava and Alcántara to her crown was a significant coup for Isabel, even if it was her husband who necessarily became Grand Master of each. Both monarchs too, styled 'the Catholic Kings' by

Pope Alexander VI in 1494, used every opportunity to wring concessions from the Papacy, to ensure their control of ecclesiastical affairs in Spain, and through that control an aura of divine authority began to attach itself to them.

In the case of **Isabel** certainly, there is no doubting her piety. For many Spanish she was a saint as well their queen. Yet the same commitment led her to sanction that most contentious of her nation's institutions, the **Spanish Inquisition**, as well as, in 1492, the expulsion from Spain of its many **Jews**. Both of these events were intimately connected to the conquest of **Granada**. In completing the *Reconquista*, and establishing the supremacy of Catholicism throughout the peninsula at a time when the empire of the Ottoman Turks was threatening Europe from the east, Fernando and Isabel were able to project themselves as international leaders determined to preserve Spain as a bastion of the Christian faith.

Of greater consequence for the future were the exploits of **Christopher Columbus** and other mariners sponsored by the Catholic Kings in opening up the New World, and founding the first European settlements in the **Americas**. From the moment of Columbus's return to Spain at the end of the first of his four transatlantic voyages of discovery in 1493 there began a scramble for overseas possessions that would occupy the minds and resources of European powers for well over 400 years. While the **Portuguese** may claim to have started the chase with their explorations of the east African coast and colonization of Madeira and the Canary Islands, there is little doubt that the initial determination of Fernando and Isabel to exploit Columbus's ambition sowed the seeds of the 'Spanish Empire'.

Despite the many successes of their reign, privately the lives of the two monarchs were blighted. Their only son and two eldest daughters died young, and their third daughter, **Catherine of Aragon**, disappeared to England, to become Henry VIII's miserably unhappy wife. Eventually the succession passed to a grandson by their youngest child, the mentally unstable Juana. The same grandson, **Charles**, also stood to inherit the duchy of Burgundy, through his mother's marriage to the Emperor Maximilian I's son Philip, and to become Holy Roman Emperor. But if this portended an unwieldy and ultimately unmanageable conjunction of crowns – dynasticism run amok – it is to Fernando and Isabel's lasting credit that Charles V's Iberian inheritance could begin calling itself **España**.

1479 Although **Fernando II**'s accession to the Crown of Aragon heralds the emergence of Spain from the union of **Aragon** and **Castile**, the two kingdoms continue to be governed separately. In Castile Fernando, as Isabel's consort, plays a leading role in shaping policy, but in Aragon Isabel plays a lesser role.

The **Castilian War of Succession** is brought to a conclusion when Isabel's rival, **Juana *la Beltraneja***, deserted by her allies, concedes the Castilian crown, and retires to a convent.

The war with **Portugal** is concluded by treaty. Portugal cedes the **Canaries** to Castile, but Castile affirms Portugal's title to Madeira, the Azores and other smaller islands in the eastern Atlantic.

1480 Isabel impresses her personality and ambitions on a full gathering of the Castilian Cortes at **Toledo**. Territorial disputes between crown and nobles are resolved by an **Act of Resumption**, allowing the Queen to repossess half of any lands unlawfully appropriated since 1464. The Cortes also agrees that a *corregidor* (royal official) should be appointed to every town and city in Castile, and that municipal offices should cease to be hereditary.

Isabel further strengthens her hand by restructuring the **royal council**, the main instrument of administration in her realm. The chief offices of government, long filled by

Fernando and Isabel with their daughter Juana

Queen Isabel (1451–1504)

During the 15th century a new kind of ruler appeared on the European stage – hardworking, diligent, proactive in policy-making, dependent on a clerisy of professional advisers, and **absolutist** in their determination to centralize power about their thrones. **Isabel of Castile** was arguably the greatest of such monarchs. The daughter of Juan II of Castile, and half-sister to Enrique IV, she imposed her personality on all those she came in contact with from her late teens onwards, combining imperious authority, piety and a relentless determination to have her way. Matronly rather than beautiful, she succeeded in winning over her husband **Fernando of Aragon** – himself an outstanding monarch – not only to her bedchamber, but also to her policies, to the extent that he became her collaborator in the forging a powerful nation-state. Significantly, Fernando co-signed many of the decrees it was her right to issue. The royal couple also paid scrupulous attention to the credentials of any potential crown appointee, maintaining a notebook of such details they took with them on their travels.

Such close attention to the minutiae of government paid handsome dividends. By excluding the sons of dukes and counts

grandee families sometimes on a hereditary basis, are replaced by secretaryships, often awarded to *letrados*, trained lawyers. The revived authority of the Castilian throne is also used to persuade **bishops** to abandon their fortresses, acquired during the *Reconquista* as protection against Muslim assault, but latterly used by some bishops to enhance their standing as regional magnates.

In the province of Andalucí, a tribunal of the **Holy Office** (Inquisition) is established, to monitor the orthodoxy of 'new Christians', whether former Muslims or Jewish *conversos*.

In Aragon however Fernando placates potential opponents by reaffirming existing rights and privileges, including con-from the administration, by installing account-keepers intensely loyal to Isabel herself, and by such measures as banning the export of gold or silver, Castilian crown revenues are estimated to have increased by a factor of 25 during her reign, enabling the queen to fund such ventures as the conquest of **Granada** and expeditions to the **New World**. In both these undertakings however it was the glory of God that drove her as much as as the glory of her throne. As soon as she became informed that the islands Columbus had discovered were inhabited, she imposed a missionary component on further expeditions. The same ardour led Isabel to license the **Inquisition**, and to order the expulsion of the **Jews** in 1492. But vile as both these initiatives must appear to posterity, they reflected Isabel's populist style of rule. During the siege of Granada she personally supervised the building of a military hospital; and she took an equally close interest in the reform of the women's religious order of the **Poor Clares**. These and other royal interventions were Isabel's means of bonding the more ordinary of her subjects to her throne – a secondary 'union' affected during her reign that in retrospect seems quite as vital as the union with Aragon.

stitutional limitations on his own powers, first in Catalunya, then in Valencia and Aragon itself.

1482 Boabdil, the son of Granada's amir **Mulay Hassan**, rebels against his father and flees to Guadix, where he is recognized as amir by his followers. As civil war spreads inside the amirate, Fernando and Isabel begin preparing for the final phase of the *Reconquista*.

A Castilian naval force imposes Spanish rule on **Gran Canaria**, the largest of the Canary Islands.

1483 Although a Castilian army is badly mauled during an offensive in Granada, Boabdil is captured, then 'turned' by Fernando. In return for territorial guarantees once Granada has fallen, Boabdil pledges to fight with the Christians against his father.

In August, with the reluctant connivance of the Pope, Castilian tribunals of the Holy Office are placed under the direction of a special royal council, the *Consejo de la Suprema y General Inquisición*. The **Spanish Inquisition**, as this body and its activities will become known, is placed under

The Spanish Inquisition

The Spanish Inquisition has passed into history as a byword for near-totalitarian intolerance and cruelty. Its reputation is not undeserved. The institution itself though was not a Spanish invention. A **Holy Office** to root out 'heresy' was first established by Pope Gregory IX in 1231, and many of its methods, including the use of torture to extract confessions, were well established by the time Fernando and Isabel gained the right to appoint an **Inquisitor-General** for the territories they ruled in 1483. For the evolution of the Holy Office in Spain that right was crucial, for it meant the Spanish Inquisition became an instrument of policy in a nonaccountable way.

Whilst originally the purpose of the Holy Office was to enforce observance of the Catholic faith among Christians, from the outset, in the hands of the first Inquisitor-General **Tomás de Torquemada**, the Spanish Inquisition particularly targeted Jewish and Moorish converts, who, in an earlier age, could have expected to practise their ancestral faiths in private without disturbance. Being the first Inquisitor-General, Torquemada was also its most ruthless. While the number of those who were burned at the stake as heretics during his stewardship has often been exaggerated, 2000 is now a widely accepted figure. But Torquemada was also largely responsible for the procedures that turned the Inquisition into a means of political repression. Those suspected of heresy – usually on the tip-off of unnamed informers who might also be paid – were detained and cross-examined secretly. If found guilty, they were then subjected to an *auto de fe*, a public ceremonial

the authority of an Inquisitor General, **Tomás de Torquemada**, a Dominican friar who will become famed for the severity of his methods. In October further offices of the Inquisition are opened in Aragon, Catalunya and Valencia.

A long-established annual trade fair, held at **Medina del Campo**, and increasingly frequented by merchants and

during which their crimes were rehearsed and a 'reconciliation' imposed. Reconciliation nearly always meant punishment of some kind or other. Although the death sentence became relatively rare – in the 16th century only around one percent of those arraigned faced execution – individuals could expect to be fined, have their property confiscated or be stripped of any titles.

To be investigated by the Inquisition spelled ruin – not least because it destroyed a person's reputation and honour, regardless of the outcome. Because of its reliance on informers, the system was far from impartial, the more so since, as time wore on, it largely reverted to its original brief of upholding Catholic morality. Once pogroms against Jewish and Moorish converts had been seen through, and a handful of Protestants prosecuted, blasphemy, fornication and other ordinary mortal sins became the Inquisition's most usual field of interest – though it was also used to discredit public figures when all else failed, most notably **Antonio Pérez** in 1590 and **Jerónimo de Villanueva** in 1644.

Almost until its eventual dissolution, in 1834, the Inquisition remained an instrument of social and intellectual control simply by virtue of its existence. Humanitarian considerations apart, its role in Spanish history is ambiguous. By promoting **unity of faith** during the turbulence of the Reformation of the 16th and 17th centuries it may well have saved more lives than it destroyed. But by instilling fear, and discouraging independence and novelty of thought, it contributed significantly to the waning of Spanish dynamism.

businessmen from Europe's leading economies, gains royal, and therefore intentional, recognition.

1484 Cardinal **Gonzalez de Mendoza**, Archbishop of Toledo, founds the College of Santa Cruz at Valladolid, aimed at raising educational standards among Spain's clergy.

The Portuguese crown, which has sponsored several maritime expeditions, refuses to support Cristóbal Colón, a Genoese mariner known to English-speakers as **Christopher Columbus** (see p.238). His plan is to reach 'Cathay' (China) and the 'spice islands' (East Indies) by sailing westwards across the Atlantic.

1485 As the war against Granada escalates, Fernando's forces capture the city of **Ronda** and its surrounding territory.

1486 Loja falls to Fernando, who, in the same year, issues the *Sentencia de Guadalupe* ('Sentence of Guadalupe'), designed to finally resolve the *remensa* peasant problem in Catalunya by abolishing the *malos usus*, also known as the 'six evil customs', enjoyed by landlords and feudal overlords. As well as granting the **remensas** freedom of movement, the *Sentencia* permits peasants to sell or sublease their land-plots, while recognizing landlords' freehold ownership.

In December, in return for military assistance in Italy, a **papal bull** grants the crown of Castile the right to make senior church appointments in territories recovered from the amirate of Granada. The same privilege will later be formally extended to Spain's conquests in the New World, and inside Spain itself.

Columbus petitions Fernando and Isabel to sponsor his plan to find an Atlantic passage to the East. The court responds by setting up a commission under Hernando de Talavera to evaluate the project. During its four-year deliberations Columbus is supported by the Castilian crown.

1487 The Granadan city of **Málaga** falls to Fernando, and its Muslim inhabitants are sold into slavery. Shortly afterwards Fernando becomes Master of the **Order of Calatrava**, and in the same year he establishes an office of the Inquisition in **Barcelona**. This inspires an exodus of wealthy and educated Jews and *conversos* from the Catalan capital, further weakening its prestige and its economy.

The Portuguese mariner **Bartholomeu Diaz** rounds the Cape of Good Hope after being blown off course by a storm.

1489 The Granadan city of **Baza** falls to Castile.

Fernando, pursuing an anti-French policy in respect of his Italian interests, concludes the **Treaty of Medina del Campo** with England in March, the terms of which include the marriage of his daughter Catherine to the heir of the English throne, Arthur. When Arthur dies shortly afterwards, his widow, known as Catherine of Aragon, marries his brother – the future Henry VIII.

Spanish soldiers returning from **Cyprus**, where they have helped Venetian forces combat Ottoman Turks, introduce **typhus** into western Europe. Aragon is ravaged by an epidemic.

1490 With the fall of **Almería** to Fernando's forces, Granada's territory shrinks to less than a quarter of what it was in 1485. Boabdil reneges on his agreement with Fernando and vows to defend his father. Unperturbed, Fernando lays siege to Granada itself, despite its near impregnability. To this end a military camp, **Santa Fe**, is built a few miles from the Muslim city. The camp rapidly becomes a small city in its own right, attracting soldiers and adventurers from across western Europe.

The **royal commission** to assess Columbus's proposed Atlantic voyage reaches a negative conclusion and Columbus is told the Castilian crown cannot sponsor him.

1491 The **Siege of Granada**, masterminded by **Gonzalo de Córdoba**, begins in earnest in the Spring. Boabdil again changes sides and joins the Christian campaign. In November the city, abandoned by the rest of Islam, signals that it is ready to negotiate surrender terms.

Spanish colonists establish **sugar-cane** plantations in the Canary Islands.

1492 On 2 January **Granada** formerly surrenders to Fernando and Isabel. Four days later, dressed in Moorish costume, the king and queen enter the city. Granada's inhabitants are granted the customary rights of *moriscos* – converted Muslims living under Spanish rule. Boabdil is 'rewarded' with the principality of **Alpujarras**, and Hernando de Talavera, the queen's confessor and a tolerant-minded reformer, is appointed Granada's first archbishop.

On 30 March the king and queen jointly sign an edict expelling unconverted **Jews** from their territories. While some Jews hurry to convert, most do not, and there follows an exodus from Spain of an estimated 100,000 refugees, including a significant number of *conversos*. The Ottoman Sultan, **Bayazid II**, is one of the few leaders to encourage Jews to enter his country.

On 16 April Fernando and Isabel agree terms with Columbus, who on 3 August sets sail across the **Atlantic** from Palos with a crew of 88 aboard three caravels, the

> **"** The Catholic monarch Fernando is wrongly considered wise, since he impoverished his country by the expulsion of the Jews, and enriched ours. **"**
>
> Sultan Bayazid II, quoted by Immanuel Aboab in
> *A Consolacam as Tribulações de Israel*

BRITISH LIBRARY

King Ferdinand directs Columbus on his search for the New World

Santa Maria, the *Pinta* and the *Niña*. On 12 October a crewman on board the *Pinta* sights the **Bahamas**, and so inaugurates the European conquest and colonization of the **New World**, even though Columbus himself will always believe his discoveries are located in the Far East.

Spanish forces eradicate **Portuguese rebels** on the Canary island of Palma.

Francisco Jiminez de Cisneros becomes Queen Isabel's confessor, on the recommendation of Archbishop Mendoza.

Elio Antonio de Nebrija publishes a Castilian **grammar**, the first of any modern European language to be printed.

1493 On 23 January, having discovered and laid claim to the large Caribbean island of **'Hispaniola'** (divided today between Haiti and the Dominican Republic), and leaving behind a colony of some 30 Spaniards, Columbus sets sail for Spain aboard the *Niña*.

Charles VIII of France, anxious to campaign in Italy without Fernando's opposition, returns the counties of Rosello and Cerdanya to the Crown of Aragon by the **Treaty of Barcelona**.

Columbus arrives back at **Palos** on 15 March. In April he is richly received by Fernando and Isabel in Barcelona, and claims for himself a reward offered for the first man to sight land on the far side of the Atlantic.

In May Pope **Alexander VI** issues papal bulls defining Spain and Portugal's spheres of authority over any newly discovered Atlantic territories. Columbus's discoveries include, as well as land, previously unknown foodstuffs such as maize, sweet potatoes, capsicums, pineapples, plantain and turtle-meat. Of more immediate significance is the discovery of gold among the islands he has explored. A second voyage is prepared under the supervision of **Juan de Fonseca** (later Bishop of Burgos), and on 25 September Columbus, confirmed as governor of territories discovered by him, sets sail from Cádiz with a fleet comprising seventeen vessels and 1500 men. Returning to Hispaniola, he founds **Isabel**, the first European township in the New World. However, the 30 Spaniards left behind the previous year at La Navidad have either died or been killed by Caribbean natives.

Boabdil relinquishes Alpujarras and, along with 6000 followers, crosses the Strait of Gibraltar to settle in Féz. To discourage any further Muslim interest in Spain, Fernando orders watchtowers to be built along the coast of Andalucí.

Spanish forces overcome Portuguese rebels in **Tenerife**, and so complete their occupation of the Canary Islands.

1494 As the power of the **Ottoman Turks** grows, Pope Alexander VI promulgates a crusade against Muslims in North Africa. With his armies tied up in Italy, following its invasion by **Charles VIII** of France, Fernando postpones taking action, even though the pope confers upon Fernando and Isabel the honorific title *Reyes Catolicos* ('Catholic Kings').

In the Caribbean, **Columbus** begins exhibiting the cruelty and arrogance that will subsequently mar his reputation. Not only does he treat the native Caribs harshly, he also orders the occasional execution of his own followers. On both counts he earns the censure of **Bernardo Buil**, a Catalan friar attached to the second voyage to oversee an evangelical mission. Columbus also stores up future trouble for himself by shipping 500 Caribs back to Spain for sale as slaves. In April he lands on **Cuba**, adjacent to Hispaniola, and in May he discovers **Jamaica**, which he calls Santiago. As Portuguese sailors prepare to follow in Columbus's track across the Atlantic, Spain and Portugal negotiate the **Treaty of Tordesillas**, dividing up the Americas between the two maritime powers in line with papal bulls issued by Alexander VI the previous year.

In Castile, the *Consulado* of **Burgos**, effectively a monopolistic chamber of commerce, is established by royal charter to promote and protect Spain's wool trade.

Fernando becomes Grand Master of the **Order of Alcántara** when the sitting Grand Master dies. He also establishes the **Council of Aragon**, made up of the viceroys of the discrete territories of the Crown of Aragon, and which is required to attend him on his travels.

Attempting to curb the excesses of **Tomás de Torquemada**, Pope Alexander VI appoints four 'assistant inquisitors' to Spain.

The Treaty of Tordesillas

The **Treaty of Tordesillas**, signed on 7 June, 1494, is one of history's more peculiar documents. In effect it divided up the Americas between Spain and Portugal – the two pre-eminent maritime powers of western Europe – at a time when the handful of islands so far discovered by Columbus were assumed to be an outcrop of the Asian continent. The year before, to contain potential conflict with **Portugal**, Fernando had exerted pressure on Pope Alexander VI to issue a series of bulls demarcating Portuguese and Spanish interests in the western Atlantic with regard to any newly discovered territories. An imaginary line was drawn 100 leagues west of the **Cape Verde Islands**. What lay to the west of this belonged to Spain, what lay to the east belonged to Portugal. After adjusting the line a further 275 leagues westwards in Portugal's favour, envoys of both countries adopted the pope's ruling at Tordesillas. In longitudinal terms this meant Spain could claim everything beyond mid-way between 48°W and 49°W, and as a result quite fortuitously ended up with the lion's share of at least **South America**. The only territory Portugal could legitimately claim was Brazil, though perhaps Brazil may be considered a big enough prize for the second-comers in the transatlantic race. Curiously, as the true dimensions of the Americas began to take shape, both sides generally abided by the terms that had been agreed, even though Portugal's colonizing in the Indian Ocean kept her abreast of Spain as an imperial power. No other nation was consulted.

1495 **Jiminez de Cisneros** (see p.240), succeeding Mendoza as Archbishop of Toledo, continues to reform the Spanish church, enforcing liturgical and monastic standards, stamping out corruption and removing 'bad' clerics.

In Italy, Charles VIII of France enters **Naples** in February, laying claim to the kingdom and driving out its Aragonese ruler Ferrante II. Fernando skilfully forges the **Holy League**, an alliance of Spain, England, Venice, the Papacy and the Holy Roman Empire against Charles VIII. In June, having secured Sicily, **Gonzalo de Córdoba** lands in Calabria with an army of 2000 mainly Castilian Spaniards.

In October Spanish settlers in Hispaniola for the first time experience serious unrest after Columbus imposes an onerous **'gold tax'** on the island's Caribs.

1496 In April Fernando and Isabel's son and heir the *infante* Juan is married to the Habsburg archduchess Margaret, a daughter of the Holy Roman Emperor **Maximilian I**. In April the dynastic bonding between the Spanish royal family and the **Habsburgs** is further augmented when the *infanta* **Juana**, Juan's sister, is married to **Archduke Philip of Burgundy**, Margaret's brother and Maximilian's son and heir.

Columbus completes his **second voyage of discovery** when he reaches Cádiz in June. He finds however that Queen Isabel, advised by Fonseca, has repudiated his earlier shipment of 500 Carib slaves, whom she orders to be returned to Hispaniola and set free.

Disregarding the papal bulls sanctioning the Treaty of Tordesillas, Henry VII of England commissions **John Cabot** (Giovanni Caboti, a Venetian mariner resident in England) to voyage to the Americas.

Spanish and Neapolitan forces commanded by Gonzalo de Córdoba drive the French out of the **Kingdom of Naples**. Ferrante II is reinstated as king, but dies before the end of the year and is succeeded by his son **Federigo**.

1497 Fernando and Isabel's only son, the *infante* Juan, dies in October. In the same year their daughter Isabel marries **King Manuel of Portugal**, having previously been married to his brother.

As the Muslims of the Maghreb feud among themselves the Duke of Medina-Sidonia captures the port city of **Melilla**, which remains a Spanish possession to this day.

Castile's monetary system is reformed, making the **gold ducat**, equivalent to 375 gold *maravedis*, a valued exchange currency in European marts. Castile's wagoners and wool-carriers are formed into a royally approved union, the ***Cabana real de Carretos***, and granted exemption from tolls and other dues.

John Cabot lands on the North American continent, and lays English claim to **Nova Scotia** and **Newfoundland**. Meanwhile the Portuguese mariner **Vasco da Gama** reaches India via the coast of Africa. As a result of da Gama's expedition, Portugal will wrest control of the **spice trade**, and establish itself as the first European colonial power in Asia.

During the course of the year, the royal Castilian army is re-organized into *tercios* (regiments). Newly armed with the **pike**, the *tercios* will gain a reputation as Europe's most formidable fighting force during the next century.

1498 Fernando and Isabel's daughter Isabel, wife of Manuel of Portugal, dies giving birth to the *infante* **Miguel**.

The **Council of the *Hermandad***, established in 1476, is dissolved. The *Hermandad* survives as a local policing entity, but with reduced powers.

On 30 May Columbus sails from San Incar with six vessels on his **third voyage of discovery**. His passengers include convicts, with whom Columbus hopes to found a settlement in the Caribbean. Sailing on a more southerly route than before, he sights **Trinidad** on 28 July, and shortly afterwards lands on the **South American mainland** near an estuary of the Orinoco river. On Hispaniola he is confronted by a rebellion among Spaniards; he responds by rounding up and hanging agitators. Taking advantage of a royal caveat allowing for the enslavement of proven cannibals, Columbus gathers more natives for shipment to Spain.

The Portuguese mariner **Duarte Pacheco** lands in South America.

Tomás de Torquemada, the first Inquisitor General, dies.

Charles VIII of France dies in April. His successor, **Louis XII**, will renew his claim to Naples, and also make a fresh claim on the **Duchy of Milan**.

1499 The Inquisition is introduced into Granada. On the orders of Jiminez de Cisneros mosques are closed, and obligatory mass baptisms of Muslims are staged. Muslims respond by rasing a **rebellion in Alpujarras**, which is swiftly and brutally crushed. Cisneros presses for a renewal of the 'African' crusade against the Maghreb. Fernando becomes Grand Master of the Order of **Santiago**.

A French army invades northern Italy and seizes Milan on behalf of Louis XII.

La Celestina, a novel in dramatic form by **Fernando de Rojas**, is published. This influential work, renowned at the time for the unprecedented depth of its characterization, tells of how a young nobleman enlists the help of an elderly bawd, Celestina, in order to seduce a young noblewoman.

1500 Following the death of their grandson *infante* Miguel, Fernando and Isabel's second daughter, Maria, is married to King Manuel. Prospects of drawing **Portugal** into the Spanish union fade, however, when Maria fails to give birth to an heir.

The Spanish court, in receipt of disturbing reports of Columbus's activities in Hispaniola, dispatches a fresh fleet under the command of **Alonso de Ojeda** in March. On board is **Francisco de Bobadilla**, the new chief colonial magistrate and replacement Governor of Hispaniola, who is ordered to investigate the 'rebellion' there. Columbus, returning to Hispaniola on 15 September, refuses to accept

Bobadilla's authority and is arrested. On his return to Spain, he is set at liberty by Fernando and Isabel.

Partly to set a standard for Spanish colonies in the Americas, the responsibilities and powers of *corregidores*, the throne's principal tool for controlling towns and cities in Castile, are codified. Isabel again forbids the further **enslavement** of 'natives'. Exceptions are made for those who resist Spanish arms, and those found to practise cannibalism – two loopholes that are exploited by avaricious colonists.

Accompanied by the Florentine **Amerigo Vespucci**, Alonzo de Ojeda explores the coast of Brazil. A few weeks later a large Portuguese flotilla led by **Pedro Alvares Cabrál** also lands in Brazil, and on Easter Monday claims the territory for the Portuguese Crown according to the provisions of the Treaty of Tordesillas. Later the same year the Spanish navigator **Vicente Yanoz Pinzón**, captain of the *Niña* during Columbus's first voyage, lands briefly on Cape St Roque (Brazil's easternmost point).

In December, Gonzalo de Córdoba, commanding an army of French and Venetian as well as Spanish soldiers, captures the eastern Mediterranean island of **Cephalonia** from the Ottoman Turks.

At the turn of the century the **population** of Castile is estimated at 4.4 million, and of Aragon 1.2 million.

1501 On the orders of Queen Isabel, acting in close consultation with Archbishop Cisneros, Muslims in Castile are told either to **convert** to Christianity or leave the kingdom. At the same time those choosing to emigrate are charged an exorbitant fine or 'licence fee', and forbidden to take their children with them. Under such pressures to conform the majority of Muslims convert, thus swelling the numbers of *moriscos* liable to investigation by the Inquisition. In October, huge quantities of books in Arabic are publicly burned in Granada by royal decree.

The main facade of Salamanca University. Its intricate decorative detailing is known as Plateresque because it supposedly resembles the work of silversmiths

DORLING KINDERSLEY

Fernando however refuses to implement the same policies in the Crown of Aragon, despite the pleas of his wife.

In Hispaniola, as native **Caribs** are decimated by diseases introduced by Spanish colonizers, and by their harsh treatment, settlers begin illegally importing **black slaves** from Africa to work their sugar and other plantations.

In July, despite a peace treaty between France and Aragon signed at Granada the previous November, a French army reinvades **Naples**, provoking fresh **Franco-Spanish hostilities** in Italy. Federigo, the Aragonese king of Naples and Sicily, is forcibly deposed, and Louis XII proclaimed king.

The **universities** of Santiago and Valencia are founded.

Fernando II of Aragon (1452–1516)

So closely did **Fernando and Isabel** work together that historians have never fully disentangled which of them was responsible for what, particularly with regard to Castilian affairs. Yet outside Spain, Fernando existed as a figure very much in his own right. In the wars that plagued **Italy** following the invasion of Charles VIII of France in 1494, it was Fernando who emerged victorious, due in large measure to the military acumen of his commander **Gonzalo de Córdoba**, but also due to Fernando's unrivalled skill at orchestrating coalitions and alliances against his enemies. Thus Fernando became, in fact as well as in title, King of Naples and of Sicily – possessions retained by Spain until the 18th century. Also on Spain's behalf, he regularized the appointment of permanent ambassadors to important foreign courts, laying the foundations of the modern **diplomatic system**. Similarly, his appointment of viceroys to govern his various kingdoms was extended to Spain's overseas possessions, and became institutionalized in the European **colonial system**.

In sharp contrast to all this, in **Castile** Fernando was, nominally at least, merely Isabel's consort. Yet although much has been

1502 In January the infanta Juana and her husband Archduke Philip visit Spain from their home in the Netherlands and are acknowledged by the Cortes of both Castile and Aragon as the heirs to the Spanish thrones.

Backed by the Spanish church, Isabel and Fernando formally **proscribe the Islamic faith** in Spain.

In February **Nicolas de Ovando** sails to Hispaniola with 32 ships and 2500 men, to take over Bobadilla's governorship.

On 8 May Columbus leaves Cádiz on his **fourth and final voyage of discovery**, on the understanding that he will not seek to interfere in Hispaniola. As well as discovering Martinique in the Antilles and other smaller islands, he

made of Fernando's frequent absences in Italy, much could also be made of the time he did spend with his wife, helping her administer her kingdom, and strengthen central government. Without question the conquest of **Granada** belongs primarily to Fernando, as does the addition of **Navarra** to the Castilian throne. There was however always a gap between what could be achieved in Castile, and what could be achieved in Catalunya, Valencia or Aragon itself.

In his own **regnal territories** Fernando either excluded Isabel's harsher policies or worked to ameliorate them, notably with regard to the persecution of Muslims and implementing the Inquisition. Whether, though, such 'revisionism' was an aspect of Fernando's supreme statecraft, inculcated into him as a boy by his father **Juan II**, or whether it followed personal inclinations, is difficult to fathom. Quite clearly he was enamoured of his slightly older spouse, but as a public figure Fernando was legendarily dispassionate – a mask worn perhaps as the surest means of regimenting the different roles expected of him in different settings.

will make landings on the shores of (present-day) Honduras, Nicaragua and Panama. When he tries to re-establish himself in Hispaniola, he is excluded by Ovando.

Although Gonzalo de Córdoba is defeated by a French army at **Terranova** in Calabria in December, he continues to advance toward Naples.

1503 On 28 April Gonzalo de Córdoba wins a resounding victory over the French at **Cerignola**. In May he enters **Naples** and reasserts full Aragonese control on behalf of Fernando.

Seville is effectively granted a port trading **monopoly** with the New World when the Castilian crown authorizes the establishment of the *Casa de Contratación* ('House of Trade'), a chamber of commerce with similar powers to the *Consulado* of Burgos.

> ❝ I was twenty-eight years old ... when I came into your Highnesses' service, and now I have not a hair upon my head that is not grey: my body is infirm, and all that was left to me has been taken away and sold. ... Hitherto I have wept over others; may Heaven now have mercy upon me, and may the earth weep for me! ❞
>
> Christopher Columbus, from a letter of 3 June 1503 written to Fernando and Isabel from Jamaica

1504 On 1 January Fernando personally receives the surrender of French forces in the Kingdom of Naples at **Gaeta**, and ascends the now vacant throne of Naples.

Queen Isabel dies at Medina del Campo on 26 November, after drawing up a will that names her youngest daughter Juana heir to the Castilian throne and its possessions. While Juana is technically queen, Fernando rules Castile in her absence, and begins styling himself 'King of Castile'.

Columbus returns to Spain from his last voyage.

1505 The Castilian Cortes, meeting at Toro, confirms Fernando's status as **regent**, but not as king. Still pursuing his dynastic grand strategy, Fernando undertakes to marry Louis XII of France's niece **Germaine de Foix** under the terms of the Treaty of Blois.

A **crusading armada** leaves Málaga to conquer the Maghreb, but besides capturing the port town **Mers-el-Kabir** achieves nothing of consequence.

1506 Expecting to rule Castile in the name of his wife Juana, **Philip of Burgundy** journeys from Flanders to Spain to confront Fernando at Villafafila. Impatient with his son-in-law, and anxious to revisit Italy, Fernando abruptly proclaims Philip King of Castile, and leaves for Naples.

On 25 September **Philip I** dies suddenly, aged 28. Queen Juana, henceforward known as 'the Mad', is deranged with grief and their six-year-old son **Charles** (Carlos) becomes heir to the Castilian throne. A council of regency is established under Cardinal Cisneros.

On 25 May **Christopher Columbus** dies in Valladolid.

1507 Returning from Italy, Fernando assumes rulership over the whole of Spain. His close political ally **Archbishop Cisneros** is appointed Grand Inquisitor.

1508 As Cuba, Puerto Rico, Jamaica and the Antilles are incorporated as Spanish possessions, the Castilian crown's absolute control over ecclesiastical appointments in the **New World** is confirmed by the papal bull *Inter caetera*.

Christopher Columbus
(Cristóbal Colón c.1458–1506)

Although Columbus was born in **Genoa**, the son of a weaver, the fact that he never once used Italian in his surviving journals and letters, but always fluent Spanish, suggests that his family came originally from Spain, and may even have been **Jewish**. Nor does Columbus appear to have felt much loyalty toward Genoa itself. As early as 1476 he experienced the first of several near-drownings whilst fighting for the Portuguese against his native city state off Cape St Vincent. Even at this early stage, inspired by the Florentine cartographer **Paolo Toscanelli**, he had conceived the notion of reaching China and the East Indies by crossing the Atlantic. That the world was round, not flat, was widely accepted by Mediterranean mariners, largely as a result of Indian and Chinese ideas transmuted to Europe through Islam. By 1480 Columbus had settled in Madeira, one of a band of mercenary adventurers who carved out personal fortunes in the employ of the **Portuguese crown**. But in 1484 the same crown declined to underwrite Columbus's ambitious proposals for a transatlantic expedition, and the next few years were spent searching for a sponsor. Not until 1492, after refusals from France and England, did Fernando and Isabel agree to arrange the necessary capital.

Prolonged negotiations were very nearly scuppered by Columbus's insistence on the best possible terms for himself – ten percent of revenues deriving from any territories discovered, and the hereditary title 'Grand Admiral of the Ocean Seas and Viceroy of the [East] Indies'. For Spain, the advantages of a successful expedition to the Indies were threefold: it would

A series of edicts devised by Cisneros, but widely ignored, prohibit *moriscos* from practising Moorish custom or wearing Moorish costume.

The University of **Alcalá**, originally founded by Cisneros in 1498 as a seminary, opens its doors to students

establish a path to the **spice islands**; it would provide overseas **colonies**; and it would open up a potential new front from which to attack the threatening **Ottoman Empire**. Although Columbus failed to find a route to the Indies, his four voyages were a remarkable achievement: the result of a mixture of sheer audacity and a degree of pure good luck. Where things went badly wrong was on dry land. Convinced that his mission was ordained by God, Columbus became tyrannical in his dealings with Caribs and his fellow Christians alike, to the extent that in 1500 he was arrested and put in irons. Although on his return to Spain, Fernando and Isabel released him, he was barred from exercising the gubernatorial authority in the New World that had been accorded him.

Contrary to myth, Columbus did not die in poverty and disgrace. But he did die disillusioned. 'They made fun of my plans then,' he wrote recalling his early efforts to win support for his project, 'but now even tailors think they can make discoveries'. At the end of his life, assuming the air of an ancient prophet, Columbus began babbling about recapturing Jerusalem. But despite the many contradictions in his life and personality, for future generations Columbus was a textbook hero, and only recently have historians begun to emphasize the more destructive aspects of his legacy. As the first of the **conquistadors** (see p.262), it can be argued that Columbus initiated three centuries of rapine that not only murdered millions of American Indians, but also wrought terrible havoc on the American ecosystem.

and rapidly earns a high reputation for scholarship, particularly with regard to the traditional schools of philosophy.

The indigenous Carib population of **Hispaniola** is estimated to have declined from 250,000 in 1493 to a mere 60,000.

1509 After personally leading a crusade to the Maghreb along-side Pedro Navarro, during which the city of **Oran** is captured, Cisneros 'retires' to teach at Alcalá, following a disagreement with Fernando over Spain's north African policy. Whereas the king wishes only to establish outposts in the Maghreb, Cisneros believes that only an 'empire' stretching south to the Atlas mountains can guarantee Spain's security.

Germaine de Foix gives birth to a son, but the child dies, leaving Fernando without an heir for Aragon.

Queen **Juana** takes up residence in Tordesillas, along with the embalmed remains of her husband Philip I. She will reside there for another 46 years.

Francisco Jiménez de Cisneros (1436–1517)

That Spain in the 16th century resisted the destabilizing effects of the **Protestant Reformation** had much to do with Francisco Jiménez de Cisneros. Queen Isabel apart, no one else did more to ensure the strongly Catholic character of the emergent nation. Yet Cisneros's contribution began relatively late in life. Having attended Salamanca University and taken Holy Orders, he spent seven years in Rome from 1459, where he came to the notice of **Pope Paul II**. Armed with an 'expective letter' from the pope urging his immediate preferment, he returned to Castile. However, the Archbishop of Toledo, Alfonso de Cavillo, took a different view, and when Cisneros pressed his case too hard he was imprisoned. Released six years later, he was eventually appointed to the Diocese of Sigüenza but resigned in 1484 to become a **Franciscan friar** at Toledo. His rise to power and influence ocurred in 1492 when Cardinal Mendoza recommended him to Isabel as her personal confessor. For the next quarter of a century he became a stalwart of the throne, shaping royal policy – in particular against the *conversos* – and also instigating a widespread **reform** of the Spanish Church, succeeding Mendoza as primate in 1495.

In 1497 and 1498 Cisneros convened two ecclesiastical synods

Alonso de Ojeda heads an expedition from Hispaniola to South America that inaugurates the beginnings of **Venezuela** and **Colombia**. A Spanish settlement is also founded at Darien in the Gulf of Uraba on the **Panama isthmus**.

1510 The Castilian Cortes grants Fernando the title 'Administrator of Castile' during his grandson Charles's minority; but as the king once again departs for Italy, Cardinal Cisneros, restored to favour, reassumes power as **regent**.

The oil-rich **sunflower** is introduced into Europe from the Americas, and becomes in due course a major cash crop.

at Alcalá and Talavera, in order to stamp out such **clerical abuses** as concubinage, simony and absenteeism. Henceforth Spanish priests were required to preach regularly and to attend confession; while monks who did not observe their vows were threatened with disrobement. At the same time, senior appointments within the church ceased being the preserve of the Spanish aristocracy. As **Grand Inquisitor** from 1507, Cisneros made the Spanish Inquisition abide more closely by its own guidelines, reducing the powers of its fourteen local tribunals; and he further strengthened the quality of Spain's clergy by founding the **University of Alcalá**. He financed and personally led the expedition (1509) that captured Oran, in Africa. Following Isabel's death, he ensured Fernando's continuance as effective ruler, and, despite disagreement on African policy, spent his last years as Spain's senior statesman, often governing in Fernando's absence. But although Cisneros personifies the severity of Spanish Catholicism, he was also a man of broad learning, especially admired in humanist circles for commissioning the **Complutensian Polyglot Bible**, in which the Hebrew, Greek and Latin versions of the scriptures were set out as parallel texts.

Fernando authorizes the transport of **black African slaves**, acquired by the Portuguese, to the New World. Labour shortages are already occurring in the Caribbean because of the high mortality rate among native workers on Hispaniola's sugar plantations. Over the following centuries the Atlantic slave trade becomes a major international business, operated for the most part by the Portuguese, the Dutch, the English and the French. While many black Africans perish during the outward bound voyages, some of those who survive are used to reinforce Spanish armies.

1511 The northern Basque city of **Bilbao**, emerging as an important exporter of iron as well as wool, is granted its own *Consulado,* similar to that established in Burgos in 1494.

In Hispaniola a Dominican friar, **Antonio de Montgesinos**, enflames colonial passions by preaching respect for 'native humanity'. While most Spaniards reject such sentiments, **Bartolomé de las Casas** is converted to the 'Indian's cause', and will spend the remainder of his life promoting peaceful colonization.

1512 In July the Duke of Alba seizes southern or 'Spanish' **Navarra** from its French rulers, the Albret dynasty, making good Fernando's tenuous claim to the throne of the principality, based on his father's first marriage to Blanche of Navarra.

1513 **Juan Ponce de León**, having sailed with Columbus in 1493 and remained in the Caribbean to become the governor of Puerto Rico, 'discovers' **Florida**, which he names after Pascua Florida, the 'Easter Season'.

In September **Vasco Núñez de Balboa** sets out from Darien with a small band of followers and a larger band of Indian helpers and crosses the Panama isthmus to become the first European to sight the **Pacific Ocean** from its eastern shores.

> " Nothing brings a prince more prestige than great campaigns and striking demonstrations of his personal abilities. In our own time we have Ferdinand of Aragon, the present King of Spain. He can be regarded as a new prince, because from being a weak king he has risen to being, for fame and glory, the first king in Christendom...At the start of his reign he attacked Granada; and this campaign laid the foundation of his power. First, he embarked on it undistracted, and without fear of interference; he used it to engage the energies of the barons of Castile, who, as they were giving their minds to the war, had no mind for causing trouble at home. In this way, without their realizing what was happening, he increased his standing and control over them. He was able to sustain his armies with the money from the Church and the people, and, by means of that long war, to lay a good foundation for his standing army, which has subsequently won him renown. In addition, in order to be able to undertake even greater campaigns, and still making use of religion, he turned his hand to a pious work of cruelty when he chased out the Moriscos and rid his kingdom of them...Under the same cloak of religion he assaulted Africa; he started his campaign in Italy; he has recently attacked France. Thus he has always planned and completed great projects, which have always kept his subjects in a state of suspense and wonder, and intent on their outcome. "

Niccolo Machiavelli, *The Prince*, trans. George Bull

1514 Despite its condemnation by Pope Leo X, the trade in **African slaves** to the New World continues to expand as Cuban 'natives' are finally overrun by Spanish colonists. Hispaniola's indigenous population drops to less than 15,000.

1515 In June Fernando formally incorporates **Navarra** into the Crown of Castile.

Juan Diaz de Solis begins exploration of the territory that will become **Argentina**.

1516 Fernando 'the Great' of Aragon dies at **Madrigalejo** in Extremadura on 23 January whilst journeying to visit his wife's tomb at Granada. Before his demise he confirms that his grandson **Duke Charles of Burgundy** should succeed him to the Crown of Aragon in preference to Charles's younger brother. He further appoints his own illegitimate son **Alfonso of Aragon** regent pending the arrival of Charles in Spain. Until such time, Castile continues to be governed by Jiminez de Cisneros. Fernando's body is taken to Granada, and buried beside Isabel.

7: Habsburg Spain

1516–1700

When, in 1516, Charles duke of Burgundy acceded to the thrones of Castile and Aragon (as **Carlos I**), Spain entered the period of its greatness. During the 'Golden Century' that followed, as well as being the mainstay of the **Habsburg** European hegemony – that at its zenith incorporated all the Iberian Peninsula, Austria, the Netherlands, the Germanic Holy Roman Empire, most of Italy and footholds in North Africa – Spain also spawned a sea-borne empire in the **New World**, laying claim to Central and much of South America, as well as developing Manila in the **Philippines** as a vital Pacific Basin entrepôt.

One advantage of Charles's territorial inheritance was that it enabled a pooling of resources, which in turn made the sea-borne imperial venture possible. Although it was hardy, even reckless Castilian conquistadors like **Hernán Cortés** and **Francisco Pizarro** who carved out new provinces in the Americas, the settlements were developed and sustained by **international consortiums** of Flemish, German, Italian and Portuguese financiers and their agents. And while the vessels that sailed to and fro across the Atlantic were built in shipyards within the Habsburg dominions, most of these were outside of Spain.

Ultimately, however, Spain's sudden and fortuitous access to resources beyond its own borders worked against the national interest. Because it relied on foreign technology and skills (including Portuguese and Italian seamanship), Spain failed to develop its own internal resources to anything like the extent achieved by its smaller competitors, notably

England and the **Dutch Republic**. Membership of the Habsburg European union also brought with it severe short-term liabilities that undermined whatever geopolitical successes Spain could claim. Inevitably the sheer extent of Charles's dominions incited the envy of the French (who were also increasingly set on an expansionist course), and war with **France** was a regular occurrence throughout the 16th and 17th centuries.

For much of the same period, Europe was torn asunder by religious conflict prompted by the **Protestant Reformation**. Launched by the monk Martin Luther against the authority and doctrines of the Roman Catholic Church, the Reformation created ideological divisions where none had existed before; and as it spread through Germany and beyond, it fuelled widespread rebellion against established rulers. The staunchly Catholic Habsburgs resisted change through force of arms, and bitter wars were fought in the **Netherlands** and the **Holy Roman Empire** – wars that Spain, to its enormous cost, helped underwrite.

Spain and the Habsburgs were also at the heart of an equally persistent struggle, against the encroachments of the Constantinople-based, Muslim **Ottoman Empire**. Under Suleiman the Magnificent (r.1520–1566) the Turks advanced on Vienna and tried to seize the island of Malta as a forward base for a projected reconquest of al-Andalus – old Muslim Spain.

Out of these and other circumstances arose the paradox that while Spain enjoyed unprecedented revenues for a European country, it very often teetered on the edge of bankruptcy. The Habsburgs' military commitments meant that an increasing proportion of its newfound wealth was already spoken for before it was even unloaded at **Seville**. While this benefited the king's European creditors, it meant that large swathes of Spain remained as impoverished as ever.

Such imbalances provoked widespread internal dissent, sparking **revolts** in Castile, Aragon, Catalunya and Andalucía. Many Spaniards also resented having to fight outside their homelands, and having to pay taxes for campaigns in Italy or Flanders. On top of this, strong regional identities within Spain further fuelled **domestic discontent**, and despite measures to foster national unity and impose more centralized forms of government, the country was scarcely more integrated in 1700 than it was in 1516.

All told, the 'might' of Spain signified more outside the peninsula than it did inside, and there is something of a mirage about the great enterprise of **'Imperial Spain'**. When, in 1700 the Habsburg monarchy imploded (largely as a result of dynastic inbreeding), Spain was ripe for the picking. But although historians conventionally characterize later Habsburg Spain as a period of progressive failure, many of the problems faced by Philip III, Philip IV, Carlos II and their administrations were not of their own making. From as early as the accession of Charles (Carlos I), Spain and its inhabitants were entering unknown territory, both literally and in terms of the administrative problems they encountered. These it negotiated as best it could, but the mistakes that it made were something which both the Dutch and the English would learn and benefit from.

The Reign of Carlos I (Charles V) 1516–1556

In dynastic terms **Charles** scooped the jackpot. From his father **Philip the Fair** he inherited Burgundy, which comprised Franche-Comté, Flanders, Luxembourg and the Netherlands. From his paternal grandfather **Maximilian I** he inherited both Austria and what was fast becoming an established Habsburg claim to the German-based Holy

Roman Empire. And from his maternal grandparents, **Fernando and Isabel**, he inherited Castile and Aragon, along with Sicily and Naples. No man since the Roman emperors had ruled over so much of Europe, and Charles took his responsibilities seriously. He strove diligently to understand the different aspirations of his separate subjects, was not afraid to appear on the battlefield when necessary, and spent much of his waking hours travelling from one kingdom to another. 'I speak Spanish to God,' he once quipped, 'Italian to women, French to men, and German to my horse'. Behind such light-heartedness lay an apprehension that his task was an impossible one, and perhaps his greatest act of policy was to abdicate, dividing his inheritance between two heirs, his brother Ferdinand and his son Philip.

Charles was usually beset by the financial difficulties incurred by almost incessant warfare, and during the course of his reign he personally signed at least 500 credit agreements. The **silver bullion** that began flowing into Spain from across the Atlantic in the 1540s arrived a decade too late, for by then the emperor was already in hock to his bankers. Sometimes his campaigns paid off, sometimes not. In 1525 an imperial army crushed the French led by François I at Pavia in northern Italy, and as a consequence **Milan** became a Spanish dependency. But a decade later France had recovered sufficiently to challenge Charles again, this time with greater success. Then again in 1547, an imperial army, commanded by the Spanish **Duke of Alba**, smashed a league of Protestant princes at Mühlberg in Germany. Five years later, however, Charles himself was trapped at Innsbruck.

One insoluble problem Charles faced was that his European domains could not be brought under a single, centralized administration. Partly this was because of the distances involved, but mainly it had to do with the nature of dynastic succession itself. Each of his territories had its own traditions and forms of government, so that, however much he might be able to redeploy men and resources within his empire, it remained at best a monarchy of many parts.

This was made clear to Charles early in his reign. The Burgundian courtiers and officials who accompanied him in 1517 were greeted in Castile with suspicion and hostility, and by the time Charles returned to Brussels in 1519, Castile was already up in arms. The ensuing **Revolt of the Comuneros** was only put down once the Castilian nobility realised that it was better to support an absent king than near-revolutionary insurgents. Much of the discontent in Spain had been caused by the notion of a foreigner ruling *in absentia*, and after the *Comuneros* uprising only Spaniards were appointed to positions of high authority inside Spain – although Burgundians continued to supply Charles's peripatetic court with its principal advisers. From 1525 the king's affairs in Spain were entrusted to the capable first minister **Francisco de los Cobos**, and the situation was eased still further when Charles's Iberian queen, **Isabel of Portugal**, was appointed regent.

All in all the emperor spent just sixteen of his forty years on the throne in Spain, and between 1543 and his abdication in 1556 failed to visit the country once. Yet even so, the three or four decades that followed the defeat of the *Communeros* were – domestically at least – among the most peaceful Spain had known for centuries; and it was during this time that its character as a international power was established.

There were three broad aspects to this. Firstly, Spain's armies acquired a reputation as a formidable fighting force: although Charles's troops were invariably drawn from across his European territories, it was the highly trained and highly skilled Spanish (formed into pike-wielding, arquebus-firing *tercios*) who became renowned for their near-invincibility.

Secondly, after a slight hiatus at the beginning of the century, interest in the **New World** revived, and it was during Charles's reign that the largest territories in the Americas were claimed on behalf of the Spanish crown. Thirdly, as Lutheranism and the Protestant Reformation spread through Europe, Spain began earning its reputation as the **'power-house of the Counter-Reformation'**. Despite the fact that the new religious theories of Erasmus and other northern humanists had entered the country, from the mid-1520s onwards, the crown, strongly supported by the Inquisition, worked to ensure that Spain would be kept free from the taint of 'heresy'. Even such innocuous pietists as the *Alumbrados*, or Illuminists, were purged; and it was a Basque Spaniard, **Ignatius of Loyola**, who in 1540 founded the Society of Jesus, or **Jesuits**, for many years the most effective propagators of the Catholic faith.

Measures undertaken by the government and the prestige of the Jesuits ensured that Spain remained staunchly and solidly Catholic. Indeed Catholicism became the bedrock of Spain's identity. There was, though, a darker side to the 'faith and certainty' on offer. Both *conversos* (converted Jews) and *moriscos* (converted Moors) continued to be harassed, and in the 1540s the old concept of *limpieza de sangre* – purity of blood – developed into a widespread movement against those suspected of having Jewish ancestry.

This unity of faith, and the relative absence of turmoil at home, enabled Spain to assume a commanding role in the protracted war against the belligerent Ottoman Empire. Not the least of Charles's anxieties were the activities of the Barbary Corsair **Khaireddin**, who regularly terrorized shipping in the western Mediterranean from bases in the Maghreb, and who acted in concert with the sultan in Constantinople. Charles's campaigns against Khaireddin, involving mixed Spanish and Italian forces, and his attempts to capture Tunis sent a clear signal to **Suleiman I** that Turkish aggression could and would be met head-on.

1516 Following the death of Fernando the Great, **Charles duke of Burgundy** is proclaimed joint-ruler of the Spanish monarchies with his mother **Queen Juana** (known as 'the Mad') of Castile.

1517 In September Charles (**Carlos I**) lands on the north coast of Spain to lay claim to his inheritance of the crowns of Castile and Aragon accompanied by a large retinue of **Flemish advisers** from Burgundy.

On 8 November **Cardinal Cisneros**, who has ruled Charles's Spanish inheritances in his absence, dies. In the months that follow, tensions grow between the Castilian nobility and Charles's 'foreign' courtiers, including his Grand Chamberlain Guillaume de Croy, Seigheur de **Chièvres**, accused by the Castilians of seeking merely to enrich themselves through the acquisition of lucrative offices. While Chièvres is appointed *contador mayor* of Castile, his nephew is made Archbishop of Toledo, and Charles's former tutor **Adrian of Utrecht** becomes Bishop of Tortosa. Another Fleming, Laurent Gorrevod, is awarded the first licence to transport **black African slaves** to Castile's possessions in the Caribbean.

The **Turkish Ottomans** take possession of Egypt, giving them a virtually unassailable position in the eastern Mediterranean.

Martin Luther sets in motion the Protestant Reformation when he attaches his '95 theses' criticizing the Catholic Church to the doors of the cathedral at Wittenberg.

1518 The Castilian Cortes, meeting to confirm Charles's accession, protests at the growing influence of his Burgundian retainers.

Charles V (Carlos V) with the heraldic emblem of the Hapsburgs top left

In May Charles travels to **Zaragoza** to assume the Crown of Aragon. Among several assurances wrung from Charles is a promise not to expel, or interfere in the lives of, the many Moors still living in Aragon and Valencia.

The 'Barbary corsair' (ie pirate) **Khaireddin**, who has been attacking Spanish and Italian shipping in the western

BRITISH LIBRARY

Mediterranean, declares himself a vassal of the Ottoman Sultan Suleiman.

1519 On 1 January Charles's grandfather, the Holy Roman Emperor **Maximilian I**, dies in Austria. Following diplomatic activity, and high-level bribery, Charles himself is elected Emperor in June as **Charles V**. For the time being Charles remains in Aragon, establishing a temporary court at **Barcelona**, to the chagrin of Castile, where opposition continues to grow, exacerbated by increased levels of taxation. The threat of open revolt festers in Toledo, where in November, backed by the powerful Ribera faction, **Juan de Padilla** demands Charles should reside in Castile, appoint only Castilians to Castilian offices, and not remit any moneys from Castile to his other territories.

During the summer an outbreak of plague in **Valencia** stirs popular resentment against the rich who are able to flee the city. Guildsmen, newly armed to combat a threatened Ottoman raid, and led by **Juan Llorenc** (a weaver), take to the streets in an attempt to create a city republic. Leadership passes from Llorenc to **Vicenç Peris** and other radicals. Although eventually the crown and nobility close ranks on their 'brotherhood', for a while Valencia is out of control.

In the New World an upsurge in colonial expansion is highlighted by the *conquistador* **Hernán Cortés**, who leaves Cuba in February for the Yucatán peninsula. Landing in April with 400 soldiers, sixteen horses and some artillery, Cortés forms an alliance with the Mexica and Tlaxcalan people against the more powerful Nahau. In November, supported by 5000 'Indians', he enters the Aztec capital **Tenochtitlan** to begin 'negotiations' with the ruler **Montezuma**. Among other contagions the Spaniards bring with them is smallpox, which ravages the Mexican population.

The founding of **Panama City** gives Spain control of the isthmus joining North and South America and access to the Pacific. In September **Ferdinand Magellan** (Fernão Magalhães) – a Portuguese navigator under contract to the Crown of Castile – sets out to find a southern passage to the Pacific. The voyage, the first fully authenticated **circumnavigation** of the world, revives Spanish interest in the **eastern spice trade**.

1520 In January Charles V (Carlos I) returns to **Castile**, but then prepares to leave for Germany (where he will be crowned Holy Roman Emperor). When he summons the Castilian Cortes to Santiago in April, in the hope of raising further subsidies, some towns and cities refuse to send representatives, while others demand that their grievances be heard. Although a subsidy is granted by the Cortes, it is flatly rejected by some municipalities, and will not be collected.

Charles sets sail with Chièvres in May, leaving **Adrian of Utrecht** to rule as regent in his absence. Within a week the **Revolt of the** *Comuneros* begins in Toledo and the north, before spreading to other cities in Castile. Led by Juan de Padilla and Pedro Laso de la Vega, the *Comuneros* establish a league that presses for Castile to be ruled by a Cortes answerable to local urban communes. A *junta* (military council) is formed, and **Medina del Campo** is devastated by royalist forces on 21 August. In September Juan de Padilla captures Tordesillas, but fails to win the support of **Queen Juana**. Some of the rebels agitate for a social revolution that targets the Castilian nobility as well as Charles's 'Flemish' government.

In May **Hernán Cortés** leaves Tenochtitlan in Mexico after hearing news that a force under Panfilo de Narvaez has left Hispaniola to arrest him. Cortés defeats Narvaez and returns to Tenochtitlan where Montezuma is assassinated by his own discontented subjects. The Mexica rise up against the Spanish, and on the night of 10 July

BRITISH LIBRARY

Hermán Cortés landing in Mexico in 1519

(known as *Noche Triste*) as many as 800 Spaniards are slaughtered. Cortés escapes, and enters into an alliance with **Ixtlilxochitl**, ruler of the second largest Aztec city, Texcoco.

The *Comuneros*

By the Spring of 1520, as Charles prepared to sail for Brussels, unrest had already broken out in several cities, including **Toledo** and **Segovia**. Within days of his departure a full-scale revolt was under way. In city after city the *corregidores* and other royal officials were driven out and *comuneros* (communes) set up in their place. At one point the regent, **Adrian of Utrecht**, was even forced to abandon the 'royal capital', Valladolid. In its early stages the uprising was distinctly patriotic and conservative, drawing support from the clergy as well as 'respectable' urbanites. **Juan de Padilla** and his associates did not seek the overthrow of the monarchy so much as a restitution of the order that had prevailed under Queen Isabel, with enhanced powers for the Castilian Cortes to ensure continuity. As the year progressed however the rebellion assumed a more revolutionary character, and by the beginning of 1521 had clearly split in two, with the **Bishop of Zamora** – usually considered the last of Spain's medieval clerical warlords – assuming belligerent leadership of the more radical wing. Critically the Castilian aristocracy, long used to their hereditary titles and enjoying the fruits of enormous estates acquired during the the *Reconquista*, opted to support Adrian and the Crown. When the king agreed not to appoint any more non-Castilians to high office and not to press for the subsidies he had been granted, it was only a matter of time before the rebellion folded. Yet while it lasted the Revolt of the *Comuneros* tore Castile apart, and for a long time townspeople remembered who had and hadn't participated. As a result the uprising became ambiguously embedded in a Castilian identity that steadfastly refused to be subsumed within either the greater Spanish monarchy or the greater Europe-wide Habsburg dominion.

1521 With the *Comuneros* movement divided, the Castilian nobility increasingly give their support to the royalist cause. The more radical *Comuneros* find a new leader in the militant Bishop of Zamora, **Antonio de Acuña**, but when he and his followers are defeated at **Villalar** on 23 April the revolt crumbles. The bishop attempts to flee to Navarra, but is captured and imprisoned. With the fall of Toledo the last of the communes is disbanded. In October, the revolt in Valencia also disintegrates, following the defeat of Vincenç Peris.

In May, Hernán Cortés lays siege to **Tenochtitlan**, now ruled by Montezuma's nephew Cuauhtemoc. The city, with its population of 200,000, capitulates in August, bringing to an end Aztec rule in Mexico and marking the beginning of a Spanish province called **'New Spain'**.

1522 In July Charles V returns to Spain for seven years with a personal bodyguard of 4000 German troops and issues a general amnesty to those who have rebelled against him. His Grand Chancellor **Mercurino Gattinara**, an Italian, undertakes administrative reforms that overhaul the Council of Castile, establishing a separate Council of Finance (1523), and a Council for the Indies (1524) specifically to oversee colonial settlements in the New World.

In the Caribbean, Havana, Santo Domingo and other Spanish settlements come under attack from **French buccaneers**, following an outbreak of war between France and the Holy Roman Empire. The buccaneers' activities establish a precedent that will later be imitated by Dutch and English privateers.

As Lutheranism spreads in Germany, an office of the **Inquisition** is established by Charles V in the Netherlands following the Spanish model.

1523 Adrian of Utrecht, elected pope the previous year (as **Adrian VI**), issues a papal bull formally incorporating the three military Orders of Santiago, Calatrava and Alcántara into the Spanish Crown. The revenues from the Orders are largely assigned by Charles V to his mainly German and Flemish bankers to secure much-needed loans.

1524 As the war between France and the Holy Roman Empire intensifies, the French king François I occupies **Milan** in October and lays siege to **Pavia** in November. Charles V responds by assembling an army made up of soldiers from across his European empire.

Foreign merchants are authorized by Charles V to trade with Spanish colonies in the **New World**, but not to settle there. Twelve Franciscans voyage to Hispaniola to begin a mission to systematically convert native Americans to Christianity. They are soon followed by Dominicans and Augustinians.

Cortés, aided by Tlaxcalan Mexicans, establishes a Spanish interest in **Honduras**, and Pedro de Alvarado marches into **Guatemala**. **Francisco Pizarro** makes his first expedition down the west coast of South America, but fails to find anything of value.

1525 Charles's army defeats and captures François I at **Pavia** on 23 February. The **Duchy of Milan** becomes an imperial dependency attached to the Spanish Crown. As the century progresses, Milan's bankers and weapons manufacturers become increasingly involved in Spanish enterprises.

Isabel de la Cruz and Pedro Ruiz de Alcaraz, two leading members of a pietist religious movement known as the *Alumbrados* (Illuminists), are arrested by the Inquisition on suspicion of being Lutherans.

1526 In March **François I**, held prisoner in Madrid, is allowed to return home to France in exchange for his two sons, who are kept as hostages in Spain.

Los Alumbrados

Even in Spain some divergence in matters of faith and practice had long been tolerated within the Catholic church. The **Inquisition** (see p.220), though a forceful institution during the reigns of Fernando and Isabel, had primarily targeted *conversos*, Jewish converts to Christianity. This changed during the reign of Charles V, when the rapid spread of **Lutheranism**, and then other Protestant sects, in Germany and northern Europe seemed to threaten the compact between Church and Crown that in Castile was particularly strong. As a result the movement known as **Los Alumbrados** (literally 'the Enlightened'), which a century earlier would have escaped serious notice from the authorities, suffered official censure.

Also known as the **Illuminists**, Los Alumbrados were pietists with mystical leanings. They believed that through constant prayer and devotion they could establish direct communication with God and so attain a level of human perfection that rendered ordinary church attendance, and observances, superfluous. One important figure within the movement was **Isabel de la Cruz**, a Franciscan nun who at the beginning of the 16th century established Alumbrados centres in Alcalá, Toledo and other mainly southern cities. Another was **Pedro Ruiz de Alcaraz**, who, enjoying the patronage of the Marquis de Villena, attracted a following at Escalona.

Under the regency of Adrian of Utrecht the Alumbrados were left alone, but they subsequently fell under the scrutiny of the Inquisition, which lumped them together not only with Lutherans, but also with Erasmians – humanist followers of the Dutch scholar **Erasmus**. In 1525 both Isabel de la Cruz and Pedro Ruiz were placed under arrest, and a fresh wave of persecutions followed in 1529, when another suspect, **Francesca Hernández**, turned informer, spuriously telling her inquisitors that the Illuminists had links with more obvious kinds of 'heretic'. That the Alumbrados survived such harassment is reflected in fresh edicts issued against them in 1568, 1574, and as late as 1623. Yet despite their deliberate abandonment of the outward forms of Catholic worship, no evidence suggests they sought either to reform or abandon the church that had nurtured them.

In April Charles V marries his cousin **Isabel**, the daughter of King Manuel of Portugal.

Francisco de los Cobos, a native of Andalucía, emerges as the king's most effective minister in Spain. Tactful and conciliatory, de los Cobos will preside over a prolonged period of relative internal peace and increasing prosperity in Spain.

Charles V, reneging on previous undertakings, decrees that all Moors in Spain must either practise the Catholic faith or leave. Notwithstanding, some *moriscos* (converts) secretly continue Islamic worship.

Pope Clement VII issues a bull affirming the king's traditional right to determine the **appointment of bishops** and other senior clerics in Spain.

Charles V decrees that any of his European subjects may settle in the New World, a right previously reserved for Castilians.

1527 In May Queen Isabel gives birth in Valladolid to a male heir, the *infante* **Philip** (Felipe).

An imperial army sacks **Rome**, where Spanish as well as Italian and German soldiers embark on an orgy of rape, looting and killing.

On a second expedition down the west coast of South America, **Francisco Pizarro** encounters evidence of a developed civilization – the Peruvian **Inca empire**. He returns to Spain the following year to gain formal approval for a third expedition and is granted the governorship of as yet unexplored territories.

Spaniards make their first incursions against the **Maya empire** in the Yucatán peninsula – the second largest kingdom in Mexico after the now hobbled Aztecs.

Work begins on a new palace for Charles V at Granada. Designed by **Pedro Machuca**, in a Renaissance style

Charles V's palace within the Alhambra is notable for its austere classicism

similar to that of Bramante and Raphael, the building remains uncompleted when work stops in 1568.

1528 Financially strained by both imperial government and military campaigns, Charles V grants the German banking house of Welser territorial concessions in what will become **Venezuela**.

1529 Charles V leaves **Spain**, entrusting its rule to the care of Queen Isabel and first minister de los Cobos.

In August the **Peace of Cambrai** terminates the war between Charles V and France. François I's sons are released on payment of a ransom. The French king undertakes not to intervene in Italy, which – apart from Rome and Venice – becomes a mainly Habsburg domain. **Milan** is confirmed as a Spanish possession, and becomes Charles V's principal military stronghold in Italy. In return, France is given that part of Charles's Burgundian inheritance that today forms the French province of **Burgundy**.

Acting on behalf of **Suleiman I**, Khaireddin captures **Penon d'Argel** from the Spanish, laying the foundation for the Ottoman conquest of Algeria. A war fleet sent by Charles to crush Khaireddin is defeated off the island of **Formentera**. Further east, the Turkish threat to Europe is confirmed when an Ottoman army besieges **Vienna**, albeit unsuccessfully. Castilian soldiers of fortune are amongst

The Conquistadors

Throughout the 16th and 17th centuries there seemed no shortage of adventurers willing to chance life and limb in the pursuit not only of new lands and previous metals, but also of championing the God they worshipped. Unlike later **Dutch** and **English** colonizers, whose activities were more singularly mercantile, the **conquistadors**, bearing the cultural inheritance of the *Reconquista*, believed they were fulfilling a divine mission. In this, as in the whole style of conquest, they emulated **Columbus** (see p.238), who, though neither a Castilian nor a Spaniard, had led the way in reconciling avarice with piety, and who also, significantly, never reneged on his loyalty to the Crown.

Such at least is evident in the careers of the two best-known conquistadors, **Hernán Cortés** (1485–1540) and **Francisco Pizarro** (1475–1541), the one credited with suborning the Aztec empire in Mexico, the other with overwhelming the Andean Inca empire. Both exhibited astonishing fearlessness, just as both were capable of insubordination toward their immediate colonial superiors. But both men too were sustained by overweening faith, and neither seems seriously to have contemplated carving out personal kingdoms in the New World, as they might so easily have done.

'I came here to get rich,' Cortés wrote, 'not to till the soil as a peasant'. Born into an impoverished hidalgo family in Medellín, he studied law at the University of Salamanca before emigrating to Hispaniola in 1504. In 1511 he fought under **Diego Velásquez** in

those who journey to Austria to resist the 'infidel'.

1530 Following an improvement in imperial relations with Rome, Pope Clement VII signs the **Peace of Bologna**, giving papal recognition to Charles V's Italian possessions.

In the New World, **Nuño de Guzmán** leads an expedition into western Mexico. Charles V's attempts to impose a ban on the import of **African slaves** in Spain's American colonies is thwarted by creditors whose commercial interests it damages.

the conquest of Cuba, then in 1519 went solo, using his charisma to assemble the force of 400 that initiated the two-year campaign culminating in the humiliation of the Aztec ruler Montezuma. A key accessory to his triumphs was an Indian princess, known to Spaniards as **Doña Marina**, whom he used as an interpreter and afterwards married. But along the way Cortés had quarrelled with Velásquez and incurred the envy of other officials, and much of his subsequent life was spent back in Spain petitioning Charles V in defence of his reputation and considerable Mexican estates.

The illegitimate son of an army captain, Francisco Pizarro joined Alonso Ojeda's expedition to Colombia in 1510, and Núñez de Balboa's epoch-making crossing of the **Panama isthmus** in 1513. From 1524 he began exploring the Pacific coast of South America. Famously, when recalled to Panama, he disobeyed orders, drawing a line on the ground with his sword and inviting those who would to follow him. Yet it was not until he had returned to Spain to gain the king's approval that his legendary assault on the Incas moved forward, by which time much of the Inca population had been devastated by a smallpox epidemic brought from Europe. His own death was ignominious: following a wrangle about spoils, Pizarro was murdered by one of his henchmen. As he lay dying, so legend has it, the Governor and Captain-General of Peru made the sign of the Cross on the ground with his own blood.

1531 Having returned to Panama, **Francisco Pizarro** sets off on his third expedition to South America with 180 men, including his four brothers.

1532 Penetrating the Inca empire of the Quechua people, Pizarro discovers that the **Incas** are bitterly divided between two rival claimants to power, the brothers **Atahualpa**, who holds the northern city of Cajamarca, and **Huascar**, who holds the 'royal' capital Cusco in the south. Exploiting this rift, Pizarro's forces journey to Cajamarca. When Atahualpa refuses to adopt Christianity at a public meeting in November, Pizarro orders his men to fire into the crowd. In the confusion Atahualpa is captured, and some 2000 Quechuans are killed before the city and its surrounding valley are permanently abandoned by its inhabitants.

1533 Atahualpa is released by Pizarro in June on condition that the room in which he has been held is filled with gold. This forms the basis of a legendary **'treasure'**, estimated at 13,000 lbs of gold and 15,000 lbs of silver, most of which is remitted to Spain with a *quinto* (one fifth) being set aside for the Crown. Atahualpa is reimprisoned, and then publicly strangled on the pretext that he has been plotting to kill his brother Huascar.

Khaireddin, appointed 'admiral of the west' by Suleiman I, consolidates his control over the Maghreb.

1534 Pizarro marches south from Cajamarca and in January enters **Cusco** where his men seize a second treasure, and where Huascar's younger brother **Manco** is placed on the throne as a Spanish puppet ruler.

In May, **Pedro de Mendoza** is authorized by the Council of Castile to explore and create settlements along the lower eastern coast of South America. Reaching the Río Plata the following year, Mendoza founds **Buenos Aires**, the capital of modern Argentina.

Khaireddin seizes **Tunis**, ousting its Berber rulers who have hitherto enjoyed Spanish protection.

1535 Francisco Pizarro founds a new Spanish settlement on the western coast of South America called Los Reyes, which will become **Lima**, the capital of modern Peru.

Charles V personally leads a campaign against Khaireddin, capturing the fortress of **La Goletta** on 14 July, and Tunis a week later. Khaireddin, however, escapes.

1536 Charles V's close ties with **Florence** are formalized by the marriage of a half-sister to the city's Medici duke. In April Italy is thrown into confusion when a French army crosses its borders. In September Khaireddin, in league with France, raids the Balearic Islands.

In Peru, the puppet Inca king **Manco** rebels against Spanish authority in Cusco. Leaving the city, he raises a large army and then returns to besiege the Spanish garrison. Although he fails to win Cusco back, he resurrects an Inca state that survives until his death in 1582.

Castile's *tercios* are reorganised as a standing army of paid volunteers. As an elite fighting force, they are increasingly deployed outside Spain, particularly in Italy and the Netherlands, where they earn a reputation for brutal invincibility.

1538 Charles V's proposed **food tax** is rejected by nobles and hidalgos determined to protect their traditional exemption from taxation of any kind. The king responds by seeking revenues outside the Cortes, which henceforward plays a less prominent role in Castilian affairs.

Reversing its previous policy, the Crown attempts to exclude all 'foreigners' from its **American colonies**. At such a vast distance such royal decision-making has little effect, and Spanish settlements become more, not less, cosmopolitan.

1539 Charles's queen Isabel of Portugal dies.

St Ignatius of Loyola (1491–1565)

A French cannonball, injuring a Basque soldier-courtier at Pamplona in 1521, gave the Counter-Reformation, and indeed Catholicism, one of its greatest champions. Until that day **Ignatius of Loyola** had groomed himself for service at the Castilian Court. Badly wounded in the left leg he was forced to abandon his military career, and turned instead to religion, following a sudden spiritual awakening. Even during his convalescence at Manresa (outside Barcelona) he began writing the *Spiritual Exercises*, a manual for those seeking God that, couched in soldierly terms, and approved by Pope Paul III in 1548, became one the Counter-Reformation's most influential texts.

Loyola spent sixteen years studying, first in Barcelona, Alcalá and Salamanca, then in Paris, Bologna, Venice and Rome, before finally entering the priesthood in 1537. He was nothing if not meticulous in his preparation, although this did not prevent him being investigated by the **Inquisition**, which briefly imprisoned him in 1527. Even as a student, though, he attracted disciples, and in 1538, he founded the **Society of Jesus** dedicated to propagating the life and teachings of Christ. By the time of Loyola's death the Rome-based Order boasted over a thousand members, and was undertaking missionary work in Ethiopia, India, the Far East and the Americas, as well as in Europe, where it was already playing a lead role in combating Protestantism.

The **Jesuits** continued to grow throughout the 16th and 17th centuries, though they suffered an eclipse during the 18th century. The Society's success can be ascribed to four factors: its authoritarian organizational character; its fervent evangelicalism; the clarity of Loyola's own teachings, redolent of the Church militant that had incubated in Spain during the period of the *Reconquista*; and its willingness to embrace new knowledge, including Europe's 17th century 'scientific revolution', making the Society a force for seemingly modern education.

Among Loyola's first followers was a fellow Basque, **St Francis Xavier**, who defined the missionary style of the Society, impressing would-be converts in India, the Malay archipelago and Japan with his 'advanced' learning. Inevitably the very success of the Jesuits generated hostility among other orders, notably the Dominicans and Franciscans, but usually the Society was protected by its unswerving loyalty and obedience to the pope, which Loyola himself enshrined in the Jesuit *Constitutions* he spent his last years formulating.

BRITISH LIBRARY

St Ignatius of Loyola holding a copy of the Jesuit *Constitutions*

The Spanish New World

Portugal was the first European nation to establish far-flung overseas colonies, when a succession of mariners began reaching down the west coast of Africa, eventually reaching the Indian Ocean. Trading ports were then established along the way – for example Goa (India), Malacca (Malaya) and Macao (China). Spanish colonization was altogether different; the Castilian conquistadors aimed to subjugate whole territories for agricultural as well as commercial settlement. In time much of the Caribbean, all of Central America, most of South America, and small parts of North America became Spanish provinces in fact as well as in title. This took time, and for a long while the Spanish presence in the Americas was restricted to coastal settlements and a handful of inland mining centres. Yet even by 1570 an estimated 150,000 mainly Castilian Spaniards were settled in the Americas, and between 1500 and 1650 some 450,000 set out to make the perilous Atlantic crossing.

What is strange is that having made it to the far shore, most remained loyal to the **Spanish Crown**, even though there was little to stop them cutting free. To an extent settlers were dependent on continuing supplies from the home country, but with French, Dutch and English freebooters soon seizing the opportunity to ferry goods to the Spanish settlements, that soon ceased to be a consideration. Spain's manufacturing base was always too slight to supply its own market. What mattered more was religious faith, and its close connection to the monarchy. Famously **Hernán Cortés** habitually carried an image of the Virgin Mary with him on his expeditions, and in a profound way the Spanish conquests were felt to be a holy mission sanctioned by

1540 In Castile Charles V's government introduces draconian **poor laws**, forcing vagrants to work, partly as a means of rectifying a chronic labour shortage. The new measures are passionately opposed by some mendicant friars who plead that the right to beg is inalienable.

In Rome a new religious order, the **Society of Jesus** (or **Jesuits**) founded by **Ignatius of Loyola**, is formally

papal rulings that the Americas were preordained as territories belonging to the Spanish and Portuguese thrones.

Out of this grew a system of **colonial administration** that partly mirrored the Castilian conquest of al-Andalus from the Moors. A key component of settlement was the *encomienda*, a legal entitlement not only to land but also to the labour of those 'Indians' already inhabiting it. But as the settlements matured, so too the Crown evolved methods of maintaining control. To prevent any one individual or group acquiring too much power, colonial authority was divided between mutually accountable governors and *audiencias*, or legal tribunals that dealt with everyday matters of law and order. But even with these provisions in place, final decision-making was reserved to the Crown itself, despite the difficulties of distance.

Inevitably the Spanish conquests had momentous consequences. The Americas became an extension of **Europe**, adding hugely to its material and manpower resources, and determining the future course of global politics. This however was only accomplished at enormous cost to the **indigenous populations**. Within fifty years the Caribs of Hispaniola, Spain's first colonial possession, had been wiped out, and all told as many as 20 million Amerindians perished as a result of Spanish incursions. While thousands died either in battle, or because of savage working conditions on Spanish plantations, up to ninety percent of the death toll were victims of such **infectious contagions** as smallpox, diphtheria, typhus and measles. On top of this, the labour shortages that ensued inspired a brutal transatlantic **slave trade**. In the centuries that followed Columbus between 13 and 14 million black Africans were forcibly shipped west.

approved by Pope Paul III.

1541 In October a combined Spanish-Italian task force is wrecked by a storm while attempting to capture **Algiers**. 150 ships and 12,000 men are lost.

Santiago, the capital of present-day Chile, is founded by **Pedro de Valdivia**, who has been sent by Francisco

> Our Old World has been responsible in the New World of the Indies for the deaths of five or six million men and women who have been wiped out in the wars and conquests waged over there, as well as through mistreatment and mortal cruelty, and other causes of the same character, intolerable conditions of work in the mines, forced labour, personal service and very many other ways in which the insatiable greed of our men from over here has inflicted itself on those wretched people in America.

> Tomás López Medel, reporting to the Crown from Guatemala c.1543, quoted in Henry Kamen, *Spain's Road to Empire* (2002)

Pizarro to enlarge Spanish territories in the far south of South America.

1542 **Francisco de Orellana**, crossing South America from the Pacific to the Atlantic, 'discovers' the **Amazon River**, named by him after local legends about fearless warrior women.

Charles V reimposes a ban on the enslavement of native Indians in the Americas as part of a comprehensive set of **'New Laws'** designed to regulate the growing number of Spanish colonies. Colonists however continue to enslave native Americans, particularly from the central isthmus.

Ruy Lopez de Villalobos, sailing across the Pacific from 'New Spain', makes landfall in the **Philippines** and claims them for Spain (see p.288). For a generation however little is done to build on Villalobos's initiative.

1543 Charles V and Cobos create a permanent **archive of state papers** in the fortress at Simanca, close to Valladolid.

The *infante* Philip marries his cousin **Maria of Portugal**.

He becomes regent in Spain on behalf of his father, and is invested with the dukedom of Milan.

1545 Vast deposits of silver are discovered at **Potosí** southeast of Lake Titicaca in modern Peru. By 1600 Potosi produces eighty percent of the colonial silver supply, and will become the largest township in the New World, with a population of 100,000.

Pope Paul III convenes the **Council of Trent**, to explore ways of combating the Protestant Reformation. It sits intermittently until 1563, during which time it upholds the authority of the Papacy, refutes Luther's doctrine of salvation by faith alone, and formulates a series of ecclesiastical reforms that provide the backbone of the **Catholic**

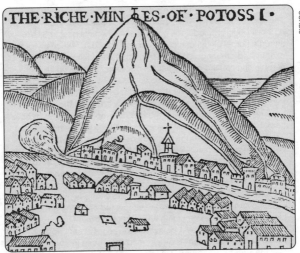

Illustration from the title page of *The Discoverie and Conquest of Peru*, published in London in 1581

Counter-Reformation. An **Index of proscribed books** is issued in Toledo, and Spain continues to be the European country least affected by Protestantism.

1546 During a major offensive against German Protestant princes, Spanish troops are deployed from the Netherlands. The imperial army is led by the **Duke of Alba**.

In the New World, further large silver deposits are discovered at **Zacatecas**, and at other sites in Mexico.

1547 Charles V and the Duke of Alba triumph over Germany's Protestant princes at the **battle of Mühlberg**.

Limpieza de Sangre

The appointment in 1546 of **Juan Martínez Siliceo** to the Archbishopric of Toledo, the premier ecclesiastical post in Spain, stirred a hornet's nest of racism and intolerance. Unlike many of the canons and prebends attached to his cathedral Siliceo came from humble origins, and quickly felt the opprobrium of his social superiors. Toledo at the time was divided between two aristocratic factions centred around the **Ayala** and the **Ribera** families. When the Ayalas realized that Siliceo was deeply **anti-Semitic**, they exploited the situation against the Riberas who were known to have Jewish ancestry. As a result Siliceo was able to force what became a notorious statute through the cathedral chapter, after the Riberas nominated a known *converso*, Fernando Jiménez, to a canonry. The essence of Siliceo's ruling was that any candidate for ecclesiastical preferment within his diocese should demonstrate *limpieza de sangre* – 'purity of blood'. But just because Siliceo was Spain's primate, his dictate rapidly snowballed into a long-lasting nation-wide movement to prevent anyone suspected of having any Jewish blood whatsoever from holding any kind of public office.

Limpieza de sangre as a policy was given royal sanction by **Philip II** almost as soon as he came to the throne in 1556. Given that the same king emerged in later 16th century Europe as the foremost champion of the **Counter-Reformation**, historians have

Juan Martínez Siliceo, Archbishop of Toledo since 1546, persuades his cathedral chapter to adopt a statute making *limpieza de sangre* ('purity of blood') a prerequisite for church appointments. Similar measures, directed against anyone of Jewish blood, are quickly adopted by other sees. **Hernándo de Valdés**, well-known for his austerity and Catholic orthodoxy, is appointed Inquisitor-General.

In Mexico, the Franciscan friar **Bernardino de Sahagún** begins systematically collecting data on the history and customs of the Nahau peoples. The great book he compiles however, *Historia de las cosas de Nueva España* ('History of

interpreted what amounted to a national phobia as an almost inevitable consequence of the religiously troubled times. But although anti-Semitism was a Europe-wide phenomenon, in Spain it had specific connotations. In particular *limpieza de sangre* was used as a weapon against the upper classes by those who sought to demonstrate that 'real' Castilians or Valencians were only to be found in the lower classes – easy to do since only nobles and *hidalgos* maintained detailed **genealogies**. This in turn locked into Spanish legalism, with the trained *linajudo* emerging as a new kind of professional, whose task was to prove, or disprove, the 'purity' of an individual's lineage.

More broadly still, *limpieza de sangre* exacerbated, and was exacerbated by, a Spaniard's all-important sense of **honour** which, since the *Reconquista*, was closely tied to the Catholic faith. In a similar way, it reflected an essentially static society that looked obsessively to its roots, not to future changes. It was not, however, universally applauded. Diego Laínez, Loyola's successor as the **Jesuits'** Vicar-General, and himself from a *converso* family, derided *limpieza de sangre* as 'el humor español' – the Spanish perversion. Yet, between 1593 and 1608 (when the witch-hunt was perhaps at its most intense), the Jesuits too felt obliged to exclude anyone with Jewish blood from their Order.

the Things of New Spain'), remains unpublished until 1829.

1548 The **Castilian Cortes**, meeting at Valladolid, complains of the dominance of Germans, Flemish and Italians in the Spanish economy.

1549 Three years before his death, the Basque-born Jesuit **St Francis Xavier** founds a Christian community in **Japan** which, within a generation, attracts over 100,000 followers.

1551 Vernacular versions of the **Bible** – increasingly used in Protestant churches in preference to the Latin or Vulgate Bible – are banned throughout Spain and its associated territories. The **Inquisition** issues a second, fuller Index of proscribed books.

Under pressure from its bankers, the Crown authorizes the export of precious metals from Castile and other parts of Spain.

1552 Charles V's costly German policies unravel when his German bankers refuse to make him further loans. When Maurice of Saxony marches on **Innsbruck**, the emperor and his half-brother Archduke Ferdinand narrowly escape capture. Charles V is forced to concede some of his American silver revenues to the **Fugger** banking family, to the detriment of Castile's economy.

1554 The *infante* Philip marries **Mary Tudor**, the Catholic heir to the English throne. Charles V rewards him with the crowns of Naples and Sicily.

In the Caribbean François Le Clerc, a French pirate, captures and burns **Santiago de Cuba**. In the following year **Havana** is attacked by another Frenchman, known as Sores, and many of its inhabitants massacred.

1554 Pedro de Valdivia, the governor of **Chile**, is captured and killed – allegedly by being made to swallow molten gold – by the **Araucanians**, a people hostile to Europeans.

Anonymous publication of *Lazarillo de Tormes*, the first **picaresque novel**. A reaction against chivalric romances, the picaresque form has as its protagonist a *pícaro* ('rogue' or 'rascal') who is forced to live by his wits.

1555 Responsibility for the Spanish crown's Italian possessions is removed from the Council of Aragon and invested in a new **Council of Italy**.

In July **Mary Tudor** is proclaimed Queen of England, and begins persecuting English Protestants. Her husband Philip is prevented by the English parliament from assuming the title King of England.

On 25 October Charles V tells an invited audience in the City Hall at **Brussels** of his plans to abdicate.

1556 Charles V formally **abdicates** on 1 January. His eldest surviving son **Philip** inherits Spain as well as of Sardinia and the Netherlands (Burgundy), while Charles's brother **Ferdinand** inherits the Archduchy of Austria, and assumes the title of Holy Roman Emperor. In September Charles returns to Castile and takes up residence in a palace adjacent to a monastery at **Yuste**, where he dies two years later.

The Reign of Philip II
1556–1598

Although only one of his grandparents, Juana the Mad, was a Spaniard, **Philip II** (Felipe II) was Spanish in a way his father never was. He grew up in Castile, spoke Castilian as his first language, and after 1559 never once left the Iberian peninsula. Instead, for long periods he immured himself in the **Escorial** – the huge monastery-palace complex he ordered to be built to the northwest of **Madrid**, which became Spain's capital in 1561. As a youth he showed some aptitude for the hunt and other princely pleasures, but as a ruler – despite maintaining a love of pageantry – he was unusually hard-working. Night after night he remained awake, reading and annotating *consulta* (advisory documents from specifically tasked councils) and other state papers. Some he approved, others he returned for redrafting. Without his signature no new policy could be actioned. But to help him in his paperwork there evolved around him an army of clerks and other desk-workers, to the extent that his administration has sometimes been called Europe's first **modern bureaucracy**.

Such a system of government was largely forced on Philip II. Like Charles V, he too governed vast territories, and a central secretariat of some kind became an essential means of control. Even though Austria and the Holy Roman Empire had passed to his uncle Ferdinand, continuing expansion of Spanish settlement in the **New World**, and the acquisition of **Portugal** and its empire in 1580, meant Philip ruled over even greater domains.

The annexation of Portugal and the final reunifying of the peninsula under one crown was one of several supposed triumphs that graced a 42-year reign. It came about however in the traditional dynastic way. Philip's claim to the Portuguese throne was through his mother, **Isabel**, and was contested against two other candidates: the Prior of Crato, and the Duchess of Braganza. A timely show of arms and the occupation of **Lisbon** secured the prize, even though Portugal remained separate from the rest of Spain legally and administratively.

Even more than Charles V, who as early as 1543 had admonished his son 'always to keep God before your eyes', Philip emerged as the principal promoter of the **Counter-Reformation**, as well as the main instigator of fresh campaigns against the Ottoman Turks. Virtually the whole of his foreign policy was dictated by an obsessive need to defend and assert Catholic values. In time, this landed the king in serious trouble. In the **Netherlands** he was faced, from 1566, by open rebellion among the Protestant Dutch. But the **Dutch Revolt**, continuing long after Philip was dead, was no mere provincial uprising. Rather the Dutch found natural allies among the Protestant princes of **Germany**, among the Huguenots of **France**, and among the **English**. Like the English too, the Dutch were adventurous seafarers, and privateers from both peoples regularly interfered with Spanish shipping.

Philip's determination to crush the Dutch committed him to interminable **wars** in northern Europe, and led to his greatest set-back, the defeat of his **Armada** by the English in 1588 – souring the relected glory he had accrued in 1571 when his brother **Don Juan of Austria** scored a memorable naval victory over the Ottomans at **Lepanto**. More seriously still, Philip's European campaigns placed an intolerable strain on royal finances. Three times during his reign the king was forced to default on his loans, despite greatly increasing bullion revenues from the New World – by the 1580s Spanish America was providing as much as eighty percent of the world silver supply. And each time he declared himself bankrupt his German, Flemish and Italian bankers tightened the noose around his neck, forcing him to grant an ever-increasing number of *asientos* – contracts that assigned future revenues to his creditors. Philip's solution – to increase levels of taxation inside Spain – inevitably made him unpopular.

Religion was no less a source of tension during Philip's reign, and in 1568 he had to confront an uprising among the *moriscos* of Andalucía which took two years to quell. The **Second Revolt of the Alpujarras**, as it was called, was largely caused by the increased vigilance of the **Inquisition**, which rightly suspected a handful of *moriscos* of colluding with the Ottomans. But the persistent harassment and persecution of great numbers of Spanish Moors had rather more to do with a continuing and racially motivated quest for *limpieza de sangre* ('purity of blood'), and the king's overarching and dogmatic mind-set. Many of the problems experienced by Philip stemmed ultimately from his refusal to grant the right of freedom of worship to the Dutch. This was ultimately to the detriment of Spanish interests, since it created a solid and eventually powerful bloc opposed to Spain.

In his style of rule the king was not overtly dictatorial, but his **absolutist piety**, echoing the conservatism of many of his Spanish subjects, was oppressive, and too many of his policies discouraged the sort of intellectual open-mindedness that was beginning to evolve elsewhere. Yet for many Spanish historians, Philip's personal misfortunes – not least the imprisonment and death of his son and heir, the *infante* **Don Carlos**, in 1568 – make him a tragic figure. Certainly from 1580, after the death of his fourth and last wife, **Anne of Austria**, his piety became more marked.

It was his last marriage which produced Philip II's eventual heir, **Philip III**. But the risks of consanguinity were not to be avoided (Anne was both his cousin and his niece), and in Spain the Habsburgs' notorious penchant for **inbreeding** brought dynasticism full-circle. In the century that followed Philip's death, the country was subjected to a succession of monarchs who were demonstrably unfit to rule.

1556 Without waiting for the return of **Philip II** from Flanders, Archbishop Siliceo requests that he declare *limpieza de sangre* (see p.272) as a royal policy. Philip II consents, commenting that 'every heresy in Germany, France and Spain has been sown by the descendants of Jews'.

1557 Faced by **bankruptcy** Philip II suspends payments to his bankers ahead of a restructuring of his debts.

On 10 August (the feast of San Lorenzo) a French army advancing into the Spanish Netherlands is halted by a mixed Flemish and Spanish army at **St Quentin**.

1558 During a witch-hunt against supposed Protestants in Seville, Valladolid and other Castilian cities, **Agustín Cazalla**, a leading intellectual and a former favourite of Charles V, is burned at the stake on the suspicion of holding Lutheran opinions.

BRITISH LIBRARY

Miniature of Philip II wearing the insignia of the Order of the Golden Fleece

In September, the *infanta* Juana, acting as Regent on behalf of her brother Philip II, sanctions an attack on **Oran** in North Africa in an effort to dent the continuing Ottoman Turkish menace. She also issues 'pragmatics' outlawing the import of all **foreign books**. Books published in Castile must be licensed by an office of the Council of Castile.

Mary Tudor dies in November, having finally failed to provide Philip II with an heir, and having failed to return England to Catholicism. Her religious adviser, **Bartolomé de Carranza**, is appointed Archbishop of Toledo by Philip, following the death of Siliceo.

1559 Juana issues a pragmatic forbidding Spanish students to study abroad. The Inquisitor-General **Hernándo de Valdés** issues a third Index of proscribed books for Spain, much fuller than an Index issued by Rome in the same year. Private as well as public libraries are rigorously scrutinized.

Anxious to concentrate his resources against the Ottomans, Philip II ends hostilities with France by signing the **Treaty of Cateau-Cambrésis** in April. To seal the peace Philip agrees to marry **Elizabeth of Valois**, the daughter of Henri II. Philip returns to Spain in September, where he begins coordinating a campaign against the Turks with his younger brother **Don Juan of Austria** and his Genoese admiral **Gian Andrea Doria**.

In August **Archbishop Carranza**, a man with many personal enemies in the Church, is arrested by the Inquisition on suspicion of heresy. He will spend the last seventeen years of his life in prison, during which time the revenues of his diocese are appropriated by the Crown. Despite Pope Pius IV's attempts to secure Carranza's release, Philip II insists that the Inquisition is in the right.

Tobacco, a plant native to the Americas, is introduced into Europe by a Sevillian doctor known as Monardes.

1560 A force led by Admiral Doria, sailing from Syracuse in Sicily, captures the fortress-island of **Djerba**, guarding the city of Tripoli (in present-day Libya). Doria's fleet is badly mauled during an Ottoman counter-attack under the corsair Dragut. 10,000 Spanish and Italian soldiers are taken prisoner and paraded in Constantinople.

Around this time **silver production** in Peru and Mexico is vastly accelerated by the application of new refining methods using an amalgam of mercury.

1561 The Ottomans raid **Majorca** in the Balearics.

1562 A reforming Carmelite nun, Teresa de Cepeda y Ahumada (**St Teresa**), founds a religious house for women at Ávila – an initiative that gives rise to a new order in the Catholic Church, the **Discalced Carmelites**.

Philip II authorizes Jesuits to undertake missionary work in the New World. In Mexico, **Fray Diego de Landa** instigates a sustained assault on the 'idolatry' of surviving Mayans. Although the Mayan elite is cajoled into outwardly accepting Christianity, it begins compiling a

> **"** I saw an angel close by me ... He was not large, but small of stature, and most beautiful ... I saw in his hand a long spear of gold, and at the iron's point there seemed to be a little fire. He appeared to be thrusting it at times into my heart, and to pierce my very entrails; when he drew it out, he seemed to draw them out also, and to leave me all on fire with a great love of God. The pain was so great that it made me moan; and yet so surpassing was the sweetness of this excessive pain that I could not wish to be rid of it. The soul is satisfied now with nothing less than God. **"**
>
> St Teresa of Ávila, from Chapter 29 of her *Life* (1565), trans. David Lewis

St Teresa of Ávila (1515–1582)

In 1535 Teresa de Cepeda y Ahumada entered a Carmelite convent in Ávila, her home town. Twenty years later she experienced the spiritual 'awakening' that inspired her to promote a reform movement within the **Carmelite Order** that would restore its original austerity and dedication to the contemplative life. Encouraged by **St Peter of Alcántara**, and with the approval of Pope Pius IV, she established a new house, St Joseph's, in 1562. Five years later she formed a close friendship with fellow Carmelite Juan de Yepes, better known as the poet and mystic **St John of the Cross** (1542–1591), with whom she set about founding further reformed convents and friaries. Teresa's insistence that only the original 'primitive' rule of the Carmelites was correct eventually led to opposition from senior Carmelites, and from this dispute a new order was founded by Teresa – the **'Discalced Carmelites'**. Discalced literally means 'barefoot', and those who followed Teresa made a point of wearing only sandals and simple garments. For challenging authority Teresa was made to withdraw to a nunnery, and Juan was briefly imprisoned. The intercession of **Philip II** in 1579, however, led to their rehabilitation, and the following year the Discalced Carmelites were awarded separate jurisdiction by the Vatican, prior to being recognized as an entirely separate order in 1593. For the last few years of her life Teresa redoubled her efforts to promote her teachings, through such books as her *Life*, *The Way of Perfection* and *The Interior Castle*. Her writings, which describe her relationship with God in intensely personal and even physical terms, are regarded as classics of mystical Catholic piety.

record of Mayan history known as *The Books of Chilam Balam*.

1563 Philip II commissions the building of **El Escorial**, a huge palace-monastery about 30 miles outside Madrid. Designed by Juan Bautista de Toledo and Bautista's more gifted pupil **Juan de Herrera** in an austerely classical style, it is completed barely a year later and becomes Philip's permanent residence. **Madrid** itself, close to the mathematical centre of the peninsula, is now the capital of Spain and its empire.

1564 Under pressure from nobles in the Netherlands, Philip II dismisses his administrator there, the unpopular Cardinal Granvelle. Unrest continues, however, as Philip's regent in the Netherlands, Margaret of Parma, continues the policy of persecuting Protestants.

Ferdinand of Austria dies. His son **Maximilian II** becomes Holy Roman Emperor.

In September **Don García de Toledo** leads a successful naval expedition against the north African fortress of Peñón de Vélez de la Gomera.

As piracy in the Atlantic and Caribbean grows, Philip II orders a new convoy system to ship bullion back to Castile. A single **treasure fleet**, carrying silver from both Peru and Mexico, henceforth sails annually from Havana for Seville.

DORLING KINDERSLEY

The palace-monastery of El Escorial is dedicated to San Lorenzo, and its design is supposedly based on the grill on which the saint was martyred

> Aside from the fact that virtually all my revenues are sold or mortgaged I owe very great sums of money and need yet more money for the maintenance of my realms.
>
> Philip II, in a report to the Council of Castile, 1565

1565 In May a major Ottoman force lays siege to **Malta**. The island is defended by the Knights of St John until the arrival of a Spanish relief force in September. During the siege, Spain's southern coast is raided by corsairs, and Moorish 'spies' are arrested in Andalucía, accused of plotting with the Turks for an invasion of the Peninsula.

Spanish troops are sent to the New World for the first time when French settlers attempt to found a colony in **Florida**. Several hundred French are massacred by a Spanish force led by **Pedro Menendez de Aviles**, who goes on to establish new Spanish settlements. Within ten years persistent attacks by North American Indians force the Spanish to abandon all but two of their colonies on the Floridan peninsula.

Spanish interest in the western Pacific is rekindled by an expedition led by the Basque adventurer **Miguel Lopez de Legazpi**, who establishes a colony on Cebu, among the Visaya islands.

1566 Cardinal Espinosa is appointed Inquisitor-General. He pursues less draconian policies than his predecessor Hernándo de Valdés.

In the Netherlands unrest continues to fester after Dutch aristocrats resign their posts in protest at the continuing application of severe heresy laws. In August, Calvinists inflict widespread damage on Catholic churches, an event conventionally deemed to mark the beginning of the decades-long **Dutch Revolt**.

1567 In August the **Duke of Alba**, a Castilian hardliner, is ordered to the Netherlands to tackle Dutch insurgency. He arrests several leading dissidents, including the Counts of Egmont and Hornes. Using harsh methods, and a force of 10,000 mainly Castilian soldiers, Alba's military successes exacerbate ill feeling among Dutch Protestants. An emergency Council of Troubles set up by the duke is quickly dubbed the **'Council of Blood'**.

In Spain the introduction of a new tax, the *excusado*, to help pay for the war in the Netherlands is widely resented.

New laws (known as 'pragmatics') designed to enforce Christian observance among **moriscos** are introduced by the Archbishop of Granada, Pedro Guerrero.

Alvaro de Mendaña, voyaging across the Pacific from Peru, discovers the **Solomon Islands**.

1568 Just before midnight on 28 January in the Escorial, Philip II, together with a group of councillors, enters the chamber of **Don Carlos**, his son by Maria of Portugal and heir to the throne, and places him under arrest. The *infante* is suspected of conspiring with the Dutch, and is widely considered unfit for office. By detaining Don Carlos, Philip demonstrates that he places his responsibilities as a monarch above those of a father. When Don Carlos dies on 24 July as a result of hunger-strikes and poor medicine unfounded rumours spread that Philip has had him poisoned. In September Philip's grief is compounded by the death of his third wife, **Elizabeth of Valois**.

In the Netherlands, Dutch resistance to what is perceived as a Spanish occupation falls under the leadership of **William I of Orange**, who, with the clandestine support of France and some German princes, begins launching small military strikes against Spanish positions. Alba responds by ordering the public execution of Egmont and Hornes in Brussels on 5 June, an action that only inflames 'anti-Spanish' feeling.

Second Revolt of the Alpujarras (1568–70)

Although the capture of **Granada** in 1492 completed the Christian *Reconquista* of Muslim Spain, the 'Moors' continued to be a feature of Iberian life and culture. However, when Archbishop Cisneros ordered the closure of all mosques in 1499, Muslims in Andalucía rebelled in what was known as the **First Revolt of the Alpujarras**. This resulted in further punitive measures, and in 1501 the Islamic faith was finally outlawed in Spain. Faced with the prospect of expulsion, many Spanish Muslims converted to Christianity. Such converts, or *moriscos*, endured as a largely unassimilated minority in the south, and in parts of Valencia and Aragon. For much of the first half of the 16th century they were left to themselves, and although a series of edicts decreed that *moriscos* should adopt Spanish customs, most continued to speak Arabic and to wear Muslim clothing. In the south they enjoyed the patronage and protection of the powerful **Mendoza family**, one of whose members usually held the post of Captain-General of Granada.

The **Second Revolt of the Alpujarras** of 1568 was sparked off by attempts to enforce the new anti-Muslim laws, or 'pragmatics', devised by **Archbishop Guerrero** the previous year. The *moriscos* had other grievances, however. For over a decade the government had damaged their main industry – the

In September relations with **England** deteriorate after the slave merchant John Hawkins is attacked at San Juan de Ulua on the Mexican coast. In November, when Spanish ships carrying silver to Flanders for the payment of Alba's army put into English ports during a storm, Elizabeth I orders their seizure by way of demonstrating her support for the Dutch 'rebels'.

On 24 December a major uprising, triggered by the 'pragmatics' of 1567, begins among the *moriscos* of Granada. Led by Fárax Abenfárax, the **Second Alpujarras Revolt** spreads quickly to other Moorish communities in Andalucía.

manufacture of **silk** – by imposing commodity taxes and banning exports. They were also aware that in court circles a campaign was afoot to undermine the standing of the Mendoza family. On the government side, there was serious concern that the *moriscos* might link up with the **Ottoman Turks**, who in 1565 had attempted to seize Malta in the western Mediterranean.

Another factor was the ardent Catholicism of **Philip II**, who saw himself as the defender of the faith, and whose values inevitably influenced official thinking. In these changing circumstances, conflict was inevitable – the more so as Guerrero gained the backing of the Inquisitor-General, **Cardinal Espinosa**. But although the government may even have encouraged a confrontation, it is unlikely that it foresaw either the scale or the ferocity of the uprising, prolonged by the infiltration of up to 4000 Muslim *anwar* ('helpers') from North Africa. In its wake tens of thousands of *moriscos* were redistributed in other parts of Spain, their homes in **Andalucía** filled by settlers from Galicia and the Asturias. Yet in the long run even these measures failed to calm Spanish anxieties. Two generations later the final act of 'ethnic cleansing' took place, with the enforced **expulsion** of all remaining *moriscos* from the peninsula (see p.312).

1569 As the Alpujarras revolt intensifies, Philip II entrusts its suppression to his brother, **Don Juan**. There is also unrest in **Catalunya** where many refuse to pay the *excusado* tax.

Fearing that French Huguenots have been disseminating Protestant ideas in Catalunya, Philip II engenders further ill-feeling by ordering the Inquisition to weed out potential heretics. Among those imprisoned are several Catalan deputies and members of the nobility.

Francisco de Toledo is appointed Viceroy of Peru. During his twelve years in office, Toledo does much to enhance Castilian royal authority in the colony, capturing and killing the last Inca emperor, **Tupac Amaru**, in 1571. He also sets up an office of the Inquisition, which he uses to rein in friars and missionaries who have been working toward establishing an independent church in the Americas, as well as to root out Jews and Protestants.

1570 Without an heir since the death of Don Carlos, Philip II marries for the fourth time. His last wife, **Anne of Austria**, is the daughter of his sister Maria and of his cousin, the Emperor Maximilian II.

Although Don Juan has made headway in the Alpujarras

The Philippines

The Philippines were first 'discovered' by **Magellan** in 1521, but it was not until the reign of Philip II, after whom the islands were named, that any attempt was made at settlement. Even as late as 1635 there were less than 200 Spanish households in the colony, all of them in or around the port city of **Manila**, the present-day capital. Unlike the Americas, Spaniards did not go there to carve out estates or raise plantations. The only local produce of any value was cinnamon, and the indigenous **Tagalog** people were neither maltreated nor pressed into anything other than voluntary service. Rather the interest of Manila was as a trading post between the New World, and by extension Castile, and the economies of the Far East – principally **China**, but also Japan and south-east Asia. American silver was shipped to Manila across the Pacific from **Acapulco**, and exchanged for such highly valued Chinese goods as porcelain, silk and later tea, brought in junks from Fujian, Guangdong and other southern provinces. Once a year a single 'treasure' galleon would then ship the Chinese goods to Acapulco – a voyage that lasted six months.

From the outset the Manila trade mostly benefited the Chinese, ensuring that the Ming and Qing empires received its share of American bullion. By 1700 more silver was being carried to Asia than to Europe, and it was as a result of this anomaly that the **Mexican dollar** became the primary hard currency in the Asia-

there is determined resistance at **Galera** from February. When the town falls in April, all of its 2500 inhabitants are killed. The revolt subsequently crumbles, and by mid-summer is effectively over. Up to 100,000 *moriscos* are forcibly relocated throughout Castile to lessen their concentration in the south.

1571 Spain, Venice and the Papacy form a **Holy League** against the Ottoman Turks, who have occupied Cyprus the previous summer. Commanded by Don Juan of Austria, a combined Spanish and Venetian war fleet

Pacific region until the beginning of the 20th century. In the port itself a burgeoning population of Chinese traders, shipwrights and other kinds of artisans, collectively known as Sangleys, outnumbered 'Spaniards' (often half-castes from the Americas), by at least ten to one. Occasionally there was friction between the Chinese and Tagalogs, who sided with the Spanish in restoring order just because, numerically at least, Spaniards provided a lesser threat. Well before the end of the 17th century, however, as both the **Dutch** and **English** made inroads into the East Indies, Manila began losing its pre-eminence. Ironically, it was only after this time that other Spanish settlements appeared in the Philippines – at least in the large northern island of **Luzon**.

In the 17th century, under Spanish supervision (but with Portuguese and Arab complicity), Manila became an outpost of the **black slave trade**. More importantly, it served as a springboard for Jesuit and other **Catholic missionaries**, eager to convert not only the Filipino peoples, but other East Asians as well. After Nagasaki joined the Manila trading 'system' in 1600, up to 100,000 **Japanese** there were persuaded to embrace Christianity. Although subsequently, during the Tokugawa shogunate, Japan closed its doors to the outside world, in Nagasaki itself a sizeable Christian community survived until 1945, when it was all but obliterated by an American nuclear bomb.

consisting of 203 galleons sails from Messina, and encounters the main Ottoman fleet in the Gulf of Lepanto (Greece) on 7 September. The **Battle of Lepanto** is hard fought, with victory only narrowly accorded to the Christians, although the Turks suffer four times as many casualties as their Christian foes. The battle is celebrated as a resounding triumph throughout Europe. Ottoman sea-power, however, remains a threat in at least the eastern Mediterranean.

Anne of Austria gives birth to a son, Ferdinand, which the king interprets as a mark of God's special favour. However, the boy does not survive infancy.

In June a Spanish force operating out of the Visayas and led by Legazpi occupies the port town **Manila**, ousting its Muslim ruler, and establishing a permanent presence there. The Spanish will lay claim to the whole of the **Philippines**, even though **Mindanao** and other islands remain under Muslim control.

1572 On 1 April Dutch pirates, known as **Sea Beggars**, capture the port of **Brill**, which becomes their new base, and the centre of resistance to Spanish rule in the Netherlands. In the winter the Duke of Alba launches a fresh campaign against Flemish Protestants, sacking the towns of Mechelen, Zutphen, Naarden and Haarlem, and butchering many of their inhabitants.

1573 The Duke of Alba is recalled from the Netherlands, having failed to crush the revolt. He is replaced by the governor of Milan, **Don Luis Requesens**, who, on the orders of Philip II, pursues more conciliatory policies. Philip II himself, faced by mounting war debts in Flanders and anxious to concentrate his forces against the Ottomans, undertakes to preserve the 'liberties' of all Netherlanders, and to appoint more of them to office. Soon afterwards Don Juan captures **Tunis** with a force of 150 galleons.

Gaspar de Quiroga is appointed Inquisitor-General. During his tenure many important works of European scholarship are removed from the Spanish Index of proscribed books, and Spanish universities are permitted to teach Copernican astronomy.

Philip II issues an **'ordinance of discovery and population'** which calls for a halt to further territorial expansion in the New World. Rather Spain's colonists should consolidate the territories they already hold. When the Vatican refuses to endorse Philip's decree the king himself assumes supreme authority over the American church.

1574 In March Philip grants an amnesty to most of the Dutch rebels. In April Spanish and other imperial troops, owed money by the government, mutiny in **Antwerp**. Requesens manages to break the mutiny, but not before troops have rampaged through the city.

The Ottomans, deploying an army of 40,000 men, recapture **Tunis** less than a year after its occupation by Spain.

1575 For the second time during his reign Philip II declares himself **bankrupt**, pending a restructuring of his debts.

1576 In Brussels, Requesens dies after a lengthy illness. He is replaced as governor by **Don Juan of Austria**, who arrives in Brussels in November just as the army again mutinies in Antwerp over pay, this time comprehensively sacking the city. Properties are looted and burned, and as many as 8000 civilians are killed in the confusion. Although the majority of the troops are Italian and German, the presence of a Spanish contingent leads to the episode being called **The Spanish Fury**. With Requesens' conciliatory gestures toward the Dutch now at risk, Don Juan makes concessions during a session of the Flemish States-General held at Ghent. According to the **'Pacification of Ghent'** freedom of worship is guaranteed throughout the Netherlands, and Spain undertakes to withdraw its troops.

El Greco (1541–1614)

One of the most idiosyncratic artists of the 16th century, **El Greco** is enduringly associated with Spain, even though he did not set foot there until his late 30s. Born in **Crete** at a time when the island was under Venetian rule, Domenikos Theotokopoulos made his way to Venice as a young man to study under **Titian**, and later visited Rome where he acquired a detailed knowledge of the Sistine Chapel ceiling and other works by **Michelangelo**. But although El Greco ('the Greek'), as he was already known, left behind him a handful of competent works in Italy, it was in Spain that he came fully into his own as an artist.

Madrid, however, did him no favours – the king disliked his work – and so he moved to **Toledo**. Perhaps this was as well, for what seems to have finally unlocked El Greco's genius was the intensity of Spanish mysticism, which flourished in the provinces in a way it never could in the austere, bureaucratic capital. Though in economic decline, Toledo was still the intellectual heart of Castile and it provided an environment in which El Greco's increasingly experimental work was more likely to be understood.

Famously, and of particular appeal to modern taste, El Greco's 'mature' paintings are strikingly bold in their use of colour, their expressive brushwork, their spatial ambiguity, and their attenuation of the human form. All these characteristics can be traced to Italian precedents, in particular the flickering surfaces and crowded spaces of **Tintoretto**'s canvases and the distortions of the **Mannerists**, but they also owe something to the traditions of Byzantine icon painting. In paintings like the *Agony in the Garden* (c.1585), or the *Adoration of the Shepherds* (1613), the figures are markedly anti-naturalistic, their elongation seeming to suggest a striving for incorporeality. It is this obsessive, phantasmagoric quality – seen at its strangest in the hallucinatory *View of Toledo* (c.1610) – that encapsulates El Greco's true originality, and which in his religious paintings perfectly captures the proximity of pain and ecstasy that lies at the heart of Catholic spirituality.

THE BOWES MUSEUM

In El Greco's *The Tears of St Peter* both the darkly dramatic setting and the physical distortion help to emphasize the saint's despair

1577 The concessions made in Ghent the previous November are ratified by the **'Perpetual Edict'**, promulgated in February. Philip II, although unenthusiastic about Don Juan's arrangements, refuses to authorize a full-scale war against England, which has been supporting the rebels. In July Don Juan, suspecting that **Antonio Pérez** and other royal advisers in Madrid are planning to grant the Dutch independence, and claiming that Dutch Calvinists have infringed the Perpetual Edict, assaults a Dutch stronghold at Namur. At once the northern provinces resume their rebellion, and Don Juan summons a fresh army under the command of the Italian aristocrat **Alessandro Farnese**.

Boosted by unexpectedly large **bullion** shipments from the Americas, Philip II makes terms with his creditors. For the following decade and more the crown remains solvent, enabling Philip to pursue more aggressive policies.

At the end of the year the English privateer **Francis Drake** sets off from Plymouth on a three-year voyage of circumnavigation during which he harries Spanish merchant shipping in the Pacific, even seizing a Potosí treasure vessel.

At about this time the Cretan-born artist Domenikos Theotokopoulos settles in Toledo, where he is known as **El Greco**.

1578 On the night of 31 March Don Juan's principal supporter in Madrid, **Juan de Escobedo**, is hacked to death by men in Antonio Pérez's pay.

On 4 August the youthful King Sebastião of **Portugal** is killed fighting Muslims during the Battle of Alcázarquivir (al-Qar al-Kabir) in Morocco. With the Portuguese throne passing to Sebastião's elderly and childless uncle, **Cardinal Enrique**, a succession crisis looms. Inside Portugal, factions begin forming in favour of three possible candidates: Don Antonio, the Prior of Crato, a royal bastard; the Duchess of Braganza; and Philip II of Spain – grandson of the Portuguese king Manuel I. Seeing an opportunity to unify the peninsula, Philip pushes his claim to be recognized as heir apparent.

In the Netherlands, Farnese routs a Dutch army at **Gembloux**. Don Juan dies on 1 October, and Farnese takes over the government.

1579 Suspecting that Antonio Pérez, the Princess of Eboli and others are in league with the Duchess of Braganza over the Portuguese succession, Philip summons **Cardinal Granvelle** from the Netherlands. Granvelle arrives in Madrid on 28 July, and on the same day Pérez is arrested and his faction banished from court.

In June Farnese captures **Maastricht**, and massacres up to 10,000 of its inhabitants. Intimidated by his action, other Dutch-held cities quickly surrender.

1580 Cardinal Enrique dies on 31 January, having reluctantly agreed to Philip II's succession to the Portuguese crown. Many Portuguese, unpersuaded by Philip's assurances that their country's autonomy will be preserved, give their support to the **Prior of Crato**. The Duke of Alba, summoned out of retirement, crosses the Portuguese border in late June. After fierce street battles, **Lisbon** is secured in August, and the Prior of Crato flees the country. Philip II, strongly backed by Lisbon's mercantile community, is proclaimed **King of Portugal** on 12 September.

Anne of Austria dies. Of the five children she has borne Philip II, only one, the future Philip III, survives into adulthood.

1581 In January a three-year truce is signed between the Holy League and the Ottoman Turks. In April Philip II meets the **Portuguese Cortes** and swears to uphold Portuguese customs and rights. Although trade tariffs between Portugal and Castile are abolished, it is agreed that the Portuguese should be governed by a separate council, and that Philip's Spanish subjects will not be granted privileges in Portugal's African, Asian and American colonies. Philip takes up residence in Lisbon while Granvelle oversees the government of Castile in Madrid.

As English **piracy** against Spanish merchant shipping increases, Philip II orders the construction of war galleons to police the Atlantic and Caribbean.

1583 Philip returns to Madrid from Lisbon in March, entrusting the government of Portugal to his nephew Archduke Albert. Back at the Escorial, the king creates a new inner council, called the *Junta de Noche*, in which Cristobal de Moura emerges as the leading figure. Cardinal Granvelle is excluded from the junta, and henceforward plays only a minor role in Spanish affairs.

The **Marquis of Santa Cruz** proposes to Philip that England be invaded as a means of depriving the Dutch of their most valued allies, of halting English 'piracy' in Spanish waters, and of restoring the Roman Catholic faith in Britain. Philip is initially sceptical, but preparations soon begin for the launch of the **Spanish Armada** (see p.299), which is preached by the clergy as a crusade against the 'infidel' Queen Elizabeth I.

1584 Philip II receives a group of well-born **Japanese Christian converts** journeying to Rome via Seville at the Escorial.

1585 In May Antwerp capitulates to Alessandro Farnese. Philip II places an **embargo** on Dutch merchant vessels entering Spanish and Portuguese ports – a ban widely disregarded in the New World where colonists are dependent on Dutch and also English traders for luxuries and vital supplies. Francis Drake crosses the Atlantic with 22 vessels and over 2000 troops and sacks **Santo Domingo**. Over the next 18 years over 200 sponsored raids against Spanish interests will be carried out by English adventurers.

1587 On 19 April Drake, ordered to destroy the Armada being prepared against England, attacks **Cádiz** harbour and causes sufficient damage to Spain's warfleet to delay Philip II's intended invasion by a year. On 17 November Thomas Cavendish, buccaneering in the Pacific, seizes the 'Manila galleon', the *Santa Ana*, as it sails from the Philippines to Acapulco.

1588 A reassembled war fleet of 130 galleons leaves La Coruña on 22 July under the command of the **Duke of Medina-Sidonia**, instructed by Philip II to sail first to Flanders, where the Duke of Parma (Alessandro Farnese)

> " As for the Expedition of Sir Francis Drake in the year 1587, for the Destroying of the Spanish Shipping and Provision upon their own Coast, as I cannot say that there intervened in that Enterprise any sharp Fight or Encounter, so nevertheless it did straightly discover, either that Spain is very weak at home, or very slow to move, when they suffered a small fleet of English to make an hostile Invasion or Incursion upon their Havens and Roads from Cádiz to Cape Sacre, and thence to Cascous, and to fire, sink, and carry away at least ten thousand Ton of their greater Shipping, besides fifty or sixty of their smaller Vessels, and that in the sight and under the favour of their Forts, and almost under the Eye of their great Admiral, the best Commander of Spain by Sea, the Marquis of Santa Cruce, without ever being disputed with in any Fight of Importance: I remember Drake, in the vaunting Stile of a Soldier, would call the Enterprise the Singeing of the King of Spain's Beard. "

Sir Francis Bacon, *Considerations Touching a War With Spain* (1629)

BETTMANN/CORBIS

A contemporary engraving of the English fleet engaging with the Armada in the Channel

waits to embark the army that will overrun England. In the Channel the **Spanish Armada** is harassed by small English naval squadrons. On the night of 7 August the already damaged fleet suffers a fire attack as it lies at anchor off Calais. The following day Medina-Sidonia runs for open waters, and the Armada heads for the North Sea. On the long voyage back to Spain many more galleons are destroyed in storms, and shipwrecked Spaniards are hunted down and killed in Scotland and Ireland.

1589 Drake commands a naval expedition that causes some damage along the coast of **Portugal**, but fails in its primary objective, which is to assist the Prior of Crato seize the Portuguese throne from Philip II.

Henri de Navarra, a champion of French Protestants, succeeds to the French throne as Henri IV, founder of the **Bourbon dynasty**. He is opposed however by a Catholic League supported by Philip II.

The Armada of 1588

In Philip II's view the **Dutch** and the **English** were pirates and heretics who conspired to undermine Spain and God alike. On the high seas both made wholly illegal attacks against Spanish merchantmen, and in the Netherlands they both fought Habsburg armies in the field The 1580s however were a time when the king felt in control of events. Not only had he added Portugal to his domains, but **Alessandro Farnese** seemed to be winning the war against the rebels. In these circumstances Philip opted to dish both his enemies at a stroke. A great fleet, or *Armada*, would sail to Dunkirk, pick up Farnese's army, cross the Channel, invade England and so prevent Elizabeth I giving any further supplies to the Dutch. Further, by commandeering **England's ports**, he would reassert supremacy at sea. And all this would be for the greater glory of God. The English would surely be led back into the Catholic fold – for it still rankled with Philip that their Parliament had refused to acknowledge him as their king following his marriage to Mary Tudor.

But the fleet that finally set sail from La Coruña in 1588 was not the fleet originally intended, which had been badly damaged at Cádiz the previous year. Mostly it was made up of Portuguese and Italian galleons, many of them older vessels contracted to the crown by private consortiums, and manned with inexperienced recruits. Large and lumbering, such vessels were no match for the nimbler well-cannoned English ships that, under the overall command of Lord Howard of Effingham, successfully adopted hit-and-run tactics against the Armada once it had entered the English Channel. But worse was to follow. Foul weather prevented Philip's admiral, **Medina-Sidonia**, from collecting Farnese's troops, and dogged his fleet as it tried to escape through the North Sea. Eventually less than half the 130 galleons that had set out from La Coruña made it back, and 15,000 men were lost.

> Great thanks do I render Almighty God, by whose hand I am gifted with such power, that I could easily, if I chose, place another fleet upon the sea. Nor is it of very great importance that a running stream should be sometimes intercepted, so long as the fountain from which it flows remains inexhaustible.

Philip II, on learning that Medina-Sidonia had returned home safely after the Armada defeat quoted in J.L. Motley, *History of the United Netherlands* (1860)

1590 In April **Antonio Pérez**, held in captivity since 1579, escapes from Madrid and flees to Zaragoza, where, as an Aragonese subject, he claims the protection of the Justicia. Pérez's sudden appearance adds to unrest that has been growing in **Aragon** for almost a decade, fuelled by distrust of Castilian officials and by a series of feuds between Aragon's leading families. Sensitive to Aragonese concerns, but loath to allow Pérez his liberty, Philip drops legal proceedings against him but persuades the **Inquisition** that he is a heretic. Pérez is arrested by the Inquisition, against which the *fueros* of Aragon offer no protection.

Faced with insolvency, Philip II persuades the Castilian Cortes to grant him a new tax, an excise duty known as the *millones* (since from the outset it is reckoned in millions of ducats) which it is the responsibility of Castile's towns and cities to raise.

In the Netherlands, Farnese, supporting the **Catholic League**, launches a two-year campaign against Henri IV of France, but fails to make lasting gains.

1591 A full-scale **revolt** erupts in Aragon on 24 May when Antonio Pérez is 'rescued' by supporters in Zaragoza. The crowd then turns on the Marquis of Almenara, Philip II's Castilian viceroy in Aragon, killing him after storming his palace. Pérez is rearrested, but on 24 September is again liberated by his followers. Willing to invoke French backing to gain his objective of a republic free from royal control, Pérez openly encourages Catalans and Valencians to imitate his rebellion. When Alonso de Vargas crosses into Aragon with a joint Castilian, Italian and German army, the Justicia, **Juan de Lanuza**, calls on his fellow-Aragonese to resist, but few outside Zaragoza respond. On 11 November Pérez flees to France, and on 18 December Lanuza is seized and executed.

1592 In January, Philip II grants a general amnesty to the rebels in Zaragoza, bringing their revolt to a close. When the **Aragonese Cortes** convenes at Tarazona, the king undertakes to respect and preserve Aragonese *fueros*. However, it is agreed that the Crown has the right to appoint a non-Aragonese viceroy, and that the appointment of the Justicia should be subject to royal approval.

The Duke of Parma (Alessandro Farnese) dies in December. Despite his brilliance as a military tactician he has failed to crush the Dutch Protestants.

1595 Although Henri IV has 'converted' to Catholicism in 1593, the Catholic League continues to oppose him. In response Henri, anxious to terminate the French wars of religion, declares war on Spain, the League's principal ally. On 5 June an army despatched by Philip II is defeated at **Fontaine-Française**.

1596 The pressure on Philip grows as France, England and the Dutch 'United Provinces' form an **anti-Spanish alliance**. The Earl of Essex commands a sea-borne operation against Cádiz, causing some damage to the port.

The *millones* **excise tax** of 1590 is confirmed as a regular source of royal revenue, and its remit expanded to include some essential foodstuffs. Despite this, in November Philip II declares himself **bankrupt** for the third time during his reign. Solvency is only restored the following years by a massive sale of *juros*, or rights to land and other forms of income enjoyed by the Crown in Castile. Castile's economy suffers severe damage, most conspicuously in the abrupt decline of the annual international trade fair at Medina del Campo.

In Andalucía, an outbreak of **plague** follows a series of poor harvests, seriously undermining the prosperity and confidence of the south.

1597 A fresh **Armada** is sent against England, but returns home after suffering storm damage.

1598 In April, Henri IV issues the Edict of Nantes, promoting religious tolerance in France. The war between Spain and France is terminated by the **Treaty of Vervins**, signed on 2 May. In the same month, in order to lighten the burden on the Castilian exchequer, Philip II's nephew **Archduke Albert** and his consort the *infanta* Isabel Clara Eugenia are declared the sovereign monarchs of the Netherlands on the understanding that the Netherlands will revert to Spanish rule if they have no children.

On 13 September Phillip II dies in the Escorial after a long illness. Spain remains at war with England.

During the course of 1598 plague spreads from Andalucía to Castile and other parts of Spain, causing tens of thousands of deaths, and further undermining the economy.

Later Habsburg Spain
1598–1700

In the sixteenth century both Charles V (Carlos I) and Philip II had promoted *hidalgos*, and other middle ranking persons, to positions of responsibility within their governments. By and large Spain's aristocrats were encouraged to pursue military careers, but were excluded from government. In the seventeenth century all that changed, due largely to the inferiority of the three later Habsburg monarchs – **Philip III** (1598–1621), **Philip IV** (1621–1665) and **Carlos II** (1665–1700) – as rulers. Philip III, the fruit of Philip II's marriage to his own niece Anna of Austria, was an uninspiring individual who at his accession readily succumbed to the personality and policies of the **Duke of Lerma**. The slightly more competent Philip IV entrusted government to the hands of the **Count-Duke Olivares** – the most effective of the later Habsburgs' first ministers, or *privados*.

The failure of Spain's royal house to supply strong rulers was reflected in a steady diminution of the throne's prestige, both at home and abroad. Although in 1625 past glories were recalled when an English naval fleet's attack on Cádiz was repulsed and a Spanish army captured the Dutch fortress of Breda, such victories proved hollow. Fifteen years later, in 1640, **Portugal** reclaimed its independence, and a major revolt in **Catalunya**, supported by the French, led to the province effectively seceding from Spanish rule for ten years. Spain also suffered by being dragged into the Europe-wide **Thirty Years War** (1618–48), during which the Dutch finally asserted their own independence, acknowledged by Spain in the Treaty of Münster in 1648. Well before the end of the century, too, the Crown had abandoned all its remaining interests in the **Low Countries**.

Such episodes however were merely the specifics of profound changes in the European balance of powers. Even before gaining their formal independence the **Dutch** had demonstrated their prowess as an emergent sea-power, taking on both Spanish and Portuguese interests in the New World and in the Far East. Yet even as the Dutch prospered, they too were challenged by another burgeoning maritime power

– the **English**, who now set about creating colonies in North America, and trading settlements in India. But if Spain's empire was challenged by more efficient rivals, an equal threat came from nearer home. **France** mounted a sustained and ultimately successful assault on the Habsburg dominance of Europe, culminating in the **Nine Years War** of 1689–1697 (also called the War of the League of Augsburg).

Louis XIV's trump card was that the rapidly ailing Carlos II had no heir, and that through his own early marriage to Philip IV's daughter **Maria Teresa** in 1660 his descendants by her had a legitimate claim to the Spanish throne. Accordingly, in 1700, when Carlos II died, Louis's grandson by Maria Teresa, **Philip of Anjou**, was proclaimed King of Spain as Philip V.

Viewed through the lens of these and other political events the history of Spain in the seventeenth century inevitably appears desultory compared to the 'Golden Century' of Charles V and Philip II. Yet whether things got appreciably worse for the majority of Spain's inhabitants is another matter entirely. The loss of the **Netherlands** eased the fiscal burden, and the period was also marked by a decrease in the activities of the **Inquisition**. Although Seville declined as the commercial capital of the transatlantic trade, that was largely because **Cádiz** replaced it. Although prices continued to rise, as they had throughout the sixteenth century – largely as a result of chronic manpower shortages – they did so at a slower pace, and the evidence is that the **economy** slowly strengthened. Although Spain generally failed to develop new manufacturing capacities, some traditional economic sectors, including shipbuilding in the Basque north, recovered former capacity. It is also the case that, once the centralizing Olivares had been dismissed, in 1643, the different provinces of Spain felt more comfortable. No longer cajoled by the Duke to join his grandiose **Union of Arms**, the peoples of Aragon, Valencia, Andalucía and later Catalunya could pursue their interests with less interference from Madrid.

Critically, Spain held on to its **Italian possessions**, despite attempted rebellions in Naples and Sicily in 1647, and despite the rising power of an independent **Savoy** and the intermittent hostility of the **Venetian Republic**. Genoa, Milan and other Italian cities continued to service Spain's economic interests, and also to furnish it with a degree of cultural sophistication not always readily available on the peninsula. Spanish art in general gravitated toward the **Spanish Baroque**, that peculiarly cloying expression of entrenched religious conservatism, but it also produced, in **Diego Velázquez**, arguably the greatest painter of the age, but also an artist who seems to have first fully understood his vocation during an Italian tour.

Velázquez's achievements were almost matched by the dramas of the best of the Spanish playwrights, **Calderón** and **Lope de Vega**. It was though **Miguel Cervantes** who, in *Don Quixote*, penned Spain's most widely acknowledged literary masterpiece. Written at the beginning of the century, the idiosyncratic novel he constructed around the 'Knight of the Sorrowful Countenance' exactly caught Spain's conscious retreat from and disillusionment with the extravagant posturing of the preceding conquistador era.

1598 Ascending to the throne of Spain and its related territories aged just 20, the lacklustre **Philip III** (Felip III)is already under the spell of the **Marquis of Denia** (Don Francisco de Sandoval y Rojas), a sophisticated Valencian grandee. Denia's son-in-law the Count of Miranda is appointed president of the Council of Castile, and in the following year Denia's uncle becomes Archbishop of Toledo. **Don Cristobal de Moura**, the most powerful figure

Miguel Cervantes and *Don Quixote*

Cervantes's masterpiece, ***El Ingenioso Hidalgo Don Quixote de la Mancha***, tells how an ageing and demented would-be knight, obsessed with the chivalric romances of the past, sets out from his home, with his faithful (and sane) servant **Sancho Panza**, for some adventures of his own. Don Quixote's state of mind means that no event or encounter is so insignificant that it cannot be instantly transmuted into something heroic, and there follows an extraordinary progress of misunderstandings and misapprehensions, until he overreaches himself and – with Sancho's help – comes down to earth with a thud. Among many the vivid episodes that have captivated readers are the knight's celebrated encounter with a field of windmills, which he mistakes for an army of giants that he must defeat single-handedly, and his determined efforts to perceive the ageing **Dulcinea** as a paragon of young and chaste female beauty.

The book is at once a satire, a parody of previous romances, an allegory, a comedy and a tragedy. Don Quixote himself is the archetypal fool, but he is also a man who remains constant to his ideals, and by the end it is the methodical and ever-practical Sancho Panza who seems the more exasperating. In a profound way Cervantes's novel is a study of disillusionment, as well as of tentative redemption. Inevitably historians have sought to link its themes and mood to the period when it was written – that

in Madrid during the closing years of Philip II's reign, is bundled off to Lisbon as Viceroy of Portugal, and the *Junta de Noche* disbanded.

1599 Denia is created **Duke of Lerma**. Known officially as the *Privado*, he establishes a precedent, followed by the later Habsburgs, whereby government is entrusted to a high-ranking royal favourite. Lerma advances the interests of his own favourites, including Don Pedro Franqueza who is created **Count of Villalonga**, but fails to address the nation's problems. Villalonga is given the responsibility of

turning-point in Spain's imperial history when the triumphs of the mid-16th century gave way to the set-backs that followed the disaster of the Armada of 1588, and in many passages faith itself seems to fall under ironic scrutiny. For some commentators *Don Quixote* is a fictional by-product of **arbitrismo**, an intellectual movement that attempted to explain, and find solutions for, Spain's moral and economic decline.

There are some obvious parallels between Don Quixote's adventures and Cervantes's own highly eventful life. The son of an impoverished doctor, Cervantes was born in Alcalá de Henares and educated in Valladolid, Seville and Madrid. He struggled to make headway in official circles before joining Don Juan's anti-Ottoman army. He fought at **Lepanto** (1571), where he sustained a wound that ruined the use of his left hand, and in 1575 he was captured by the Turks, and imprisoned at **Algiers** for five years. Returning to Spain he began to write – plays and poems as well as novels – while continuing to work as a rather inefficient public servant (*Don Quixote* was started while Cervantes was in jail for poor accounting). It was not until the publication of part one of *Don Quixote* in 1605 that he gained public recognition. Even after this financial hardships dogged Cervantes for the rest of his days, despite the fact that *Don Quixote* had been translated into both English and French by the time of his death in 1616.

reforming royal finances, but uses his position to embezzle the king's revenues.

1600 Lerma and Philip III order a fresh campaign against **Protestant rebels** in the Netherlands. In the Caribbean, where the Dutch have been trading illegally for several decades, Dutch captains increasingly turn to piracy.

1601 Spanish forces intervene unsuccessfully on behalf of Catholic interests in **Ireland** opposed to the island's colonization by the Protestant English.

Philip III is persuaded by Lerma to move his court from Madrid to Valladolid, away from the influence of his grandmother, Maximilian II's widow, the dowager **Empress Maria**.

1602 Sebastian Vizcaino sets out on a northwards voyage from western Mexico during which he explores much of the **Californian coastline**. It is largely as a result of this expedition that the Spanish are later inspired to attempt to create a new colony in western North America.

The **Dutch East India Company** is founded in Amsterdam. Over the coming decades the Dutch will establish themselves as the principal European power in East Asia, at the expense of Spanish and Portuguese interests.

The Spanish governor of **Milan**, Pedro Henriquez de Azevedo, extends the duchy's territory to include Finale, Piombino and Monaco, giving it direct access to sea-ports and so strengthening Milan's position *vis-à-vis* Venice and Savoy.

1603 For the funeral ceremonies of the Empress Maria, **Tomás Luis de Victoria** composes music for the *Officium Defunctorum* ('Office of the Dead'), a work widely regarded as one of the masterpieces of late Renaissance polyphony.

1604 In the Netherlands, Albert of Austria appoints a Genoese financier, the **Marquis of Spinola**, to command his mainly Belgian army. In August Spain and England conclude a peace treaty. In September Spinola attacks and captures the Dutch port city of Ostend.

1605 Miguel Cervantes (1547–1616) publishes the first volume of his novel **Don Quixote**. A second volume will be published in 1614, two years before his death.

1606 The court returns to Madrid.

PRIVATE COLLECTION

Don Quixote pays court to two whores, whom he mistakes for ladies, outside an inn

1607 Villalonga is brought to trial for misappropriating crown revenues and forced to pay back 1.5 million ducats, an amount equal to one sixth of the crown's annual budget. Faced once again by insolvency, the crown suspends debt repayments to its bankers and other creditors. Lerma continues in power, persuading Philip III that all is well by

" As thus they discoursed they discovered some thirty or forty windmills that are in that field, and as soon as Don Quixote espied them he said to his squire: 'Fortune doth address our affairs better than we ourselves could desire, for behold there, friend Sancho Panza, how there appears thirty or forty monstrous giants, with whom I design to fight and deprive them all of their lives, with whose spoils we will begin to be rich; for this is a good war, and a great service unto God, to take away so bad a seed from the face of the earth.'

'What giants?' quoth Sancho Panza. 'Those that thou seest there,' quoth his lord, 'with the long arms; and some there are of that race whose arms are almost two leagues long.' 'I pray you understand,' quoth Sancho Panza, 'that those which appear there are no giants, but windmills, and that which seems in them to be arms are their sails, that are swing about with the wind, and do also make the mill go. 'It seems well,' quoth Don Quixote, 'that thou art not yet acquainted with matters of adventures. They are giants, and if thou art afraid go aside and pray, whilst I enter into cruel and unequal battle with them.' And saying so he spurred his horse Rozinante, without taking heed of his squire Sancho's cries advertising him how they were doubtlessly windmills that he did assault and no giants; but he went so fully persuaded that they were giants as he neither heard his squire's outcries not did discern what they were, although he drew very near to them, but rather said as loud as he could: 'Fly not, ye cowards and vile creatures, for it is only one knight that assails you.' **"**

Miguel Cervantes, *The History of Don Quixote of the Mancha*,
trans. Thomas Shelton (1612)

sustaining a lavish court style, paid for by the sale of offices and the debasement of Castilian coinage.

1609 Unable to pursue an effective military policy because of its debts, the crown agrees to a **twelve-year peace** with the Dutch, signed on 9 April at Antwerp. On the same day, partly to compensate for Spain's loss of face, an edict for the expulsion of Spain's *moriscos* is promulgated in Madrid. Eagerly supported by the clergy, and by the poor, the expulsion order is put into effect throughout the peninsula except Portugal. Over the next five years up to 300,000 'converted' Moors are forced to leave their homeland.

1610 In Paris, Henri IV is assassinated by a Catholic extremist on 14 May. As his son Louis XIII succeeds to the throne, his widow **Maria de Médicis**, a fervent Catholic committed to a Franco-Spanish alliance, assumes power as regent.

1611 In an attempt to reduce **royal expenditure**, aristocrats and hangers-on at court are ordered to return to their estates and live off their lands. For a few months Madrid becomes almost deserted, but by the end of the year the court is back in full swing.

1612 Maria de Médicis scores a political triumph when she arranges simultaneous marriages between her son Louis XIII and Philip III of Spain's eldest daughter Ana, and between Philip III's son and heir the *infante* Philip and her daughter **Elizabeth of Bourbon**.

1613 In Italy, war erupts between Spanish-ruled Milan and Savoy after Savoy's ruler, Carlo Emanuele I, occupies the

> The monarchy of Spain, which embraces all nations and encircles the world, is that of the Messiah, and thus shows itself to be the heir of the universe.
>
> Tommaso Campanella, *Discourses* (1607), quoted in Anthony Pagden, *Spanish Imperialism and the Political Imagination* (1990)

The Expulsion of the Moriscos

Following the fall of Granada in 1492, Spain's Muslims were given a stark choice: either embrace Christianity, or leave. Many chose to convert so that during the course of the 16th century *moriscos*, as they became known, accounted for between two and three percent of Spain's population. Their distribution in the territories that made up the Spanish monarchy was, however, uneven. In Castile and Catalunya their numbers were few, even after the forced relocations that took place after the **Second Alpujarras Revolt** of 1568; but in Aragon and especially Valencia *moriscos* were concentrated in sizeable numbers. Where they constituted distinct communities it was suspected, not without reason, that they secretly continued to practise Islam, but this was tolerated because such communities also made a meaningful economic contribution, either as artisans and small-time traders, or as labourers on the huge estates of Valencian and Aragonese aristocrats.

In court and ecclesiastical circles, however, the *moriscos* were perceived as a security threat: not only might they provide a fifth column inside Spain for the Ottomans, but in Aragon some *moriscos* had expressed enthusiasm for rule by French Protestants, whose reforming religion was closer to their own Muslim instincts. It is also the case that many poorer Spanish, confronted by the spectacle of such prosperous *moriscos* as there were, felt that they had been deprived of jobs and other opportunities by those who too often seemed unwilling to assimilate themselves to Spanish culture. In any event, a majority of Spaniards welcomed news of their expulsion in 1609. Only those landowners threatened with the loss of their *morisco* workforce protested, but their objections were ignored, drowned out by the general rejoicing, led from the pulpit by the Archbishop of Valencia, **Juan de Ribera**. Within the space of five years an estimated 275,000 *moriscos* were hounded out of Spain. Most crossed to North Africa. There, some became subjects of the Sultan of Morocco, some died of famine and exhaustion, some were butchered by Berber tribesmen, and some, settling at the port of Sale, became pirates, known as the Sale Rovers.

disputed principality of **Monferrat**. Although Savoy is defeated, the conflict arouses strong anti-Habsburg and anti-Spanish feelings in Italy.

1615 In July a small Dutch fleet, marauding in the **Pacific**, destroys a Spanish fleet off Lima.

1616 The Valencian painter **José de Ribera** (1591–1652) settles in Naples where he remains till the end of his life.

1618 As bullion revenues from the Americas level off and the Crown continues to overspend, the Lerma creates a special advisory council known as the *Junta de Reformación*, instructed to prepare a detailed report on Castile's economic ills and possible cures. But before the *Junta de Reformación* can deliver its report, Lerma falls from power on 4 October following a palace coup masterminded by his own son, the **Duke of Uceda**.

In Italy, there is a revolt against Spanish rule in the **Valtelline** – the long valley running northwards from Milan toward Austria. Milan's governor, the Duke of Feria, crushes the revolt and establishes new Spanish garrisons.

In Europe, the **Thirty Years War** is sparked when Protestants in Bohemia revolt against their Catholic ruler, the Habsburg Archduke Ferdinand (later Emperor Ferdinand II). Although the war, which in reality consists of a number of separate conflicts, is often confined to Germany, where it takes on a religious complexion, it masks a struggle between the Habsburgs and the French Bourbon monarchy for European domination. Spain is initially involved only indirectly, supplying arms and men to the Austrian Habsburgs; as the conflict widens however it will be drawn into direct hostilities with France. The Thirty Years War also fuels a renewed determination amongst the Dutch to establish the **United Provinces** as a fully independent state.

1619 The *Junta de Reformación* produces its findings in February. While it identifies several abuses, it fails to recommend the root-and-branch solutions advocated by some. The Duke of Uceda, now firmly in control at court, largely ignores the junta's report.

In the summer, Philip III leaves Madrid for an extended visit to **Lisbon**, partly to secure the Portuguese Cortes' agreement to the eventual succession of his son Philip. The king's youngest son, Ferdinand, is appointed Cardinal-Archbishop of Toledo aged just ten.

4000 soldiers on their way to the New World are drowned during a great storm in the Atlantic.

1621 Taken ill on his return journey from Lisbon, Philip III dies in the Escorial on 21 March, and is succeeded by **Philip IV** (Felipe IV), aged sixteen. Although more able than his father, Philip IV's youth makes him vulnerable to the intrigues of his favourite, the Andalusian aristocrat Gaspar de Guzmán, **Count-Duke Olivares**. Rather than openly assume the powers of a *Privado* for himself, however, Olivares persuades Philip IV to appoint his ailing uncle, **Don Baltasar de Zúñiga**, as chief minister.

In April the Twelve Year Peace with the Dutch United Provinces expires and is not renewed, mainly because of continuing Dutch interference with Spanish shipping. Amongst Philip IV's first acts is to confirm **Spinola** as commander-in-chief of the army in the Netherlands – since Archduke Albert has died without heir earlier in the year, direct rule over the Netherlands has reverted to the Spanish crown. At once plans are made to attack and reduce a Dutch stronghold at **Breda**.

In September the French **Catholic League** intervenes in the German wars by marching into Bohemia and Austria, forcing the Spanish Netherlands to respond in kind. Spinola crosses the Rhine at the head of an army of Belgian and Spanish troops, in support of Frederick of Bohemia,.

1622 Don Baltasar de Zúñiga dies in October and **Olivares** openly assumes the role of Philip IV's *Privado*. The effective ruler of Spain for the next twenty years, Olivares introduces some much needed fiscal reforms, purging the Crown of unnecessary expenditures, and expanding Spain's navy. His domestic policies are designed to centralize royal power, while foreign policy focuses on countering French aggrandisement.

Privateers are authorized by the Crown to operate out of the Basque port of **San Sebastián** against Dutch and English shipping in the Atlantic, North Sea and Baltic. Their activities continue for 70 years at the rate of four missions a year.

1623 In February Olivares promulgates **23 articles of reform** based on the findings and recommendations of the defunct *Junta de Reformación*. Among the measures imposed are a drastic cut-back in the number of civic officials, a ban on foreign manufactured imports, the enforced closure of brothels and new sumptuary laws outlawing excessive costumes. In many parts of Castile such measures are simply ignored.

1624 Olivares presents a secret memorandum to the throne urging greater unity within Philip IV's Spanish kingdoms. Aragon, Catalunya, Valencia and Portugal should be subject to the same tax regimen as Castile; and more non-Castilians should be given positions in government. In a separate initiative known as the **Union of Arms,** Olivares promotes the concept of a single Spanish army composed of troops from all the king's dominions, including the New World.

Relations with **England** deteriorate sharply following a failure by the Prince of Wales to secure the hand of a Spanish *infanta* in marriage, and England's subsequent decision to lend its support to the embattled Elector of the Palatinate in Germany, currently fighting against Spinola.

1625 Following a nine-month siege, the Dutch fortress city of **Breda** capitulates to Spinola on 5 June. The event is commemorated nine years later in a large canvas by the court painter Velázquez (see p.328).

In October a combined English and Dutch naval force attempts an assault on **Cádiz**, but is driven off by Spanish galleons and bad weather. Loyal Belgian privateers, operating out of Dunkirk, begin successfully harrying English and Dutch merchant shipping.

1626 Endeavouring to promote the Union of Arms, Philip IV and Olivares convene the **Cortes** of Catalunya, Aragon and Valencia. Aragon and Valencia reluctantly agree to

Conde-Duque de Olivares (1587–1645)

Although Don Gaspar de Guzman y Pimental was born into the top flight of Castilian society – his father was Spain's ambassador to Rome and his mother came from the prestigious Fonseca family – as a second son his career options were limited. In his teens he prepared to enter holy orders, and early on his obvious abilities were rewarded by his appointment as a canon of Seville. The death of his elder brother in 1606, however, dramatically transformed his life. Abandoning an ecclesiastical career, Don Gaspar, now Count Olivares, attached himself to the household of the *infante* **Philip** in Madrid. Of those charged with the prince's upbringing Olivares swiftly emerged as the favourite, or *valido*, and when Philip succeeded to the throne in 1621 it was natural he should play a prominent role in government.

In fact, Olivares effectively ruled over the Spanish empire for over twenty years until he was ousted in 1643. Unlike his predecessors as *Privado*, Lerma and Uceda, he took his responsibilities seriously, and endeavoured to make the monarchy work. He introduced **economic reforms** which, if they didn't exactly turn deficits into profits, at least kept the ship of state afloat; he attempted to contain the rising power of France by

grant new subsidies, although they refuse to allow men conscripted in Aragon and Valencia to serve outside their territories. In May the Catalan Cortes, held in Barcelona, outrightly rejects Olivares's proposals, seeing in them only an attempt to impose Castilian rule. Notwithstanding, in July Olivares publishes an edict announcing that the Union of Arms has come into effect.

1627 In January the Spanish crown again suspends loan repayments to its foreign bankers. The action is taken primarily to free the monarchy from its indebtedness to **Italian financiers**. The crown's military and other commitments, and the poor performance of the Castilian economy, quickly force him to reverse his position.

strengthening the **Habsburg alliance** with Austria; and by creating a more **centralized government** he sought to erode the differences between Castile, Aragon, Catalunya, Valencia and Portugal.

In such policies Olivares was up to speed with what was happening elsewhere in Europe. Yet none of them met with lasting success. After his departure the Crown once again got into severe financial straits, exacerbated by Spain's costly involvement in the **Thirty Years War** (1618–48), while his vision of a unified monarchy not only prompted **rebellion** in Catalunya and Andalucía, but also hastened Portugal's push for **independence**. Despite such failures, though, Olivares is remembered as one of the few true heavyweight Spanish statesmen of the 17th century. In part this had to do with his personality – dominating, moody, and inconsistent; and toward the end he was exhibiting all the traits of a manic depressive. Equally he is remembered as a **patron** of the arts and literature. It was Olivares who introduced Velázquez (see p.328) to Philip's IV's court, and who advanced the career of Spain's greatest playwright, Calderón de la Barca (see p.333).

When the **Duke of Mantua** dies without an immediate heir, the dukedom is claimed by a Frenchman, the Duke of Nevers, thus posing a threat to Spain's hold over the north of Italy.

1628 In March the governor of Milan, **Don Gonzalo de Córdoba**, intervenes directly in Mantua, sparking a three-year conflict between Spain and France.

In September Dutch 'pirates', in reality a force commissioned by the Dutch West Indies Company and commanded by **Piet Heyn**, capture the entire Spanish treasure fleet in Maatanzas Bay after it has set sail from Havana. The booty seized is used to enhance Dutch sea-power in both the Atlantic and Pacific oceans.

1630 Having failed to make headway in the Mantuan war against French intervention, **Spinola** dies in September.

Working in Cairo and Damascus, Ahmed ibn Mohammed **al-Makkari** compiles his *History of the Islamic Dynasties in Spain*, incorporating long extracts from now lost works of earlier Islamic historians.

1631 Seeking new revenues, Olivares imposes a **salt tax**, provoking riots in the Basque province of Viscaya.

The **Mantuan War** is concluded by the Treaty of Cherasco, which confirms Nevers as the new Duke of Mantua.

1632 The course of the Thirty Years War alters dramatically in the Habsburgs' favour when the Swedish king **Gustav Adolphus**, who has intervened effectively on behalf of the German Protestants, is killed at Lützen in November.

1633 Philip IV's younger brother **Fernando** (known as the *Cardenal-Infante*) is appointed regent in Brussels. Spanish troops in northern Italy are redeployed in Germany in defence of Bavaria against France.

1634 Increasingly frustrated by the cumbersome traditional councils that advise the monarchy on policy, Olivares creates the *Junta de Ejecución*, an executive body that rapidly displaces the Council of State.

In May the Holy Roman Emperor Ferdinand II and Germany's Protestant princes agree a cease-fire at Prague. In August Spain and England enter into a pact whereby the English agree not to support the Dutch. On 6 September a joint Habsburg army comprising Spanish and Austrian troops gains a decisive victory at **Nördlingen**, ending Sweden's ambitions to become a major European power.

At Castile's expense, a naval expedition is dispatched to Brazil in an attempt to recover Portuguese territories (mainly present-day Guyana) lost to the Dutch.

The appointment of the Habsburg **Princess Margaret of Savoy** as Governor of Portugal provokes disquiet among the Portuguese nobility.

1635 France enters into a pact with the Dutch in February, dispatches an army into Italy in March, and formally **declares war** against Spain on 19 May. In June what remains of the Spanish Netherlands are invaded by the Dutch from the north and by the French from the southwest.

A second expedition is sent against the Dutch in **Brazil**, but is no more successful than its predecessor.

1636 Mounting a counterattack, Spanish forces in Flanders invade France, reaching to within a few miles of **Paris** in August. In September a second Spanish army captures St Jean-de-Luz north of the Pyrenees.

1637 French troops cross into Catalunya. Seeing the Franco-Spanish war as a Castilian concern, most **Catalans** refuse a call to arms.

PRADO, MADRID/BRIDGEMAN ART LIBRARY

Portrait of Count-Duke Olivares by Velázquez. Olivares is depicted as if leading troops into battle, and the portrait may relate to the relief of Fuenterabbia in 1638

In October the Dutch recapture **Breda**, held by the Spanish since 1625.

In Portugal there is anti-Castilian rioting in **Évora** and other cities, in part provoked by Olivares's attempts to force Portugal into the Union of Arms.

1638 French troops besiege **Fuenterabbia** in Guipuzcoa (Navarra), inflicting severe damage on several Basque shipyards. In August a Spanish fleet is destroyed in the Bay of Gueteria. Although Catalans continue to refuse Philip IV military aid, Fuenterabbia is relieved in the autumn.

In December, the German prince Bernard of Weimar captures **Breisach**, severing the overland Spanish supply line between Milan and Brussels, and forcing Spain to supply its Netherlands army via the English Channel.

1639 As the Franco-Spanish war escalates, a larger French army invades Catalunya, laying siege to **Salses** in July. Though Salses falls to the French, Catalans still show reluctance to defend their homeland, and Olivares is forced to introduce draconian measures to secure **conscripts** for a countersiege in the autumn.

In October, the Dutch inflict a crushing defeat on the main Spanish fleet commanded by Don Antonio de Oquendo during the **Battle of the Downs**, off the English coast. Many of the ships ordered by Olivares in his drive to regain naval supremacy are destroyed or captured.

1640 The French garrisoning Salses capitulate to Spanish forces in January. In the same month a secondary war fleet, combining Castilian and Portuguese vessels, is forced by Dutch warships to abandon an attempted reconquest of **Pernambuco**, the main Dutch settlement in Brazil.

In February and March unrest spreads in **Catalunya** as Olivares billets his Castilian army on Catalan households prior to a fresh campaign against France. As the viceroy, the Count of Santa Coloma, loses control, Olivares orders the arrest of a *disputat* (deputy), Francesc de Tamarit. This increases Catalan resentment, now orchestrated by **Pau Claris**, a forceful priest from Urgel. In late April, a royal official is murdered at Santa Coloma de Farnès, which is sacked and burned by Castilian troops in revenge. Their action sparks a **general uprising** among Catalunya's rural communities, which form an army that takes control of Barcelona, and frees de Tamarit from prison. Olivares decides to moderate his policies, but to little avail: on 7 June violence erupts in **Barcelona**. Properties belonging to royal officials and other Castilians are burned, and the viceroy, Santa Coloma, is assassinated while attempting to flee by boat. Order inside the city is restored by members of the Catalan nobility, but outside Barcelona a peasant army continues to rampage. The **Duke of Cardona** is appointed viceroy, but dies suddenly on 22 July as the rebels seize Tortosa. As Olivares reluctantly orders the Marquis de los Vélez to organize a fresh military force to bring the revolt under control, Pau Claris enters into secret talks with the French.

A second revolt erupts on the other side of the Peninsula, in the form of the **Portuguese Revolution**, actively supported by Cardinal Richelieu of France. As the Marquis of los Vélez advances into Catalunya, a leading Castilian adviser, **Miguel de Vasconcellos**, is murdered in Lisbon, prompting a general uprising. The viceroy Margaret of Savoy, with few troops to protect her, agrees to return to Castile, and the Duke of Braganza is acclaimed **King João IV** of Portugal, ending the union with Spain that has lasted since 1580.

In Catalunya, the situation worsens when the citizens of Barcelona riot against those Catalan aristocrats who, fearing a rebel takeover, have begun closing ranks with the Crown. Beginning on 24 December, a reign of terror envelops the city, during which scores of 'Castilian sympathisers' are murdered.

1641 On 16 January, as the Castilian army closes on Barcelona, Pau Claris proclaims a Catalan republic under the protection of France. **Cardinal Richelieu** however refuses to commit French troops for the defence of Barcelona until Claris amends his proclamation to a declaration of allegiance to the French crown. Three days later French and Catalan troops confront and disperse the Marquis de los Véles's army outside the city, in the **Battle of Montjuic**. Shortly afterwards Pau Claris dies, and the Catalan Revolt begins to weaken as rival factions are opposed by Catalunya's own grandees. For a decade French troops remain in Barcelona and other parts of Catalunya, claiming the province as their own and waging a war of attrition against royalist forces.

Olivares is confronted by a third uprising in **Andalucía**, where the two leading grandees, the Duke of Medina-Sidonia and the Marquis of Ayamonte, have been hatching a plot to establish an independent kingdom. Although their conspiracy is foiled, Olivares faces censure by a majority of Castilian nobles and only survives in power through Philip IV's support.

In the **Far East**, the Dutch establish their authority in Malacca and Formosa (Taiwan), to the detriment of Spanish as well as Portuguese trading interests.

1642 In April, Francisco de Melo, a Portuguese general appointed to command Spain's Netherlands army, defeats the French at Honnecourt, leading to their eviction from Flanders. Fighting the Spanish in Catalunya, the French capture Perpignan in September, and annex the province of **Roussillon** to the French crown. In October the Marquis of Leganés, attempting a counteroffensive, is defeated outside Lerida. The death of the belligerent Cardinal Richelieu on 4 December offers hope that the French campaign may slacken.

1643 On 17 January Philip IV gives in to his queen's insistence that he dismiss Olivares, who is exiled to Toro, where he will die in July 1645. Instead of appointing a replacement *Privado*, Philip IV declares that he will govern his dominions personally. In the event, Philip struggles to perform his duties, and increasingly relies on the services of a younger courtier, **Don Luis de Haro**, a nephew of Olivares. With Philip's approval, Don Luis sets his sights on mending the rifts that have developed between Spain's component crowns.

Francisco de Melo advances into France from Flanders and lays siege to Rocroi in the Ardennes. On 19 May however his army is humiliated by a relief force commanded by the Duke of Enghien. A few days after the **Battle of Rocroi**, Louis XIII dies, and is succeeded by his four-year old son **Louis XIV**.

1644 Jerónimo de Villanueva, formerly Olivares's right-hand man in government, and an enemy of Don Luis, is investigated by the Inquisition on charges of heresy and stripped of his offices.

Negotiations to end the Thirty Years War begin in **Westphalia**. They will drag on for another four years, during which Spain's representatives convince the Dutch and others of the growing ambition of France, whose armies now occupy the Rhine.

1645 The **Inquisition** is ordered to investigate the fallen minister Olivares, but in July he dies before proceedings can begin.

In September, the poet and satirist **Francisco de Quevedo** (b. 1580) dies in Villanueva de los Infantes. Quevedo, an outstanding writer of Castilian Spanish, is remembered for his *Sueños* – coruscating portraits of contemporary morals and corruption – and for his picaresque novel *La Vida del Buscón* ('The Swindler') published in 1626.

> Here you will find all the tricks of the low life or those which I think most people enjoy reading about: craftiness, deceit, subterfuge and swindles, born of laziness to enable you to live on lies; and if you attend to the lesson you will get quite a lot of benefit from it. And even if you don't, study the sermons, for I doubt if anyone buys a book as coarse as this in order to avoid the inclinations of his own depraved nature.

Quevedo, Prologue to *The Swindler*, trans. Michael Alpert (1969)

1646 In September, a combined French and Dutch force captures **Dunkirk**, undermining Spain's capacity to combat Dutch sea-power.

Philip IV's only son and heir, **Baltazar Carlos**, dies.

1647 Excessive taxation imposed by the Spanish monarchy to pay for the war against France prompts a rebellion in **Naples** led by the fish merchant Tomasso Aniello. In October Aniello declares the kingdom of Naples to be a republic under French protection. There are also armed uprisings in **Sicily**.

Unable to service its debts, the Spanish crown declares itself bankrupt.

1648 In April Spain recovers control of Naples.

As peace negotiations in Westphalia draw to a conclusion the Spanish and the Dutch reach a separate agreement, the **Treaty of Münster**, signed on 24 October. By its terms the full independence of the United Provinces (present-day Holland) is recognized in perpetuity. Despite the **Peace of Westphalia**, which determines the boundaries and religious following of Germany's many smaller states, conflict between Spain and France continues, exacerbated by the discovery in August of a plot by the **Duke of Hijar** to seize power in Aragon with French help.

1649 Philip IV marries his second queen, his niece **Mariana of Austria**. During the year **plague** ravages the south. In Seville half or more of the population dies.

1651 The final campaign to restore royal authority over **Catalunya** and expel the French is led by the Marquis of Mortara and Philip IV's illegitimate son **Don Juan José of Austria.**

1652 After a prolonged siege the French garrison at **Barcelona** surrenders to Don Juan José on 13 October.

1653 As the last French troops withdraw from Catalunya, Philip IV undertakes to uphold Catalan liberties, and under these conditions Catalunya returns to the Spanish monarchy.

The crown, at war with **England** where a republican government has replaced the Stuart monarchy, yet again declares itself bankrupt.

1654 The English, having fought against and beaten the Dutch at sea, resume their interest in the Caribbean. A fleet dispatched by Oliver Cromwell fails to take Hispaniola but captures **Jamaica**.

1656 As war between Spain and England intensifies, Admiral **Robert Blake**, blockading Spain's ports, captures part of the American treasure fleet in September, aggravating Philip IV's financial difficulties.

1657 In March, England and France enter into an alliance against Spain. In April Blake destroys the entire Spanish silver fleet as it shelters off **Tenerife** in the Canaries.

1658 An Anglo-French army commanded by Marshal Turenne resoundingly defeats a Spanish-Belgian army during the **Battle of the Dunes** on 14 June. As a result French territory in Flanders is extended.

1659 The long war between Spain and France is ended by a treaty negotiated on the Isle of Pheasants in the Bidasoa River. Known as the **Treaty of the Pyrenees**, it cedes Artois in Flanders and the Catalan county of Roussillon to the French crown, and specifies that Philip IV's daughter **Maria Teresa** should marry Louis XIV.

1660 The Portuguese, with assistance from both France and England, resist military intervention from Spain. The Anglo-Portuguese entente damages Spanish trading interests in Manila. Because of this, and to contain Bourbon power, Spain enters into an alliance with the Dutch Republic in December, dramatically reversing former policy toward the Dutch.

The painter **Velázquez** dies in Madrid.

1661 Don Luis de Haro dies. His positions and responsibilities are divided between the **Count of Castrillo** and the **Duke of Medina de las Torres**.

1663 Don Juan José leads an army into Portugal to recover the throne for Philip IV, but is defeated at **Amexial**.

1665 The Spanish are again convincingly defeated in Portugal at **Villaviciosa** on 17 June, ending the last major campaign of recovery.

Philip IV dies on 17 September and is succeeded by **Carlos II**, his four-year old son by Mariana of Austria, who becomes regent during the boy's minority. Carlos himself grows up feeble in mind and body. Following Philip IV's wishes, government is entrusted to a *Junta de Gobierno*, a cabinet of mixed Castilian, Aragonese, Catalan and Valencian councillors under the tutelage of the **Count of Castrillo**. It is however the regent's Austrian Jesuit confessor, **Father Nithard**, who increasingly wields most influence at court.

Diego Rodriguez de Silva Velázquez
(1599–1660)

By the early 17th century a distinctive school of painting had emerged in Spain – sometimes called **Spanish Realism** – in which figures, often in shallow, darkened spaces, are isolated by strong lighting. It's an approach seen at its most powerful in the austere, monastic paintings of **Francisco de Zurbarán** (1598–1664), and in the more dynamic figure paintings of **José de Ribera**.

It was a manner followed in his early work by the most celebrated Spanish artist of his day, **Diego Velázquez**. Paintings like the *Waterseller of Seville* (c.1619) are direct and unidealized images with a limited range of largely earth colours. Velázquez may well have continued in this vein had he not been summoned to Madrid in 1623 by his fellow Sevillian, the **Conde-Duque Olivares**. Within a few years he was the principal court artist, and had established a personal relationship with **Philip IV** which enabled him to bring a new degree of informality to court portraiture. It also gained him access to the **royal collection**, where the paintings of **Titian**, with their rich colours and loose brushwork, made a particularly strong impact. Velázquez also benefited from direct contact with **Rubens** who was in Madrid in 1628 on a diplomatic mission.

Rubens encouraged Velázquez to make the first of two journeys to Italy in 1629–31, where he was able to study the Italian tradition at first hand as well as acquire works for Philip IV. He travelled widely and absorbed much. The results are immediately discernible in a work like *Los Borrachos* ('Feast of Bacchus'), which combines a greater depth of colour and freer handling of paint with the realism for which he was already known. The painting's matter-of-factness also reveals a typically anti-classical approach to mythological subject matter.

Velázquez's increasing facility as a painter can be clearly seen by comparing the portraits of Philip IV painted throughout his career. While the pose of the king is always fairly conventional, in the later portraits the colour intensifies, the picture surface becomes more animated, and there is an increasing emphasis in conveying atmosphere and a sense of the space around the figure. This virtuosic rendition of light and air reaches its apogee in the large group portrait known as **Las Meninas** (1656), where it is used to unify the stiff formality of the interior with the gestural spontaneity of the figures – including the painter himself – in a way that suggests a suspended moment in time.

FRICK COLLECTION

This Velazquez portrait of Philip IV was painted in 1644 during a succesful campaign against the French in Catalunya

1668 Spain formally recognizes Portugal's independence. The king's illegitimate half-brother, **Don Juan José**, excluded from government, and a sworn enemy of Father Nithard, flees Madrid for Catalunya, where he attracts a large following, influenced by his self-projection as a second Don Juan of Austria.

Diego de San Vitores, a Jesuit, leads an expedition into the Pacific from Acapulco and lays claim on behalf of Philip IV to **Guam** and other islands in the Mariana group (named after the Queen Regent).

1669 **Don Juan José** returns to Madrid to seek a power-sharing arrangement with the Queen Regent. Stopping at Torrejón de Ardoz on 24 February, he calls for the dismissal of Father Nithard, who the day after himself flees Madrid. Backed by popular support, Don Juan José enters the capital in apparent triumph. Prevailing upon Mariana to appoint a reformist *Junta de Alivios*, he fails to assert his own authority. The Queen Regent, unwilling to share power, is protected by a royal bodyguard under the command of the **Marquis of Aytona**.

1670 Outmanoeuvred by Mariana, Don Juan José accepts the post of Viceroy of Aragon, removing him from Madrid. Unable to govern by herself, Mariana of Austria turns to the son of an Andalucian army officer, **Fernando de Valenzuela**. Valenzuela's meteoric rise to power is resented by the aristocracy, but he curries favour with the Madrid populace by staging **bullfights** and distributing bread at the crown's expense.

The English, establishing a settlement at Charleston in South Carolina, begin making alliances with **North American Indians** against Spain, even though in July they gain trading concessions in the New World by the **Treaty of Madrid**.

1672 France mounts a full-scale invasion of Holland. In response Spain and the Dutch confirm their mutual defence pact by the **Treaty of the Hague**, signed in August. In September Spain declares war on France. By the beginning of the following year there is fighting in both Flanders and Catalunya.

1673 In September a combined Dutch-Spanish army commanded by the **Prince of Orange** forces France to withdraw from the Rhine.

1674 Celebrating his fourteenth birthday **Carlos II** formally comes of age, although power continues in the hands of the Queen Regent and Valenzuela.

In August the Dutch-Spanish army wins another victory over France at **Seneff**. Spanish attempts to recapture Roussillon from the French crown are undermined by renewed unrest in **Sicily**. Troops are withdrawn from the Pyrenees to crush a potentially fatal rebellion. France takes advantage by invading Franche-Comté in Spanish Flanders.

1675 A French war-fleet, sent by Louis XIV to aid Messina in Sicily, defeats a Spanish fleet off **Lipari** on 11 February.

1676 A combined Spanish and Dutch fleet commanded by Martijn de Ruyter is first defeated at sea off **Agosta** (Sicily) on 22 April, then mutilated on 2 June at **Palermo** where it has sought shelter. For the first time France enjoys **naval supremacy** in the western Mediterranean.

In December Castile's grandees, angered by the power exercised by Valenzuela, whom they regard as a commoner, collectively demand that **Don Juan José** be recalled to Madrid. Don Juan José, who has been campaigning against the French in Catalunya, marches on the capital, and Mariana of Austria capitulates. Valenzuela is arrested and exiled to Manila.

1678 In September the war between Spain and France is brought to an end by the **Peace of Niemegen**. Spain surrenders **Franche-Comté** to Louis XIV.

1679 Don Juan José dies unexpectedly in September, and the lacklustre **Duke of Medinaceli** becomes Carlos II's chief minister. Unable to stand up to the grandees, Medinaceli

Spanish Theatre

It was through regular contact with **Italy**, and *commedia dell'arte* in particular, that commercial theatre developed in Madrid and other Spanish cities from the mid-16th century. Audiences flocked to courtyards to watch either entirely new works, or re-renderings of established favourites. As in England, plays were commissioned for a meagre sum by the actor-managers of travelling companies, with little further benefit to their authors – although the most renowned actor-manager of the time, **Lope de Rueda** (c.1510–65), wrote his own.

None of the above really explains the extraordinary explosion of play-writing talent that occurred from the end of the 16th century onwards, a 'Golden Age' contemporaneous with the 'Jacobethan' theatre of Shakespeare, Marlowe and Jonson. Spain's relative isolation from the mains currents of European thought meant that her playwrights, unlike their English counterparts, were largely uninfluenced by classical literature and drama. Instead the Spanish three-act **comedia** derived from more local literary traditions – ballads, chivalric romances, the picaresque novel – in which tragedy and comedy intertwine in often complicated plots. Spanish drama also included one-act farces called **entremeses**, and one-act **auto sacramentales**, 'sermons in verse' that were played in the street on the feast of Corpus Christi.

Spain's first great dramatist, **Lope de Vega** (1562–1635), was also its most prolific, writing as many as 1800 plays – about 500 of which have survived. Not surprisingly, many have a spontaneous and energetic quality, with well-drawn – if often stereotypical – characters. Most of his plays fall into the category of *comedias de*

allows the **Council of State** to resume some of its power. The great offices of state however are increasingly sold to the highest bidder, or awarded by heredity.

1680 The Council of State **devalues** the currency by fifty percent following a sharp recession in part caused by the inability of Castilian textiles to compete with their Euro–

capa y espada ('cloak and dagger dramas'), light comedies of love and intrigue, but his best work draws on Spanish folklore and history. Among the most celebrated is *Fuenteovejuna*, which tells of a village's rebellion against a tyrannical nobleman.

Lope's successors include his follower **Tirso de Molina** (1584–1648), whose *El burlador de Sevilla* ('The Trickster of Seville') is the first drama to include the philander Don Juan, and **Ruíz de Alarcón y Mendoza** (c.1581–1634), who is credited with making the comedia a less artificial form. But it is **Calderón de la Barca** (1600–81) who, in the opinion of many, brought Spanish theatre to its highest point. Calderón's plays are more tightly structured than Lope's as well as more philosophical, and they combine a formal ingenuity with intense lyrical fluency. *El alcade de Zalamea* ('The Mayor of Zalamea') is a compelling study in the tensions between love, honour and religious morality, while his masterpiece *La vida es sueño* ('Life is a Dream') explores the individual's relationship with fate, in a bizarre tale of an imprisoned prince in which illusion and reality become indistinguishable.

In 1625 Calderón was spotted by **Olivares** (see p.316), and was recruited into the service of King Philip IV. Much of his best work was performed on an artificial lake at the newly constructed **Buen Retiro** palace near Madrid, but with the king's death in 1644, theatrical performances were banned for six years – partly in response to criticism by the church. Calderón took holy orders in 1651, and although he started writing again shortly after, by the time of his death Spanish theatre had lost much of its energy and originality.

pean rivals. In Castile prices collapse and the Crown declares itself insolvent. In Madrid and Toledo riots occur as businesses are made bankrupt. In these circumstances Seville relinquishes such control as it still enjoys over the New World trade to **Cádiz**, a more accessible port for the non-Spanish merchants into whose hands the great bulk of trade has fallen.

Beginning in August there is an uprising among the previously peaceful **Pueblos** in the province of New Mexico, initially directed against Franciscan and Jesuit missionaries who themselves have instigated violent measures against 'native idolatry'. Led by a medicine man called Popé the revolt lasts sixteen years.

1681 Death of the dramatist **Calderón de la Barca**.

1682 Death of the painter **Bartolomé Esteban Murillo** (b.1617). From about 1650 Murillo abandons the harsh modelling of Spanish Realism for a softer, more diffused approach (*estilo vaporoso*) that proves highly popular.

1683 Fighting again breaks out in Catalunya and Belgium as Spain and France return to war.

1684 Hostilities between Spain and France are terminated by the **Treaty of Ratisbon**. Philip IV cedes **Luxembourg**, formerly part of the Spanish Netherlands, to Louis XIV.

1685 The Duke of Medinaceli falls from power. He is replaced by the more energetic and forceful **Count of Orepesa**, who repairs some of the worst failings of the Castilian economy.

1686 In July the Habsburg Emperor Leopold I of Austria forms the **League of Augsburg**, a defensive pact against the blatant expansionism of Louis XIV. Philip IV joins the League alongside several German princes, England and Holland.

1687 Taking advantage of the fact that most of Leopold I's forces are fighting the Ottoman Turks, Louis XIV launches an invasion of the German **Palatinate** in October.

1689 Having contained the Turks, Leopold I, together with the Dutch, declares war on France in May. Spain and England shortly follow suite. The resulting conflict, spreading

The Nine Years War (1689–97)

Although the **Nine Years War** eventually petered out in a stalemate between its principal antagonists, Louis XIV and Emperor Leopold, the most obvious loser was Spain, whose reputation as a spent superpower now seemed confirmed. Not only was Carlos II forced to give up what became known as **Haiti**, but the battle of Fleurus in 1690 spelled the end of Spanish rule in any of the **Netherlands**. Indeed, had Louis XIV not decided to withdraw his forces from Catalunya at the end of the war, the consequences for Spain could have been much more serious.

Yet Louis XIV could not be called the overall victor of the conflict, at least on his own terms. The war had come about precisely because of a determination among several states, including the United Provinces (Holland) and England, to contain French expansionism, and in this they had succeeded. It was the Dutch king of England, **William III**, who, in the war's closing stages, did most to promote the ideals of the Grand Alliance, among which was the relatively novel concept of a **balance of power** between European nations. In one respect, however, the Nine Years War was a throwback to the past. Unlike the earlier, longer and much bloodier Thirty Years War, it was barely informed by religious affiliations. The Catholic Holy Roman Emperor freely made alliances with Lutheran princes in Germany, just as Carlos II cooperated with the Calvinist Dutch. Rather, at the heart of the conflict was the old spectre of **dynastic rivalry**, in this case between the houses of Habsburg and Bourbon – a rivalry that by 1700 was set to tear Europe apart, just because both houses still saw the Spanish throne as a possession worth having.

across much of Europe, but with the heaviest fighting in Catalunya and Flanders, will be known variously as the **Nine Years War** and the **War of the League of Augsburg**.

Carlos II's wife **Maria Luisa de Orléans** dies without providing an heir.

1690 A combined Spanish and Dutch army led by the Count of Waldeck is heavily defeated by the French at **Fleurus**. What remains of the Spanish Netherlands is placed under Bavarian administration.

1691 Orepesa is removed from power by a resentful Council of State, whose members' interests have been eroded by him. The Council prevails upon the king not to appoint a replacement minister. For a while power in Spain is shared out among Castile's **grandees**.

Carlos II's choice of **Mariana de Neuberg** – sister to the Emperor Leopold and daughter of the Elector palatine – as his second wife enrages Louis XIV, who hopes for an eventual Bourbon succession in Madrid. Louis escalates the war against Spain, and in July a French fleet bombards Barcelona and Alicante, killing many inhabitants.

In the New World, **Texas** (named after the Tejas Indians) is declared a Spanish province as a counter to growing French influence in the North-American midwest.

1692 Despite continuing French successes in the land-war, the comprehensive defeat of the main French fleet by an Anglo-Dutch force at **La Hogue** in May ends France's naval supremacy.

The sculptor-architect **José Benito Churriguera** begins work on the *retablo major* (main altarpiece) of the church of San Esteban in Salamanca. Along with his two brothers he establishes an exuberantly Baroque style of highly decorated forms, known as **Churrigueresque**, which exerts a

The magnificent Churrigueresque altarpiece of San Esteban, Salamanca

strong influence on Latin American architecture in the following century.

1697 At the beginning of the year France invades Catalunya and captures Barcelona. Louis XIV, knowing that Carlos II is unlikely to produce an heir, has begun scheming for a Bourbon succession to the Spanish throne, and peace negotiations to end the war in Europe are already under way. From September onwards a series of treaties are signed at **Ryswick** (Rijswijk), bringing the Nine Years War to a close. Although some territory in the Pyrenees is restored to the Spanish crown, Spain cedes Haiti – the western part of Hispaniola – to the French crown.

As Carlos II's health deteriorates – he is now regularly seized by fits – the question of his successor becomes uppermost in the minds of Europe's rulers and statesmen. While Louis XIV begins pressing the claims of the younger of his two grandsons, **Philip of Anjou**, the Emperor argues in favour of his own son, **Archduke Charles of Austria**. Carlos himself however prefers a third candidate, the youthful **Prince Joseph Ferdinand** of Bavaria.

1698 In October Louis XIV and Emperor Leopold secretly agree that the Spanish monarchy and its territories should be divided equally among the three main aspirants to the succession. When Carlos II learns of this arrangement he makes a fresh will in November, reaffirming his wish that Joseph Ferdinand inherit all his dominions.

Spanish interest in fully colonizing Florida revives with the founding of a new settlement at **Pensacola** in the Gulf of Mexico.

1699 The sudden death of Joseph Ferdinand in February leaves just two viable candidates for the Spanish throne, Archduke Charles and Philip of Anjou. Louis XIV and the Emperor again reach a secret agreement, partitioning the Spanish monarchy.

New Orleans is founded by Pierre Le Moyne as a French settlement at the mouth of the Mississippi. Leading to the creation of Louisiana, Le Moyne's initiative establishes a buffer between Spanish settlers in southern North America and English expansionism further north.

1700 In May Carlos II, determined that the crown should not be divided, heeds the advice of his Council of State and nominates Louis XIV's grandson Philip of Anjou as his heir. Despite the protests of his Habsburg wife, of the Dutch and of the English, he draws up a new will on 2 October. He dies on 1 November, and Anjou is proclaimed **Philip V** (Felipe V) of Spain.

8: Spain and the early Bourbons

1700–1808

The accession of the Bourbon **Philip of Anjou** to the Spanish throne in 1700 threw much of Europe into disarray and made war inevitable. Overnight the **Habsburgs** had lost half their domains. Nor did it help when **Louis XIV** refused to exclude the possibility of his grandson Philip V (Felip V) succeeding to the French throne as well. Britain also felt aggrieved, since it was now faced by the prospect of being squeezed out of its lucrative – if often illegal – trade with Spain's possessions in America, where it was beginning to assemble colonies of its own. The upshot was the **War of the Spanish Succession**, beginning in 1702, during which a Grand Alliance, that included Austria, England and the Dutch Republic, endeavoured to replace Philip with the Habsburg **Archduke Charles**, son of the emperor Josef.

By the time the war ended in 1714 Spain's **Italian territories** had passed to Austria, and Britain had acquired **Gibraltar** as a base from which to influence the Mediterranean. But Philip V was still king in Madrid, and Spain's American territories remained intact. Paradoxically, the conflict strengthened the new dynasty's hand. **Aragon**, **Catalunya** and **Valencia** had sided with the Habsburgs, and in reclaiming them the crown was able to suppress their Cortes, and many of the *fueros* that had previously sustained disunity. War had softened the country up for the kind of royal **absolutism** that was the hallmark of Bourbon rule. Instead of the old, cumbersome system of councils that had advised the Habsburg monarchs, administrative powers were vested in secretaries (i.e. ministers) answerable directly to the king, either individually or in cabinet.

These provisions did not, however, reflect any great strength in the person of the king himself. Rather they were introduced from France, in the first instance by councillors sent to Spain by Louis XIV. Neither Philip nor his immediate successor **Fernando VI**, who came to the throne in 1746, was an imposing figure. Rather, each allowed himself to be dominated by his wife – **Elizabeth Farnese** and **Maria Barbara of Braganza** respectively – and it was not until the accession of **Carlos III** in 1759 that Spain had, after over 150 years, a capable ruler.

Carlos III was the best of the early Bourbons, and his reign is sometimes regarded as a second golden period. Yet although he authorized some socially beneficial reforms, set the empire on a more prosperous footing, and began rolling back the power and influence of the Church, his domestic policies were broadly defensive – a matter of maximizing state revenues and doing the minimum necessary to protect the Bourbon regime from a new tide of political radicalism that would soon unleash the French Revolution. After Carlos III's death, Spain was once again encumbered with a weak king. **Carlos IV** was in thrall not only to his queen, **Maria Luisa of Parma**, but also to her favourite (and possible lover) **Manuel de Godoy**.

Throughout the 18th century Spain found itself at odds with Britain and her allies. Sometimes it was dragged into conflict through a **Family Pact** with Bourbon France; sometimes it initiated hostilities in an effort to recover its former prestige. Thus Spain became embroiled in a war against a **Quadruple Alliance** in 1718, the **War of the Polish Succession** in 1733, the **War of Jenkins' Ear** in 1737, the **War of the Austrian Succession** in 1740, the **Seven Years War** in 1761, and the **War of American Independence** in 1780. Though the fortunes of war were, inevitably, mixed, each inflicted a terrible strain on already stretched resources. And however much was spent, Spain was unable to impede Britain's steady rise toward becoming the superior world power.

Ironically, Spain was eventually overrun not by Britain, but by **France**. None of Spain's leaders was capable of appeasing the new militaristic French Republic that, from 1795 onwards, fell increasingly under the influence of **Napoleon Bonaparte**. As a result in 1808, with the utmost contempt for the Spanish military, and deftly manipulating a face-off between the king and his rebellious son, **Fernando VII**, Napoleon imposed French rule by enthroning his own brother, Joseph Bonaparte.

In retrospect, the Bourbon succession proved a poisoned chalice – since the continuation of a Bourbon monarchy in Spain provided Napoleon with a pretext for belligerence. Nevertheless, Spain in the 18th century was tolerably well-governed, even if this was done through perpetuating what in European intellectual circles became known as the *ancien régime*. The gap between rich and poor remained stark, and may have widened. On the other hand, the **Inquisition**, despite being active against the more extreme utterances of the Enlightenment, gradually lost its power. Opportunities in the American colonies were now available to all Spaniards, and there was a steady improvement in the **manufacturing capacity** of the north and the east of the country.

But apart from the introduction of a more centralized style of government, change was extremely slow. By 1800 ninety percent of the population still lived in the countryside, beyond Spain's relatively small towns and cities, and **agriculture** remained the principal employment. One-and-a-half percent of the population, were clerics of some description – priests, monks or friars – and the **Church** still controlled up to a fifth of Spain's domestic wealth. Compared to Italy, Britain, Holland or even France, there was hardly an educated middle class to speak of, outside of a bureaucratic corps trained to serve the state.

As the closing years of the century showed, Spain remained vulnerable to the traditional scourges of **famine** and **epi-**

demics that thrived on failed harvests. Least affected was the **aristocracy**. An ambitious programme to tax hidalgos, nobles and even grandees was abandoned in 1754. While most continued living off the fruits of their large estates, some gravitated to the Bourbon court, which was lavishly maintained in the French manner. A new palace was built in the heart of Madrid, away from the older Escorial, and at Ildefonso, near to Segovia, Philip V constructed *La Granja* as his summer residence. But if periwigs became commonplace, many other items did not, least of all books and pamphlets on such troublesome subjects as the rights of man or democracy. After 1716 the Cortes of Catalunya, Aragon and Valencia were subsumed in the Cortes of Castile, which in turn was convened only three times during the century – twice to affirm the accession of a new king. To the Bourbons, the idea of representation of the people remained unnecessary and unwelcome.

1700 Philip of Anjou, the younger grandson of Louis XIV, is proclaimed **Philip V** (Felipe V) of Spain in accordance with Carlos II's will. Since the French king has previously given William III of England an assurance that Spain would be partitioned, and since the Habsburg emperor Joseph is dismayed at this expansion of Bourbon power, Europe faces crisis.

1701 In February, shortly after his seventeenth, birthday Philip V enters **Madrid**, bringing with him a body of French courtiers and officials, among them **Jean Orry**, who sets about forming an administration, and the **Princesse des Ursins**. Philip's accession is confirmed by the Cortes of Castile, and in October by the Cortes of Aragon, Catalunya and Valencia meeting in joint session at Barcelona. In exchange the king is required to affirm the existing laws and customs of his various peninsular territories. Notwithstanding, Philip V grants France an *asiento de negros* – the right to trade black slaves in Spain's American colonies.

> **"** At the very least your decisions must be taken in agreement with me; and it is little enough to insist that one of my representatives attends your cabinet. **"**
>
> Louis XIV, writing to Philip V, February 1703

In September diplomats representing Austria, England and the Dutch Republic meet in the Hague, where a new **Grand Alliance** is formed to contain Louis XIV.

1702 Backing the Habsburg claimant to the Spanish throne, Archduke Charles, the Grand Alliance declares war on Louis XIV and Philip V in May, triggering the twelve year **War of the Spanish Succession**. Determined to reclaim Milan, Naples and Sicily for the Habsburgs, the Emperor dispatches an army to **Italy**.

1703 Fearing that Louis XIV intends to place a Bourbon monarch on its own throne, **Portugal** joins the Grand Alliance. Spanish colonies in North America come under attack from the English.

1704 In March Archduke Charles lands at Lisbon, and shortly after Alliance troops begin crossing the border. Philip V personally leads a counter-attack, supported by the **Duke of Berwick** (a bastard son of England's deposed Catholic king James II). An Anglo-Dutch fleet, commanded by John Byng, fails to capture Cádiz, but manages to seize **Gibraltar**. On 13 August the Duke of Marlborough crushes Louis XIV's main European army at **Blenheim**, and in the following month English and Dutch warships destroy a Spanish treasure fleet in the Bay of Vigo. Sweeping army reforms replace Spain's once-vaunted *tercios* with more modern regiments.

1705 Catalunya and Valencia, already softened by anti-Bourbon uprisings, fall to the Alliance. Although the Cortes of both provinces declare in favour of Archduke Charles, in Catalunya pro-Bourbon insurgents effectively harass Alliance positions.

1706 On 23 May Marlborough scores a second sweeping victory over Louis XIV at Ramillies, removing the Netherlands from Bourbon control. Philip V attempts to regain **Barcelona**, but is pushed back to **Zaragoza**, which itself falls in June leaving the Alliance with temporary control of Aragon. In June the Allies take Salamanca, and enter **Madrid** on 27 June, forcing the court to flee to Valladolid. In Italy, Prince Eugene crushes a Franco-Spanish army outside Turin on 7 September, forcing the Bourbons out of Italy. In the Balearics Majorca is seized by Alliance forces. Despite these setbacks Philip V shows unexpected resolve, rallying his forces and, with the help of his popular wife, **Maria Luisa of Savoy**, winning over Castilian hearts and minds.

1707 By the terms of the **Treaty of Milan** (March), the Bourbons surrender their interests in northern Italy, to the advantage of the Duchy of Savoy. In the summer an Austrian army occupies Naples.

On 25 April a Franco-Spanish army, commanded by the Duke of Berwick, defeats an Alliance force at **Almansa** – a victory that saves Philip V's throne and restores Valencia to Bourbon rule. Shortly after, the recapture of Zaragoza by Berwick returns Aragon to the Bourbons. Philip V uses these victories to formally abolish Aragonese and Valencian *fueros* in an edict issued on 29 June. The *fueros* of Catalunya are also suppressed, even though Catalunya remains in revolt. The Council of Aragon, established in 1494, is also abolished, ending any notion of the province's continuing autonomy.

War of the Spanish Succession (1702–14)

Hostilities began in 1702, after Austria, England and Holland revived the Grand Alliance against Louis XIV. Inevitably the conflict spread to the Caribbean and North America (where it was known as **Queen Anne's War**), with England pushing down from its East Coast colonies toward the Gulf of Mexico. Yet when peace was finally restored, in 1714, there was no clear winner. Louis XIV was bowed, but not beaten. England had emerged as a powerful state, but as yet without a significant empire to call its own. The Habsburgs still ruled Austria and Germany, and Philip V was still king in Spain.

Spain, though, was the country most affected. In 1702 its army and navy were both in poor condition, and to defend itself it had to rely on France, yet French support had to be paid for out of Spanish revenues and Spanish taxes. As the fighting intensified, so old divisions opened up between **Castile** and the principal 'provinces' – **Valencia**, **Catalunya** and **Aragon**. A majority of aristocrats played a watching game, withdrawing to their estates until they knew which way the wind was blowing. After the war's conclusion, only four of their number were indicted for disloyalty to the crown. And yet a great number of Castilians did enlist in Bourbon royalist armies, and it was the Habsburg forces of **Archduke Charles** that assumed the role of unwelcome invader. Other factors included the presence of Protestant heretics among Charles's troops, and the popularity of the Queen, **Maria Luisa of Savoy**. Famously, when 'imperial' troops occupied Madrid, the city's many prostitutes worked overtime to sap the strength of the interlopers.

At the war's end Spain was much reduced. Its Italian territories were lost, as was any Spanish claim to the Netherlands, and in the complicated peace negotiations taking place at **Utrecht** and **Rastadt**, **Britain** managed to obtain the most important Atlantic trading concessions. Yet in an unanticipated way the war gave the crown an unprecedented opportunity to forge a new kind of unity in Spain. Without it the *Nueva Planta* of 1716 would have been unworkable, and although the English continued to be a thorn in Spain's side throughout the following decades, the same period was marked by domestic recovery and growth.

In August Maria Luisa gives birth to an heir, Luis Fernando. Philip's growing military strength is supplemented by French reinforcements, and the arrival from France of **Michel-Jean Amelot** as his principal military adviser. In October Archduke Charles evacuates Madrid and sets up a court at Barcelona, where he is proclaimed Carlos III of Spain.

1707 In July Marlborough defeats Louis XIV's main army at Oudenarde. Britain also occupies **Menorca** in the Balearics in September. In Spain, the autumn brings a poor harvest, leading to widespread famine.

1709 Marlborough wins a fourth great victory over the Bourbons at **Malplaquet** in September. Faced with defeat in northern Europe and perhaps in Spain, the elderly Louis XIV contemplates suing for peace and suspends his support for Philip V.

1710 As tensions within the Bourbon camp intensify, Philip V declares his 'independence' from France. On 20 August the Alliance mount a counter-offensive from Barcelona and seize Zaragoza. As Philip V prepares to evacuate Madrid for a second time, Queen Maria Luisa appears on a balcony with Luis Fernando and rallies the people. Notwithstanding, a Habsburg army occupies the capital. Louis XIV is persuaded to intervene, sending a senior general, the **Duc de Vendôme**, to assist Philip V. On 10 December a Franco-Spanish army smashes the Alliance at **Villaviciosa**, forcing the Habsburgs to abandon both Madrid and Zaragoza.

1711 The Emperor Joseph dies in April, and Archduke Charles succeeds him to the crown of Austria and the Holy Roman Empire as **Charles VI**. Fearing that if he wins the war in Spain the Habsburg empire of Charles V will be revived, Britain begins withdrawing from the Grand Alliance, working instead for a peace.

1712 As peace negotiations commence in August, hostilities in Europe are largely suspended.

1713 Britain, France and Austria agree peace terms by the **Treaty of Utrecht**, signed on 11 April. Through this and subsequent treaties Philip V is confirmed as King of Spain and its American possessions, on condition that he renounces any claim to the French throne. He is stripped of his Italian possessions: Naples, Milan and Sardinia are ceded to Austria, and Sicily passes to Savoy. Gibraltar and Menorca are confirmed as British possessions, and Britain secures an *asiento* giving it a near-monopoly in the black slave trade with Spain's American colonies. Despite these provisions, the emperor Charles VI refuses to abandon his claims to the Spanish crown and so the war in Spain continues.

1714 Queen Maria Luisa dies of tuberculosis in January. In February Philip authorises the creation of a pan-Spanish Royal Navy.

On 7 March Charles VI agrees to forfeit his claim to the Spanish throne by the **Treaty of Baden**. Although Habsburg forces are withdrawn from Barcelona and other garrisons, **Catalunya**, knowing it will lose its customary rights, continues to defy Philip V, declaring war on him in July. On 12 September Barcelona falls to royalist forces and the civil war that has plagued Spain since 1704 ends.

In imitation of the French system of government, **Secretaries** (i.e. ministers) of state, finance, war and the Indies are appointed by Philip V in November, diminishing the power of Spain's traditional councils. Only the **Council of Castile**, tasked with administering justice throughout Spain, retains its authority.

1715 In January Philip V marries his second wife, **Elizabeth Farnese**. The queen immediately asserts her forceful personality by persuading her husband to send the Princesse des Ursins and other French courtiers home. Her own Italian adviser, **Julio Alberoni**, imposes himself on the king's administration.

BETTMANN/CORBIS

Portrait of Elizabeth Farnese with a lapdog

European tensions are eased by the death of Louis XIV and the succession of his five-year-old great grandson, Louis XV.

1716 On 16 January Philip V decrees a *Nueva Planta* ('New Plan') that formalizes absolutist changes to the Spanish monarchy. Viceroys are replaced by Captains-General in the provinces, all of which now become subject to the jurisdiction of the Council of Castile. Catalunya is particularly hard hit, with the abolition of Catalan *fueros*, its *generalitat* and its currency. The Catalan language is banned in law-courts and other official environments, and Catalan universities are closed.

Elizabeth Farnese gives birth to Philip's first son by her, **Charles of Bourbon Farnese**.

1717 Thirty-seven years after Cádiz has replaced Seville as the principal port for Spain's transatlantic trade, the *Casa de Contratación* (the monopolistic 'House of Trade' instituted in 1503) is finally moved there. José Patiño, appointed intendant to Cádiz, builds new dockyards and sets about creating a new navy designed to match Britain's.

Encouraged by the queen, Julio Alberoni masterminds a campaign that recaptures **Sardinia** from Austria. The island is assigned to Charles of Bourbon Farnese.

Philip V exhibits symptoms of mental instability for the first time.

1717 In pursuance of the queen's determination to create an Italian inheritance for her son, a task force for the invasion of **Sicily** is launched in July. To uphold the Treaty of Utrecht France, England, Savoy and Austria form a Quadruple Alliance against Spain in August. In September Admiral Byng destroys most of Spain's new fleet off Cape Passaro.

In North America a Spanish settlement is founded at **San Antonio** in Texas, later known as the Alamo.

Philip V and Elizabeth Farnese

The **Bourbon** succession of 1700 brought fresh blood to the Spanish throne, but no huge improvement in the moral character of its incumbent. In the past the French monarchy had been bedevilled by rivalry between royal sons, and **Louis XIV** was determined there should be no repetition. As a boy Philip had it drummed into him not to expect anything for or of himself, and he became an introspective, ultimately damaged individual. He briefly showed resolve when Louis XIV threatened to leave him in the lurch in 1710, but thereafter he became a divided man, torn between his wives and his confessor – unable to leave the royal bedchamber one day, and unburdening himself of his perceived guilt the next. As a result he was dominated by both his queens, **Maria Luisa of Savoy** and **Elizabeth Farnese** (also known as Isabel), yet was capable of treating each with great cruelty.

It was Elizabeth Farnese (1692–1766) who left a deeper mark on Spain. When she arrived in Madrid in December 1714 everybody was expecting the 22-year-old Italian princess to be a docile bedmate for the insatiable (yet monogamous) monarch. But for the next three decades she dominated Spanish politics, sometimes manipulating her husband through his libido, at others providing him with sufficient affection to nurse him through

1719 The Duke of Berwick leads a **French army** across the Basque frontier and occupies Fuenterrabia in June and San Sebastián in August. A British naval squadron destroys dockyards at Santoña on Spain's north coast, and Vigo and other towns are occupied in September. The Quadruple Alliance makes the dismissal of Alberoni a precondition for peace negotiations, which begin in December.

As Spain seeks to expand its manufacturing base a **royal textile factory** is established at Guadalajara.

1720 The **Treaty of the Hague** is signed on 17 February. Philip V relinquishes all claims to his former territories in

recurrent bouts of **insanity** – when Philip V, kicking and screaming, would lock his doors and refuse to attend state business. Though she suffered physical abuse, she endured it, not just because she saw it as her marital duty, but also to realize her own ambitions. Through his first marriage Philip already had heirs to the throne – Luis and Fernando. What, therefore, was to become of Elizabeth's own sons by him, particularly her eldest, Charles? Her plan was to secure an **Italian inheritance** for him, bending Spanish foreign policy and using Spanish arms to achieve her aims. In 1733 it paid off. Charles became **King of Naples and Sicily**, and then, when Fernando died without a male heir in 1759, King of Spain.

For thirty years Elizabeth Farnese was monarch in all but name. Her early favourites – **Alberoni** and **Baron Rippardá** – were foreigners, which made her unpopular among Spaniards, who referred to her as 'La Parmesana', after her native city. From 1726 onwards, however, she was responsible for appointing a series of more gifted administrators, beginning with **José Patiño**; and the result was that when her husband's death forced her to retire from the court, in 1746, Spain was in measurably better shape than when he had come to the throne.

Italy, and Emperor Charles VI gives up his claim to the Spanish Crown. The duchies of Parma, Piacenza and Tuscany, however, are set aside for Charles of Bourbon Farnese. Savoy is given Sardinia in return for handing Sicily over to Charles VI. French troops withdraw from Spain.

1721 Work begins on a spectacularly carved, Baroque altarpiece, known as the *transparente*, within the ambulatory of Toledo Cathedral. Designed by **Narciso Tomé**, it is completed in 1732.

1724 In January Philip V unexpectedly **abdicates** in favour of his eldest surviving son by Maria Luisa, Luis Prince of the Asturias. Although Philip and Elizabeth Farnese 'retire' to *La Granja*, a newly built palace at **Ildefonso**, they continue to manipulate affairs through the secretary of state, **José Grimaldi**. On 31 August Luis dies of smallpox, and his brother **Fernando** is proclaimed king instead. In September Philip V reassumes the throne, despite the opposition of many grandees who begin forming a faction around his 'dispossessed' son Fernando. As Philip and Farnese return to power, the Dutch-born Johann Wilhelm, created **Baron Ripperdá**, emerges as a new royal favourite, mainly because he claims that he can secure Elizabeth Farnese's son Charles's succession to the Holy Roman Empire. Before the end of the year Ripperdá concludes the **Treaty of Vienna**, which he persuades the Queen is in her favour. The treaty however only provokes foreign apprehensions.

The **Cortes** of Aragon, Valencia and Catalunya are formally subsumed within the Cortes of Castile, which convenes briefly for only the second time since Philip's accession. Navarra and the Basque provinces are permitted to retain their *fueros* on account of their loyalty to Philip V during the War of the Spanish Succession.

The **Count of Montemar** leads 30,000 men on an expedition to North Africa. The swift capture of Oran and Mers-el-Kebir partially restores Spain's military pride.

1726 Ripperdá, having failed to fulfil his promises to the queen, is dismissed in May. Government is entrusted to the more capable hands of **José Patiño**, who concentrates on introducing fiscal reforms and strengthening the navy for defensive purposes.

1727 Against a background of increasing hostilities in the Caribbean, Spanish forces begin the **Siege of Gibraltar** in an attempt to remove its British garrison; but although the siege is sustained for fifteen months the British hold out.

1727 Largely to protect Philip V, who is suffering a second spell of mental instability, the court removes from Madrid to **Seville**.

The Royal Guipuzcoan Company of Caracasis is established as a venture capital enterprise along Dutch and English lines. It provides Basque merchants with a near-monopoly in the burgeoning **chocolate** trade with Venezuela.

1729 The heir to the throne, Prince Fernando of the Asturias, marries the Portuguese heiress **Maria Barbara of Braganza** in January. Among those who accompany her to Spain is the Italian composer **Domenico Scarlatti**. Scarlatti settles permanently in Spain, where he writes the dazzling keyboard sonatas for which he will be remembered.

The **Treaty of Seville** concedes fresh trading rights to Britain in the Spanish Americas.

1730 An improvement in **American bullion revenues** contributes to the increased stability of the Spanish government from about this time.

1732 Through the **Declaration of Seville**, and following the death of the heirless Duke of Parma, Britain agrees to help Charles of Bourbon Farnese secure Parma, Tuscany and Piacenza, promised to him in 1720. In return the Spanish Crown agrees to pay Britain reparations for damage caused to its shipping in the Caribbean and Atlantic. An English fleet ferries 6000 Spanish troops to the Italian mainland.

1733 Although the court returns to Madrid, Philip V and Elizabeth Farnese increasingly reside at *La Granja*. Prince Fernando is placed under house arrest as plots to dethrone King Philip are hatched in his name.

France persuades Spain's government to enter into an alliance against the Austrian Habsburgs during the **War of the Polish Succession**. The agreement, known as the

Family Pact between the Bourbon crowns, is formalized at the Escorial on 7 November.

1734 After Spanish forces win a convincing victory against Austria at Britanto in Italy, Charles of Bourbon Farnese is proclaimed **King of Naples**. A second campaign overruns **Sicily**, which is added to Charles's dominions. To the annoyance of Castilians no attempt is made to reintegrate the 'two Sicilies' with the Spanish crown.

1735 The Italian architect **Filippo Juvarra** is employed to transform the palace and gardens of *La Granja* into a far grander royal residence.

1736 José Patiño, who has reluctantly helped Elizabeth Farnese achieve her Italian ambitions, dies in November.

Juvarra's garden façade of the palace of *La Granja* suggests a mini-Versailles

Government however continues to run smoothly under those trained by him.

1737 Robert Jenkins, an English sea captain, testifies to the House of Commons that in 1731 he was attacked by Spaniards trading in the Americas and had his ear cut off, precipitating the **War of Jenkins' Ear** two years later.

1737 Philip V descends into his final **madness** from which he never fully recovers.

1739 Spain and Britain endeavour to resolve their differences by the **Convention of Pardo**, but when Spain fails to hand over promised reparations Britain declares war in October. In November Admiral Vernon captures **Portobello** in the Gulf of Mexico. Although hostilities between the two countries will last nine years, fighting is largely confined to the Caribbean.

1740 In Europe, the War of Jenkins' Ear merges with the **War of the Austrian Succession**, in which Britain supports the Austrian Habsburgs against France and Bavaria.

In order to counter British naval attacks, the **annual convoy system** for shipping bullion from Havana to Cádiz is abandoned. By sailing singly more Spanish ships evade capture.

1741 Hoping to add Milan to her son's possessions, Elizabeth Farnese persuades Philip V and his government to dispatch an army to northern Italy to wage war against Austria.

José del Campillo y Cossio, an effective and imaginative administrator, emerges as the senior minister in Philip V's government. The reforms initiated by him provide a foundation for a revival of Spain's colonial trade that lasts until the end of the century.

1743 José del Campillo dies in April. The equally able, but more conservative, Zenón de Somodevilla – soon created

Marquis of Ensenada – assumes overall responsibility for government.

In May George Anson heads an expeditionary force into Pacific and captures the treasure galleon *Covadonga* as it leaves Manila.

The Bourbon **Family Pact** between Spain and France is renewed in October when Louis XV agrees to help Farnese in her Italian campaigns.

1746 Philip V dies on 9 July. His eldest surviving son by Maria Luisa, **Fernando V**, is proclaimed king and promptly orders his stepmother to leave Madrid. Elizabeth Farnese retires to *La Granja* and quickly becomes a focus for largely ineffectual intrigue against the king. The Marquis of Ensenada is retained as first minister, although Fernando also promotes Ensenada's main rival **José de Carvajal y Lancaster**. Despite such apparently decisive interventions, Fernando will be remembered for his weak character easily dominated by his queen, Maria Barbara of Braganza, who fails to provide him with an heir.

1747 Both the War of Jenkins' Ear and the War of the Austrian Succession are brought to an end by the **Treaty of Aix-la-Chapelle**. Charles of Bourbon Farnese is confirmed as Duke of Parma and Piacenza, but is excluded from Milan. Following the treaty, Ensenada makes rebuilding the navy a government priority. The number of Spanish warships is soon quadrupled, many of them constructed on the English pattern.

1749 In October Fernando VI announces wide-ranging **tax reforms** devised by Ensenada in his capacity as Secretary of Finance. Various existing **taxes**, including the *alcabala* and the *millones* (see p.300), are to be abolished, replaced by a single tax, called the *catastro*, based on **income** levied on the whole population (including hidalgos and aristocrats). Before such taxes can be raised it is decided to create a comprehensive register of existing properties and wealth. Ensenada also introduces a French system of provincial intendants, charged with raising revenues, and directly answerable to the king and his ministers. Aristocratic and ecclesiastical landlords however continue to evade taxation.

1750 In January Spain and Portugal agree to resolve boundary disputes in South America. As a result some 30,000 **Guarini Indians**, hitherto nurtured by Jesuits, are expelled from Brazil and forced to resettle in Paraguay. Jesuit protests provoke strong anti-Jesuit sentiment in Madrid.

1753 In consideration of a payment of 2.3 million *pesos* to the Vatican, Pope Benedict XIV signs a **concordat** giving the Spanish crown complete control over all church appointments, revenues and expenditures in Spain.

1754 Following the death of José de Carvajal in April, a clique led by the **Duke of Huéscar** persuades Fernando VI to dismiss Ensenada. His revolutionary plans for income tax are subsequently shelved, along with the register of properties commissioned by him and completed at the beginning of the year. Notwithstanding, it is estimated that Ensenada's reforms concerning colonial administration have increased royal revenues by eighty percent. A new, markedly conservative administration led by Huéscar takes shape, with important posts going to the **Count of Valparaiso** and **Ricardo Wall**, a minister of Irish descent.

1755 As anti-Jesuit sentiment grows in Madrid, Fernando VI is persuaded in September to dismiss his powerful **Jesuit confessor** Padre Rávago.

1756 The **Seven Years War** between France, Austria, Sweden and Russia on one side and Britain and Prussia on the other begins. Spain remains neutral at first.

1757 **Queen Maria Barbara**, having willed that her considerable wealth be sent to Portugal, dies on 27 August. Fernando VI becomes deranged, and government grinds to a halt.

1759 Fernando VI dies on 10 August. His half brother Charles of Bourbon Farnese, King of the Two Sicilies and Duke of Parma, succeeds to the throne as **Carlos III**. Taking a more active interest in government than his

The Enlightenment in Spain

Although there were many fine painters and writers during the three centuries that Spain functioned as a world power it failed to produce a single thinker of international stature. It also failed to contribute significantly to the development of **science and technology**, two fields that in the 17th and 18th centuries were propelling western Europe into global prominence. Partly this was a matter of chance – genius follows its own dictates – but more largely it had to do with the intransigent nature of Spanish culture, and the rigidity of Spanish power structures. **Roman Catholicism** remained the dominant ideology until well into the 19th century, and there was less social mobility in the peninsula than in Italy, France, Holland, England or Germany. Populous towns and cities – always the incubators of new ideas – were few and far between. Even by 1800 only two conurbations, **Madrid** and **Barcelona**, boasted populations in excess of 100,000.

Even so, and despite the best efforts of the Inquisition and some government officials, Spain could not remain wholly immune to the **European Enlightenment**. Spain's absolute monarchs nurtured a paternalistic notion of themselves, and this meant taking some account of the 'improving' ways and means being developed elsewhere. In the first half of the 18th century in particular, there was a surge in new institutions which provided Spain with at least the semblance of a modern nation. A **National Library** was created in 1711, a **Spanish Academy** in 1713, and an **Academy of History** in 1735. In the same period **Benito**

predecessor, he retains most of Fernando's ministers, only getting rid of Valparaiso. Upon his accession he abdicates the throne of Naples in favour of his third son Fernando.

1760 Carlos III's wife **Maria Amalia of Saxony** dies. Of their thirteen children only seven survive childhood. At the king's request, Pope Clement XIII authorizes the proclamation of the Immaculate Virgin Mary as the patron saint of Spain and the Indies.

Jerónimo Feijó, a Benedictine professor, compiled his immensely popular 9-volume *Teatro crítico universal* (1727–39), an encyclopedia that provided Spanish readers with a digest of the latest in scientific and technological knowledge.

Later in the century it was government ministers – often trained lawyers – who adopted 'progressive' ideas – notably **Pedro Rodriguez de Campomanes**, who encouraged the spread of relatively open-minded 'Economic Societies', and **Gaspar Melchior de Jovellanos**, whose *Informe en el expediente de ley agraria* (1795) not only proposed a rational reform of agriculture but dared to criticize the church and aristocracy for inhibiting productivity. Private printing presses, too, began publishing independent newspapers and journals, among them Luis Cañuelo's *El Censor* (1781–7), which attacked the government for not introducing greater reforms. On the practical level there were some startling innovations, not least the creation of Madrid's celebrated **Botanical Gardens** by Fernando VI, and of **model townships** along Spain's highways during the reign of Carlos III. Yet the works of such political radicals as Voltaire, Montesquieu and Diderot were vigorously suppressed in Spain, and once the **French Revolution** began censorship once again held sway. In retrospect, the Bourbon regime behaved much as other repressive regimes do. While it was prepared to adapt new technologies from outside, it baulked at genuine social awakening.

1761 Carlos III decrees that royal authority must be obtained for the circulation or publication of papal documents in his Spanish territories.

On the king's initiative the **Family Pact** with France is renewed as Spain prepares to enter the Seven Years War against Britain. Carlos agrees to help France regain its Canadian possessions, lost to the British following defeat at Quebec in 1759.

1762 Sensing Carlos III's intentions, Britain pre-emptively declares war on Spain in January. British forces seize Havana in August and Manila in October, paralysing Spain's trade system. To alleviate food shortages in part caused by war, the *fiscal* of the Council of Castile, Pedro Rodriguez de Campomanes, creates a free grain market in Spain, abolishing import tariffs.

Leopoldo di Grigorio, one of Carlos III's Italian advisers, and soon created the **Marquis of Squillace**, emerges as a powerful figure at court even though he holds no official position.

1763 The Seven Years War is ended by the **Treaty of Paris**, signed on 9 February. Manila and Havana are returned to Spain, but in North America Florida is ceded to Britain, which is also awarded territory east of the Mississippi. West of the Mississippi Spain is compensated with the territory of Louisiana, gifted to it by France.

In August Squillace is appointed secretary of war, replacing Ricardo Wall, who is held responsible for Spain's war failures. Grimaldi comes back as secretary of state and effective first minister.

1764 The costly Royal Palace in Madrid is completed.

1765 A royal decree opens up the Spanish Caribbean trade to Barcelona and seven other port cities in Spain, formally ending the monopoly of Cádiz.

1766 At the beginning of the year unrest spreads through Spain, induced by food shortages and additional taxes imposed as a result of the Seven Year War and expensive re-armament programmes. The **Madrid Uprising** of 20 March is sparked by the Marquis of Squillace when he prohibits the wearing of long capes and slouch hats in an attempt to prevent criminals disguising themselves. A mob of 5000 destroys Squillace's residence, and the minister flees to his native Italy. Next day the mob swells to 25,000. Ten Walloon Guards are killed outside the Royal Palace, and **Miguel Cayetano Soler**, president of the Council of Castile, is assassinated. Carlos III appears on a balcony and promises to dismiss his foreign ministers and allow people to wear what they like, then flees to his palace at Aranjuez. There is rioting in other cities, notably Barcelona, Zaragoza, Bilbao and Cádiz. On 11 April the **Count of Aranda** is appointed as Soler's replacement, and under his authority order is gradually restored. In May Carlos withdraws his concessions, and reneges on a promised general amnesty. A commission of inquiry into the causes of the disturbances, headed by the secularist reformer **Campomanes**, delivers its report on 31 December. It concludes that the Jesuits are chiefly to blame.

1767 In March a royal decree orders the expulsion of Spain's 4000 or so Jesuits. As well as provoking the Madrid Uprising, the **Jesuits** are accused of disloyalty to the throne in South America. As significant is their unswerving obedience to the pope, which has already led to their expulsion from Portugal and France. Land and other property belonging to the Jesuits is sequestered by the crown. In schools and universities Jesuit teachers are replaced by laymen, and the Jesuits' wealth is partly used to fund new schools and hospitals.

1767 Courting popular opinion, a royal decree reduces the powers of the **Inquisition** and relaxes its Index of prohibited publications.

1769 Reforms are introduced into Spain's **universities**. Greater emphasis is placed on science and technology, as well as the study of medicine. College entry is also made easier for the sons and daughters of commoners.

1770 British settlers are driven off the **Falkland Islands** in the south Atlantic by Spanish soldiers after Spain 'buys' the islands off France. War with Britain is only averted when Spain allows a British garrison to return.

1771 The king's oldest surviving son, **Prince Xavier**, dies of smallpox.

1773 Although he has proved himself an efficient administrator, the Count of Aranda is relieved of his posts in Madrid and sent to Paris as ambassador. As an 'Aragonese faction' begins forming around the king's new heir, Prince Carlos of the Asturias, Grimaldi re-emerges as Carlos III's first minister.

1775 A punitive expedition sent against **Algiers** – led by Alejandro O'Reilly and promoted by Grimaldi – turns into a military disaster, with 1500 men lost.

1776 Spain begins offering clandestine support for **North American** rebel colonials in their war of independence against Britain. In South America, the seizure of Colonia

> ❝ Throughout the kingdom it is said there are two factions at my Court. This will only cause damage, to yourself more than myself, since you will one day inherit it from me. Fostering differences between father and son now will inevitably encourage others in the future to goad members of your family into doing precisely the same to you. ❞
>
> Carlos III, writing to the infante Carlos, July 1776

from Portugal gives Spain control of the Río de la Plata (River Plate) and its estuary.

In December José Moñino, lately created the **Count of Floridablanca**, replaces Grimaldi as secretary of state.

1777 A royal decree, aimed at countering British aggrandisement, formally licenses free trade among all the territories of the Spanish crown with the exception of Mexico. Benefiting Barcelona and other peninsular cities, the decree hastens the emergence of a prosperous **Spanish trading bloc**.

Pablo de Olivade, a reforming minister and close colleague of Campomanes, is publicly humiliated following his arrest by the Inquisition two years earlier. Sentenced to eight years' imprisonment on spurious charges of heresy, Olivade escapes to France where he joins in a propaganda campaign against Spanish conservatism.

As British forces are tied down fighting American rebels, Spain consolidates its hold over northern **California**.

1780 As it becomes clear that Britain is set to lose its north American colonies, Spain openly enters the **American War of Independence**.

1781 The Spanish capture of Pensacola, leading to the recovery of **Florida** from the British, is hailed as a great victory. It is offset, however, by uprisings in two of Spain's own colonies, Peru and Venezuela.

1782 Spanish forces occupy **Menorca** in the Balearics, but again fail to dislodge the British from **Gibraltar**.

To help pay its war expenses the government begins issuing bonds (*vales reales*) which become established as a currency – the first time **paper money** is used in Spain.

1783 In March Carlos III issues a decree asserting that **manual labour** is honourable, and that hidalgos should not consider it demeaning to engage in trade.

Carlos III (1716–88)

Carlos III has always been thought the best of the 18th century Spanish Bourbon monarchs, and the only one who was not inordinately beholden to his wife or wives – unsurprisingly, since **Maria Amalia of Saxony**, to whom he was devoted, died in 1760 two years after his accession. Thereafter Carlos remained a chaste widower. Significantly too, by 1758 he already had 25 years' experience as a ruler – in **Naples** he had established a third, generally well-regarded Bourbon regime that continued under his younger son Fernando. Notwithstanding, his reign got off to the worst possible start. Inheriting his mother **Elizabeth Farnese's** ambitiousness, he took Spain into the near-global **Seven Years War** just when the armies of Britain and Prussia were proving invincible. For two years Spain was devastated by a naval blockade that severed the Atlantic trade, and at the end of it Carlos had nothing to show except the loss of **Florida**. These setbacks, though, inspired him to revive Spain's standing as a first-rate power. In the years that followed he repaired Spain's economy, revived the American empire by introducing a system of free trade between its constituent parts, reinforced Spain's domestic government, and reduced the power of the Church both by expelling the Jesuits and by gaining important concessions

In September the **Peace of Versailles** concludes the American War of Independence. Florida and Menorca are confirmed as Spanish possessions, although Spain is forced to cede the Bahamas to Britain, as well as to reaffirm British trading privileges in its American colonies.

The reforming minister Campomanes is appointed president of the Council of Castile.

1784 A fresh campaign is mounted against Algiers in an attempt to assert Spanish authority over the Maghreb, but meets with no more success than the campaign of 1775 – partly because Muslim Algerians are given

from the papacy. As a result, at his death in 1788 Spain was indeed once more a nation to be reckoned with, even if it fell short of its 16th century imperial grandeur.

A well-known portrait by **Francisco de Goya** (see p.374) depicts the king as a countryman, attired in casual gear, and seemingly unconcerned with the trammels of power. The reality was rather different. Although Carlos was an obsessively keen hunter, riding out twice a day, he was equally a hard worker, dedicated to consolidating the **absolutist monarchy** he had inherited. Again like his mother, he had a knack of appointing capable ministers – notably the **Counts of Aranda** and **Floridablanca** – but he also chose them because of their proven loyalty to the throne in general and his own ideas in particular. Toward the aristocracy at large he displayed a patient, tolerant attitude, so long at least as they behaved with decorum in Madrid – the Dukes of Osuna and Arcos were both temporarily banished from court for openly liaising with **actresses**. But toward his other subjects he could be distinctly duplicitous. Having made concessions to the **citizens of Madrid** during their uprising in 1766, he reneged on them as soon as it was safe to do so, and many of his so-called reforms were thinly-disguised means of social control.

military support by France.

1785 Spain is badly affected by the first of three consecutive **bad harvests**, leading to food shortages, famine, the spread of epidemics and sporadic rioting.

1786 Carlos III's health goes into decline after he begins having fainting fits.

1787 Spain's long-emergent system of cabinet government is given formal expression by the creation of a *Junta de Estrada*. The crown prince, previously excluded from government, attends its sessions as his father continues to sicken.

Unauthorized **clerical assemblies** are prohibited by a decree drawn up by the anti-clerical Campomanes.

1787 Carlos III dies on 14 December and is succeeded by his forty year-old son **Carlos IV**. Floridablanca is retained as chief minister.

1789 The **Cortes of Castile**, representing all of Spain's provinces, convenes for only the third time in the 18th century, but is dissolved soon after it has affirmed Carlos IV's accession to the throne.

In Paris, the **French Revolution** begins when Louis XVI is forced to accept a constitution by a radical National Assembly amid scenes of public disorder and violence. Taking note of these events, and their threat to Bourbon rule in Spain, Floridablanca orders the reinforcement of troop levels in the Pyrenees.

1790 Tax protests produce a winter of violent discontent in Galicia.

1791 In February, as French revolutionary ideas radiate through Europe from Paris, Floridablanca orders the suppression of private printing presses. Only official newspapers are allowed. The **Inquisition** is re-empowered, and used by government to suppress revolutionary literature imported from France and impose strict **censorship**. Two progressive ministers, Campomanes and Gaspar Melchior de Jovellanos, are removed from office. Other intellectuals are harassed.

1792 On 28 February Floridablanca is imprisoned on a charge of abusing his power, as Carlos IV endeavours to appease French politicians angered by Floridablanca's opposition to France's recently instituted constitutional monarchy. Floridablanca's fall is partly a consequence of an aristocratic faction led by the **Count of Aranda**, who takes over as first minister. The *Junta de Estrada* is replaced

> It is said that the century of enlightenment has taught man his rights. But it has deprived him of true happiness and contentment and of his personal and family security. In Spain we do not want so much enlightenment – insolence in deeds, words and writings against legitimate powers.
>
> Floridablanca, writing to the Spanish ambassador in Paris, 1791, quoted in John Lynch, *Bourbon Spain* (1989)

by an old-style **Grand Council**, whose members include several grandees not directly involved in government.

Aranda works to appease the new government in France in the hope of saving the Bourbon monarchy there. In August however **Louis XVI** is deposed and a **Republic** declared. On 15 November Carlos IV dismisses Aranda. **Manuel de Godoy**, a favourite of the queen, emerges as the new man at court.

In the Maghreb, Oran is evacuated in February after the government decides its garrison is too expensive to maintain.

1793 Louis XVI is executed on 21 January. On 7 March the French Republic, already at war with Britain, declares war on Spain, encouraging the two countries into an unlikely alliance. Despite the activities of French agents, no revolutionary uprising occurs in the peninsula; rather support for the king, and even Godoy, is emphatic. In April Spain goes onto the offensive, occupying **Roussillon**. In August an Anglo-Spanish fleet captures the important French port of **Toulon** together with its naval arsenal. The Anglo-Spanish entente however deteriorates amid mutual distrust and recrimination.

Manuel de Godoy (1767–1851)

No other Spanish figure in the age of Napoleon has excited such revulsion or such sympathy as **Manuel de Godoy** – the archetypal self-server who nonetheless demonstrated unswerving loyalty to his royal patrons. Born into impoverished minor nobility in Badajoz, in 1784 he went to Madrid to seek his fortune, enlisting in the palace guard. Soon after he was 'noticed' by the heir presumptive's wife, **Maria Luisa of Parma**. He fell off his horse on parade, but remounted so smartly that the future queen couldn't help but lose her heart – so the story goes. Almost certainly they became lovers, though that did not prevent **Carlos IV** from sharing Maria Luisa's admiration. To the consternation of the court Godoy became secretary of state in 1793, aged 25, and in 1795 was given the soubriquet **'Prince of Peace'** after negotiating the Treaty of Basle.

Other titles followed, among them *generalísimo*, even *alteza serenísima* ('serene highness'). In power, Godoy ran a court of his own, his antechamber crowded with beautiful women petitioning on behalf of their husbands, and he wasted few opportunities to enlarge his wealth. In 1797 he further scandalized society by marrying **Maria Teresa de Borbón**, a cousin of the king, while continuing to support a mistress, **Pepita Tudó**. Except for the years 1798–1800 he retained and augmented his offices, right up until the moment Napoleon annexed Spain. In retrospect he has been blamed for all the calamities that led to surrender, although the policies he pursued were largely those dictated to him. Despite his complete lack of qualifications for running a government, he learned quickly, at least when it came to the minutiae of daily business. Subsequently he joined Carlos IV and Maria Luisa in exile in **Rome**, and only left when the ex-king died in 1819. The remainder of his days were spent in **Paris**, where he lived off a meagre pension. In 1847 **Isabel II** restored some of his titles and properties in Spain, but by then Godoy, now in his eighties, preferred to stay put, mulling over what might have been, and what never was.

1794 Counterattacking, the French Republic reoccupies Roussillon, then invades Navarra and Catalunya. In November French troops seize **Gerona**, but fail to capture Barcelona.

1795 Spain concludes a separate **peace treaty** with France, signed at Basle in Switzerland on 22 July after French forces take Vitoria. **Santo Domingo** in the Caribbean is ceded to the Republic in return for the French evacuation of Catalunya, but Spain loses no other territory. Godoy, who has brokered the treaty, is hailed as the **Príncipe de la Paz** ('Prince of Peace') by Carlos IV and Maria Luisa.

1796 In February the revolutionary 'conspiracy of San Blas' led by **Juan Piconell** is foiled by government agents.

Spain and France enter into an alliance against Britain by the **Treaty of Ildefonso**, signed on 18 August. In effect Spanish armed forces are put at France's disposal. Accordingly, on 5 October Spain declares war against Britain.

1797 An English fleet commanded by Horatio Nelson routs the Spanish navy off **Cape St Verde** in February. Cádiz and other ports are blockaded, severely damaging Spain's transatlantic trade, as well as its finances. To keep Spain's colonies on side, 'neutral trade' with the United States of America is legalized.

> ❝ The Spaniards are most obstinately attached to their old customs. I heard of two men who left a manufactory at Guadalaxara because the Proprietor of it chose to introduce wheelbarrows. 'No,' they said,'they were Spaniards, and it was only fit for beasts to draw carriages!' ❞
>
> Robert Southey, *Letters Written During a Journey to Spain* (1797)

At the year end Jovellanos and the equally left-leaning Luis de Urquijo, known for his translations of Voltaire, are invited to join a new 'reform government' at France's insistence. Conversely, those Jesuits expelled in 1767 are allowed to return to Spain.

1798 On 28 March Godoy resigns from the government following a contretemps with Queen Maria Luisa, but also because France wants his dismissal. Urquijo becomes first minister and the previously disgraced Miguel Cayetano Soler the finance minister. In September Carlos IV decrees the sale of property belonging to religious charitable institutions, the proceeds being exchanged for government bonds at three percent per annum. Although the bonds rapidly lose their face value, this and other measures help create a free market in property in Spain.

1799 Francisco de Goya (see p.374) is appointed First Painter at the court of Carlos IV.

1800 Following a series of French defeats, Urquijo is dismissed by Carlos IV and subsequently imprisoned. **Godoy** is restored to favour in December after agreeing to help Napoleon Bonaparte campaign against Portugal.

A **yellow fever** epidemic kills up to a quarter of the population in some areas of Andalucía.

At the turn of the century Spain's population is estimated at 10.5 million, a rise of 3 million since 1700.

1801 In May Godoy personally leads an army against Portugal which surrenders within 3 weeks – a campaign known as the **War of the Oranges**. Godoy is rewarded with the title *generalísimo,* and also becomes Spain's High Admiral.

Spain returns **Louisiana** to France, which sells it to the United States in 1803. In North America Spain's sole surviving territory is **California**. In an attempt to extend California northwards, Spanish settlers reach Vancouver Island.

1802 In March France and Britain suspend hostilities through the **Peace of Amiens**, signed without reference to Spain. Knowing that war will return, the Spanish government desperately attempts to enlarge its military, leading to anti-conscription unrest in Valencia and the Basque province of Viscaya.

PRIVATE COLLECTION

Goya's *The Disasters of War* were produced in response to the Spanish resistance to Napoleon. Plate 15 is entitled simply 'Y no hai remedio' ('And it can't be helped'). Fear of censorship meant that the etchings were not published in Goya's lifetime

Francisco Goya y Lucientes
(1746-1828)

In one of his famous series of etchings called *Los Caprichos*, **Francisco de Goya** depicts a sleeping man behind whom a cloud of bats and owls hover menacingly. Inscribed on the stone block against which the man leans are the words *El sueño de la razon produce monstruos* ('The Sleep of Reason Produces Monsters'), a statement that encapsulates Goya's lifelong concern with the darker side of his own imagination and with what he called the 'human errors and vices' that surrounded him.

Born in Fuendetodos, Goya studied painting first at nearby Zaragoza, then in Madrid and Italy. In 1775, with the help of his brother-in-law, and sometime teacher, **Francisco Bayeu**, Goya secured employment at court, joining a small group of artists who produced brightly coloured and idealized genre scenes as designs for **tapestries** for the royal palaces. Goya's regular exposure at court to the paintings of Velázquez (see p.328) helped him to develop an increasingly fluent and delicate touch, and he was soon the portrait painter of choice with both the fashionable and the prestigious.

By the time he was appointed **First Painter** to Carlos IV in 1799, Goya was already suffering from the deafness that was to blight the rest of his life and intensify the essential pessimism of his vision. He now had the official task of depicting the

1803 Hostilities between France and Britain resume in May. Spain only remains neutral by paying a substantial **subsidy** to France for 'protecting' its American interests, set at six million *livres* a month.

A failed harvest leads to **famine** in Castile and parts of Andalucía.

1804 On 18 May Napoleon Bonaparte is proclaimed Emperor in Paris. In December Spain is persuaded by

profoundly unattractive royal family, which he did with a ruthless acuity. Indeed some have seen his famous large canvas of *The Family of Carlos IV* (1800), in which the gorgeousness of the costume painting is in sharp contrast to the vacuous expressions on display, as satirical in intent. What is more likely is that it reflects the traditional Spanish predilection for realism at its most uncompromising. Satire and social criticism are very much in evidence in the etchings, however; in particular in *Los Caprichos* which attack religious superstition, and *Los desastres de la guerra* ('The Disasters of War'), which for the first time capture, as images, the full viciousness and horror of war.

Goya retained his position at court during the French occupation, and after the restoration of Fernando VII in 1814, but, as a liberal intellectual, he was profoundly disenchanted by the violence and repression of those years. In 1819, following a serious illness, he bought a small house on the edge of Madrid, the *Quinta del Sordo*, which he proceeded to decorate with a series of wall-paintings in which his view of the essential destructiveness and brutality of man is given full rein in darkly foreboding paintings like *Saturn Devouring his Children*. His final years were spent in France, as a voluntary exile, and he died at **Bordeaux** in 1824.

him to re-enter the war against Britain after four Spanish treasure ships are intercepted setting out from Buenos Aires.

1805 British naval supremacy is underlined when the combined fleets of Spain and France, ordered by Napoleon to clear the way for an invasion of England, are defeated by Lord Nelson during the **Battle of Trafalgar** on 21 October. In Spain, a conspiracy against Carlos IV by the heir apparent **Prince Fernando** and his followers is uncovered.

While the prince's fellow conspirators are punished, no action is taken against Fernando other than having him removed from Madrid.

1807 A papal bull issued in February authorizes the Spanish crown to appropriate one seventh of Church properties to help pay for its wars. Godoy, who has devised this scheme, immediately loses the support of clerics and some aristocrats, who begin plotting his removal.

The **Treaty of Fontainebleau**, concluded on 27 October between Spain and France, provides for the eventual partitioning of Portugal between the two states, with the Algarve being given to Godoy. Two days later Prince Fernando, now discovered to be actively encouraging opposition to Godoy, is placed under arrest.

In November a Franco-Spanish army occupies Portugal, forcing its royal family to flee to Brazil. A large part of the French army however remains encamped on the Ebro in Spain.

1808 On 17 March an uprising in Aranjuez engineered by the 'Fernandistas' and secretly supported by France forces Godoy to hide in his own attic. Discovered two nights later he is imprisoned. As rioting intensifies, Carlos IV abdicates in favour of his son. The French army enters Madrid on the 23 March and Fernando (*el Deseado*, the 'desired one') is proclaimed King the next day. When **Fernando VII** is unable to shake off French control, Carlos IV rescinds his abdication. Carlos, Maria Luisa and Godoy are seized by French troops and taken to Paris. Napoleon then 'invites' Fernando to a meeting at Bayonne. With both Spain's kings on French soil, Napoleon is able to dictate terms. Fernando VII is persuaded to relinquish his crown to the Emperor, who immediately transfers it to his brother **Joseph Bonaparte**. The Spanish royals are interned in France.

CORBIS

PRISION DE GODOY

A popular print showing the arrest and imprisonment of Manuel Godoy (kneeling), who is confronted by the new king, Fernando VII

9: Later Bourbon Spain

1808–1931

Napoleon's decision to annex Spain in 1808 was one of his costliest errors. Almost immediately large parts of the country rose up in spontaneous revolt, initiating a protracted **guerrilla war**. As seriously, Napoleon's principal enemy, **Britain**, which until then had been hostile to Spain, now became its ally. For the following six years French and British armies fought each other across the Iberian peninsula, tying down Napoleon's troops when they were needed elsewhere. Eventually the Bonapartists were defeated, and Portugal as well as Spain was 'liberated'. In the wider picture, the **Duke of Wellington**'s prestigious victories proved the necessary prelude to Napoleon's final defeat at Waterloo in 1815.

A year before Waterloo **Fernando VII** returned to Madrid, and Bourbon rule resumed. The Spain Fernando came back to however was vastly different from the Spain he had been persuaded to leave. In his absence a provisional government had been created by urban *juntas* opposed to **Joseph Bonaparte**, with a new Cortes, or national assembly, first convened in Cádiz. In 1812 the same body issued a **Constitution** which, though scarcely revolutionary, nonetheless set limitations on royal power. Moreover, the Cádiz Cortes engendered an entirely new element in Spanish politics. The **Liberals**, as they called themselves, were not traditional stakeholders in the national power-structure, but mainly professional types drawn from the upper ranks of Spain's small urban constituency.

This, for Spain, was the most important domestic consequence of France's intervention. The Liberals were not a group who had been waiting in the wings. Rather they were created by the circumstances that arose in 1808. The unprecedented freedom of expression that occurred in the debating chamber at Cádiz inspired Liberalism, not the other way round. But having once tasted power, Liberals were loathe to give it up, and much of Spain's political history for the following century and beyond was consumed by a seemingly irresoluble contest between Liberal parliamentarians on the one hand and an intransigent Crown on the other.

As early as 1843, however, Spain's political landscape had become markedly more complex than the simple matrix of a liberal-royalist face-off may suggest. The Liberals themselves had divided into two broad camps, calling themselves **'Moderates'** and **'Progressives'**. While the Moderates became, to all intents and purposes, conservatives, the Progressives pushed for more radical change, and the throne was sometimes able to hold its own by playing the one off against the other. But there were other developments too. The 1840s saw the emergence of a group calling themselves **Democrats**, prepared to espouse republican ideals, and sometimes also prepared to enter into an alliance with the Progressives, who, like the Moderates, still upheld the ideal of a constitutional monarchy. Then toward the end of the century, in Barcelona and other cities, there emerged forms of **proletarian socialism**, including **anarchism**, influenced and inspired by political ideologies spawned outside Spain, but which increasingly exposed Liberals of every kind as upholders of entrenched, upper middle-class values.

All this was further complicated by the persistence of **regionalism** in Spanish politics, particularly in Catalunya. But there was also movement on what could be termed the far right. From the moment of **Isabel II**'s accession in 1833, many traditionalists – especially in Navarra and Aragon as well as even in Catalunya – vehemently objected to the succession of a female. Support grew for the queen's uncle, Fernando VII's brother **Don Carlos** – and out of this sprang the phenomenon of the **Carlists**. Between 1833 and 1839, and again in 1872–76, the Carlists plunged Spain into civil war, and there were attempted uprisings in other years, creating a well-defined reactionary tradition that continued into the 20th century.

Liberals of every hue prided themselves on being **constitutionalists**, but the problem was no constitution they could devise was sufficiently inclusive to contain all the active political forces. Periodically, therefore, the Bourbons were able to take advantage of prevailing turmoil. Conversely, the forces ranged against them sometimes proved irresistible. In 1868, during a 'Glorious Revolution', they were even expelled. In their place **Amadeo of Savoy** was invited to occupy the throne, and when, in 1873, fed up with the cut and thrust of Spanish politics, he abdicated, the **First Republic** was proclaimed. But this only lasted a year, whereupon the Bourbons returned.

The 'restoration' of **Alfonso XII** in 1875 was effected by a series of *pronunciamentos* (literally 'pronouncements', in reality *coups d'état*) issued by army generals. Not for the first time, and certainly not for the last, the course of Spanish politics was determined by the intervention of the military. Indeed the *pronunciamento*, usually though not invariably associated with conservative and reactionary interests, became an established feature of Spanish life.

Although in 1900 Spain was still a predominantly **agricultural** nation with a large peasantry, modernity could not be kept in check forever. Matters came to a head in July 1909, During what became known as the **Tragic Week** Barcelona erupted. The barricades went up, followed by the inevitable authoritarian backlash. No other event so underlined the gulf between government in Madrid and Spain's emerging proletariat. Liberal politicians, for all their original good intentions, had failed to respond to change. As significantly, they had failed to install any mass party mechanisms, with the result that Spain's first mass parties were organized by the left and far left. Consequently there was little if any means of integrated dialogue between Spain's ruling elite and those it claimed to represent. Such was the political background of **Primo de Rivera**'s dictatorship, which lasted until 1930, and was in some ways a genuine attempt to promote unity among a fragmented, volatile nation that threatened, at any moment, to disintegrate.

The 19th century also witnessed the disintegration of Spain's colonial empire. During the six critical years of the Bourbons' absence from 1808 Spain's **American colonies** acquired an appetite for autonomy. Francesco de Miranda, San Martín and, especially, **Simón Bolívar** saw, and realized, an opportunity to create independent republics. By 1824 Cuba, Puerto Rico, the Philippines and a handful of smaller islands in the Pacific were all that remained of Spain's once-vaunted empire. Then, in 1898, Spain's 'disaster' year, even these were stripped away, through a brief but humiliating war against the **USA**.

The military's response was to shore up a new protectorate in **Morocco**. But even so close to home things could go terribly wrong. In 1921 thousands of Spanish troops were slaughtered by tribal insurgents during a campaign ordered by **Alfonso XIII**. Not just in Barcelona, but all across Spain the public outcry at the death of so many conscripts was deafening, and the only way the king could save his skin was to give Primo de Rivera and his revivalist policies *carte blanche*.

It didn't work. Primo de Rivera lacked the political skills to forge a consensus, and in 1930 Alfonso XIII surrenderd to pressure from other generals and got rid of him. But the real pressure was from below, as sweeping **socialist victories** in municipal elections the following year made manifest. Rather than stay on and fight, the king fled, and the inglorious **Second Republic** was born.

1808 Following the French occupation of Spain, and the proclamation of **Joseph Bonaparte** as king, anti-French riots occur in Madrid on 2 May, which are ruthlessly suppressed the following day. Further uprisings occur in Valencia, Oviedo, Zaragoza, Seville and other cities, and by June French garrisons are under attack across the country, marking the beginning of the **War of Spanish Independence**. Provincial *juntas* are formed to provide government in liberated areas, and royalist propaganda in support of the ousted Fernando VII is widespread. Joseph Bonaparte wins the support of some aristocrats and bureaucrats, but these are derided as *afrancesdados*. The great majority of Spaniards are opposed to what they consider an alien rule imposed by force.

In May the Portuguese, overrun by the French in 1807, appeal to **Britain** for help. On 4 July Britain unilaterally ends hostilities with Spain, and dispatches a force under the command of Sir John Moore to the peninsula.

On 19 July a Spanish loyalist army defeats a French army at **Bailén** on the main highway between Madrid and Andalucía. As Joseph Bonaparte flees the capital for the greater safety of **Vittoria**, French prisoners-of-war are sent to Cádiz, which remains a loyalist stronghold throughout the war. Further Spanish battlefield successes however will be sparse. Instead, loyalists turn to **guerrilla** tactics, keeping French detachments pinned down across Spain.

In September, representatives from the provincial *juntas* convene at Aranjuez, where a Supreme Junta is proclaimed in the name of King Fernando under the presidency of the

MEPL

Joseph Bonaparte, Napoleon's older brother, was appointed King of Spain in June 1808. His reign ended with the defeat at Vittoria in 1813

former minister the **Count of Floridablanca**. Composed largely of conservatives, the new Junta ends the sale of church properties and enlists the Inquisition's help in suppressing publications favourable to the French.

In November **Napoleon** himself enters Spain at the head of 150,000 troops. In December he reoccupies Madrid and issues an edict dissolving the Inquisition. The Central Junta abandons Aranjuez and moves south to **Seville**. Floridablanca dies on the way. A portion of Napoleon's army is sent to Portugal to combat the British.

1809 In January French troops advance into **Andalucía**. The Supreme Junta falls back to **Cádiz**, where it summons a Cortes representing all Spaniards, including those in America. Colonists in Buenos Aires, Caracas and some other South American cities refuse to acknowledge the legitimacy of the Junta while remaining at least nominally loyal to Fernando VII.

Cádiz is besieged, but the French are unable to reduce its defences.

The British army is driven out of Portugal into **Galicia**, where it narrowly escapes annihilation during fierce fighting at **La Coruña**. On 16 January Sir John Moore is killed in battle, and command passes to **Sir Arthur Wellesley**. Wellesley evacuates his troops by sea, but returns later with reinforcements and recaptures Lisbon. Driving the French out of Portugal, Wellesley defeats them at **Talavera** on Spanish soil on 28 July – a victory that secures Portuguese independence and its victor the title **Duke of Wellington**.

1810 Napoleon, having left Spain the previous autumn, and having now defeated **Austria**, resumes personal command of the campaign against the British in Portugal, but although he overruns key fortresses on the Spanish-Portuguese border, he is unable to dislodge Wellington from Lisbon. French troops occupy the Basque provinces and Catalunya.

In May, a Creole priest, **Miguel Hidalgo y Costilla**, launches a full-scale rebellion in **Mexico**, aimed at securing independence from Spain. In **Venezuela** and **Argentina** opposition to the Cádiz junta, which now proclaims itself a Regency, grows.

The Cortes of 'free Spaniards', including 24 representatives from the Americas and two from Manila, convenes in Cádiz on 24 September. During the open debates that follow a new reformist group emerges. Soon known as **Liberals**, these are led by Agustín Argüelles and Father Diego Muñoz Torrero. Mainly as a result of their influence, the Cortes declares that Spanish sovereignty resides among its members, and proclaims press freedom. The Cortes remains committed, however, to restoring Fernando VII to the throne as a constitutional monarch.

A **yellow fever** epidemic kills more than 25,000 people in Barcelona and Cádiz.

1811 Wellington renews his offensive against the French. Defeating them at **Fuentes de Onoro** on 5 May, he captures Almeida.

> 66 Our ministers may depend upon it that they cannot establish elsewhere such a system as they have here; that they cannot anywhere keep in check so large a proportion of Bonaparte's army, with such small comparative British means; that they cannot anywhere be principals, and carry on the war upon their own responsibility, at so cheap a rate of men and means as they can here; that no seat of operations holds out such prospects of success, whatever may happen elsewhere, even for the attainment of those objects which would be in view in transferring the seat of war to the north of Europe. 99
>
> The Duke of Wellington, writing to Lord Sydenham, 7 December 1811

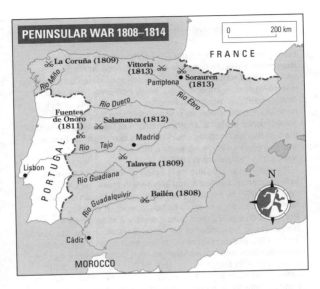

PENINSULAR WAR 1808–1814

0   200 km

FRANCE

La Coruña (1809)

Vittoria (1813)

Pamplona

Sorauren (1813)

Río Miño

Río Ebro

Río Duero

Fuentes de Onoro (1811)

Salamanca (1812)

Madrid

Río Tajo

PORTUGAL

Lisbon

Río Guadiana

Talavera (1809)

Río Guadalquivir

Bailén (1808)

N

Cádiz

MOROCCO

A provisional junta at Caracas in Venezuela under the leadership of **Francisco de Miranda** declares independence on 7 July, and incites other Spanish American colonies to do the same. Paraguay declares independence on 14 August, and in Chile a 'conservative' junta is overthrown. In Mexico however the rebel leader Hidalgo is captured and executed by troops loyal to Cádiz.

Bad harvests induce famine in Castile. Several thousands die of starvation in Madrid, a city of 200,000 without an adequate water supply.

1812 In March the Cádiz Cortes promulgates a **Constitution** that will be widely admired by European liberals. According to its provisions Spanish sovereignty ultimately

The Peninsular War of 1808–14

Having wrested control of the French Revolution, **Napoleon Bonaparte** aimed to bring the whole of Europe within an over-arching **Continental System** – a federation of states under his own revolutionary imperial aegis. Many non-French, however, including Britons, Austrians, Prussians and Russians, saw in Napoleon's great vision, as well as a threat to their own governmental systems, another instance of Gallic hegemonism of the sort that had inspired Louis XIV. As a consequence Europe was plunged into endemic warfare that only ended with Napoleon's final defeat in 1815.

The Peninsular War, known in Spain as the **War of Spanish Independence**, formed a vital segment in these Napoleonic Wars. In 1807, by the Treaty of Fontainebleau, Spain agreed to allow French troops to cross its soil in order to subjugate **Portugal**, an ally of Britain, and therefore a strategic threat to Bonaparte. In November of the same year Lisbon was occupied, and in 1808 Britain responded by dispatching an army. But by then Napoleon had seized Spain as well, with the result that the ensuing conflict became a struggle to liberate both Iberian nations. Yet although Britain assumed the major military role, its motives were by no means altruistic. At stake was Britain's own survival, as a nation and as a colonial power. Nor is it true, as sometimes thought, that Britain achieved success single-

resides in the *patria*, or nation, represented in a single-chamber assembly, all of whose members should be elected – although the franchise excludes females, servants, criminals and the insane. Ministers may be appointed by the King, but are answerable to the assembly. Aristocratic and other privileges are abolished, as is the Inquisition, and the influence of the Church is to be contained. But although it is specified that all Spaniards must adhere to the Catholic faith, the latent **anti-clericalism** of the Constitution pro-

handedly. Although Spanish armies seldom won battlefield victories, Spanish **guerrilla forces** wore the French down, forcing them to spread their manpower, attacking their convoys, and intercepting their dispatches.

Without such determined resistance the outcome might have been very different. As early as July 1808, during the siege of Zaragoza, it was a Spaniard, **José de Palafox**, who coined the phrase 'War even to the knife!' At the beginning of 1809 the British suffered near-disaster at La Coruña, although once Sir Arthur Wellesley had been put in command the situation improved. Wellesley, an aristocratic disciplinarian, had spent his apprenticeship in **India**, where he had learned the importance of maintaining supply lines in difficult terrain. He might regard his own troops as 'the scum of the earth', but he also understood their needs, just as he understood the strengths and weaknesses of his own position. His trump card was British naval supremacy, gained at **Trafalgar** in 1805, which meant as long as he hung on to Lisbon and its surrounding defences – the **Torres Vedras** – then essential supplies were guaranteed. But events elsewhere played an equal part. Warring against Austria and Russia Napoleon could never give Spain his undivided attention, just as the war in Spain in turn undermined his other campaigns.

vokes a backlash in ecclesiastical circles, creating a rift between Church and Liberals in Spain.

Commanding an army that includes Portuguese and Spanish as well as British troops, Wellington defeats the French at **Salamanca** on 22 July, and enters Madrid in August.

In Venezuela, Francisco de Miranda is captured and sent for trial in Cádiz. Leadership of the colonial rebels passes to

Simón Bolívar. In Mexico, rebellion is revived by José Maria Morelos. In Central America and Chile Spanish loyalists contain rebel forces.

1813 On 21 June Wellington defeats the main French army at **Vittoria**, forcing Joseph Bonaparte to flee for his life to Paris. On 10 November the last significant French garrison in Spain capitulates at **Pamplona**, following which Wellington marches into France, where he crushes a force commanded by Marshal Soult. As a result of these victories Spain is liberated from French revolutionary rule.

Following nationwide elections, a new **national assembly** meets in Madrid in October. There are however fewer Liberals than in its predecessor, mainly due to an effective propaganda campaign launched by the Church, and the inability of a mainly illiterate electorate to cast their votes.

A congress of **Mexican** colonial rebels formally declares their independence on 14 September. Simón Bolívar captures Caracas and establishes a dictatorship he intends to extend throughout Spanish South America.

1814 Released by Napoleon, **Fernando VII** returns to Spain and begins conspiring with traditionalists for the restitution of full Bourbon absolutist rule. On 4 May he issues a decree declaring the Cortes of Cádiz and the Constitution of 1812 illegal. The Council of Castile and other instruments of royal power are revived. A majority of Spaniards accept his ruling, although there are disturbances in Madrid. Leading Liberals are arrested, and some are deported to Spain's outposts in the Maghreb. The king also restores the **Inquisition**, which he tasks with suppressing Liberal publications and Masonic lodges, and the Papacy re-licenses the **Society of Jesus**. Jesuits once again preach and teach in Spain.

Freed from fighting the French, Spanish troops are sent to the Americas to assert royal authority, although news of Fernando's high-handed policies stimulates further rebellion.

1815 Napoleon is defeated at **Waterloo** on 18 June by a mixed British, Prussian and Dutch army, finally ending the prospect of a Europe-wide dictatorship.

10,000 Spanish soldiers reclaim **Venezuela**, forcing Simón Bolívar to flee to British-governed Jamaica.

1817 Chile gains its independence following a rebel victory over Spanish troops at Chacabuco on 12 February.

1818 Argentina gains its independence. Simón Bolívar re-establishes himself in the Orinoco basin.

1819 Supported by Britain, Bolívar crosses the Andes and defeats a Spanish army at the **Battle of Boyaca River** on 7 August. He occupies **Bogotá** on 10 August and is proclaimed president of a new republic that incorporates Colombia, Venezuela and what will become Ecuador.

35 years after construction began, the **Prado** is completed in Madrid and opens to the public as a Royal Museum, housing the throne's unique collection of paintings by Spanish, Italian and Dutch masters.

1820 On 1 January **Rafael de Riego**, the commander of a royal army awaiting embarkation for South America, rebels against Fernando VII by declaring his allegiance to the 1812 Constitution. His proclamation, or *pronunciamento*, amounts to a coup, and is quickly supported by other senior officers. The constitutional movement spreads to towns and cities particularly in northern Spain, and on 7 March the king concedes a return to constitutional rule. Following a general election, a strongly Liberal Cortes opens in Madrid on 9 June. The **Inquisition** is permanently abolished, **Jesuits** are expelled from

JOE STAINES

In 1810 Simón Bolívar headed a diplomatic mission to London. This statue, in London's Belgrave Square, was erected in 1974

Spain, and many smaller monasteries are closed. Ecclesiastical property is sold to pay off part of the accumulated national debt, and reforms to urban administration are proposed. Freedom of the press is restored, and free public education provided to encourage the spread of literacy. As the members of the assembly push for further reforms, however, a division appears in Liberal ranks between **Moderates**, led by Francisco de la Rosa, and more radical **Progressives**, headed by Rafael de Riego and known temporarily as *Los Exaltados*. The Moderates, fearful that radical legislation will lead to anarchy, propose that the 1812 Constitution be amended along British lines by limiting the electoral franchise to property owners and creating an upper house in the legislature. De Riego argues that the Constitution should stand unchanged.

1821 **Mexico** declares its independence on 24 February and Agustín de Iturbide becomes its provisional president. At the same time the independence of Spanish Texas and California is also asserted. On 22 July San Martín proclaims the independence of **Peru**. On 24 September Guatemala declares its independence. Other Central American states, including Nicaragua and the Honduras, follow suit.

1822 Rafael de Riego and the progressive *Exaltados* win a majority of seats in the Cortes in fresh elections. Their victory however provokes a conservative reaction supported by the Church. Royalist guerrilla groups become active, and in northern Catalunya an anti-constitutional 'regency' is proclaimed.

In the Caribbean **Santo Domingo**, half of Spain's first colony Hispaniola, is overrun by forces from neighbouring Haiti.

1823 As Spain lurches toward civil war between progressives and traditionalists, Fernando VII requests help from Louis XVIII. The French king responds in April by despatching the **'Army of One Hundred Thousand Sons of St Louis'**, backed by a Holy Alliance approved by the pope. The Cortes reassembles at Cádiz, taking the king as a prisoner. On 31 August parliamentarian forces are defeated at **Trocadero**, and Cádiz surrenders. Rafael de Riego is taken back to Madrid and dragged to his execution in a basket pulled by a donkey. Restored to his throne, Fernando VII annuls the 1812 Constitution, but is persuaded by France to moderate his absolutist policies. Although some properties are restored to the Church, no attempt is made to revive the Inquisition, and Fernando accepts the need for a bicameral assembly. Notwithstanding, the last ten years of his reign will become known as the **'Ominous Decade'**.

1824 On 9 December the last significant royalist army in South America is defeated by Simón Bolívar at **Ayucucho** in northern Peru – a victory that leads to the creation of the **Republic of Bolivia**. Spain's only remaining colonial possessions outside north Africa are Cuba, Puerto Rico and the Philippines.

1827 Supporters of the king's brother **Don Carlos Maria Isidro de Bourbón**, heir presumptive to the throne since Fernando VII has no children, stage an uprising in **Catalunya**. Known variously as *Agraviados* and *Apostólicos*, the rebels espouse absolutist values, including the restitution of the Inquisition.

1829 Fernando VII marries his niece **Maria Cristina of Naples**.

1830 In France the overthrow of the Bourbon monarchy during the **July Revolution** gives Spanish Liberals hope, even though an attempt to overthrow Fernando VII in Madrid fails. In October Fernando's position is strengthened when Maria Cristina gives birth to a child, named **Isabel**. For the first time a **pragmatic sanction** of 1789, allowing for a female succession, is made public as Maria Cristina schemes to exclude her brother-in-law from the throne. Don Carlos refuses to accept the decree. To win greater support Fernando orders the release of leading Liberals detained in prison since 1823 and issues an amnesty to those who have fled abroad.

1832 Toward the end of the year the king sickens and Maria Cristina assumes the responsibilities of government.

1833 Fernando VII dies on 29 September. His two-year-old daughter is proclaimed **Queen Isabel II**, and Maria Cristina becomes Regent. Don Carlos and his supporters begin a six-year civil war against the new regime.

1834 As the **First Carlist War** intensifies, Britain lends support to Maria Cristina by suspending its Foreign Enlistment Act, enabling Sir George de Lacy Evans to form an international brigade in support of Isabel II.

1835 To win popular support Maria Cristina appoints **Juan Mendizábel** prime minister. A businessman who has made money in London, and known as 'Jupiter of the Progressives', Mendizábel introduces radical policies that include the abolition of aristocratic entail in the inheritance of land and the enforced sale of ecclesiastical lands. He also encourages the growth of a market economy by severely limiting the trading privileges of Spain's long-established trade guilds.

1837 The Carlists attempt to capture Madrid, but fail. As their campaign loses support, the throne issues a revised **Constitution** that guarantees the Moderate Liberals – in reality middle-class oligarchs – a say in government. The Progressives however continue to build support in Spain's towns and cities.

1839 The Carlists surrender to **General Baldomero Espartero**, a loyalist hero and also the 'sword' of the Progressive Liberals, bringing the First Carlist War to an end.

1840 Espartero, now styled the **Duke of Victory**, issues a *pronunciamiento* and seizes power in Madrid. Although Maria Cristina and several leading Moderates are exiled to France, Espartero's Progressive regime is rapidly suborned by factional squabbling and the general's own political indecisiveness.

1843 In July the 'sword' of the Moderates, **General Rámon María Narváez** (Duke of Valencia), issues a *pro-*

The Carlists

For some traditionalists the accession of a three-year-old girl to the throne in 1833 was unacceptable. Instead they supported the claim of Fernando VII's younger brother **Don Carlos**, invoking the Salic Law (an ancient French custom that forbade female succession), and declaring war against the Regent **Maria Cristina** and her government. They were defeated in 1839, and Don Carlos, known also as the Conde de Molína, abjured his claim to the throne in favour of his own son, another Don Carlos, known variously as the **Conde de Montemolín** and Carlos VI. The second pretender however was no more successful than his father, and having twice failed to wrest the crown from Isabel II, in 1846–8 and 1860, died childless in 1869. At this point the Carlist mantle passed to his brother, **Don Juan de Bourbón**, who passed it on to his own son, the third Don Carlos and fourth pretender. In 1872 the Carlists mounted another all-out attempt to seize the throne, but at the end of the **Second Carlist War**, Carlos VII, or the **Duke of Madrid** as he styled himself, was condemned to permanent exile, eventually dying in Italy without any sons in 1909.

The Carlists appealed to **reactionary elements** in Spanish society, including some members of the Church hierarchy. By

nunciamento and overthrows Espartero's government. Espartero is exiled, and **Maria Cristina** recalled as Regent.

1844 Narváez creates the **Guardia Civil** (Civil Guard), a police force modelled on the French gendarmerie used to maintain order in the countryside. Dressed in patent leather hats and green capes, the Guard soon becomes a symbol of centralized oppression, and is particularly detested by the **Basques**.

1845 Encouraged by Maria Cristina, Narváez promulgates a new **Constitution** that militates against the interests of the Progressives and strengthens the throne. A revised electoral

hinting that they favoured the restitution of provincial *fueros*, they also won support from **separatist groups** in Aragon, Catalunya and the Basque provinces. Claiming to represent true Bourbon values was seen as a viable political alternative in 1833, but as the century progressed they were increasingly out of tune with the times. They were finally sidelined by **Alfonso XII**'s endeavours to sustain a constitutional monarchy after 1874, and by the emergence of a more liberal brand of Catholicism. While to some extent their failure can be attributed to their inability to attract meaningful support from outside Spain – a sign that dynasticism was now a spent force in Europe – their persistent rebelliousness had important consequences. If the **First Carlist War** of 1833–9 almost wrecked state finances, it also produced the first in a long line of Spanish generals ready and willing to meddle in politics. It was largely because of his victories against the Carlists that **Baldomero Espartero** became Regent in 1840. Indeed, it has been argued that by keeping regional aspirations alive the Carlists created a situation in which sooner or later a military dictator was the inevitable solution to Spain's fractured and fractious political society.

franchise based on property qualifications restricts voting to no more than one percent of the adult male population. In a further package of reforms, the appointment of town and city mayors is given to the crown, and the National Militia, perceived as an instrument of the Progressives, is suppressed. Amid the outcry that follows, a group calling themselves the **Democrats** emerges in Spain for the first time.

1846 A small uprising lasting two years begins in Catalunya, launched by 'partisans' loyal to the second Carlist pretender, **Don Carlos Conde de Montemolín** (see p.396). There is also unrest in Galicia, which Narváez personally suppresses.

1848 In February **Louis Philippe** of France is forced to abdicate as a new republic is created. As revolutionary movements spread throughout Europe, Maria Cristina revokes the 1845 Constitution and Narváez assumes dictatorial powers.

In April, the **Great Fair of Seville** is held for the first time. Providing a showcase for bull-fighting, horsemanship and flamenco dancing, the fair will become a main annual tourist event.

Spain's first **railway** opens between Barcelona and Mataró in October.

1851 Pope Pius IX issues a **Concordat** whereby the Vatican acknowledges the legitimacy of ecclesiastical land sales in Spain in return for an undertaking from the government to pay clerical wages.

1854 Amid scenes of widespread unrest the increasingly unpopular government of General Narváez is overthrown following a *pronunciamiento* issued by a fellow general, **Leopoldo O'Donnell**, in June. **Baldomero Espartero**, recalled from exile by O'Donnell in the hope of creating a broad liberal alliance, sets up a new administration in November. Seizing power, Progressive Liberals institute a **revolution** known as the *Biennio*, since it lasts two years (see p.400).

1855 A further Carlist rebellion is attempted and fails.

1856 In July, after less than two years as prime minister, during which he has revived the National Militia, **Espartero** is forced to retire by a reactionary cabal infuriated by his promulgation of a revised constitution that allows for universal male suffrage. Among those who support Espartero's removal is **O'Donnell**, who assists in the immediate suppression of the new constitution, and of the National Militia. During the crisis **Isabel II** emerges as a figure in her own right, determined to preserve the traditions and privileges of the throne despite the opposition of a majority of Spaniards. In October O'Donnell himself is dismissed from office, and **General Narváez** is reinstated as first minister.

1857 As opposition to the royalist government spreads there is an **uprising in Seville**, organized by the Democrat leader Sixto Cámara.

1858 Leopoldo O'Donnell returns as prime minister for five years after Isabel II realises she cannot rule Spain without Liberal support. To restore order he promotes a 'Liberal

> ❝ The Alameda, or church show, and the bullfight, are the chief relaxations. These will be best enjoyed in the Southern provinces, the land also of song and dance, of bright suns and eyes, wholesale love making, and of not the largest female feet in the world. ❞
>
> Richard Ford, *A Handbook for Travellers in Spain* (1855)

The Biennio of 1854–56

While **1848** was the great year of European revolutions, the 'Spanish Revolution' didn't occur until six years later, and even then proved short-lived. Perhaps this was because, like most regime changes in Spain, it was achieved by a military *pronunciamento*. Having overthrown the government of Narváez, the moderate **Leopoldo O'Donnell** turned to the immensely popular progressive **Baldomero Espartero**, who at the time was living in exile in England, in the hope of creating a broad alliance among Spain's disunited Liberals. Surprisingly, Espartero's second administration proved far more productive than his first (1840–43), with over 200 new laws being passed, to the lasting benefit of Spain's infrastructure. The railway-building programme, begun in 1848, was greatly extended; the electric telegraph was introduced; new roads were commissioned; scrubland was afforested; and Madrid got its first piped water. Company laws were relaxed to encourage commerce, and several new banks came into being, improving the availability of credit to entrepreneurs. Yet for **Isabel II**, and increasingly for O'Donnell, the pace of change was too much, and following pressure from conservative army officers, Espartero was dismissed in July 1856.

By the end of the year O'Donnell too had gone, and the old guard was back in power. Spain's mid-century revolution was over. Yet in retrospect it was scarcely a revolution at all. No serious attempt had been made to address the real causes of Spain's backward condition. The crown remained intact, much-needed agrarian reform was neglected, and the Church retained much of its influence. Espartero's government also failed to attend the two most important sources of popular grievance – **inequitable taxation** and **army conscription**. For true radicals and progressives the Biennio was a disappointment even while it lasted, and its most enduring legacy was to expose the Liberals – many of whom now had significant land-holdings – as a narrow, sectarian interest group. Soon other kinds of ideologue would strive to fill what was becoming a political vacuum.

Union' of Moderates and Progressives. Although his policy of inclusiveness works for a while, when Progressives fail to win senior office they begin turning to **General Juan Prim y Prats**, a chemist's son, as their new 'sword'. General Prim increases his appeal by repudiating any alliance with the Democrats.

1860 The second Carlist pretender, the **Conde de Montemolín**, is captured and exiled for plotting sedition.

1862 Isabel II dismisses O'Donnell and replaces his government with an administration made up of court cronies. The **Progressives** attempt to incite a national uprising, but when that fails renew their alliance with the Democrats.

1866 In June O'Donnell is re-appointed prime minister, but dies in office early the following year.

An economic boom that has lasted well over a decade gives way to **recession**, fuelled by growing difficulties in European financial markets. Some Spanish banks collapse, and the building of new railways ceases. **Unemployment** in Barcelona, Burgos and other industrializing cities encourages social and political unrest.

1868 Opposition to Isabel II and her government intensifies from the beginning of the year. In some towns and cities Democrat *juntas* are established under the leadership of **Francsico Pi y Margall**, a politician heavily influenced by the **anarchist** writings of Pierre-Joseph Proudhon. In September, following the formation of a coalition of Progressives, some other Liberals and Democrats, Prim y Prats issues a *pronunciamiento* that heralds the **Glorious** (or **September) Revolution**. Isabel II is deposed and driven into permanent exile.

In October a ten-year Creole insurrection begins in Cuba, where Spanish colonials, dependent on selling their sugar to North America, have become increasingly vexed by the interferences of *peninsulares* – administrators sent from Spain. The **Cuban Revolt** undermines the Glorious Revolution by preventing its leaders from implementing two of their principal pledges – the abolition of tax on foodstuffs and an end to military conscription.

1869 The September Coalition issues a new **constitution** that provides for the retention of the monarchy if a suitable king can be found. It also legislates for **religious toleration** and **full male suffrage**. Some Democrats, dismayed that the constitution has not gone further, begin openly espousing **republicanism**. A smattering of republican uprisings are ruthlessly suppressed as actual government remains in the hands of the military.

1870 The search for a king is ended when **Amadeo of Savoy**, a member of the powerful Hohenzollern family, agrees to become Spain's constitutional monarch. He arrives in Spain in November. On the day he enters Madrid General Prim is assassinated by an anarchist. Amadeo's accession to the throne is opposed by the Carlist faction.

1872 The third Don Carlos, and fourth Carlist pretender, openly rebels, launching the **Second Carlist War** – a bitterly fought contest that lasts four years but is mainly confined to Catalunya and Basque areas in the northeast.

1873 In February, exasperated by the difficulties of governing Spain, King Amadeo abdicates, leading to the creation of a short-lived **First Republic**. In Catalunya, Valencia and Andalucía self-governing Democrat cantons are proclaimed in some towns and cities. The **'cantonalist revolt'** in turn gives rise to a federalist movement calling for Spain's various provinces to be given autonomy. Order is restored by **General Pavia** through the simple expedient of firing several shots in the Madrid Cortes and then imposing military rule.

> He who would really see Spain, must go prepared to rough it, must be unembarrassed by a courier, must be content with humble inns, coarse fare, windows often glassless, vehicles always jolting, and above all must put all false Anglican pride in his pocket, and treat every Spaniard, from the lowest beggar upwards, as his equal. He must take Spain as he finds her; she is not likely to improve; she does not wish to improve; the only way of finding pleasure in her is to take her as she is, without longing for her to be what she is not.
>
> A.J.C. Hare, *Wanderings in Spain* (1873)

1874 In January a further military coup unfolds when **General Manuel Paria y Rodriguez de Albuquerque** expels Republican deputies from a reconvened Cortes in Madrid and then hands over power to **General Francisco Serrano**.

At the end of the year there is yet another *pronunciamento*, issued in Sagunto by Brigadier Arsenio Martinez Campos. The First Republic is dissolved and on 29 December **Alfonso XII**, Isabel II's son by the Duke of Cádiz, is invited to accede to the throne. But although the **Restoration** is effected by the military, and wholly supported by the Church, its guiding hand is **Antonio Cánovas de Castillo**.

1875 Following Alfonso XII's return to Spain from exile, part of which has been spent undergoing military training at Sandhurst College in England, Cánovas de Castillo is appointed prime minister – a post he retains until 1881. The military is encouraged to disengage from public life and Spain enjoys economic revival, led by Barcelona's factory-building entrepreneurs.

1876 A **'royalist' constitution**, largely devised by de Castillo, is promulgated. Integral to its success is a political system that allows for the regular alternation of Liberal and Conservative administrations. Called *turno pacifico* (peaceable alternation), it operates through the interior ministry's ability to secure desired electoral outcomes through the machinations of centrally appointed **caciques** ('local bosses'). A form of institutionalized corruption, *Caciquismo* will be slowly undermined by the growth of mass political parties, over which neither the king nor his ministers can exercise control.

Antoni Gaudí (1852–1926)

The son of a coppersmith, **Antoni Gaudí** was a Catalan through and through – imaginative, bold, eclectic, quirky, separatist and left-of-centre. Born in Reus, he gravitated to Barcelona as a student when the city was fast becoming one of Europe's foremost cultural centres. He remained there for the rest of his life, and today Barcelona is still adorned with many of his visionary and highly idiosyncratic buildings. To label his art is counter-productive. He was at once central to the cultural expression of Catalan nationalism, variously called the **Catalan Renaissance** and **Catalan Modernismo**, and stood apart from it. Similarly his work reflects several sources without ever being dominated by any one of them. John Ruskin and William Morris, the Frenchman Eugène Viollet-le-Duc were important influences, as were **Neo-Gothic** and the *mudéjar* art of Christian-Moorish Spain. In so far as his work can be characterized by any one trait, then that would be its preference for an apparently anarchic profusion of curves and rounded shapes, mostly inspired by natural forms. By largely avoiding straight, external lines of power, Gaudí sought a state of spontaneity subliminally opposed to the conventions of patronage and hierarchy. For decoration, broken cups and plates were as good as any traditional materials and motifs. Yet as the surviving models Gaudí made for his projects make

1878 The **Cuban revolt** ends after Spain's colonial authorities make concessions to the rebels, enabling them to trade more freely with the United States.

1879 **Pablo Iglesias**, a printer and son of a washerwoman, founds the **PSOE** (Partido Socialista Obrero Español – Spanish Socialist Party). Despite being organized as a 'mass party', its electoral successes are initially scant, partly because a still largely illiterate electorate shuns polling stations.

1881 Práxades Mateo Sagasta heads a Liberal government

abundantly clear, his buildings embody an intense structural logic underpinned by awesomely complex geometries.

After his death 'contemporary' architecture was dominated by the aggressively linear geometry of the **International Modern style**, which for a time obscured Gaudí's extraordinary output – despite the enthusiasm of the Surrealists and the architect Le Corbusier. More recently his originality has been almost universally admired. His last major work – currently in the process of completion with the help of advanced computer programmes – was the church of **La Sagrada Familia** ('Holy Family'), known locally as the 'Cathedral of the Poor'. Seemingly a construction of pure caprice, the building was supported largely by public subscription since Church authorities refused to fund what they considered total mayhem, even though Gaudí was himself an intensely devout Catholic. But if the Sagrada Familia is a prime example of the architectural mind at play, the **Parc Güell**, begun in 1900, but discontinued in 1914, deserves equal attention. Commissioned by his long-standing patron, the textile manufacturer **Eusebio Güell**, it was planned as an entire hillside garden suburb in which the details of a distinctly organic design were deliberately left blank for implementation by Barcelona's gifted craftsmen. In the name of co-operative design, Gaudí demonstrated his commitment to the principle of collective, communal creativity and to Barcelona's rich craft tradition.

FRANCESCO VENTURI/CORBIS

The astonishing roof of Gaudí's Casa Batlló, completed in 1906, is meant to suggest the spine and scales of the dragon defeated by St George – the patron saint of Catalunya

that lasts four years. Press freedoms are restored and rights to free association are legislated.

1884 The Josephines, a Catholic lay order, commission the Catalan architect **Antoni Gaudí** to design the church of the *Sagrada Familia* in Barcelona.

1885 The ***turno pacífico*** enables a conservative government to take over from Sagasta's Liberal administration without any disturbance to public order.

Alfonso XII dies in Madrid on 25 November. His wife, **Maria Cristina of Austria**, who is carrying his child, is appointed Regent.

1886 The Queen Regent is delivered of a boy on 28 February. Almost at the hour of his birth **Alfonso XIII** is proclaimed king, and the constitutional monarchy continues.

Novelist **Benito Peréz Galdós** publishes *Fortunata y Jacinta* ('Fortunata and Jacinta'). Widely regarded as his masterpiece, the novel is a multi-layered dissection of Madrid society in the 1870s.

1888 Iglesias and his markedly republican PSOE establish a workers' union, the **UGT** (Unión General de Trabajadores), in Barcelona – a general workers' trades union that, while embracing the industrial strike as a political weapon, also promotes self-help and adult education amongst its members. In Barcelona, as well as other cities, unionism is fiercely opposed by industrialists.

An internationally sponsored **Universal Exhibition** confirms Barcelona's reputation as a cosmopolitan city and trade centre.

1891 The return of a Liberal government enables legislation that grants **universal male suffrage**. Although this has some effect on urban elections, in the countryside Liberal and Conservative deputies can usually retain their seats.

The Spanish-American War of 1898

The Spanish-American war was over almost before it began. On 15 February 1898, an American warship, the **USS Maine**, mysteriously sank in Havana harbour. As the American press began filling with apocryphal stories of Spanish atrocities, both nations started rattling their sabres. Then on 9 April Spain suddenly conceded the Cubans' demands for autonomy within a Spanish union. Undeterred, the US government demanded that Cuba be given full independence. Spain declared war against the USA on 24 April, and the USA reciprocated the following day. On 1 May America's Pacific fleet drove the Spanish out of **Manila**, and by the end of July Cuba had been 'liberated'. By the terms of the **Treaty of Paris**, signed in December, Cuban independence was affirmed, while **Puerto Rico** and **Guam**, as well as the Philippines, were all assigned as American colonies.

The war heralded America's advent as a world power, and gave it a new set of heroes – **Admiral John Dewey**, the victor of Manila Bay, and **Theodore Roosevelt** and his 'Rough Riders'. Famously, in March 1898, the press baron **William Randolph Hearst** cabled one of his reporters, Frederic Remington: 'You furnish the pictures and I'll furnish the war.' For Spain the defeat was traumatic, and 1898 became known simply as 'The Disaster'. What remained of its empire had been stripped away, and, perhaps inevitably, profound self-examination followed. What exactly was wrong with the *patria* that it had suffered such humiliation? The Carlists – or what remained of them – called for Alfonso XIII to be replaced with a king of their own choice. But despair gave way to calls for 'national regeneration'. In the decades that followed a literary group known as the **'Generation of 1898'**, and which included Pio Baroja and Joaquin Costa y Martinez as well as **Ortega y Gasset** (see p.400) and **Miguel Unamuno**, wrote enthusiastically of traditional Spanish values. More ominously, the military experienced an almost pathological need to demonstrate that it wasn't as inept as events had appeared to demonstrate.

1893 Against a background of renewed calls for **Catalan autonomy**, scores are killed and injured when the Lyceum Theatre in Barcelona is bombed by an anarchist – an outrage that gives police a pretext for rounding up hundreds of known dissidents.

1894 **Catholic Action**, a right-wing political party dedicated to fostering Catholic solidarity among the laity and to opposing radical secularism, is founded.

1895 A second revolt erupts in **Cuba**. The rebels, envying the freedoms of the United States, derive clandestine support from Washington.

1898 Following an escalation in tensions between Spain and the **United States**, the two countries go to war. In the space of a few months Spain is forced to relinquish **Cuba**, **Puerto Rico** and the **Philippines**.

1900 At the turn of century two-thirds of Spaniards are still illiterate and tied to agricultural labour. Spain's **population** is estimated at around 17,000,000 – a 70 percent increase on 1800, partly attributable to the cessation of epidemics and famine, and improved healthcare.

1901 Francese Cambó de Asis and Prat de la Riba found the *Lliga Regionalista*, a mass party that campaigns for Catalan autonomy and Spanish federalism without advocating violence or other illegal means.

> **❝** The Spanish-American War was not a great war. A large number of our troops took the hazard of watermelons in Georgia and Florida, and fought the malaria and mosquitoes, but very few Spanish. **❞**
>
> Congressman James L. Slayden, speaking in the House of Representatives, 1906

1902 Aged 16 **Alfonso XIII**, a young man preoccupied with military affairs, assumes such powers as the Constitution of 1876 permits him.

1903 Victories for **republican candidates** in a general election inaugurate a period of sustained instability in Spanish politics. Over the coming 21 years no fewer than 33 different administrations will be formed.

1906 On 31 May Alfonso XIII marries **Victoria Eugenia de Battenberg**. Their wedding is marred by an assassination attempt against the king – the first of several that will dog the remainder of his reign. Partly as a result of this episode the ruling Liberal government extends the army's powers to act against subversives.

1907 The *Lliga Regionalista* splits into two factions. Abiding by his constitutional and legalistic principles, Francesc Cambó forms the ***Solitaritat Catalana***, designed to appeal to a broad spectrum of Catalan society. Excluded from this compact is **Alejandro Lerroux**, founder of the **Radical Republican Party**, and a charismatic left-wing Catalan nationalist prepared to advocate violence as a means to Catalan autonomy. By appealing directly to Barcelona's 'alienated proletariat', Lerroux is seen to be abetting urban terrorism.

The painter **Pablo Picasso**, resident in Paris since 1904, completes *Les Demoiselles d'Avignon*, a revolutionary painting, influenced both by African sculpture and the late work of Cézanne, and named after a Barcelona brothel. This marks a crucial stage in the history of **Cubism**, a new way of painting in which objects are fragmented into facets, as if viewed from different perspectives simultaneously.

1908 Completion of the Palau de la Musica Catalana in Barcelona. Designed by **Lluis Domènech i Montaner**, this richly decorated building is a masterpiece of Catalan Modernismo.

1909 To counter tribal insurgency in **Morocco**, on 9 July the conservative prime minister **Antonio Maura** orders the dispatch of an expeditionary force largely made up of conscripts and reservists. There are anti-war protests in Valencia, Aragon and Catalunya. As news reaches Spain of a military disaster at **Melilla** anti-government feeling explodes in Barcelona, unleashing what becomes known as *semana trágica* – **tragic week**. The UGT and Lerroux's anarchists join forces and on Saturday 24 July a general strike is called in the city. Two days later, when the military governor, Luis de Santiago, declares a state of emergency, the strikers and their political supporters respond by setting up **barricades**, sealing off many parts of the city. During the ensuing disorder twelve churches and forty convents are destroyed. By Friday, with fresh army units drafted into Barcelona, order is restored. Over 1700 protesters are arrested and tried, and five are executed. When further demonstrations are mounted to protest the severity of the government's response, **Alfonso XIII** replaces Antonio Maura with the more liberal Sigismundo Moret as prime minister.

1910 The anarcho-syndicalist **CNT**, *Confederación Nacional de Trabajo* (National Labour Confederation), is founded in Barcelona. More radical and more militant than the UGT, it explicitly seeks to destroy the existing establishment, if necessary by violence.

1912 The **assassination** of José Canalejas, a leading political reformer, provokes a division among Liberal politicians and leads to the founding of the **Reformist Republican Party**, a middle-class association that includes among its early members **Manuel Azaña**, later to become prime minister.

Following negotiations with France, a Spanish **protectorate** is declared in Morocco, although ongoing insurgency there continues to drain Spain's resources.

1914 To the advantage of its industrialists, Spain remains neutral during the five-year **Great War** (World War I) that consumes most of the rest of Europe from August onwards. The **Hispano–Suiza** factory in Barcelona, already famous for its luxury automobiles, will manufacture engines for France's first warplanes, and Spanish textile companies will produce many of the army greatcoats worn on the Western Front. But while entrepreneurs and factory-owners get rich, workers and agricultural labourers are adversely affected by steep **price rises** induced by the war. In Catalunya industrial relations deteriorate sharply, and employers use thugs as well as the lock-out to deter organized strikes.

1916 The composer **Enrique Granados** is killed when the ship taking him from England to France is torpedoed by a German submarine. His masterpiece *Goyescas*, a suite of piano pieces inspired by the paintings of Goya, was composed two years earlier.

1917 As successive governments prove unwilling or unable to effect popular reforms, the socialist UGT abandons its 'parliamentary' strategy and joins forces with the more radical CNT to call a nationwide **general strike**. During the strike a republican Catalan 'assembly' is briefly established, and the Spanish **communist party** makes its presence felt for the first time (although its membership remains small). Within the army some officers begin forming *juntas de defensa*, in effect military unions dedicated to national regeneration.

1919 Although the Great War is formally concluded, social and industrial unrest continues to fester in Spain. The ruthless suppression of another general strike in Barcelona induces the inevitable backlash of assassinations and other acts of terror as large parts of the city become the fiefdoms of rival gangs. **Antonio Maura** returns to power as prime minister after neither conservatives nor liberals can secure enough seats in the National Assembly (Cortes) to form an administration.

In London **Manuel de Falla**'s ballet *El sombrero de tres picos* ('The Three Cornered Hat'), based on the novel by Pedro de Alarcón, is premiered by the *Ballet Russes*. Designed by Pablo Picasso, the ballet establishes Falla's international reputation.

1920 The economic prosperity induced by the Great War runs out of steam as France, Italy and Britain begin recovering their manufacturing capacity. Unemployment in Barcelona, Bilbao, Madrid and Cádiz adds to Spain's worsening social condition.

1921 The massacre of thousands of Spanish soldiers by tribal insurgents in Morocco as they retreat from a frontier post at **Annual** during a campaign ordered by the king provokes demands for army reform from both within and outside the military.

José Ortega y Gasset publishes *España Invertebrada* ('Invertebrate Spain'), one in a series of polemical writings designed to refute revolutionary rationalism.

1922 Francesc Maciá founds the **Catalan Action Party**, a socialist organisation that campaigns for the establishment of a republic of Catalunya within a federation of other such Spanish republics.

1923 The **PSOE** (Socialist Party) gains seven seats in the National Assembly during a national election after its leader, **Indalecio Prieto**, repudiates the communist philosophy of Karl Marx and embraces the principles of republicanism.

On 12 September, one week before an inquiry into the Moroccan fiasco of 1921 is due to publish its report, **General Primo de Rivera** issues a *pronunciamento* in Barcelona that leads to a military coup against the government. With the full support of **Alfonso XIII**, he

José Ortega y Gasset (1883–1955)

For much of the 20th century Ortega y Gasset was Spain's most popular intellectual. In part this was down to his enormous energy in setting up and running journals and periodicals, as well as writing a constant stream of essays and books. His reputation was established by a series of publications produced in the 1920s and 1930s, among them *España Invertebrada* ('Invertebrate Spain', 1921), *La dehuminizació del arte* ('The Dehumanisation of Art', 1925) and *La Rebelión de las masas* ('The Revolt of the Masses', 1929). In these he mounted a spirited defence of traditional humanistic culture against what he saw as the importunism of **socialist ideology**. The democratic tendency, Ortega y Gasset argued, gave rise, and could only give rise, to conformism, intolerance and vulgarity. As Professor of Metaphysics at **Madrid University** from 1910 onwards, he endeavoured to base his cultural polemics in philosophical argument. Rejecting the German rationalism he had studied abroad in his youth, he proposed that absolute reason should be abandoned in favour of the logic of the here and now. 'I am I and my circumstances', he wrote – an apothegm that has led to his being called the father of **Spanish existentialism**.

More interesting was his commentary on **cultural modernism**. The intrinsic 'difficulty' of such modernists as James Joyce and Pablo Picasso was welcomed by Ortega y Gasset precisely because it 'excluded' the masses by expressing individualism. In contrast, 'socialist art' with its grinding realism can teach us nothing, just because it panders to popular taste. Largely because of this analysis, the simplistic suspicion still lingers that modernism and elitism are intertwined. Everything else Ortega y Gasset wrote however now gathers dust. In 1936 he fled to Argentina in the interests of self-preservation, but was welcomed back to Spain by **General Franco** (see p.446) in 1945, and in his sixties he founded the **Institute of Humanities** in Madrid (where he was born and died). Although Ortega y Gasset was himself too individualistic to be pigeon-holed as a fascist, his reputation since the dictator's death in 1975 has never recovered from the taint of association.

establishes a personal dictatorship that, in its first months, suppresses the 1876 Constitution, ends press freedom and places all of Spain's provinces under army rule through a **Military Directory**. The same instrument is used to discipline commanders in Morocco.

1925 Primo de Rivera, who has already announced his intention of 'retiring' once he has returned Spain to stability, replaces the Military with a **Civil Directory**.

In Morocco, the war against the insurgents turns in Spain's favour with the capture of the rebel leader **Abd el-Krim**.

1926 The painter **Salvador Dalí** visits Paris where he becomes closely associated with the **Surrealists**. Heavily influenced by **Freud**, Dalí attempts to reproduce the unconscious on canvas, employing a highly detailed and academic technique. He was expelled from the Surrealist movement in 1938 for his reactionary politics

1927 Fighting in north Africa ends as Spain's army asserts control over the whole of Spanish Morocco. Confident that his policies are working, Primo de Rivera convenes a **National Assembly** with a view to creating a new constitution more favourable to corporate interests. The work of the assembly however is hampered by a lack of support for the dictator's policies among its members.

1928 With the support of some army commanders, **Sánchez Guerra**, the leader of Spain's conservatives, attempts the overthrow of Primo de Rivera. Although the

> A society without an aristocracy, without an elite minority, is not a society.
>
> Ortega y Gasset, *The Revolt of the Masses* (1929)

Primo de Rivera (1870–1930)

Born in Cádiz, Miguel Primo de Rivera y Orbaneja was a career soldier for whom love of the *patria* meant very nearly everything. Appointed **Captain-General of Barcelona** in 1922 he witnessed at first hand the effects of anarchy on its streets. Like others of his class and profession he entertained a profound fear of **socialism**, which, through the Bolshevik revolution, had already overturned tradition in Russia. But almost as perturbing was the apparent inability of Spain's constitutionally elected government to provide stability. With the backing of fellow-generals, in September 1923 he issued a *pronunciamento* and embarked on a seven-year dictatorship. Crucially he enjoyed the support not only of **Alfonso XIII**, but also of the Church, the landed aristocracy and big business – at least in the early years. He restored public order, improved **industrial relations** (to the delight of the UGT he suppressed the CNT), brought the war in **Morocco** to a successful conclusion and initiated a programme of **public works** that was of real benefit to Spain.

Where Primo de Rivera stumbled was in the political arena – he simply didn't know how to maintain a following. He attempted to create a **Patriotic Union** party, but without any grass roots machinery; he upset entrepreneurs and industrialists by imposing state controls that undermined profitability; he lost the support of moderate Catalans by clamping down on Catalan institutions; and, most seriously of all as regards his own survival, he infuriated the military by insisting that merit, not length of service, should be the determining factor in promotion. But if some of his policies were unnecessarily repressive, on the plus side he was probably sincere when he said he would retire voluntarily once his job was done. Privately he enjoyed the reputation of a *bon viveur*, and historically he has enjoyed an altogether favourable comparison with his eventual dictatorial successor, **Francisco Franco** (see p.446). Whether though Primo de Rivera would have gone without being pushed is hotly debated. The signs were that the more unpopular he became, the more determined he was to see his programme through.

The dictator Primo de Rivera at work at his desk

coup fails, it is indicative of the dictator's declining support even among right-wing elements.

1929 Unrest in the military grows when Primo de Rivera endeavours to introduce **army reforms** that seek to abolish automatic promotion by seniority and other traditional privileges. The dictator's regime is further damaged by economic problems induced by a **global recession**.

1930 On 28 January Alfonso XIII dismisses Primo de Rivera from office and entrusts government to **General Dámaso Berenguer** on the understanding that Berenguer will do everything in his power to save the throne. Anti-monarchists, including some army officers, form an alliance at San Sebastián on 17 August, but their rebellion is crushed by royalist forces at **Jaca** on 12 December. Primo de Rivera himself dies in exile in Paris in March.

1931 The **PSOE** and other republican and socialist parties win sweeping victories in municipal elections held on 12 April. Realising the extent of the political forces ranged against him, **Alfonso XIII** goes into voluntary exile two days later, although he refuses to offer his formal abdication. On 19 April the **Second Republic** is proclaimed.

10: Spain in the Modern Era

1931–2003

When the **Second Republic** was proclaimed on 19 April 1931 there was a huge air of expectancy, and also of apprehension. What was missing was any tradition of consensus politics, and it was this that made a mockery of attempted democracy. Each time an election was held, or a government was formed, the winners refused to take into account the needs and aspirations of their defeated rivals, and the losers refused to accept the will of the people. Within months the political scene became crowded with a plethora of bickering factions and parties. The Republic was also seen as an opportunity by Catalan and other regional separatists to raise their voices. In the country at large there was a marked imbalance between the relatively wealthy, developed north, northeast and east and the still predominantly agrarian central plains and south; and to complicate matters further the Republic came about just as Europe was being tugged apart by two relatively new ideologies – **communism** in Russia, and **fascism** in Hitler's Germany and Mussolini's Italy. For many, democracy was by no means an obvious or even desirable path.

Notwithstanding such adverse circumstances, the governments of **Alcalá Zamora** and **Manuel Azaña** did make some headway, even though they were dependent on fragile accommodations within mainly left-wing coalitions. For some, though, change was not fast enough, while for others – conservatives and traditionalists – change of any sort was anathema. The first unambiguous sign of the troubles that lay ahead came in April 1932, when **General José**

Sanjurjo, resorting to the familiar means of a *pronunciamento*, attempted a military coup. The coup failed, and in the short-term brought the warring factions of the left to some sort of collective sense. But as the pendulum swung one way, so it swung the other. Returned to power, Azaña pursued a politics of inclusivity, but only toward more radical groupings. By the summer of 1936 the old guard – which included churchmen as well as the army – had had enough. **General Emilio Mola** decided to act. Unlike Sanjurjo, though, he laid his plans carefully, even if his objective was to install Sanjurjo as head of state. In the end Mola's **Nationalist army rebellion** of July 1936 triggered a **Civil War** that was to last until April 1939. The war was a national calamity: as well as claiming half a million lives, it caused untold damage to the country's towns, cities and infrastructure, and led to the repressive dictatorship of **General Francisco Franco**, which only ended with his death in 1975.

Franco was an *Africanista*, a soldier who had fought in Morocco, had risen to be chief-of-staff, but was then virtually exiled to the Canary Islands. What no one had anticipated were the man's formidable political cunning or his sheer good luck. He was not a remotely glamorous individual – at his death he was described as 'the sphinx without a secret' – but the dice always seemed to roll his way. Just three days after Mola launched his revolt Sanjurjo was killed in a plane crash, and nine months later Mola himself was killed in the same way. Meanwhile, in November 1936, **José Antonio Primo de Rivera**, son of the 1920s dictator, and founder of the neo-fascist **Falange** mass party, was shot in a Republican prison in Alicante. As a result Franco was able to suborn the Falange to his own ends. But just as crucial as any of these deaths was Franco's dependence on **Hitler** and **Mussolini.** The Nationalists only won the ensuing Civil War because of the military assistance forthcoming from Germany and Italy. From its beginning the conflict was internationalist. But whereas the Republic had only the intermittent support of the far-off **Soviet Union** and the passion of the **International Brigades**, the Nationalists could rely on Hitler's formidable **Condor Legion**, and on 50,000 Italian troops.

Franco, or **El Caudillo** ('the leader') as he became known as, reaped the benefit, and, after 1939, Spain was run as a one-man state. During World War II both the Axis and the Allies were kept at arm's length: Britain's fears of losing **Gibraltar** were exploited to secure badly needed grain and oil supplies from the United States, while Germany was grudgingly provided with war materials and secret bases for its submarines. After 1945, Franco won at least a degree of respectability in the West by his virulent anti-communism during the **Cold War**. He manipulated those around him in a similar fashion. Although he had assumed leadership of the Falange in 1936, the party was never his only means to power. Rather he used it to control the traditionalists in his government, just as he used the traditionalists to control the Falange. What guaranteed Franco's survival, however, was his guarded promise that, after his death, the **monarchy** would be restored. Spaniards of different political persuasions had only to wait and change would come.

In the event, the outcome, accomplished without bloodshed, was little short of astonishing. **Juan Carlos**, a grandson of Alfonso XIII, was proclaimed king two days after Franco's demise in November 1975. Three years later, with the king's full backing, and thanks to his prime minister **Adolfo Suárez**, Spain was provided with a **democratic constitution**, progressive in nature, that largely overcame the nation's abiding regional differences in part by pandering to their aspirations.

MODERN SPAIN

FRANCE

BASQUE PROVINCES
San Sebastián
NAVARRA
Pamplona
LA RIOJA

Girona
CATALUNYA
Zaragoza
Lérida (Lleida)
Barcelona
ARAGON
Tortosa
Tarragona

Guadalajara
Teruel

BALEARIC ISLANDS
Palma

VALENCIA
Valencia
LA MANCHA
Albacete

Alicante

Murcia

Almería

N

ALGERIA

0   150 km

Melilla (Sp.)

Since 1978 Spanish politics have abided by the norms of democratic accountability. Successive governments of the left and of the right, led respectively by **Felipe González** (1982–1996) and **José Maria Aznar** (from 1996), have inclined to centrist positions. Much against the rub of Spanish history consensus politics appear to have taken root. Along the way interest has been excited by scandals, as Spanish politicians have proved no less immune to the corruptions of power than their counterparts elsewhere. But the greater fly in the ointment – apart from **Colonel Tejero**'s last-ditch attempted coup in 1981 – has been the continuing militancy of **Basque nationalists**, once lauded as the torchbearers of anti-authoritarianism, but now increasingly perceived as irrational die-hards.

In retrospect, Spain's recent and seemingly abrupt transition from dictatorship to modern functional democracy merits closer investigation. As Franco aged, so the day-to-day management of Spain passed to younger, more progressive hands. A key episode occurred as early as **1957**, when, guided by **Luis Carrero Blanco**, a group of neo-liberal technocrats assumed ministerial responsibilities. The same **technocrats**, many of whom belonged to the Catholic **Opus Dei** lay order, were scarcely committed to the ideals of democracy, but out of their reforms flowed the basics of Spain's regeneration. Spain also benefited from a deepening friendship with the **USA**, which, during its Cold War with the Soviet Union, embraced any regime whose credentials were stridently anti-communist. But perhaps as significant as these was a less dramatic process of economic and cultural reintegration with western Europe. Through the tourist explosion of the 1960s, which brought millions of holiday-makers to Spanish resorts; through the hundreds of thousands of 'poor' Spaniards who sought work 'abroad' before returning home; through the inexorable diffusion of 'foreign' consumer goods and marketing techniques; through the advent of TV; through academic exchange; and also through sporting contacts, Spain rediscovered the wider world as Franco's xenophobia withered on the vine.

1931 Following the proclamation of the **Second Republic** on 19 April a coalition government is formed made up of left-wing and moderate parties and factions, among them the PSOE (Socialists), the Left Republicans and Alejando Lerroux's Radical Republicans. **Alcalá Zamora**, a Catholic moderate, assumes the responsibilities of prime minister. **Manuel Azaña y Diaz**, the leader of the Left Republicans, is appointed Minister of War, and **Miguel Maura** becomes Minister of the Interior.

In May a series of attacks by the extreme left on ecclesiastical buildings creates divisions within the government. In the **general election** that follows the Socialists and Left Republicans strengthen their position in the Cortes. When members press for radical reforms, particularly with regard to the Church, Zamora and Maura resign, although shortly afterwards Zamora is voted the Republic's first President. **Azaña** becomes prime minister in October, and **Francisco Largo Caballero**, leader of the UGT (General Workers' Union), becomes Minister of Labour. Legislation is passed to give workers and unions more rights. Azaña also attempts to modernize the army by reducing the number of officers, but although generous pensions are offered those willing to take early retirement many senior military personnel express discontent.

In December a new **republican constitution** is ratified by the Cortes. Women are given the vote, and permitted to stand as candidates in elections. The Church is separated from the State, and freedom of worship is guaranteed. A progressive divorce law is promulgated and education in state-run colleges and schools is secularized. To prevent its

threatened secession **Catalunya** is granted limited autonomy, exercised through a regional assembly known as the
Generalitat. The constitution and its related legislation are
however opposed by Lerroux's increasingly right-of-centre
Radical Republicans as well as by conservatives. The
government is also faced by severe shortfalls in revenue,
exacerbated by inherited deficits.

1932 A **communist uprising** in Catalunya's Llobregat valley in January is crushed within five days by the Civil
Guard, although this provokes anarchist agitation in
Barcelona, Madrid and other cities. In Andalucía there is
mounting unrest among poorly paid farm labourers. There
are also increased tensions between the two largest unions,
the **UGT** and the **CNT**, now dominated by the Fed-
eración Anarquista Ibérica (Federation of Iberian
Anarchists). Strikes are accompanied by street violence.

As the political situation in Spain deteriorates, capital goes
abroad as the rich seek to protect their wealth. Fearing a
Bolshevik style revolution, conservatives begin rallying to
Acción Popular, a right-wing 'mass' party founded by
José Maria Gil Robles y Quiñones, a Catholic lawyer.
Dedicated to protecting the interests of the Church, the
landed aristocracy and the bourgeoisie, Gil Robles pro-
pounds 'accidentalism', a political theory that devalues the
existing government by arguing its transience.

When Azaña attempts to push through his army reforms
there is renewed discontent in the military. On 10 August
General José Sanjurjo issues a *pronunciamento* at Seville.
His coup fails however and Sanjurjo flees to Portugal.

1933 In January the Civil Guard quells disorder in a village
near Cádiz. Over twenty agricultural workers and members
of their families are killed. In February right-wing factions
combine to form **CEDA** – Confederación Española de
Derechas Autónomas (Confederation of Autonomous Right-

> **No other dialectic is admissible save the dialectic of fists and pistols when justice or the *patria* is offended.**
>
> José Antonio Primo de Rivera, speech in Madrid, 29 October 1933

Wing Groups). CEDA is led by **Gil Robles**, whose Acción Popular gives it an immediate backbone. Increasingly CEDA obstructs further radical legislation in the Cortes and in June **Largo Caballero**, leader of the UGT, resigns from the government out of disillusionment. Rejecting what he calls 'bourgeois democracy' as a viable means for achieving socialist aims, he begins mending fences with the anarchist CNT.

On the far right, the former dictator Primo de Rivera's son **José Antonio Primo de Rivera** creates the **Falange**, modelled on the Italian Fascist Party of Benito Mussolini. Whereas Mussolini's followers wear black shirts, Falangists wear blue shirts.

By October Azaña no longer commands a majority in the Cortes, and President Zamora calls for **elections** to be held in November. CEDA gains seats at the expense of the Socialists, but Gil Robles declines to form a government. Instead an administration is created by **Lerroux**, now perceived as the principal defender of middle-class interests, although his government is only sustained by CEDA's support. Under pressure, Lerroux begins reversing many of Azaña's reforms. In response, revolutionary **workers' councils** are established by miners in the Asturias, while right-wing Catalan nationalists cause unrest in Barcelona.

1934 In October CEDA formally joins Lerroux's administration, taking over the ministries of Labour, Justice and Agriculture. As the government lurches further to the right, the left responds with a series of strikes, demonstrations and, in the Asturias and Basque provinces, local insurrections.

Diego Hidalgo, the Minister of War, appoints **General Francisco Franco** to quell the unrest. Using Moroccan mercenaries Franco unleashes a brutal campaign against striking miners in the Asturias that includes shelling residential districts in Oviedo and other towns. Within two weeks Franco brings the province to heel. Reprisals against militant leaders continue into the next year. Franco is appointed Commander-in-Chief of Spain's army in Morocco.

1935 On 8 May Gils Robles enters Lerroux's government, replacing Hidalgo as Minister of War. The military is purged of suspected left-wingers, and Franco is promoted Chief of Staff. As the year progresses the government's image is tarnished by a series of corruption scandals, and in December Zamora orders a general election to be held the following February. Amid mounting chaos the Left begins re-uniting around a new socialist coalition, the **Popular Front**, organised by Azaña and Indalecio Prieto.

1936 Despite its exclusion from the Popular Front, the CNT instructs its members to vote for it on 16 February. The Popular Front narrowly defeats the Right, and with the support of the PSOE, is able to form a government. Back in power, Azaña adopts a markedly more radical rhetoric than in 1931–33, partly to build up support among the impoverished rural communities in the south, and among the independently-minded peoples of Galicia and the Basque provinces.

On 14 March **José Antonio Primo de Rivera**, leader of the Falange, is arrested and imprisoned at Alicante.

On 10 May Azaña takes over the presidency from Zamora, and his deputy **Santiago Casaves Quiroga** becomes prime minister. Franco is relieved as Chief-of-Staff and posted as commandant-general to the Canary Islands. Despite these and other moves Azaña and Quiroga fail to win the support of union-leader Largo Caballero, who presses the government to adopt explicitly revolutionary policies.

LIBRARY OF CONGRESS

A Republican poster of 1936 ridiculing the Nationalists and their supporters, who include the Nazis, the Church, Italian Fascists and Moroccan troops

Armed right-wing gangs set about creating disorder. The Falange gains new members, despite or because of Primo de Rivera's imprisonment. CEDA loses ground to the 'National Block', an 'anti-democratic' party set up by **José Calvo Sotelo**. Gil Robles responds by adopting fascist rhetoric, and is hailed as *Führerprinzip* at mass rallies. There is also a revival of the old **Carlist faction** (see p.396), sometimes called 'The Traditionalists'.

During May, as street-battles between Falangist and Socialist youth groups erupt in Barcelona, Burgos and other industrial cities, **General Emilio Mola** conspires to overthrow the government and make the exiled José Sanjurjo head of state. He is eagerly supported by **General Juan Segui** in Morocco, but is unable to enlist the whole-hearted commitment of Francisco Franco.

> ❝ The fighting had barely started when the newspapers of the Right and Left dived simultaneously into the same cesspool of abuse. We all remember the Daily Mail's poster: 'Reds Crucify Nuns', while to the Daily Worker Franco's Foreign Legion was 'composed of murderers, white-slavers, dope-fiends, and the offal of every European country'. As late as October 1937 the New Statesman was treating us to tales of Fascist barricades made of bodies of living children (a most unhandy thing to make barricades with), and Mr Arthur Bryant was declaring that 'the sawing-off of a Conservative tradesman's legs' was 'a commonplace' in loyalist Spain. The people who write that kind of stuff never fight; possibly they believe that to write it is a substitute for fighting. It is the same in all wars. The soldiers do the fighting, the journalists do the shouting, and no true patriot ever gets near a front-line trench, except on the briefest of propaganda-tours. ❞
>
> George Orwell, *Homage to Catalonia* (1938)

On 12 July the murder of a loyalist army officer, José de Castillo, is followed within hours by the assassination of José Calvo Sotelo, the most forceful of the rightist leaders. Franco is persuaded to join Mola's conspiracy, and on 17 July a military revolt is launched by the Spanish army in Morocco, triggering the **Spanish Civil War**.

On 18 July army garrisons across Spain declare in favour of Mola's *pronunciamento*, though the rebels fail to take control in Madrid, Barcelona, Valencia and Bilbao. **Franco** leaves the Canaries and flies to Casablanca to assume command of Spain's African forces. Already he has concocted a strategy with Mola whereby two rebel, or **Nationalist**, armies will converge on Madrid, one from the south, the other from the north. Franco's immediate problem however is to transport his men from North Africa to Spain across the Straits of Gibraltar. Aboard many warships, ratings mutiny against officers determined to joined the uprising, while some vessels remain loyal to the **Republic**.

On 20 July **José Sanjurjo**, returning from exile in Portugal, is killed when his overloaded plane crashes. Three days later Mola sets up a *Junta de Defensa Nacional* (National Defence Council) at **Burgos** as the supreme body of the his Nationalist uprising. Shortly afterwards Franco makes his first, unilateral overtures to the fascist regimes in Italy and Germany. Both **Mussolini** and **Hitler** agree to provide air cover for the movement of his troops across the Straits of Gibraltar. On 5 August, protected by Italian and German warplanes, Franco begins ferrying his army to southern Spain, and establishes his headquarters at **Seville**. On 10 August Franco captures **Mérida**, where his Moroccan soldiers indulge in wanton savagery against suspected Republicans. When **Badajoz** falls on 14 August some 2000 killings follow, and similar scenes attend the fall of **Talavera** on 3 September. In the north, Mola secures many cities in Old Castile and Navarra with the help of

Carlist sympathizers. The Nationalist rebels encounter stiff resistance however in Galicia, the Asturias and the Basque provinces, while Catalunya, Valencia and large parts of central Spain remain Republican.

On 19 August, the poet, dramatist and painter **Federico García Lorca** – a Republican sympathizer and known homosexual – is murdered in Granada on the orders of the Nationalist civil governor. A friend of Salvador Dalí and Luis Buñuel, Lorca's poetry presents the beauty and harshness of Andalucian life through vivid, often surrealist, imagery. His 'folk tragedies', *Bodas de sangre* ('Blood Wedding', 1935), *Yerma* and *La casa de Bernarda Alba* ('The House of Bernarda Alba', 1940), are widely regarded as amongst the century's greatest plays.

President Azaña appoints an **emergency cabinet** headed by José Giral. Where the army does not remain loyal to the Republic, militias of mainly untrained workers are created and these prevent the larger cities falling into Nationalist hands. As the militias take control of the streets, some atrocities are perpetrated against known and perceived rightists. During the course of the war some 4000 priests and 2500 monks and nuns will be murdered. In Barcelona, Madrid and other cities anarchists and extreme socialists, while remaining loyal to the Republic, institute **revolutionary councils** and collectivize factories and farms. The CNT energetically promotes the view that Mola's rebellion will only be crushed by instigating immediate full-scale revolution. Such initiatives are opposed by the **Spanish Communist Party**, which supports the government's appeals to the Soviet Union for aid – initially rejected by **Joseph Stalin**. On 5 September, Azaña invites **Largo Caballero** to form a new government of unity. Drawing support from the CNT as well as his own UGT union, Caballero begins building a **Popular Army** to take over from the militias.

> **The horses are black.**
> **The horseshoes are black.**
> **On the capes shine**
> **stains of ink and wax.**
> **They have lead skulls**
> **which is why they don't cry.**
> **With their souls of patent-leather**
> **they come along the street.**

Federico García Lorca, *The Ballad of the Civil Guard*, trans. Roger Bardon (1967)

Mola takes the northern port of **San Sebastián** on 12 September, giving him control of the Basque province of Guipúzcoa. In the south, Franco diverts his forces from marching on Madrid toward **Toledo**, where the Alcázar (citadel) is under siege from Republican forces. On 21 September he meets with Mola and other Nationalist leaders at **Salamanca**. Playing up his relations with Hitler and Mussolini, Franco persuades his colleagues to appoint him overall commander of the rebel forces, and also to secretly elect him head of a provisional government. The Alcázar is relieved on 29 September – a victory proclaimed by Franco as part of a 'crusade' against infidel communists, and endorsed by Toledo's archbishop, **Cardinal Gomá**. On 1 October Franco is invested as *Jefe del Estado* – Chief of State – by the nationalist Junta. He adopts the fascist salute, and encourages the use of his 'African' nickname, **El Caudillo**.

On 6 October Franco resumes his march on **Madrid**. Advised of Franco's adoption of the trappings of fascism, Stalin offers support to the Republic. From mid-October **Soviet weapons**, including tanks and warplanes, are

> **We have four columns advancing on Madrid. The fifth column will rise at the proper time.**
>
> Emilio Mola, in a radio broadcast, October 1936.

shipped into Cartagena, Valencia, Barcelona and other Mediterranean ports. Handled by the Spanish Communist Party, many of the armaments are forwarded for the defence of Madrid, whose outskirts are penetrated by Nationalist forces at the beginning of November. Madrid resists the Nationalists' onslaught, and prevents encirclement by Franco's army. The capital's morale is boosted by the arrival of the first **International Brigades** on 8 November.

By mid-November, following fierce fighting on the outskirts of northern and southern Madrid, the battlefront 'stabilizes' as both sides dig in to protect their positions. On 20 November **José Antonio Primo de Rivera** is shot in the prison at Alicante.

In December **Mussolini** agrees to send ground troops to support the Nationalist cause. 50,000 Italian troops will fight in Spain.

1937 On 3 January Franco orders a fresh assault on Madrid. 30,000 men die before the front again stabilizes two weeks later. Opening up a new front to the east of Madrid, nationalist forces advance along the **Jaruma valley** on the main Valencia road on 6 February, but fail to break through Republican lines.

On 7 February **Málaga** falls to Mussolini's Italian troops. Those left inside the town are massacred, while those attempting to flee are shelled from both air and sea.

The International Brigades

In the 1930s many younger radicals in Europe and further afield, unaware of the full extent of the atrocities perpetrated by Joseph Stalin against his own people in the USSR, firmly believed **Communism** was the key to the future. As the Spanish Civil War got under way, and the Nationalists' close links with Hitler and Mussolini became apparent, there was a natural tendency among such idealists to fight on the Republican side, the more so as the **Comintern** (Communist International) provided a means – the International Brigades. There were seven brigades in all, divided by nationality, including the 'Abraham Lincoln Brigade' for Americans, and the 'Garibaldi Brigade' for Italians. The main recruitment centre was the Comintern's Paris office, which organized rallies sometimes graced by the electrifying presence of **'La Pasionara'** – in reality Dolores Ibarruri, a founder of the Spanish Communist Party in 1920 and famed for her exhortation 'It is better to die on your feet than live on your knees'. Not everyone who signed up was a card-carrying communist, but 60 percent were, and a further 20 percent joined the Party once they had arrived in Spain.

In all there were around **20,000 volunteers**, half of them French. The first group of 500 arrived at Albacete on 14 October 1936, and 1900 volunteers helped defend **Madrid** during the siege that began three weeks later. The Brigades also made valuable contributions to the Republican cause during the **Battle of Guadalajara** – when they helped repel an Italian armoured corps – and in fighting along the **Ebro** in 1938. By then however the number of fresh recruits had begun to dwindle, partly because it was becoming obvious that Franco would win the war, and partly because of an increased appreciation of the dangers involved. Thousands of volunteers never returned home. Among those who did was the writer **George Orwell**, whose *Homage to Catalonia* (1938), a classic account of the infighting on the Republican side, became the best known English-language account of the war, rivalled only by **Ernest Hemingway**'s engrossing but less dispassionate novel *For Whom the Bell Tolls* (1940), derived from its author's experience of the Civil War not as a fighter but as a reporter.

On 8 March, to relieve the pressure on his troops at Jaruma, Franco persuades three Italian divisions to launch a diversionary offensive at **Guadalajara**, 50 km to the northeast of Madrid. On 12 March the Republican Popular Army counterattacks, inflicting massive damage on the Italians. Franco is suspected of withholding Spanish reinforcements.

On 31 March Mola launches a major offensive to overcome remaining Basque resistance and gain control of **Bilbao** and other key industrial centres. **Durango** is subjected to aerial bombardment by the German **Condor Legion** (see opposite).

On 19 April, using intimidation as well as argument, and guided by his brother-in-law **Ramón Serrano Suñer**, Franco welds the Falange, the Carlists and other rightist groups into a single party – the *Falange Español Tradicionalista y de las Juntas de Ofensiva Nacional Sindicalista* (FET y de las JONS) – with himself as its supreme leader.

On 26 April the Condor Legion and some Italian warplanes assault the traditional Basque capital **Guernica**, killing over 2500 civilians with incendiary bombs in a deliberate act of terror designed to induce Basque surrender. International indignation is compounded when Franco first tries to conceal what has happened, then points an accusing finger at the Basques themselves.

On 3 May a **'secondary' civil war** erupts in Barcelona, between orthodox Communists and an anarchist coalition of the CNT and POUM (Partido Obrero de Unifición Marxista) intent on setting up a revolutionary workers' government to replace the Republic's Popular Front. CNT and POUM are smashed, and on 17 May Largo Caballero, who has supported the anarchists, is forced to relinquish his premiership in favour of **Juan Negrín**, who forges a new union of Socialists and Communists. The POUM leader, Andreu Nin, is abducted by Soviet agents and murdered. The Catalan Generalitat is dissolved.

The Condor Legion

Within days of the beginning of Mola's insurrection Franco contacted Berlin as well as Rome to request air support to assist him move troops from Morocco to Andalucía. Hitler realized that this would enable the **Third Reich** to test its rapidly evolving weapons systems in battle conditions. Accordingly, in November 1936, he authorized the dispatch of an entire battle group – the infamous **Condor Legion**. Its main components were four bomber squadrons and four fighter squadrons – Junkers, Heinkels, even, slightly later on, the awesome Messerschmitt 109. German pilots and ground-staff, anti-tank and anti-aircraft units, and motorized artillery all accompanied the aircraft. Although nominally under German field command – **General Hugo Sperrle**, and later **Wolfram von Richthofen** – the Legion did what the Nationalist high command asked it to do. From the outset the German contingent willingly embraced Franco's style of war, which was to terrorize the enemy regardless of whether targets were military or civilian. Madrid, Barcelona, Valencia, Bilbao and other Republican strongholds were regularly subjected to heavy and sustained aerial bombardment – the beginnings of what subsequently became known as *Blitzkrieg*. The most notorious instance occurred at **Guernica**, where, on a market-day in April 1937, an entire town was levelled and half its inhabitants killed during a three-hour attack. In an attempt to cover up what it had done, the Condor Legion sent in sweepers to remove incriminating evidence, but the chance presence of four British and Belgian reporters during the raid meant that the atrocity could not be kept from the world. Notwithstanding, the Legion continued deploying its might in similar fashion until the end of the war, taking out Soviet warplanes as it did so. In large measure the Nationalist victory was made possible by Hitler's gift. Yet as the war progressed Franco was made to pay for it. In what became known as the **Montana Project**, Germany demanded mining rights in captured northern territories as well as in Morocco. Spain was also expected to provide wolfram and other minerals essential to Hitler's re-armament programme – a means of reimbursement that continued during World War II.

On 3 June **Emilio Mola** is killed in an air-crash flying from Vitoria to Burgos, reinforcing Franco's position as undisputed leader of the Nationalist cause.

On 18 June **Bilbao** falls to Franco's army, signalling the collapse of the Republicans' 'northern' front.

In June **Pablo Picasso** finishes his large canvas *Guernica*, an indictment of the bombing of the Basque town, which is exhibited at the Spanish pavilion of the Paris **Exposition Internationale**.

On 6 July the Republic's Popular Army, commanded by **Vincente Rojo**, launches a counteroffensive against **Brunete**, west of Madrid. During a 19-day battle thousands are killed on both sides before the Popular Army retreats.

On 24 August Rojo launches a fresh Republican offensive out of Catalunya aimed at capturing **Zaragoza**.

On 26 August, following the fall of Santander, the **Basques** surrender to the Nationalists. Franco orders brutal reprisals against Basque militiamen, sowing the seeds for the Basques' enduring hatred of his regime.

On 2 September Franco decides to 'clear' the **Asturias** – an operation completed by the end of October. Republican sympathizers are rounded up and used as forced labour in the province's coal mines.

On 6 September Rojo's forces capture **Belchite**, but fail against Zaragoza.

In November Franco prepares to renew the assault on Madrid.

On 15 December Rojo, hoping to relieve pressure on Madrid, mounts a Republican counteroffensive in southern Aragon, capturing **Teruel**. On 29 December, believing the opportunity exists to break the Popular Army, Franco orders his main forces into Aragon.

The Spanish Pavilion

The **International Exhibition** of 1937, with its theme of modern technological achievement, took place in Paris between May and November. Dominating the exhibition grounds were the towering, and bombastic, pavilions of Germany and the USSR. The **Spanish Pavilion**, in comparison, was a small structure designed by **José Luis Sert** in a distinctly modernist style. The Civil War delayed the opening of the pavilion, and it also provided the subject matter for many of the exhibits, which emphasized the brutality of Franco's Nationalists and the assumed efficacy of the Republic's social policies. Beginning with the tall abstract sculpture by Alberto Sanchez Perez that stood outside the entrance, most of the art on display could be described as avant-garde. **Joan Miró** contributed a large canvas, *The Reaper*, of an uplifted arm and clenched fist; there was a fountain and mobile by the American artist Alexander Calder; while in the auditorium documentary films, including *Madrid '36* by **Luis Buñuel**, were screened at regular intervals.

As Spain's most famous artist, **Pablo Picasso** (whom the Republican government had recently appointed director of the Prado) was under pressure to make a significant contribution to the pavilion. When news of the aerial bombardment of the Basque town of **Guernica** (see p.436) reached Paris, it prompted a vast street demonstration of protesters, and provided Picasso with a powerfully resonant subject. Three months, and over forty preliminary studies, later *Guernica* was erected in the pavilion. Working on a large scale, and with reference to both specifically Spanish imagery as well that of the old masters (Goya's *3rd of May* was a particular influence), Picasso produced a painting that has become a universally recognized emblem of the horror of war. Initial reaction was largely negative, however, with both the German and the Soviet responses predictably hostile. When the exhibition closed *Guernica* toured Europe and the USA as a means of raising awareness of the Spanish civil war, finishing up at the Museum of Modern Art. It remained there for over forty years, only returning to Spain in 1981.

1938 On 31 January Franco creates a cabinet that replaces the military *junta* as the principal instrument of Nationalist government. His brother-in-law Serrano Suñer is appointed Minister of Interior. Other posts are divided among Falangists, armymen and Carlist traditionalists.

On 7 February the Republican lines in Aragon are broken, and two weeks later Teruel is recaptured after some of the bloodiest fighting in the war. On 6 March Republican spirits are lifted by the sinking of the Nationalist battle-cruiser the *Baleares*. On 15 March Franco orders his forces to drive down the **Ebro** toward the sea with a view to forcing a wedge between Barcelona and Valencia. On 15 April the Nationalist army reaches the Mediterranean. Rather than march north against Barcelona, Franco chooses to bombard **Valencia**, the lesser target, on 23 June. The following night, Rojo launches the last main Republican offensive out of Catalunya across the Ebro at **Gandesa**. Again Franco allows himself to be diverted, and there follows a six-month battle which results in the rout of the Popular Army. During the fighting, Republican morale is severely dented by news of the **Munich Agreement**, between Hitler and British Prime Minister Neville Chamberlain, which dispels hopes of an immediate anti-Fascist war in Europe. In October Negrín orders the withdrawal of the **International Brigades**, and on 17 November the Internationals wave goodbye to crowds gathered in Barcelona. Shortly afterwards the USSR ceases giving support to the Republic. On 23 December the Ebro front collapses, and Nationalist forces swarm into Catalunya.

1939 In mid-January **Tarragona** falls to the Nationalists. On the 25 January the Republican government abandons Barcelona for **Gerona**; Nationalist soldiers enter Barcelona, now largely deserted, the next day. Although Republican forces under **General Mioja** continue to control parts of central Spain, as well as Madrid, President Azaña flees to France on 6 February, quickly followed by Negrín and

Rojo. On 13 February Franco issues a **'Law of Political Responsibilities'**, promising reprisals against all republicans (including trades unions members). Not only is **'serious passivity'** deemed a crime, but the law is made retroactive to October 1934. Across Nationalist Spain, a witch-hunt begins which will account for the imprisonment and execution of tens of thousands of non-Nationalists in the coming years.

On 4 March tensions in what remains of the Republican camp boil over into open fighting. In **Madrid** communists and non-communists kill each other. On 27 March Franco's troops begin marching into the capital, which, on the point of starvation, offers only token resistance. On the same day Franco signs up to the **Anti-Comintern Pact**, created by Hitler and Mussolini, and a few days later signs a bilateral Treaty of Friendship with Nazi Germany. On 1 April the **Spanish Civil War** is officially ended, although republican enclaves will continue fighting until 1951.

On 8 August Franco assumes the right to issue decrees without reference even to his cabinet. On 3 September **World War II** commences when Britain and France enter into hostilities against Germany. Franco declares **Spain's neutrality** while agreeing to supply Germany (and later Italy) with war materials, and also with fuelling bases for its submarines. On 8 October he announces a 10-year economic plan based on the principle of economic autarky (self-sufficiency), and at the same time introduces food rationing. Ten days later Franco takes up residence at **El Pardo**, a country house outside Madrid where he holds court for the next thirty-five years.

1940 In February Franco promulgates the **Law of the Repression of Freemasonry and Communism** in an attempt to legitimize his regime's continuing persecution of its ideological enemies. On 1 April construction begins of the *Valle de los Caídos* (Valley of the Fallen'), a vast monument to Nationalist soldiers killed during the Civil War.

Sited in the valley of Cuelgamuros, the project will take twenty years to complete using forced labour at a cost of US$ 200 million. Its internal basilica, hewn from solid granite, is 262 metres long, and 41 metres high at its maximum. The complex is surmounted by a 150-metre-high Cross.

During May **Cardinal Segura** of Seville breaks ranks with his fellow bishops and criticizes Franco's government on humanitarian grounds. On 24 May Britain appoints **Sir Samuel Hoare**, a senior politician, as its ambassador to Madrid, tasked with keeping Franco out of hostilities. On 8 June R.A. Butler suggests in the House of Commons that the future of **Gibraltar** may be discussed after World War II provided Spain remains neutral. On 13 June Franco affirms Spain's neutrality while continuing to give Germany and Italy clandestine support. Two days later Spanish forces occupy the free port of **Tangiers** in Morocco in order 'to protect its neutrality'. The real aim is to add French Morocco to Spanish Morocco. In August **Hitler** begins pressurizing Franco to enter the war on the Axis's side. On 23 October the two leaders meet at **Hendaye**, a French resort. Franco makes clear to Hitler that the recovery of Gibraltar, the annexation of French Morocco to Spain and the provision of weapons for his depleted army are among his conditions. Hitler rejects Franco's terms, but a protocol is issued stating that Spain will enter the war 'when the time is right'. In the same month deteriorating economic conditions and a failed harvest lead to preliminary negotiations with the **USA** to supply Spain with grain.

1941 In January the Red Cross delivers the first **US grain consignments** to Spain. On 12 February Franco meets Mussolini at **Bordighera** in Italy. The Spanish dictator repeats his pledge that Spain will enter the war when conditions are right. On 26 March Franco issues the **Law of State Security**, allowing for political dissidents to be tried by military tribunals. On 7 April **Britain** grants Spain trade credits worth £2.7 million. In May, following tensions between members of his cabinet, Franco appoints Colonel Valentin Galaza as Minister of Interior in place of his brother-in-law **Serrano Suñer**, who becomes Foreign Minister.

Following Germany's **invasion of Russia** on 21 June, in August Franco sends the **Blue Division**, made up of Spanish troops, to fight alongside Hitler's forces on the eastern front. To Britain and America Franco justifies his action by claiming Spain's troops are engaged only in a war against communism. In November the Falange is purged of anti-Francoist elements.

The Japanese attack **Pearl Harbour** on 7 December. America's consequent entry into the war on the Allied side gives Franco reason to delay declaring war on Britain.

1942 In February the USA makes **oil shipments** to Spain conditional on its being allowed to monitor the uses to which it is put. In May tensions between the Falange and monarchist elements within the army erupt into street battles in several cities, mirrored by student unrest in Madrid and Santiago. On 16 August Falangists throw two bombs into a crowd at a Carlist monarchist meeting at **Begoña**. Yielding to pressure from the army, Franco dismisses the pro-Falange Serrano Suñer from his cabinet in September. **General Francisco Gómez Jordana**, known to favour the Allies, becomes Foreign Minister.

1943 Allied successes against Hitler in Russia and North Africa, and against Mussolini in Italy, finally persuade Franco not to enter World War II. Following **Mussolini's downfall** in July, he begins soliciting Allied friendship. On 26 September he orders the withdrawal of the **Blue Division** from German lines, although Spanish soldiers are allowed to remain on the Russian front as volunteers. In the same month Spanish Republicans who have been supporting the French Resistance overrun the **Val d'Asran** in the Pyrenees, starting an eight-year guerrilla war against Franco's regime.

On 17 March Franco announces that a **Cortes** will be summoned. Its membership however consists of those appointed directly by the dictator, those who are *ex officio* loyalists, and those nominated by Falangist syndicates.

1945 On 15 March **Don Juan de Borbón** – the third son of Alfonso XIII and pretender to the Spanish throne – issues the **Lausanne Manifesto**, denouncing Franco's regime and promising a return to constitutional monarchy. In April, anxious to appease Allied sensibilities, Franco issues the *Fueros de los Españolas* ('Rights of the Spanish'), a supposed charter of liberties that describes Spain as a Catholic democracy in which personal freedoms are guaranteed to those who do not oppose the government. In Europe, **World War II** ends on 7 May with the defeat of Hitler. On 18 July Franco dismisses those ministers known for their pro-Axis sentiments, but fails to convince Britain, the United States or France that Spain should be admitted to the **United Nations** (UN).

1946 Early in the year senior army officers are dismissed from Franco's cabinet for expressing support for the restoration of the Spanish monarchy. On 26 February France seals its borders with Spain. On 12 December the UN votes by a majority to exclude Spain from all UN bodies. Spain however is supported by most Latin American countries in the General Assembly.

1947 In May, as Spain's economy continues to suffer, there is **industrial unrest** in Madrid, Catalunya and the Basque provinces, despite a prohibition against strikes. Striking miners are brutally suppressed by the **Civil Guard**. Employers refusing to dismiss strikers are imprisoned.

In June **Eva Perón**, wife of the Argentinian dictator Juan Perón, visits Spain and provides Franco with a much needed propaganda coup. Through the period of Spain's post-war isolation **Argentina** remains a vital source for grain supplies and other merchandise.

On 6 July, attempting to 'prove' Spain's democracy, Franco stages a **national referendum**. Voters, who are intimidated at polling stations, are asked whether they would prefer a Catholic or a Communist state.

1948 In February, Russia's invasion of Czechoslovakia heightens **Cold War** tensions between East and West. Determined to resist the spread of communism, the USA begins looking upon Franco's regime more favourably, although in March President Harry S. Truman affirms Spain's exclusion from the **Marshall Plan**, designed to resuscitate Europe's ailing economies.

On 25 August Franco and Don Juan de Borbón agree that the pretender's 10-year-old son **Juan Carlos**, whom Franco is already thinking of as his eventual successor, should leave Portugal and be privately educated in Spain under the Caudillo's supervision.

1949 On 8 February the **National City** and **Chase Manhattan Banks** loan US$25 million to Franco's regime with the approval of the US government. In March **NATO** (North Atlantic Treaty Organisation), a defence pact against the USSR, is established without reference to Spain following objections from Britain and France.

1950 Franco's offer to send troops to **Korea**, where a war between communists and American-backed nationalists has broken out on 24 June, is spurned. On 24 November however the **UN** votes to rescind its diplomatic boycott against Spain. In the same month the US government authorizes a $62 million loan to help Franco modernize Spain's military.

1951 In March Barcelona experiences a **general strike** in which 300,000 workers, dismayed by the sharply rising cost of living, participate. A show of military strength ends the strike, but in April there is further industrial unrest in the **Basque provinces**, supported by Basque separatists.

Francisco Franco (1892–1975)

The man who dominated Spain for close on forty years – Francisco Paulino Hermenegildo Teódulo Franco Bahamonde – was born in El Ferrol in Galicia. His father worked in the naval pay corps. The young Franco attempted to sign up for the navy proper, but failing that enrolled at the Military Academy in Toledo, graduating 251st out of a class of 312. Serving in **Morocco**, however, he more than made his mark, as a fearless soldier and keen disciplinarian. He became commander of the recently formed **Spanish Legion**, and by 1926 was the youngest general in the army. In 1934, using brutal methods, he crushed a workers' uprising in the **Asturias**, paving the way for his promotion to Chief-of-Staff under the right-wing Lerroux/Gils Robles government of 1935. The following year however his career nose-dived. Manuel Azaña punished Franco for what he had done in the Asturias by banishing him to the Canaries with strict orders not to leave his post. Despite this rebuff, Franco, whose natural instinct inclined to caution, delayed joining Mola's insurrection until the last minute.

Franco emerged as military and political leader of the Nationalists, acquiring control of the fascist **Falange** in the process, and in 1939 set up a near-unassailable personal dictatorship. Crucially, he did not attempt to impose a single, uniform political doctrine on those who carried out the business of his government, but allowed men of varying opinions to work side by side while reserving unlimited powers of patronage to himself. It was, though, during the Civil War that his true character emerged. Twice he deliberately delayed attacking **Madrid**, and in 1938, having swept down the Ebro to the Mediterranean, he chose to assault Valencia rather than Barcelona, which at the time was his for the taking. The war, therefore, lasted far longer than was militarily necessary. But Franco's object was to destroy as well as defeat the enemy. Communists, socialists, Jews and 'freemasons' – a term Franco used to denote liberals – were all vermin who had no place in the Spain of his distinctly medieval imagination.

To achieve his ends Franco used **Moroccan mercenaries** to slaughter his at least nominally Christian foes. Yet in victory he proclaimed himself Spain's divinely ordained saviour. Coins minted during his regime bore the legend 'Caudillo by the Grace of God.' This, though, squared ill with his appearance. Hitler called him a 'fat little sergeant', and the American journalist John Whitaker (who accompanied the Nationalist army) described him as "Excessively shy...his voice is shrill and pitched on a high note which is slightly disconcerting since he speaks very softly – almost in a whisper." To enhance this rather unprepossessing image, Franco regularly dressed up in elaborate uniforms. On hunting expeditions – his favourite pastime – his aids worked overtime, laying baits to ensure the presence of easy prey. He stalked wild geese with a machine-gun and during the difficult closing months of 1940 wrote a novel – *Raza* ('Race'): a thinly disguised effort at self-glamourization published under the pseudonym Jaime de Andrade.

Franco addressing a Falangist celebration in Madrid

MEPL

In November Franco offers Britain a 99-year lease-back arrangement if it will return **Gibraltar** to Spanish sovereignty. The offer is rejected.

1953 On 22 February prominent monarchists are placed under arrest in Madrid and other cities. On the 27 August Franco's government signs a concordat with the **Vatican** guaranteeing the Church a role in Spain's educational institutions. Catholicism is confirmed as the official state religion.

On 26 September Spain and the USA sign the **Pact of Madrid**, a bilateral agreement that allows America to acquire four air-force bases on Spanish soil in return for grant aid worth US$625 million.

Carrero Blanco, who will prove Franco's staunchest ally in the coming years, becomes chief of his political staff.

1954 As Franco pushes his regime's Catholic credentials, **Rafael Carlo Serer** establishes *Opus Dei*, a secular order that advocates the pursuit of personal excellence by adhering to Catholic values. Perceived by Franco as a useful instrument to contain both monarchists and Falangists, *Opus Dei* rapidly acquires official sanction.

On 21 November municipal elections are held in Madrid for the first time since 1939. Voting however is restricted to heads of families and married women, and voters are intimidated by Falangist hardliners.

The birth of Franco's first grandson – **Cristobal Martinez Bordiu** – by his only daughter prompts speculation that the Caudillo will create a new dynasty. On 29 December however Franco agrees with Don Juan that **Juan Carlos** will stay in Spain to attend military academies and university.

1955 Spain is admitted into the **UN** in December in the wake of intense politicking by the USA.

1956 On 8 February **students** in Madrid, protesting for better living conditions and the liberalization of academic courses, clash with Falangists. During a scuffle at the Faculty of Law a Falangist – Miguel Alvarez Pérez – sustains a gunshot wound. Following this and other incidents of student unrest, Franco appears to back calls made for the instigation of a full totalitarian state made by his Minister-Secretary **José Luis de Arrese** and others. Arrese however is opposed by Carrero Blanco, and by a coalition of monarchists and Opus Dei members.

On 2 March France concedes **French Morocco**'s independence under its sultan **Mohammed V**. On 5 March a nationalist revolt erupts in **Spanish Morocco**. Lacking the resources for a colonial war, Franco hands over rule to Mohammed, although the formal independence of Spain's last important colony is not promulgated until April 1957.

In April there is a wave of **strikes** in the Basque provinces and the Asturias calling for higher wages. Strong-armed methods used to suppress the strikes only encourage **Basque nationalism** (see p.464).

1957 Advised by Carrero Blanco, Franco overhauls his cabinet in February. Arrese and other Falange hardliners are replaced by Opus Dei members, including **Laureano López Rodó**, who comes in as 'technical director', and **Nariano Navarro Rubio**, Minister of Finance. Although it is not immediately obvious, the reshuffle constitutes a major shift in the regime's policies. The new breed of ministers, known as **technocrats**, even **neo-liberals**, are committed to industrial reform, to encouraging foreign investment and to participating in western Europe's new capital markets, as well as modernizing education and social welfare. A **Decree-Law of the Juridical Regime of the Administration of the State** issued on 27 February formalizes the cabinet system, giving greater individual responsibility to ministers and preparing the way for Franco's eventual role as a figure-head in government.

Luis Buñuel (1900–1983)

One of Europe's outstanding film-makers, Luis Buñuel shot to prominence with his first production, ***Un Chien andalou*** ('An Andalucian dog'), in 1928. Made in close collaboration with Salvador Dalí (see p.415), this short piece, with its tumble of disconnected, chilling images, including an ant's nest pitted in a human hand and most famously the apparent slicing of a woman's eyeball with a razor, exactly captured the spirit of **surrealism** on film. Subsequently Buñuel turned toward more structured narratives as he repeatedly savaged Spain's Establishment. His Surrealism remained a guiding principle, however. Again and again his satires, sometimes aping conventional cinematic realism, explode on the screen in sudden phantasmagoric bursts – a dramatic tendency encouraged by the more absurd trappings of his most persistent target, the **Catholic Church**.

Buñuel's radicalism frequently landed him in trouble. When his fiercely anti-clerical second film, *L'Age d'or* ('The Age of Gold', 1930), was screened in Paris police had to clear the auditorium. *Las Hurdes* ('Land Without Bread', 1932), a no-holds barred portrait of impoverished Spanish villagers, earned Buñuel the opprobrium of the government, and forced him into voluntary exile. For almost twenty years he lived in France, the US and Mexico, either undertaking commercial work or not making any movies at all. But in 1950 he returned to the international scene with a vengeance. Still in Mexico, he scraped together enough money to create ***Los olvidados*** ('The Young and the Damned'), a searing indictment of the criminal justice system through its sympathetic presentation of juvenile delinquency.

From then on there was no holding Buñuel back. In 1960 he embarrassed **Franco**'s regime, which had allowed him to return to Spain, by winning the prestigious Palme d'Or at Cannes with ***Viridiana***, memorably presenting the Last Supper as a beggar's banquet. Subsequent productions included *El ángel exterminador*

('The Exterminating Angel', 1962), in which a roomful of bourgeois socialites are trapped by their own vacuity, *Simón del desierto* ('Simon of the Desert', 1965), depicting the religious insanity of an anchorite, and *Belle de Jour* (1966), in which Catherine Deneuve plays a wealthy Parisienne who takes a day job as prostitute. Repeatedly Buñuel came up with titles that lured his art-house audiences into iconoclastic ambush – *Le Charme discret de la Bourgeoisie* ('The Discreet Charm of the Bourgeoisie', 1972), for instance, or *Cet Obscur Objet de Désir* ('That Obscure Object of Desire', 1977). Guerrilla tactics coupled with a profound understanding of sado-masochism were integral to his cinema.

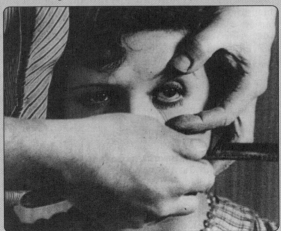

BRITISH FILM INSTITUTE

The infamous eye-slitting sequence from Buñuel's *Un Chien Andalou*

commitment to Catholicism and 'social justice', presented to the Cortes on 17 May confirms the ascendancy of the technocrats. As their rationalizing policies begin taking effect, however, unemployment and inflation rise. Following a further wave of strikes in the Basque provinces, and in Catalunya, limited collective wage bargaining is introduced. Secretive and communist-dominated **Workers' Commissions** are established in factories and other workplaces.

1959 Negotiations for loans from the **IMF** (International Monetary Fund) begin in January. On 6 March Franco accepts a **Stabilization Plan**. Placed on international exchange markets, the *peseta* devalues by half, and public spending is slashed in line with IMF requirements. As a result of these and other measures Spain's economy begins to revive. **Tourism** takes off, and industry benefits from a dramatic increase in **inward investment**, although some industries (notably tobacco and petrol) continue to be run as state corporations. Economic growth is initally confined to specific regions, with Catalunya, Valencia, the Basque provinces and Madrid the main beneficiaries, along with holiday resorts on the Mediterranean littoral. Spain's new wealth gradually spreads out in the form of improvements to national education and healthcare programmes, and over the coming years there is marked **urban migration** as younger people abandon still impoverished rural areas.

In Madrid, the first **synagogue** to be permitted in Spain since 1492 is opened on 2 October.

A group of militant **Basque nationalists** (see p.464) found **ETA** (Euskadi Ta Askatasuna), a Marxist organization committed to achieving Basque independence, by violent means if necessary.

1960 *Viridiana*, a film by **Luis Buñuel**, wins the Palme d'Or at the Cannes International Film Festival, but is immediately banned by the Spanish government.

1962 A year of endemic industrial action sees an advance in genuine workers' representation at the expense of Falangist syndicates. Many employees prefer to settle with their employees rather than lose production.

On 14 May Juan Carlos marries **Princess Sofia of Greece** in Athens.

In October **Pope John XXIII**, anxious to promote social justice, inaugurates the **Second Vatican Council**. Many of the Council's pronouncements offer both implicit and explicit criticisms of Franco's regime, encouraging a new generation of priests to engage in oppositional politics in Spain.

1963 The torture and execution of a communist politician, **Julián Grimau**, provokes an international outcry during which Franco's past is exhumed in the world's press. On 11 April John XXIII issues his encyclical *Pacem in Terris* ('Peace on Earth'), calling for human rights to be observed in all Catholic nations. On 3 May Franco's government agrees that **political trials** should in future be conducted in civil rather than military courts. In September two alleged anarchists are garotted. In the same month Spain permits the USA to construct a base for its **Polaris nuclear submarines** in Spanish waters in return for further aid.

1964 On 24 May **Juan Carlos** stands beside Franco during the annual Civil War victory parade in Madrid. In June Spain hosts the **European football championships**, the national team beating the USSR in the final by two goals to one. As tourism becomes a billion dollar business, Spain (including Majorca, Menorca and Ibiza in the Balearics) receives **15,000,000 visitors** during the course of the year. Britons, French and Germans begin acquiring retirement homes on the **'Costa del Sol'**. Its international stock beginning to ride high, the government pushes for membership of the **European Community** (EC, later EU), but admittance is blocked by Holland and Belgium.

> Just as hilliness is overstressed to such an extent as to eliminate all other types of scenery, the human life of a country disappears to the exclusive benefits of its monuments. For the Blue Guide, men exist only as types. In Spain, for instance, the Basque is an adventurous sailor, the Levantine a light-hearted gardener, the Catalan a clever tradesman and the Cantabrian a sentimental highlander. We find again here this disease of thinking in essences, which is at the bottom of every bourgeois mythology of man (which is why we come across it so often). The ethnic reality of Spain is thus reduced to a vast classical ballet, a nice neat commedia dell'arte, whose improbable typology serves to mask the real spectacle of conditions, classes and professions. For the Blue Guide, men exist as social entities only in trains, where they fill a 'very mixed' Third Class. Apart from that, they are a mere introduction, they constitute a charming and fanciful decor, meant to surround the essential part of the country: its collection of monuments.

Roland Barthes, 'The Blue Guide', in *Mythologies* (1957)
trans. Annette Lavers (1973)

1966 New laws allow for greater **press freedom**, although proprietors remain liable to prosecution for printing inflammatory material.

In Barcelona there are serious **student disturbances** after a free student union at a Capuchin convent is evicted by police on 9 March. For the first time Spanish students stage sit-ins.

1967 In September the people of **Gibraltar** vote over-whelmingly to remain under British rule. **Carrero Blanco** is made Vice-President. On 22 November a *Ley Orgánica del Estado* (**Organic Law of the State**) is presented to the

Cortes. Echoing Franco's theory of an 'organic democracy', this opens up one third of the Cortes's membership to direct election by heads of families and their wives. Political parties, though, remain outlawed, and legally only the Caudillo can sanction new laws.

1968 On 30 January Juan Carlos's son **Felipe** is born. In April **Pope Paul VI** requests that the papacy be allowed to appoint Spain's bishops, but Franco refuses, preferring to stick by the existing system whereby he selects one candidate from a list of three supplied by papal nuncios. In the summer continuing student unrest, mirroring student violence in Paris and other west European cities, provokes the temporary **closure of Spain's universities**.

1969 On 24 January, following an escalation in student disturbances and attempts to forge bonds between student and workers' unions, a **state of emergency** is declared, lasting two months. Unrest is stimulated by rumours of Franco's declining health.

On 7 June Spain closes its border with Gibraltar.

To ensure political stability, on 17 July Franco confirms to the Cortes that his designated **successor** is Juan Carlos, who is given the title *Príncipe de España*. Juan Carlos swears to uphold the traditions of the existing regime, now called the *Movimiento*.

On 29 October Franco appoints more technocrats to his cabinet, producing what becomes known as the *gobierno monocolor* – 'monochrome government'. In the Falangist backlash that follows several militant right-wing groups, some of them controlled by Carrero Blanco, emerge, including the *Guerrilleros de Cristo Rey* and the neo-fascist *Fuerza Nueva*.

1970 The government secures preferential trading terms with the **EC**, raising hopes for Spain's eventual admittance into the Community.

During the summer Franco's security forces begin arresting leading Basque nationalists. On 18 September **Joseba Elósegi**, a member of ETA, sets fire to himself in front of the Caudillo during a *jai alai* (pelota) tournament. At the end of the month US President **Richard Nixon** and Secretary of State **Henry Kissinger** are received by Franco in Madrid. In November sixteen ETA members, including two priests, are put on trial for terrorist offences. The trial creates international sympathy for the **Basque cause**, and in December Franco is forced to commute the death sentences handed down to three of the accused.

1971 On 13 September a joint assembly of Spain's bishops and priests issues a statement asking for **public forgiveness** for the role played by the Church in supporting Franco during the Civil War and its aftermath.

1972 Franco's personal reputation is tarnished when his brother, **Nicolás Franco**, is found to be at the heart of a financial scandal involving the disappearance of 4 million kilos of olive oil held in reserve. During a judicial investigation six witnesses die in mysterious circumstances.

In September Spain signs a trade agreement with the **USSR**, Franco's ideological enemy.

1973 In a June cabinet reshuffle, orchestrated by Vice-President **Carrero Blanco**, some Falangist hardliners are appointed to senior government positions.

In the early morning of 20 December Carrero Blanco is killed in Madrid when an **ETA bomb** underneath his car explodes. The assassination coincides with the scheduled opening of the trial of ten union leaders accused of being communists. Fernández Miranda becomes provisional prime minister, but on 27 December is replaced by **Arias Navarro** who orchestrates a crackdown against political dissidents. López Rodó and other technocrats are dismissed by Franco, although room remains for some neo-liberals.

The painter **Pablo Picasso** dies in France aged 92.

1974 Spain's economy worsens as oil prices rocket in the wake of the Yom Kippur Arab-Israeli war of October 1973. As the 'oil crisis' bites workers become more militant, and the government more authoritarian. On 2 March a Catalan anarchist, **Salvador Puig Antich**, is executed despite protests from the international community. The Caudillo's visibly declining health and assurances of the restoration of the monarchy perhaps prevent serious unrest.

1975 On 31 May US President **Gerald Ford** pays a state visit to Madrid. Although he has a formal meeting with Franco, he spends more time with Prince Juan Carlos. In September three ETA terrorists are executed. Wired up with electrodes to monitor his heart-rate, **Franco** attends his last cabinet session on 17 October. During the meeting, news breaks that **Spanish Sahara** has fallen to Moroccan insurgents and the Caudillo has a heart attack. He dies in the early morning of 20 November. Two days later Juan Carlos is proclaimed **King**.

1976 In June and July, pro-democracy demonstrations take place in Madrid, Barcelona and other cities, following which Juan Carlos dismisses Carlos Arias and appoints **Adolfo Suárez**, a lawyer and former state broadcasting chief as his prime minister. Supported by the clergy and by liberals, Suárez devises a **Law of Political Reform** stipulating a bicameral (two-chamber) parliament to be elected on full adult suffrage. The Law is accepted by the Cortes, despite Falangist opposition, and by 94 percent of the electorate during a **national referendum** held in December. The Law also legalizes political parties, including the long-banned Socialist PSOE.

1977 Suárez creates the **UCD** (*Unión del Centro Democratico*), a centre-right party, and secures 34 percent of the national vote in a **general election** held on 15 June. His nearest

❝ We don't ask for a 'yes' to our party, but to the participation of all citizens in the construction of a text that is for everyone, including those that do not like it, but this is the greatness of democracy, that it defends those who attack it. ❞

Felipe Gonzalez, then General Secretary of PSOE, in *El País*, 5 December 1978

rival, the PSOE, polls 28 percent of the vote, while the hard right (Francoist) *Alianza Popular* manages only 8 per-

The 1978 Constitution

The Constitution ratified at the end of 1978 transformed Spain's political institutions. In place of the anachronistic regime that, by the time of Franco's death, hovered somewhere between being an outright dictatorship and an unelected oligarchy the country received a **progressive democratic system** based on the principle of **consensus** and specifically geared for the growth of a plurality of **political parties**. As befitted Spain's internal diversity the new constitutional provisions were complex. Although the monarchy was retained, its authority was severely limited, with the proviso that the king continued as nominal commander-in-chief of Spain's armed forces. At the national level legislative power was invested in a wholly elected bicameral *Cortes Generales*. The upper house, or **Senate**, has 257 members, 200 of them directly elected by simple majorities (first-past-the-post) in one-member constituencies, the remaining 57 being nominated by provincial governments that are themselves elected. In contrast, the lower house, or **Congress of Deputies**, having a maximum of 400 members, is elected according to a system of **proportional representation**. Voters vote for **party lists** in multi-member constituencies. The duly elected Congress then elects a Prime Minister (also called President). In both Senate and Congress the

cent. With the support of Catalan and Basque nationalist deputies Suárez forms a 'broad church' government.

1978 Following detailed consultations with other political leaders and parties, Suárez and his cabinet draw up a **new constitution** designed to implement full democracy within the framework of a constitutional monarchy with an emphasis on **regional autonomy**. The Constitution is ratified by the Cortes, and by an 88 percent yes-vote in a national referendum on 6 December.

1979 In March, fresh **elections** are held in accordance with the newly promulgated Constitution. The results vary little from those of 1977 and Suárez continues in power.

maximum term of office is four years.

These parliamentary provisions, though, are only one aspect of the 1978 Constitution, which strives for an American-style balance of powers. A 12-member **Constitutional Court**, is, like the US Supreme Court, empowered to determine constitutional issues, and to hear cases pertaining to matters of basic human rights. Four of the court's members are nominated by the Congress, four by the Senate, two by the judiciary, and two by the cabinet of the day. The Constitution also enshrines a tranche of **freedoms**, including the freedom of worship and the right to belong to a trades union (so long as it is democratically structured). Amongst its most important articles, though, are those that authorize strong regional government. Accordingly, Spain is partitioned into seventeen **autonomous communities** – for example Catalunya, Valencia, Galicia and Andalucía – each with its own elected assembly, and which together provide mid-level government for Spain's fifty-odd provinces. In view of the **regionalist tensions** that have dominated Spanish history, the decision to go for at least a semi-federal rather than a centralized (and therefore authoritarian) system of government is widely perceived as the crowning glory of 1978.

Colonel Tejero, brandishing a pistol, harangues the deputies in the Cortes

1981 Suárez resigns in January after his UCD party splits into centrist and rightist factions. In the confusion that follows **Antonio Tejero**, a Lt-Colonel in the Civil Guard, attempts a Falangist coup by storming the Congress of Deputies of the *Cortes Generales* in Madrid on 23 February. For several days the situation inside Spain remains precarious as a majority of army commanders refuse to declare their allegiance, either to Tejero or the state. **King Juan Carlos**, however, intervenes in his role as commander-in-chief to restore democracy – an action that enhances his standing.

In September Picasso's *Guernica* (see p.439) arrives in Madrid from New York's Museum of Modern Art where it has been housed since 1939.

1982 Under scratch governments formed out of coalitions Spain joins **NATO**, and **divorce**, always opposed by the Catholic Church, is legalized. In October, the PSOE, led by the radical lawyer **Felipe González**, wins a landslide victory in fresh elections. Prime minister for fourteen years, González introduces many social reforms, especially as regards healthcare and unemployment benefits, but fails to implement the sweeping socialist policies promised during his first election campaign.

1983 Death of the painter **Joan Miró** aged 90. After an early involvement with Surrealism, Miró developed his own unique vocabulary of abstract forms and symbols.

1986 Opposed to Spain's membership of NATO, González holds a national referendum in which a narrow majority vote to remain within the alliance. Spaniards also vote in favour of joining the **EU** (European Union, formerly EC), to which González is committed. Among the benefits enjoyed by Spain as a result of EU membership are large subsidies granted by the **common agricultural policy**.

1988 **Pedro Almodóvar** establishes his reputation as the most talented Spanish film director since Buñuel with *Mujeres al borde de un ataque de nervios* ('Women on the Edge

> " Personally, transgression isn't my aim, for it implies the kind of respect and acceptance of the law I'm incapable of. This may explain why my films were never anti-Franco. I simply didn't even recognize his existence. In a way, it's my revenge against Francoism. I want there to be no shadow or memory of him. "
>
> Pedro Almodóvar in an interview with Frédéric Strauss (1995)

EL DESEO

Pedro Almodóvar filming outside La Sagrada Familia in Barcelona

of a Nervous Breakdown'). His films' subversive and often outrageous take on Spanish life provides particularly strong roles for women.

1989 González becomes **President of the EU** on the principle of annual member-rotation of the presidency. The PSOE wins a national election with a reduced majority after facing a strong challenge from the *Partido Popular* (PP), an amalgamation of the UCD and the *Alianza Popular*.

The painter **Salvador Dalí** (see p.415) dies in Figueras in his Teatre Museu Dalí.

1991 **Secondary education** is made compulsory up to the age of 17.

1992 The rehabilitation of Spain's international reputation is enhanced by the **Barcelona Olympics**, by **Expo '92** (held at Seville) and by the designation of **Madrid** as European City of Culture for 1992. Less political capital is made out of attempts to celebrate the 500th anniversary of **Columbus**'s first voyage to the Americas (see p.224) as media attention outside Spain focuses on the destruction of Amerindian communities.

1993 The PSOE loses its parliamentary majority, due largely to a wave of corruption scandals building since 1989. Chief amongst these is the **GAL affair**, which reveals that a covert security agency – the **Grupo Antiterrorista de Liberación** – authorized by the cabinet has systematically employed torture and murder in its suppression of Basque nationalists. The PSOE is also accused of illegal fund-raising by setting up bogus business consultancies. González manages to continue as prime minister by forming a pact with the **CiU** *(Convergencia I Unió)*, a right-wing Catalan nationalist party led by **Jordi Pujol**.

1994 **Ceuta** and **Melilla**, Spain's two surviving enclaves in North Africa, are granted limited autonomy.

1996 Pujol withdraws his support for González and the PSOE, forcing a March general election. The right-wing Partido Popular, led by **José Maria Aznar**, dramatically increases its share of the vote at a time of high inflation and unemployment, although Aznar is only able to form a government through a coalition with Pujol's CiU and other regional parties. Committed to deregularization, Aznar revives the economy by instituting tight monetary controls and curbing trade union power.

In the election, **Herri Batasuna** ('Unity of People'), ETA's 'political' wing, polls less than 12 percent of votes cast in the Basque provinces which, since 1980, have enjoyed regional autonomy.

1997 Following a resurgence of **terrorist incidents** perpetrated by ETA, mass demonstrations against Basque militants are staged inside as well as outside the Basque provinces. The imprisonment of Herri Batasuna's leaders however provokes renewed calls for an independent Basque homeland.

Basque Nationalism

Claiming to be **Europe's oldest surviving people**, and speaking a language (Euskera) only distantly related to any other, the Basques inhabit a region – which they call **Euskadi** – straddling the Pyrenees that dips south to the Ebro and stretches west to the Asturias. Throughout their history they have clung to their traditions and sometimes sought independence from the more forceful powers surrounding them. Notable Basques include the Jesuit saints Ignatius Loyola (see p.266) and Francis Xavier, the philosopher Miguel de Unamuno, and the revolutionary 'La Pasionaria'. In Roman times they were known as the **Vascones**, and were never fully pacified. Against the Visigoths they waged an almost ceaseless war of resistance – aided by their mountainous terrain – and only became Christianized after the Islamic conquest of al-Andalus. The long campaign to rid the Iberian peninsula of its Muslim rulers drew the Basques closer to their northern neighbours, the Christian Kingdoms, and by the 16th century they had become to all intents and purposes part of Spain itself. In the 18th century they enjoyed royal protection, and were allowed to maintain their *fueros* as a token for their support for the **Bourbons** during the War of the Spanish Succession. But in the 19th century they threw in their lot with the **Carlists** (see p.396), since when nothing has quite gone their way.

The modern separatist movement goes back to 1895, when **Sabina Arana**, as much a cultural as a political nationalist, founded the conservative **Basque Nationalist Party** (PNV). Amid

Spain signs up to the EU's **single European currency** (European Monetary Union), slated to come into effect in 2002.

1998 The independence of Spain's **judicial system** is seen to work when two former government ministers, Rafael Barrionuevo and Rafael Vera, are jailed for their complicity in the **GAL affair**.

the confusion of the Second Republic Basque autonomy was briefly established in 1936, but for the next four decades Basques suffered the full opprobrium of **General Franco**. The destruction of **Guernica** in 1937 was just one of many horrors inflicted during the Civil War, and oppression continued after the war ended. At stake were the mineral riches, particularly of Viscaya province, and well-developed steel and shipbuilding industries. In 1959 a group of young intellectuals founded **ETA** (Euskadi Ta Askatasuna – 'Euskadi and Liberty'), which adopted a Marxist liberation platform and, eight years later, turned to terrorism to achieve its ends. Since then ETA and the authorities, usually represented by the **Civil Guard**, have fought a running battle, suspended only briefly in 1998. While ETA is accredited with 800 killings, including the assassination of **Carrero Blanco** in 1973, on the other side suspected Basque nationalists have been hunted down, imprisoned without trial, tortured, and sometimes murdered. But whereas Spain's transition to democracy in 1978 did little to abate the face-off in the immediate term, more recently ETA has lost ground politically. On the one hand there has been a steady inflow of workers from Andalucía and elsewhere into Basque cities, altering their demographic complexion; on the other, the grant of Basque autonomy, effected in 1980, and Spain's membership of the **EU** have promoted a sea-change in the attitudes of a majority of Basques. Today, Basque militants represent not so much a minority people as a minority within a minority.

As support for Basque militancy dwindles, **ETA** announces a unilateral cease-fire in October. In the Basque provinces, an alliance known as the *Mesa de Estella* (or *Pizarra Estella*) is formed between Herri Batasuna and Basque democrat parties.

2000 The **Partido Popular** wins a clear majority in a mandatory national election held in March, enabling Aznar to discontinue his alliance with the CiU and continue as prime minister. The year is marred by a spate of terrorist incidents as **ETA** returns to violence.

CORBIS

José Maria Aznar was one of the few European leaders to give unequivocal support to George Bush during the 2003 Iraq war

2001 Aznar pledges to support US President George W. Bush's **war against terrorism**, following the destruction of the World Trade Center in New York on **11 September** by members of Osama Bin Laden's al-Qaeda terrorist network. Because of Spain's proximity to North Africa it is felt to be especially vulnerable to **Islamic extremists**, and from November terrorist suspects are arrested with increasing frequency. At the same time the government stiffens measures against **illegal immigrants** coming from Morocco, Algeria and Tunisia.

2002 At the beginning of the year the *peseta* is replaced by the **euro**. Its introduction induces an extraordinary flurry in cash purchases of houses, cars and electronic goods as Spaniards who have participated in a **black market** outside the tax regimen scramble to rid themselves of stockpiles of the outgoing currency.

The Spanish economy at large is adversely affected by a global downturn largely brought about by the 2001 attack on New York, and the government is damaged by allegations of sleaze and corruption made in the media.

Aznar presses Britain for the return of **Gibraltar** to Spanish sovereignty. The British government's initially positive response changes when it becomes clear that the majority of Gibraltarians have no wish to join Spain.

2003 Aznar gives his firm support to US President George W. Bush and British Prime Minister Tony Blair in their campaign against **President Saddam Hussein** of Iraq, despite the inability of UN weapons inspectors to uncover 'weapons of mass destruction'. Notwithstanding, on 20 March an **Anglo–American invasion of Iraq** commences with an aerial assault on the Iraqi capital Baghdad, and by 14 April nearly all of Iraq is under the Allies' control.

Against a background of anti-war protests **local elections** are held on 25 May. While the Spanish left, in particular the Socialist Party led by **José Luis Rodríguez Zapatero**, makes gains, Aznar's Popular Party confounds opinion polls by holding on to power in a majority of constituencies. Aznar's charismatic wife, **Ana Botella de Aznar**, known variously as 'La Botella' ('the bottle') and 'Hilaria' (after Hilary Clinton), gains a seat on the Madrid council. In the Basque provinces, ten percent of votes cast are spoiled by followers of the outlawed **Herri Batasuna party**.

In a new and controversial biography of Juan Carlos, the English historian **Paul Preston** alleges that the king shot dead his younger brother Alfonso in April 1956. The book becomes a best-seller, but enrages many conservatives and some liberals.

books

books

The following is a selective list of books about Spain's history and its culture. Wherever a title is in print, the UK publisher is given first, the US publisher second (except where the title in question is published elsewhere). Where a title is available in one country only, the country is indicated. Where a title is published by one publisher in both the UK and US, then the name of publisher only is given. Books that are out of print are designated o/p. Surprisingly, there is no good single-volume account of the whole of Spanish history written in English that can be particularly recommended. There is however a valuable fourteen-volume history published by Blackwell (UK and US) under the General Editorship of John Lynch, which is the best introduction for the serious student currently available. Outstanding titles in this series are recommended under the appropriate sections below.

General History

Raymond Carr (ed), *Spain: A History* (Oxford University Press). This contains nine chapters each written by a different expert, accompanied by generous illustrations. It is a good introduction to Spanish history, but also decidedly skimpy.

John A. Crow, *Spain: The Root and the Flower* (California University Press). A synoptic, readable and engaging account of the development of culture and society in Spain from Roman times.

Mark Ellingham and John Fisher, *The Rough Guide to Spain* (Rough Guides). The ultra-dependable travel guide furnishes excellent historical information apropos specific sites and contains useful sections on Spanish architecture, cinema and even wildlife.

M. Vincent and R.A. Stradling, *Cultural Atlas of Spain and Portugal* (Andromeda, UK). A detailed and impressive, though expensive, compendium that is organized historically. Good on illustrations as well as maps.

Prehistoric and Roman Spain

M.E. Aubet, *Phoenicians and the West: Politics, Colonies and Trade* (Cambridge University Press). A broad-picture account of Phoenician trading activities in the western Mediterranean with invaluable insights into how the Phoenicians developed Cádiz and other Iberian ports.

Maria Cruz Fernández Castro, *Iberia in Prehistory* (Blackwell). This absorbing study of the peninsula's early history provides archeologically-based reconstructions of the first human settlements, and covers the subsequent intrusions of Phoenicians, Greeks and Carthaginians.

Roger Collins, *Spain: An Archaeological Guide* (Oxford University Press). New findings and shifts of emphasis tend to date any archeological guide quickly, but, limited to 130 well-known sites, Collins's sure-footed survey has staying power.

A.T. Fear, *Rome and Baetica: Urbanization in Southern Spain* (Oxford University Press). A detailed, academic appraisal of how towns and cities, and an urban lifestyle, developed in the most prosperous region of Roman Spain.

S.J. Keay, *Roman Spain* (British Museum Publications; California University Press). An extremely sound, engaging and finely illustrated introduction to Roman Iberia.

David Lewis-Williams, *The Mind in the Cave: Consciousness and the Origins of Art* (Thames and Hudson). In this wide-ranging and compelling exploration of the Cro-Magnon cave art that spread from France into Spain, Lewis-Williams argues that rock murals from 25,000 years ago indicate nothing so much as the prevalence of a lost shamanism.

J.S.Richardson, *Hispaniae: Spain and the Development of Roman Imperialism* (Cambridge University Press). Richardson rightly focuses attention on what Spain did for the Roman empire as much as what the empire did for Spain.

J.S. Richardson, *The Romans in Spain* (Blackwell). Richardson's account of the Roman occupation of Spain is both scholarly and readable. More importantly it shows how Hispania was not just one colony among many, but an integral part of the developing empire.

Visigoth, Medieval and Islamic Spain

Roger Collins, *Early Medieval Spain: Unity in Diversity 400–1000* (Macmillan, UK). In this general history Roger Collins shows how the Visigoths survived the Arabic Conquest to seed the tiny Christian states that eventually drove the Muslims out of Spain.

Roger Collins, *Visigothic Spain, 409–711* (Blackwell). Collins provides a very creditable general introduction, underlining the fact that, despite their reputation as 'barbarians', the Visigoths were far more the preservers of Roman civilization than its wreckers.

Roger Collins, *The Arab Conquest of Spain 710–1031* (Blackwell). In this volume Collins reveals how contact between Hispania's Muslim invaders and its ousted rulers was from the beginning complex and ambiguous.

Richard Fletcher, *Moorish Spain* (Phoenix; California University Press). Fletcher provides an extremely readable, erudite and sympathetic introduction to the Muslim occupation of the Iberian peninsula.

Richard Fletcher, *The Quest for El Cid* (Oxford University Press, UK). With consummate skill Fletcher investigates the discrepancies between the real and the imagined figure of El Cid.

Edward James (ed.), *Visigothic Spain: New Approaches* (Oxford University Press). While Roger Collins's study of Visigoth Spain (see above) is the most general introduction to the period, this collection of essays by distinguished scholars shows that Visigoth studies are alive and growing.

Cyril Glassé, *The Concise Encyclopaedia of Islam* (Stacey International). Although it shies away from 'sensitive' political issues, this is the most comprehensive one-volume reference work on Islam in print and contains many useful entries both on the general features of Islam and on specifically 'Spanish' subjects.

J.N. Hillgarth, *The Spanish Kingdoms* 1250–1516 (o/p). Published in 1976 by OUP, this scholarly two-volume work shows its age, but is still an important study, particularly with regard to the breadth of the sources it draws on.

Angus MacKay, *Spain in the Middle Ages: From Frontier to Empire* (Macmillan, UK). Although written a quarter of a century ago, MacKay's book continues to provide a reliable and readable account of the rise of the Christian States and some of the currents that made Spain an unexpectedly strong state at the close of the 15th century.

Angus MacKay, *Spain: Centuries of Crisis, 1300–1474* (Blackwell). McKay's excellent appraisal of late medieval Spain and the centuries immediately preceding Fernando and Isabel brings a difficult period to life through well-selected sources.

Andrew Wheatcroft, *Infidels: The Conflict between Christendom and Islam 638–2002* (Viking; Putnam). Wheatcroft's beautifully researched account of mutual recrimination and malediction between the two largest branches of monotheism contains a useful section on the breakdown of Moorish-Christian relations in Spain.

Justin Wintle, *The Rough Guide History of Islam* (Rough Guides). This vade mecum to the whole history of Islam shows precisely how the Arab Conquest of Spain ties in with the bigger Islamic picture.

Kenneth Baxter Wolf (trans.), *Conquerors and Chroniclers of Early Medieval Spain* (Liverpool University Press, UK). Wolf assembles and translates key Christian writings from both immediately before and after the Arab Conquest, including the all-important 'Chronicle of 754'.

Imperial Spain

Fernand Braudel, *The Mediterranean and the Mediterranean World in the Age of Philip II*, trans. Siân Reynolds (University of California Press). Braudel's masterpiece challenged the way history is conventionally conceived and written, dwelling upon the informal relations between societies rather than their political posturing. Philip II features, but in a strangely peripheral way.

John Edwards, *The Spain of the Catholic Monarchs 1474–1520* (Blackwell). Edwards is a slightly dry author, but this is a conscientious, and sometimes sceptical, review of the reigns of Fernando and Isabel, who are too often assumed to have forged 'Spain' on their own.

J.H. Elliott, *Imperial Spain 1469–1716* (Penguin). Originally published in 1963, Elliott's highly acclaimed account of Spain's 'Golden Age' and its immediate aftermath remains popular, even though both in its detail and in some of its broader assumptions it has been superseded by more recent studies.

J.H. Elliott, *The Count-Duke of Olivares: The Statesman in the Age of Decline* (o/p). The value of Elliott's biography is that it focuses on a figure who is seldom regarded as belonging to the top-flight of European statesmen.

David Howarth, *The Voyage of the Armada* (Penguin, US). Howarth provides the necessary counterpart to Anglo-centric accounts of the 1588 debacle.

Henry Kamen, *Spain's Road to Empire* (Allen Lane; Putnam). Published in 2002, this is likely to remain the most important general history of the Habsburg Spanish empire for a while. Attacked by some Spanish historians for down-playing Spaniards' contribution to Spanish expansionism, it has also been criticized for not being revisionist enough.

Henry Kamen, *The Spanish Inquisition* (Weidenfeld & Nicolson; Mentor). The most readily available history of the Inquisition is widely admired for its insistence that the Inquisition was not as efficient, and therefore not as deadly, as is often supposed.

Henry Kamen, *Spain in the Later Seventeenth Century 1665–1700* (o/p). Always keen to buck the trend, Kamen argues that later Habsburg Spain was not quite the shambles suggested by other historians.

Henry Kamen, *Philip of Spain* (Yale University Press). Kamen's 1997 biography of Philip II was the first major assessment of the most powerful ruler of the later 16th century, which succeeds brilliantly in drawing a portrait rooted in the values of Philip's own times.

Elie Kedourie (ed.), *Spain and the Jews: the Sephardi Experience, 1492 and After* (Thames and Hudson). This important collection of essays examines a topic that, prior to the death of Franco, too few of Spain's own historians were willing even to contemplate.

Peggy K. Liss, *Isabel the Queen* (Oxford University Press). An academic study of the most important woman in Spanish history, but also the best available biography in English.

Geoffrey Parker, *The Army of Flanders and the Spanish Road, 1567–1659* (Cambridge University Press). Parker highlighted how the acquisition of Milan was vital for maintaining a creditable Habsburg military presence in the Netherlands.

J.H.Parry, *Europe and the Wider World 1415–1715* (o/p). First published in 1949, this brief but classic exposition contextualizes the achievements of seafarers in Spain's employ within the broader development of European maritime technology and enterprise.

Kirkpatrick Sale, *The Conquest of Paradise: Christopher Columbus and the Columbian Legacy* (Papermac; Plume). Sale was in the forefront of those who, around the time of the quincentenary of Columbus's 'discovery of America', saw it not as a great triumph for Europe, but as a disaster for native Americans and their habitat.

R. Stradling, *Europe and the Decline of Spain: A Study of the Spanish System 1580–1720* (o/p). Stradling demonstrates, in his 1981 publication, how the rise of other European powers, notably France and Britain, left Spain stranded as a major player in continental politics and war.

Hugh Thomas, *The Conquest of Mexico* (Hutchinson; Random House).

Thomas concentrates his formidable scholarship and narrative abilities on one segment of Spain's seizures in the Americas, and brings home the extent to which the Mexicans themselves were imperialists in their own right.

The 18th and 19th centuries

Sebastian Balfour, *The End of the Spanish Empire* (Oxford University Press, UK). Balfour provides a useful overview of how and why Spain lost virtually all its American colonies in a few short years following the Peninsular War.

Charles Esdaile, *The Peninsular War: A New History* (Allen Lane: Putnam). This latest in a long line of histories of the Peninsular War written by Englishmen again succumbs to the glorious magnetism of Wellington, but also gives full credit to the part played by Spanish *guerrillas*.

Douglas Hilt, *The Troubled Trinity: Godoy and the Spanish Monarchy* (University of Alabama Press, US). Hilt's is as good as any introduction to the most quintessentially romantic of Spain's politicians, and to the court that he dominated with such seeming ease.

Henry Kamen, *The War of Succession in Spain* 1700–15 (o/p). It was with this book that Kamen, an acknowledged authority on the Habsburgs, first announced his arrival as a serious and radical historian of Spain in 1969.

V.G. Kiernan, *The Revolution of 1854 in Spanish History* (o/p): Published by OUP in 1966, this is a scholarly and detailed look at the attempts to curtail the monarchy during one of the many crises faced by the Spanish Bourbons in the 19th century.

John Lynch, *Bourbon Spain 1700–1800* (Blackwell). As Spain lost its grip on Europe and the wider world, so historians have tended to focus their energies on other periods. Lynch's book however is as tidy a summary of the first Spanish Bourbon century as one might wish for.

The 20th century

Gerald Brenan, *The Spanish Labyrinth* (Cambridge University Press). A personal memoir of the Civil War by 'one who was there', Brenan's book, first published in 1943, is full of insight as well as experience.

Raymond Carr, *Spain 1808–1975* (Oxford University Press). Carr provides an unsurpassed account of the political impasse that led to the Spanish Civil War and its aftermath. His *The Civil War in Perspective* (Weidenfeld & Nicolson, UK) is also recommended as a summary overview of its subject.

John Hooper, *The New Spaniards* (Penguin). Hooper's portrait of the generation of Spaniards that grew up as Franco was dying is well-informed, perceptive and affirmative.

Gerald Howson, *Arms for Spain: the Untold Story* (John Murray, UK). Relying particularly on under-utilized Russian sources, Howson argues that the International Brigades were routinely betrayed by all and sundry in their endeavours to fight fascism in Spain.

Mark Kurlansky, *The Basque History of the World* (Vintage, UK). Kurlansky's idiosyncratic portrait of the Basques is a delight. It tells the whole Basque story, from pre-Roman times to the present, while simultaneously doubling as a Basque cook-book.

Paul Preston, *Concise History of the Spanish Civil War* (Fontana, UK). This as the single best introduction to the Civil War, although the unabridged version, *The Spanish Civil War* (o/p.), published in 1986 is even better.

Paul Preston, *Franco: A Biography* (Fontana Press, UK). Preston's immaculately researched and universally acclaimed 1000-page biography of Europe's third-rate fascist dictator unquestionably deserves the plaudits it has received, inside as well as outside Spain.

Paul Preston, *The Triumph of Democracy in Spain* (Routledge). Preston usefully brings the story of Spain in the 20th century to its unpredictably satisfying conclusion.

Hugh Thomas, *The Spanish Civil War* (Penguin, Touchstone). Although

Thomas's account of the Civil War has been somewhat superseded by the work of other contemporary historians, it remains a riveting read, and an invaluable guide to the internecine politics of the period.

Art and Culture

Germain Bazin, *Baroque and Rococo* (Thames and Hudson), trans. Jonathan Griffin. An elegant and lucid overview of a period of art history that is notoriously difficult to define, Bazin's short study helps establish the parameters of Spanish Baroque art and architecture.

Julia Blackburn, *Old Man Goya* (Jonathan Cape, UK). This highly personal and idiosyncratic book attempts to penetrate Goya's burgeoning mental anguish following the onset of deafness.

Jonathan Brown, *Painting in Spain 1500–1700* (Yale University Press). A classic account of the subject written with refreshing clarity. The same author's *Images and Ideas in Seventeenth-Century Spanish Painting* (o/p) is an invaluable, if specialist, aid for unpicking some of the hidden meanings of Spanish Baroque art.

Ian Gibson, *Federico García Lorca* (Faber and Faber; Pantheon). Gibson's sensitive biography of Spain's leading 20th century poet is the finest available in English. The same author's *The Assassination of Federico García Lorca* (Penguin UK) is a painstaking reconstruction of Lorca's murder.

Robert Hughes, *Barcelona* (Harvill; Vintage). Of many portraits of the Catalan capital, this is perhaps the pick of the bunch, exploring the city as a series of intermeshing cultural statements.

John F. Moffitt, *The Arts in Spain* (Thames and Hudson). A short but lively overview of Spanish art and architecture, from cave painting to the end of the 20th century.

John Richardson, *A Life of Picasso 1907–1917* (Pimlico; Random House). The second volume of what promises to be a literary and art-critical monument covers ten of the most crucial years of Spain's foremost modern artist.

Literature

The Poem of the Cid, trans. Rita Hamilton and Janet Perry (Penguin). Although it is hard to choose between several translations of *La Poema*, the advantage of this one is it also provides the original Spanish text.

George Borrow, *The Bible in Spain* (o/p). First published in 1843, Borrow's account of working in Spain and Portugal on behalf of the British and Foreign Bible Society, and of being imprisoned for his efforts, is a bizarre travel adventure, as well as a classic of its time.

Miguel de Cervantes, *Don Quixote*, trans. John Rutherford (Penguin). Of the modern translations of Cervantes's masterpiece this has to be first choice.

J.M. Cohen (ed.), *The Penguin Book of Spanish Verse* (Penguin). As an introductory compendium of Spanish verse down the centuries Cohen's compilation does everything one might wish, including the provision of original Spanish texts.

Federico García Lorca, *Selected Poems*, Christopher Maurer (ed.) (Penguin). A bilingual selection of the work of Spain's best-loved modern poet, employing several different translators.

Washington Irving, *The Alhambra,* a.k.a. *Tales of the Alhambra* (The Library of America, US). Mixing story-telling and a memoir of the author's own sojourn in Granada, Irving's Alhambra has long been regarded as a captivating classic. This edition includes other major works by Irving.

Benito Pérez Galdós, *Fortunata and Jacinta*, trans. Agnes Moncy Gullón (Penguin). Sometimes compared to Balzac, Galdós is regarded as the greatest Spanish novelist of the 19th century, and this his finest book.

Saint Teresa of Ávila, *The Life of Saint Teresa of Ávila*, trans. J.M. Cohen (Penguin). Still read by Spaniards, the saint's autobiography offers rare insights into the world of 16th century Catholic spirituality.

Amin T. Tibi, *The Tibyan: Memoirs of Abd Allah ibn Buluggin* (Brill, Leiden). The engrossing memoirs of the last of the Zirid amirs of Granada are here well presented and translated from the Arabic original.

index

Entries in colour represent feature boxes

g

h

m

n

t

u

V

W

X

Z